P9-DNA-058

DOGFIGHT OVER TOKYO

DOGFIGHT OVER TOKYO

THE FINAL AIR BATTLE OF THE
PACIFIC AND THE LAST FOUR MEN
TO DIE IN WORLD WAR II

JOHN WUKOVITS

DA CAPO PRESS

Copyright © 2019 by John Wukovits

Cover design by Chris Shamwana
Cover image: ©Kevin M. McCarthy, Olga Klyagina, railway fx,
    George Muresan, bunnavit pangsuk, Khunying kai, Angel DiBilio,
    Serjio74, Triff, Paul Drabot / Shutterstock
Cover copyright © 2019 Hachette Book Group, Inc.

Hachette Book Group supports the right to free expression and the value of copyright. The purpose of copyright is to encourage writers and artists to produce the creative works that enrich our culture.

The scanning, uploading, and distribution of this book without permission is a theft of the author's intellectual property. If you would like permission to use material from the book (other than for review purposes), please contact permissions@hbgusa.com. Thank you for your support of the author's rights.

Da Capo Press
Hachette Book Group
1290 Avenue of the Americas, New York, NY 10104
HachetteBooks.com
Twitter.com/HachetteBooks
Instagram.com/HachetteBooks

Printed in the United States of America

First Edition: August 2019

Published by Da Capo Press, an imprint of Perseus Books, LLC, a subsidiary of Hachette Book Group, Inc. The Da Capo Press name and logo is a trademark of the Hachette Book Group.

The Hachette Speakers Bureau provides a wide range of authors for speaking events. To find out more, go to www.hachettespeakersbureau.com or call (866) 376-6591.

The publisher is not responsible for websites (or their content) that are not owned by the publisher.

Print book interior design by Trish Wilkinson.

Library of Congress Cataloging-in-Publication Data has been applied for.

ISBNs: 978-0-306-92205-3 (hardcover), 978-0-306-92204-6 (ebook)

LSC-C

10 9 8 7 6 5 4 3 2 1

To my companion of more than two decades,
Terri Faitel—
her unquestioned support and editorial skills
helped me more than she may know

CONTENTS

PREFACE

SINCE THIS BOOK is written from the viewpoint of the Air Group 88 pilots, especially the last four men to die in the war, I faced what for me was the difficult task of casting Admiral William F. Halsey in the villain's role. I have admired Halsey since my high school years, and in my later biography of the man I took pains to ensure a fair evaluation—hero during the first two years of the war, but flawed commander in the second half. Overall, though, I argued that his leadership from late 1941 to mid-1944 earned him a spot in the naval pantheon alongside John Paul Jones and George Dewey. This book required me to portray him as less heroic, because that is how the aviators of Air Group 88 saw him.

At the same time, Admiral Halsey was also the main influence in my writing this book. When researching his life for my biography, I was moved that the admiral made a point to urge that the final aviators to die in the war should never be forgotten. That remark stuck in my mind, and when thinking of an idea for my next book, I wondered if the experiences of those four fliers might produce a compelling story. I knew that if I could locate sufficient information on at least two of the four naval aviators, that I had the foundation for a book. Happily, I uncovered a vast amount of material—letters, official documents, reminiscences, interviews, and photographs—from the Hobbs and Mandeberg families, and additional information from the remaining two families. Combined with other official material from government records and from aviator recollections, I possessed all I needed to produce this book.

While the volume relates the accomplishments of Air Group 88—a collection of fighter, dive-bomber, and torpedo plane pilots aboard the USS *Yorktown* (CV-10)—while off the Japanese coast from July to

October 1945, it is anchored by the experiences of those final four men to perish in the war. I thus see most of the action through their eyes and through the reactions of their families in the United States.

I need to clarify how I define the aviators as the last four men to die in the war. I use that description in the narrow sense that they were the last men killed while conducting a wartime mission. They lifted off the *Yorktown* during wartime, and they died during that mission. In no way do I mean to detract from the hundreds of thousands of World War II veterans who succumbed in the following decades from wounds suffered during the war. They are casualties of World War II every bit as much as are these four carrier pilots. This book simply relates the story of four men who perished while carrying out their orders during the final wartime action.

Many people deserve my thanks. The expansive Hobbs family in Kokomo, Indiana, freely opened their doors to me and shared Billy Hobbs's diary, letters, flight log, and other mementos. So, too, did the Mandebergs on the West Coast, the Leviens in New York City, and the Reverend Robert Vrooman in New York State. Especially worthy of mention are Nancy Hobbs Exmeyer, the sister of Wright Hobbs, and Sonya Levien, Eugene Mandeberg's fiancée. I was honored to interview Nancy and Sonya, who so deeply knew and loved two of the four aviators.

A special thanks goes to the Air Group 88 survivors who willingly gave their time to share their recollections during interviews. My sessions with them, either in person or by telephone, were highlights of my time researching this incredible story. The men include William Watkinson and Earl Godfrey of VF-88; Gerald Hennesy, Bernard Hamilton Jr., and Merald Woods of VBF-88; and Arthur Briggs of VB-88. The widows of two VF-88 aviators, Margaret Odom and Betty Proctor, were also helpful, as was John Haag, whose father, Lieutenant (jg) John Haag, flew with the fighting squadron.

Todd Cummins, executive director of the USS *Yorktown* Association, and his staff aboard the aircraft carrier at Patriots Point Naval & Maritime Museum in Mount Pleasant, South Carolina, provided valuable aid in locating records and photographs of Air Group 88. My agent, historian, and most of all, friend, Jim Hornfischer, encouraged me at every step of the way, for this book and for every previous volume. In the process, he helped me attain a dream I had long held of writing books about the Pacific War. The comments of my editor at Da Capo Press, Robert Pigeon, improved the manuscript, and publicist Sarah Falter brought her stellar talents to promoting this book. Cartographer extraordinaire Jeffrey Ward designed the maps that accompany the text.

Two individuals who are no longer with us helped start my writing career. My writing mentor, Tom Buell, whose powerful biographies of Pacific commanders fueled my desire to write about that conflict, offered comments about my early writings—exhausting numerous red pens in the process—and put me in touch with people and organizations that furthered my career. My history adviser at the University of Notre Dame, Dr. Bernard Norling, mailed cogent comments on various topics in his lengthy single-spaced, typewritten letters. I owe much to these two amazing historians.

My family has been at my side throughout this decades-long literary quest. The pride in me exhibited by my daughters, Amy, Julie, and Karen, has made every moment of the writing process worthwhile. Their joy, in turn, has filtered down to the next generation, as my grandchildren, Matt, Megan, Emma, and Katie, text or telephone their joy at my accomplishments. The unquestioned support of my big brother, Tom, a naval aviator residing in San Diego, blends with the memory of my parents, Tom and Grace, and of my younger brother, Fred, to prod me to excellence. Terri Faitel, my companion of more than two decades—and the person to whom this book is dedicated—has as always added her incisive comments to the manuscript as well as offered her support. I am fortunate to have their encouragement, and I love them all.

John F. Wukovits
Trenton, Michigan
October 30, 2018

CHRONOLOGY

1943–1944

JUNE 1943 TO JULY 1944: Flight training for Wright Hobbs, Eugene Mandeberg, and other aviators-to-be.

1944

AUGUST 15: Commissioning of the first three squadrons: VF-88 at NAS Atlantic City, NJ; VB-88 at NAS Wildwood, NJ; VT-88 at NAS Quonset Point, RI.

AUGUST 19: VT-88 moves to NAAF Martha's Vineyard, MA.

NOVEMBER 15: VF-88 moves to Otis Field.

DECEMBER 1: VB-88 moves to Otis Field.

DECEMBER 8–9: VT-88 moves to Otis Field.

DECEMBER 12: VB-88 reduced from 36 to 22 men.

1945

JANUARY 2: The fourth squadron, VBF-88, commissioned at Otis Field.

FEBRUARY 1–15: Air Group 88 moves to California.

FEBRUARY 20: Air Group 88 leaves the West Coast for Hawaii.

FEBRUARY 24: Air Group 88 arrives in Hawaii for training.

APRIL 30: Air Group 88 leaves for Saipan.

MAY 12: Air Group 88 arrives in Saipan for training.

JUNE 12: Air Group 88 leaves for the Philippines.

JUNE 16: Air Group 88 arrives in the Philippines.

JUNE 17: Air Group 88 joins the USS *Yorktown* (CV-10).

JULY 1: Air Group 88 leaves for Japan.

JULY 10: Air Group 88 attacks Tokyo-area airfields.

JULY 14–15: Air Group 88 attacks Hokkaido and Northern Honshu.

JULY 18: Air Group 88 attacks *Nagato* and Yokosuka Naval Base.

JULY 24–25: Air Group 88 attacks Kure Naval Base.

JULY 24: Ensign Edward Heck is rescued by a Dumbo aircraft in the Inland Sea.

JULY 25: Lieutenant Howard M. Harrison is rescued by a Dumbo aircraft in the Sea of Japan.

JULY 26: President Harry Truman and British prime minister Winston Churchill issue the Potsdam Declaration calling for Japan's unconditional surrender.

JULY 28: Air Group 88 attacks Kure Naval Base and Honshu airfields.

JULY 30: Air Group 88 attacks Tokyo-area airfields and shipping.

JULY 30: Lieutenants (jg) Donald R. Penn and Henry J. O'Meara are rescued by a Dumbo aircraft in the Sea of Japan.

AUGUST 6: The United States drops an atomic bomb on Hiroshima.

AUGUST 9: The United States drops an atomic bomb on Nagasaki.

AUGUST 9–10: Air Group 88 attacks Hokkaido and Central Honshu.

AUGUST 13: Air Group 88 attacks Tokyo Plains Airfields.

AUGUST 15: Air Group 88 attacks Tokyo-area airfields; the war ends while Air Group 88 aviators prepare to attack Tokyo airfields; the final four men to die in the war are shot down and killed.

SEPTEMBER 2: Japanese officials sign the surrender document in a ceremony held aboard the USS *Missouri* (BB-63).

OCTOBER 1: The *Yorktown* and Air Group 88 leave Japan for the journey back to the United States.

OCTOBER 20: The *Yorktown* and Air Group 88 pass beneath the Golden Gate Bridge and arrive in the United States.

PART I
TO THE WAR

CHAPTER 1

"And Then Came the War"
Training for Combat, 1943–1944

ATLANTIC CITY'S CLARIDGE HOTEL boasted a proud heritage at the famed New Jersey resort center. Its twenty-four stories of rooms, restaurants, and shops dwarfed other structures that crowded the Boardwalk area by the ocean and stood as a landmark that attracted tourists by the score. Hotel management and workers had accommodated parties and functions for decades, from wedding receptions and family reunions to small gatherings of people seeking a restful weekend free from the burdens of everyday life.

The group that walked in on September 1, 1944, differed in crucial ways from its predecessors, however. Whereas most affairs featured an assortment of ages, youth prevailed among the sixty-eight uniformed naval officers who entered the establishment for their fighter squadron commissioning party. They were not there to celebrate a wedding or other joyous occasion, but to mark the origins of their air squadron and to embrace the realization that they would, within months, be posted to the Pacific, sent there to operate in the dangerous skies over Japan. Strafing enemy shipping, bombing oil refineries, and engaging Japanese Zeros—then the superior fighter aircraft of the war—in spectacular dogfights awaited this group of young officers, but from the laughter and joking that rose as they filed into the banquet room, an observer could never deduce the serious nature of the business that soon would be theirs.

Like all fighter pilots, they crowed of aerial feats to come and bragged that no enemy pilot was their equal. The younger and less experienced the aviator—and the more alcohol he ingested—the more boastful he became, for each had yet to learn what any veteran of the war could quickly explain: air combat is nothing to take lightly.

Fighting Squadron 88, like most Navy squadrons in the latter half of the war, featured a core of experienced aviators blended in with a mass of neophytes. The youngsters, like twenty-two-year-old Ensign Wright C. "Billy" Hobbs Jr., a Hoosier who grew up on an Indiana farm, or the fun-loving, cigar-chomping Lieutenant (jg) Joseph G. Sahloff from New York, so thin he was compared to Ichabod Crane, viewed the veterans with awe. Hobbs and the other newcomers wondered if they had the guts and skill to match Lieutenant (jg) Marvin R. Odom, who had only a few months earlier helped break up a formation of fifteen Japanese fighters and notched the first of his Pacific kills. Everyone discussed Lieutenant John P. Adams's feats during the war's first months, when he amassed two Navy Cross decorations—the Navy's highest honor—and one Distinguished Flying Cross in combat over the Gilbert and Marshall Islands and in the crucial May–June 1942 Battles of the Coral Sea and Midway, where he destroyed two enemy aircraft.

This, however, was a time for fun, laughter, and above all, exaggeration. They knew that the United States had gained the upper hand in the Pacific, but in their opinion, victory was far from certain, at least until Fighting Squadron 88 arrived to settle the score. If anyone doubted their feelings, all one had to do was read the poem titled "Fighting Eighty-Eight," a fitting ode to his squadron and to the men who would fly the planes into battle, written by Lieutenant Paul E. Williams and printed in that night's program.

Fighting Hellcats riding high
Japs, come meet your fate
Other outfits, step aside
For Fighting Eighty-Eight.
Tojo's pilots, one and all
Have hara-kiri dates
They've received the word that here
Comes Fighting Eighty-Eight.
Of this one thing you can be sure

That lead will perforate
The hide of every Jap who faces
Fighting Eighty-Eight.
Bombers and torpedo planes
Hurry, don't be late
For your path will be cleared out
By Fighting Eighty-Eight.
And if St. Peter's Angels have
All left the Pearly Gate
You'll find them out there, flying wing
On Fighting Eighty-Eight.[1]

The squadron was a part of Air Group 88, a unit that would eventually comprise four squadrons. Ensigns Hobbs and Sahloff already exhibited some of that cocky attitude so prevalent among fighter pilots, whose task would be to clear the way for the squadron bombers and torpedo planes that followed them to the target. They would be the first to grapple with the enemy; they would be the first to engage Zeros and face Jap antiaircraft fire.

They were ready, they were eager, they were young.

"BILLY WAS BORN TO FLY"

Norman Rockwell, whose celebrated paintings depicted homespun America, would have felt right at home with Billy Hobbs and his family. Born August 15, 1922, to a farming family in Kokomo, Indiana, Billy Hobbs swam and fished in Little Wildcat Creek, which lazily meandered through the 160-acre Hobbs farm just outside of town. "We had sleds and would go on down the hill," said Nancy Exmeyer, Billy Hobbs's younger sister. "In the summertime we'd swim. We had a briar patch and a big woods."

When the leaves turned golden and wintry temperatures turned the creek to ice, he and his siblings—three sisters and two brothers—donned skates and raced its length, although the shallow depth sometimes produced a choppy surface. Should the creek lose its allure, those nearby woods and its hidden secrets captured their fancy.

More importantly Billy's parents, Wright Sr. and Hattie, fit the Rockwell scheme by fashioning a sheltered world for their children. "We had great parents," added Exmeyer. "If someone today says I'm just like them, I say, 'Thank you.'" They stressed the importance of treating people kindly and of developing good manners. Be good to people, keep your word, and work hard: those were the traits inculcated by the parents.

Kokomo residents knew the father through his work on hybridization of corn. Farsighted and inquisitive, he experimented in increasing the yield before anyone else in the area, and no one was surprised when his feats garnered notice in the local newspaper.

Since her husband spent most of his days in the fields, Hattie, like so many mothers, was the one who dealt with the everyday issues presented by Billy or one of his siblings. She dispensed the advice; she patched scraped elbows and bandaged cut fingers. She was especially close to Billy, her firstborn, even though she would never admit it, but the two developed a strong bond during Billy's emergent years.

The Hobbs family escaped the worst ravages of the Great Depression because of the family farm. They experienced hardship—pretty much everyone in the Kokomo area suffered in the 1930s—but they fared better than their neighbors, with whom they frequently shared the bounties from their fields and from their collection of animals. "We'd give food to the neighbors who were hard off," said Exmeyer. "Nothing fancy. Meat and potatoes. My parents gave to people, and gave and gave. When we were poor, there were others who were real poor."

Billy, who shared one of the three bedrooms with his brothers while his parents and his sisters occupied the other two, exhibited his parents' kindness and responsibility, and developed an interest in new challenges from his father. His siblings looked up to their well-mannered big brother as their role model, and they tried to emulate his politeness and friendliness. "Billy was always after us, for the best," said Nancy Exmeyer. "He was pushing everyone. He wanted perfection, ever since he was a kid. He was friendly, courteous, and modest. There were times as a young girl I wished he wasn't my brother, because he could be so strict, but Billy was a good big brother to have."[2]

The student at West Middleton High School compiled above-average grades in his four years, excelling in physics, and helped his dad at the farm. Flashing a charming grin beneath blue eyes and a crop of brown hair, Hobbs liked the Talbert sisters and went out with other girls, but everyone at school and home knew what most grabbed his attention—flying. "Billy was born to fly," said Nancy Exmeyer. "He knew he was going to fly. He just knew. He was always making the paper airplanes. We were only three-and-one-half miles from the airport, and he'd see those planes take off and land. We knew Billy was destined to fly. We knew."[3]

Billy loved fashioning airplanes from almost anything, including matchboxes, and launched a stream of concoctions skyward, most of which gained minimal altitudes before crashing to the fields. The aerial antics of barnstorming pilots lifting off from nearby DeGrasse Airport so captivated the youth and further entrenched an affection for flying that some later believed Billy saw flying as his ticket out of the back-breaking labors and long hours of farming. After cashing his first paycheck working odd jobs while in high school, Billy snuck over to Clyde Shockley's makeshift airfield, later named Ruzika Airport, not far from the farm and surreptitiously took flying lessons, keeping his antics hidden from his parents because he feared they would put an immediate halt to the activities. Exmeyer always suspected that Hattie knew what her son was up to, but said nothing to her husband to avoid any confrontation between father and son. "He got his pilot's license before he ever got out of high school," said Hobbs's sister, Joyce Clelland. "He was slipping over and taking flying lessons all that time. Bill was really determined to fly. He had his pilot's license before we all knew it." Once he learned the rudiments of flying, Billy, eager for any opportunity to lift into the air, often traipsed to the airfield and took a plane up without first checking with Shockley.

Billy knew his path by the time he graduated from West Middleton High School in the spring of 1940. "And then here came the war," said Clelland.[4]

"ONE SIMPLE MISTAKE WHEN FLYING COULD BE FATAL"

For more than a year, Billy grabbed the opportunity to fly whenever his work allowed. He continued his lessons and became one of the few

Kokomo boys his age to solo in a plane. With the surprise Japanese attack against the Hawaiian naval base at Pearl Harbor, Billy's thoughts, like those of so many of his former classmates, turned to the military. He and his buddies never questioned the choice; it was their duty, if physically able, to enter one of the military branches and help defend their nation. Nineteen-year-old Herbert Wood of Iowa, for instance, who would later join Hobbs in the same carrier air group, enlisted after watching newsreels of the war in his local theater.

The Army and Marine Corps stood as excellent options, but Billy Hobbs had his eye on only one choice—the air. In September 1942, he enlisted in the Navy's V-5 Aviation Cadet program, which in the early stages of the war accepted males with a high school diploma. After successfully passing a battery of psychological and aptitude tests showing they possessed the skills to meet the Navy's requirements, the Navy sent the hopefuls to local junior colleges or universities to begin four months of half a day's instruction in mathematics, physics, navigation, and aerology and half a day of flying with an instructor. The lanky Hobbs, listed as 6'0" tall and weighing 145 pounds on the Navy's official entry card, thought that the Navy and its carriers offered enticing chances for him to keep flying, and even better, he did not have to leave Indiana for these initial months of training. He could fill his mornings and afternoons with aviation, yet be close enough to home that he could see family and friends, almost as if he were embarking on a trial run of what the military would be like. Hobbs understood that his chosen field of combat—the sky—brought risks that ground troops did not face, but he had the desire and the fortitude to accept the challenge.

Hobbs joined a group called the "Lombardiers," a central Indiana naval aviation unit named after the late Carole Lombard, actress and wife of noted film star Clark Gable. The commanding officer invited Clark Gable to attend the induction ceremony to be held during halftime of the Kokomo-Logansport football contest, but Gable was unable to accept. Along with eighteen other Kokomo males, Hobbs was sworn in on October 16, 1942.

From that point, Hobbs's instruction continued at Ball State Teachers College about fifty miles southeast of Kokomo. Navy instructors intensified the training for the civilian pilot trainees, cramming 240 hours of instruction into eight weeks, in addition to the flying based out of nearby Muncie Airport. Hobbs handily advanced through every stage of his instruction until, on January 18, 1943, he received a certificate from the Civil Aeronautics Administration naming him a student pilot. He was now ready for the next step—Naval Preflight School in California, followed by primary flight training at the Naval Air Station in Livermore, thirty miles east of San Francisco. Hobbs's ties to Kokomo would remain strong, but they now stretched across the continent.

WITH BILLY HOBBS set to leave Kokomo for California, for the first time the war personally impacted the Hobbs family. Hattie's worries over the welfare of her son intensified. "Mom and Dad didn't want Billy to go into the service," said Nancy Exmeyer. "Oh Lord, no! They were scared to death for him, but they knew he would have to go sooner or later. We weren't surprised that Billy wanted to fly."[5]

Billy reported to Naval Preflight School in June 1943, which one pilot labeled "the most dreaded and supposedly the toughest part of the training program."[6] Now formally under the aegis of a military organization, Billy and the young aviators-to-be spent the next three months learning the Navy's procedures and rules. Half each day Hobbs and the group engaged in arduous physical training—calisthenics, running, and hiking over hills tested each person's stamina, while sporting contests offered a spirit of competition to boys who wanted to match their skills against their fellow cadets.

Classes occupied the remainder of the days, where instructors hurled official terminology, military customs, saluting, close-order drill, aerology, navigation, and a hundred other items at Cadet Hobbs and the other overwhelmed candidates. Hobbs had to be able to identify every combat plane then in use, either by the United States or by one of her adversaries, and within a second recognize the aircraft from any angle. The instructors constantly reminded them that if they thought this was difficult now, in combat, where hesitation meant death, they would have no time to think about their foe.

They also had to master the series of training manuals offering advice about everything from how to handle an emergency landing in the ocean, to marksmanship and avoiding sharks. A booklet titled "There's

No Substitute for Marksmanship!" emphasized the need for accuracy and explained that "one blow gun which <u>HITS</u> is better than one 16-inch gun which <u>MISSES</u>." Hobbs learned that "the plane is just a platform to get your guns up where you can hit the enemy hard and quickly,"[7] and that to destroy a German or Japanese plane, he had to perfect the techniques of leading his target with his firing.

Should they be hit in combat and forced to make a landing in the ocean, "Dunking Sense" warned them that "the danger is that the plane will go over on its back, or nose down and dive." The booklet cautioned to "be prepared for the sea to be a lot rougher than it appeared from aloft," and when boarding the life raft, to use the lifeline and wriggle up over the side as nearly horizontal as possible rather than attempting to climb vertically, which could capsize the raft. Once inside, for protection from the sun, they should rub "exposed surfaces with any oily part of a raw fish, especially the fatty layers just under its skin."

Hobbs and his fellow cadets took most of the advice to heart, but they wondered about the section that dealt with one of nature's most feared predators—the shark. "Treat sharks with plenty of respect," the booklet urged, and added that if "you do happen to go overboard or if the raft capsizes—splash and kick as much as you can while getting back aboard."[8]

The booklet covering capture by an enemy seemed more helpful than any advice concerning sharks. Should they be taken prisoner, they were to give out only their name, rank, and serial number. However, the booklet warned, "the enemy has devised a bag of tricks that would probably extract information from a mummy." The booklet added, "Your captors have one interest in you—to get information that will help them destroy your comrades and your home and family." In words that Hobbs must have found naïve, if not comical, the booklet contended that "it isn't hard to keep quiet, and it isn't hard to escape. Actually, being captured is an excellent chance for you to pull off something pretty special."[9]

Once Hobbs's preflight training ended, he was sent to the Naval Air Station at Livermore east of San Francisco for primary training. One of those newer airfields hastily constructed after Pearl Harbor to train the overflow of pilot candidates that long-established and overcrowded fields could not handle, NAS Livermore's one-square-mile rested amid fertile farmland surrounded by majestic hills. The military facilities, including barracks and athletic fields, contrasted with the bounties nature placed in the region, but wartime demands left little room for sentimentality. The Navy needed more airfields to train the thousands of men needed to finish the task of defeating the Germans in Europe and the Japanese in the Pacific.

Five stages of training, ranging from aircraft familiarization and navigation to combat techniques and formation flying, now tested Hobbs. An array of airborne exercises challenged everything he had learned about flying, as instructors who assumed Hobbs knew nothing of his craft asked him to execute rolls, loops, and other maneuvers, and then either approved his performance or handed him a "down." If Hobbs received a down, he had to earn two "up" marks to move on. If not, he had to go before a board that would decide his fate. Scuttlebutt had it that at least half the cadets would wash out of the program and earn a speedy ticket out of Livermore.

Classroom instruction filled many of their morning schedules. Hobbs listened attentively when legendary Marine aviator Captain Joseph J. Foss—a Medal of Honor recipient for his flying feats over Guadalcanal in late 1942 and the United States' leading ace with twenty-six kills—lectured the group on tactics. Billy considered Foss a role model and hoped to emulate him when he entered combat.

Within a few days of his June arrival, Hobbs was in the air with his instructor, learning how to fly an aircraft called the "Yellow Peril," a name concocted from the brilliant yellow fabric that covered the biplane in hopes of making it easier to spot in the air and thus reduce the occurrence of accidents. Carrying both instructor and cadet in open cockpits, the N2S Stearman aircraft sported a 220-horsepower engine that produced a top speed of 124 miles per hour for the twenty-five-foot-long trainer. Like every other cadet, Hobbs prepared two parachutes for his June 18 flight—one for himself and a second for his instructor, a man named Holladay—climbed into the rear seat, and strapped himself in as the instructor, flying from the front seat, taxied down the runway. Once in the air, Holladay communicated with Hobbs through the gosport, a stethoscope-like tube attached to Hobbs's ears through which he listened while Holladay spoke.

LIKE HOBBS, SINCE youth Lieutenant Gerald C. Hennesy wanted to
be a fighter pilot. He read all the stories about the famed World War I
flying aces, including American Eddie Rickenbacker, who gained fame
shooting down German aircraft. "I admired their bravery and skill," said
Hennesy. Trying to emulate his heroes, Hennesy "did everything I could
to make sure I was assigned to a fighter squadron."[10] Hennesy learned
in primary flight training that when flying, a fighter pilot needed to be
aware of everything occurring in the air space surrounding him, and that
he had to be confident that he could best any foe he met in battle.

Some of the rawest cadets erred in thinking that, because they had
not yet left the United States and entered the combat zone, they were
somehow immune to dangers. They did so at their own peril, for dangers
lurked above Indiana farms and California airfields, far from the sounds
of war that reverberated thousands of miles from American shores.

"When I first started flight training I did lose a fellow student who
was a friend of mine," said Hennesy. "He was on a required training
flight in a 'Yellow Peril,' an open-cockpit Stearman biplane. The object
of the lesson was to practice what to do in the event of an engine failure.
The instructor would cut the engine to simulate a failure and the student
was to immediately push the joystick forward to nose down and keep air
flying speed. My friend did this, but unfortunately he had not fastened
his seat belt and was thrown out of the plane. Too close to the ground,
his parachute was unable to fully open and he was killed. His death saddened me deeply, and the event brought into focus the realization that
one simple mistake when flying could be fatal."[11]

IN TWELVE JUNE days, Hobbs flew nineteen flights averaging ninety
minutes each, including eleven solos, all in the "Yellow Peril." Holladay and other instructors showed him how to land Navy style, which
required the pilot to land with the tail down in a stall, and asked Hobbs
to execute other maneuvers that required mastering before he could advance to the next phase of their training. Combat hovered in the distant
future, but Hobbs had taken a step closer to that dogfight he so desired.

"BILLY, WHAT DOES THE MEDAL MEAN?"

Twenty miles northwest of Hobbs, Eugene Mandeberg, called Mandy by his friends but Eugene by his parents, experienced similar training. Some in his family thought that the military and air combat were awkward companions for the quiet, studious native of Detroit, Michigan, who loved to make people laugh, not by telling jokes but with clever comments about people and actions he observed. Contemplation, books, and writing were his tastes, but like Hobbs, Mandeberg placed his future on hold to don a uniform and fight for his country. Whereas Hobbs selected a fighter because of the one-on-one thrill of aerial action, Mandeberg held a deeper motivation. He told his brother, Mitchell, that he did not want to be responsible for anyone else's life, as he would be if he were to pilot a dive-bomber or torpedo plane containing a rear seat gunner. In a fighter, he alone would suffer the consequences of his actions.

No one in his family was surprised that Eugene had given part of his free time at preflight school at St. Mary's College east of San Francisco to editing the post newsletter, *The Eaglet,* for he had always loved writing. While most of his high school classmates had assumed he would join his father in running the successful family furniture business, Mandeberg, who took his Jewish faith seriously, turned to writing, where he could express his views on society's ills. "He was very witty," said his niece, Jean Mandeberg. "He was a promising writer. He was hired by the University of Michigan's newspaper, *Michigan Daily,* to do a column. He had a social conscience. His stories were ahead of his time."[12] Before being called into the service, he and his cousin, Michael, had put down a deposit on a loft in lower Manhattan so that Mandeberg could pursue his love of writing and Michael hone his painting skills.

While he studied flying and combat techniques, the newsletter allowed him to indulge his more academic pursuits. Mandeberg crafted such crisp submissions that a caption underneath a photo of Eugene called him "an excellent organizer and writer" who had produced "splendid feature articles."[13]

Mandeberg always had a penchant for profiling the ills of society. In 1940 and 1941 he penned a series of articles for *Michigan Daily* profiling bigotry and government abuses. He attacked a suggested plan to remove aliens from factories making war materials, claiming that those people would have difficulty finding new jobs and asserting that "these people are human beings, even if they are not citizens; even if they have foreign names." In an article titled "Bringing Up Nazis," Eugene attacked parents who shunned their basic responsibilities and failed to properly raise their children. In another article, "Anti-Strike Legislation—Is It Fair to Labor?," he took the less-popular path in suggesting that if the government adopted anti-strike laws to ensure an uninterrupted flow of armaments from defense industries, that it had an inherent duty to pass "parallel laws regulating the manufacturers employing these men who cannot strike."[14]

Before entering the military, Mandeberg wrote stories that he hoped to place in national magazines. He railed against prisoners being held on death row, only later to be found innocent of their crimes; about the owner of a hamburger joint who refused service to an Italian American because of the man's heritage; and about a town council that debated minor issues while ignoring a proposal to pass a widow's pension for an elderly woman in financial difficulty. "Mrs. Holmes . . . who the hell is she?" asked one council member when he saw her name on the agenda.[15]

In his 1940 story "Private Party," detailing a fictional lynching in Georgia of a black man accused of raping a white woman, Mandeberg crafted a bitter attack against bigotry. Even though the whole town knew the accuser was lying, a mob dragged the man from jail, hanged, and burned him. The story ended when the narrator, Ralph Hudson, a man who opposed the lynching, asked one of the participants, "How can you do that to a man?" The man replies, "Why, Hudson, he isn't a man—he's a nigger."[16]

One short story Eugene wrote before entering the military suggested that, with war clouds gathering, the serene young man had already pondered what he might one day soon be asked to do. Titled "First Leave," the story highlighted a young soldier named Billy, who returned home after completing training camp, proudly wearing his uniform, from which hung a shiny medal.

"Billy, what does the medal mean?" his mother asked.

"Mean? It means that I hit the bull's-eye more times than anybody else," replied Billy. "It means that I can shoot faster and better than most fellas."

"You mean you can kill more men than the other boys."

"Oh mother, please. This is only range shooting. I'm not killing anybody."

"But you know how, don't you Billy? They even gave you a medal for it."

"Mom, I told you. We were only shooting at targets."

Later, after Billy retired to his room, the mother tiptoed up, peered in, and saw her son rubbing the medal with his sleeve to increase its shine. The mother turned away, crying softly, and muttered to herself, "Oh dear God, he doesn't understand, he doesn't understand."[17]

The themes foreshadowed what Eugene and his loved ones were about to experience. They also illustrated that while Billy Hobbs viewed the war as an opportunity to fly, Eugene Mandeberg considered it his duty to combat evil.

IN MID-1943, THE pace intensified for both Hobbs and Mandeberg. On the final two days of July, Hobbs advanced from the biplane, which reminded people of World War I flying days, to the monoplane trainer, an N2T Tutor aircraft, nicknamed the "Tiny Timm" after the plane's manufacturer, Otto Timm. The open-cockpit monoplane still held an instructor and cadet like the "Yellow Peril," but its plastic-bonded plywood created a material that was stronger and lighter than traditional plywood. Until he soloed in a single-seater, however, when he alone could control the aircraft, Hobbs would not feel he had truly joined the community of naval aviators.

With a last flight on September 7, Hobbs was at last ready for his next stop, NAS Corpus Christi, where he would learn gunnery and combat techniques and become familiar with more technologically advanced aircraft than the trainers with which he had begun. While some men joined Hobbs in Corpus Christi, Mandeberg and others traveled to NAS Melbourne in Florida. Whether in the sunshine of Florida or Texas, Hobbs and Mandeberg were about to learn how to take an aircraft into combat and turn what the Wright Brothers had envisioned as a boon to society into a military platform capable of inflicting death.

"I'M NO LONGER A VIRGIN, IN GUNNERY"

The sultry Corpus Christi climate failed to dampen Billy Hobbs's enthusiasm as instructors emphasized the traits of a successful combat pilot. They told the cadets that if they wished to pit their talents against a skilled German or Japanese pilot, they must keep physically fit to better withstand the rigors of flying in combat, and must know the strengths and weaknesses of their foe's airplanes. They stressed that they had to be aware of everything around them in the sky, and able to instantly recognize an aircraft as friend or foe. They repeatedly emphasized that they must so completely comprehend everything about a plane that they could fly it without thinking, as if they and their aircraft were one entity. Finally, instructors told the initiates that, starting here in Corpus Christi or Melbourne, they had to develop a killer temperament in the air, for an enemy pilot who escaped one encounter might later return to kill either them or their buddies.

Any hopes of immediately leaping into a combat-ready plane dissipated when they stepped behind the controls of the two-seater SNV trainer built by Vultee Aircraft. Hobbs, Mandeberg, and the other cadets so detested the irritating shaking of the canopy at high speeds that they nicknamed the trainer the "Vultee Vibrator."

From mid-September through November, Hobbs and Mandeberg flew the SNV the first four times with an instructor before soloing in the new trainer. They and their classmates flew planes over the Gulf of Mexico, handing Hobbs and Mandeberg their initial experiences of navigating over water, a trickier skill than flying over land that was partly designed to prepare them for carrier operations.

"Had a big morning flying today," Mandeberg wrote his parents from his post at NAS Melbourne, Florida. "First we went up to 25,000 feet on an oxygen hop and played around up there. Then we went up again, only to 10,000 feet this time, and chased tails for an hour. It was good exercise." In a sign that Mandeberg was beginning to master the ability to scrutinize the sky, he added, "I can now look six different ways at once. Very good training."[18]

Hobbs was ecstatic that, at last, he was beginning to experience what he considered something akin to combat flying. In Corpus Christi, he was gaining insight that would enable him to challenge German Messerschmitts in Europe or Japanese Zeros in the Pacific. As young as Hobbs then was, he saw only the glamour of flying while overlooking the risks of piloting a combat plane. The inherent dangers became evident when Hobbs and Mandeberg had to sit in the cockpit and, accompanied by the instructor, fly the SNV with the cockpit covered with a canvas hood. The exercise was designed to simulate those times in the air when, due to cloud cover or darkness, the pilot had to resort to instrument flying, during which the unskilled aviator tended to rely on instinct or what he thought he saw instead of trusting the information from his instrument panel. Stories had already circulated of those pilots who, while flying in thick clouds, ignored their gauges and wound up flying straight into the ground.

Another cadet at Corpus Christi at the same time, James W. Vernon, said that "instrument flying strained my mind and emotions. I flew in the rear cockpit of the Vibrator under a canvas hood that shut out all sight of land and sky." Blind to what was outside while under the hood, the pilots were forced to abandon their instincts and trust their instruments, which Vernon described as "the eyes of unfriendly beasts." After a few attempts the cadets shed their fears of leaning on metallic devices and, as Vernon wrote, "I learned to believe what the instruments indicated and to ignore my body sensations, because they lied."[19]

Night flying and purposely putting the trainer into dives and stalls joined instrument flying in testing the skills and courage of the cadets. Accidents became so common at Barin Field, one of Hennesy's training fields thirty miles west of Pensacola, that cadets relabeled the strip "Bloody Barin."[20] Consequently, Hobbs was happy to log in his flight book that in November he had passed both instrument flying and radio use.

Hobbs and Mandeberg advanced closer toward combat flying when they graduated from the "Vultee Vibrator" to the more solidly-constructed all-metal SNJ Texan, a monoplane that, unlike the Vultee, looked similar to a fighter and contained many of the same features that American fighter aircraft possessed. The plane helped cadets transition from biplanes to monoplanes, and, with retractable landing gear and two forward-firing .30-caliber guns, introduced gunnery to Hobbs and the others. Vernon claimed the switch from monoplanes to biplanes was "like swapping a jackass for a mustang," and that "fun flying had returned after all those dreary hours under the instrument hood."[21]

An instructor accompanied Hobbs on his first three flights in the SNJ before the Indiana aviator soloed on January 9, 1944. In the coming weeks, the focus of training switched from basic piloting to gunnery. Firing paint-tipped bullets at a fabric sleeve towed by another plane—different colored paint allowed each cadet to determine how many times he hit his mark—Hobbs and Mandeberg pitted their ability to hit the targets against that of their classmates. One by one, the aviators charged the sleeve, and rather than trying to point the guns at the target and pulling the trigger, they aimed the entire plane, determined the distance to the target, the speed at which the tow plane moved through the air, and the point at which the bullets would intercept the sleeve. Cadet Herbert Wood said that it was much like hunting birds with a shotgun or throwing a touchdown pass to a receiver dashing down the field. "You don't point the gun at the bird because, if you do, the bird is ten feet ahead of it. You fire ahead of it and, when the shot gets there, it hits the bird."[22] Instructors warned that their lives in combat depended on their becoming so skilled in gunnery that they could hit the sleeve with one short burst rather than wasting bullets and running out of ammunition.

The energy level rose as the cadets approached their first attempts at using their airplane as a combat weapon. "And tomorrow we start gunnery," Mandeberg wrote to his parents from Melbourne. "That's the biggest part of the flight program. It ought to be fun." Mandeberg so enjoyed his initial runs at a sleeve that he joked in a letter to his mother, "Everything is fine here. I got some hits in gunnery, so I'm no longer a virgin," and then to allay her fears quickly added, "in gunnery."[23]

As they neared the end of training at Corpus Christi, Mandeberg, who had been moved from Melbourne to the Texan airfield, and Hobbs flew solo most of the time. Hobbs's final eighteen flights, occurring in nine days near the end of March 1944, led to the day every cadet awaited—being commissioned as ensigns and receiving their wings as Navy aviators. On April 1 a proud Billy Hobbs accepted certificates stipulating that he had passed the test in instrument flying in single-engine planes, a card naming him as a naval aviator, and most importantly, the wings he could attach to the uniform he would now wear as a naval ensign.

Notices appeared in the *Kokomo Tribune* and in the local newspapers of every newly commissioned ensign. "Eugene Esmond Mandeberg, son of Mr. and Mrs. Nathan Mandeberg, . . . has been commissioned an ensign in the United States Naval Reserve, from the Naval Air Training Center, at Corpus Christi, Tex.," announced the *Detroit Free Press* on April 11, 1944.[24]

Now officially a part of the Navy, the former cadets listed their top three choices for aircraft. Hobbs and Mandeberg placed fighters as their top choices. Once they learned the aircraft in which they would continue their training, Hobbs and Mandeberg would move to the final phase of preparation before joining the fleet for either European or Pacific combat.

"I WOULD RATHER SIT MY HIND END IN AN F6F"

Operating out of the next post, NAS Miami, was the closest to experiencing combat conditions Hobbs and Mandeberg would have without leaving the United States. In southern Florida, their time flying in trainers had ended. From here on, the newly commissioned ensigns would practice with the same fighters, dive-bombers, or torpedo planes that currently battled Hitler's forces in Europe and the Japanese in the Pacific.

Before traveling to Miami, Hobbs enjoyed a few days back home, feasting on Hattie's cooking and meeting hometown friends. After an all too brief break, on April 6 Hobbs packed his suitcase and said his goodbyes. Among the items he took was a new diary with the inscription, "Presented to Ensign Wright Hobbs, From Mother & Dad, April 6, 1944."[25] Hattie and Wright hoped that their son would fill the blank pages with his actions and thoughts as he completed training and left the United States for the combat zone.

Hobbs had a busy first week in Miami. "Arrived here at N.A.S. Miami today. Like it very much," he entered in his diary on April 8. Hobbs was selected as squadron leader three days later, one day before beginning five days of ground school. "Went to ground school all day. Very boring," he wrote on April 12. He enjoyed examining the Douglas SBD-5 Dauntless aircraft, the Navy's main dive-bomber for the first three years of the war, adding in his diary, "Had ground check-out on SBD-5. Looks like a rugged plane but can't tell til I fly it." On April 16 Hobbs, accompanied by an instructor, piloted that plane for the first time, one day before taking the same aircraft up in his first solo. "Had first dual hop in SBD today," he wrote of that flight. "Nice plane but rather slow."[26] Hobbs sought speed, and while the SBD might boast an enviable war record, he preferred to fly in a single-seater fighter.

Hobbs's correspondence from Miami with his parents differed from the letters he mailed to his siblings, especially his brother, Henry. While shielding Hattie from the risks he faced in training, he divulged more to Henry. "Have been flying some and going to ground school a lot," he wrote Hattie from Miami. "Also been having some pretty tough swimming classes. They have a pretty tough course here but it is under such pleasant surroundings and conditions that a fellow doesn't mind it."[27]

Knowing that Henry would keep certain details from his parents, Billy discussed the hazards of flying. "I will give you the word on the SBD-5 (that is what we are flying)," he wrote on May 6. "She is a rugged air plane, but slow as all hell as compared to the Jap fighters. It really hustles a fellow to get 225 M.P.H. with a 500# bomb and a full load of gas. The rate of climb is very slow. We heard that when the Japs see the SBD's coming, they get out all the B-B guns they can find." Billy at least loved the speed the SBD achieved when making near vertical dives. "If anybody asks how fast a plane I am flying just say I did 455 M.P.H. That was nearly straight down from 18,000 feet." While admitting the plane's defects, Billy also wagered he would not have to take one into combat. "There is no doubt that I will fly either a Helldiver [Curtiss SB2C Helldiver dive-bomber eventually replaced the SBD] or F6F [Grumman F6F Hellcat fighter, the Navy's principal fighter aircraft] in the fleet. Both are darn good planes. I would rather sit my hind end in an F6F. They are so easy to handle."[28]

Though divulging to Henry that he, like every other naval aviator, daily faced peril, Hobbs continued to sanitize his letters to Hattie. "We (Briggs & I) are going up for a high-altitude oxygen flight in a few minutes," he wrote Hattie in a letter that marginally hinted at the dangers. "We go up to about 20,000 feet. It is more or less to get us used to using our oxygen equipment. In case anybody passes out, our gunners can take over."[29]

Diary entries from April 28 to May 2 again referred to the hazards of his occupation. "Started on a navigation hop but was forced to turn back," he recorded in one of the entries. He admitted that on the second of two gunnery flights, he "got lost from tow plane on the last hop," and that on April 29 he "nearly got killed today. Engine quit on take-off."[30]

The most perilous portion of training proved to be the exercise called field carrier landing practice, where the ensigns had to land their planes on fields on which were marked the outlines of aircraft carrier decks. Lieutenant (jg) Odom asserted that "I was scared to death all the time" at setting down on a small patch of land bordered on both sides by trees. With the signal officer standing along the runway relaying signals indicating if the plane was in the proper position, "We used to do that for hours on end. Day in. Day out."[31]

Hobbs found an outlet from the rigors of flying in dancing, nightclubs, and females. He spent some evenings with Mary Glynn, a local girl he had met on April 14. "Was out to Colonial Club with Mary last nite," he entered in his diary. "Nice time." On a date with Mary a few days later, he "did O.K. Met her sister who is quite fast." He also dated a girl he referred to as "CM," and two days later accompanied Anne McDonald and Kathy Morcott to the "5 O'Clock Club." Later in the month, he "went out to Surf Club in afternoon with Kathy & CM. Hit Kitty Davis that night. Had one hell of a time."[32] Hobbs referred to a popular Miami Beach nightclub owned by a woman named Kitty Davis and her husband that catered to the burgeoning number of naval aviators posted to the area. She was so renowned in southern Florida that Hobbs left with an autographed photo of Davis and the ensign sitting at one of the tables.

"Say, what do you mean, kidding me about drinking rum," he wrote to brother Henry in May. "That blonde didn't even drink any. Another couple did all that drinking. My gal wouldn't drink, wouldn't dance, but was really built so I figured she might do the other thing (you can guess what that was) so that is what we did. Ain't I a bad boy!"

Commenting on his social life was not the only boasting Hobbs did to his brother. He also bragged about what he would do once he reached the combat zone. When he learned that Henry had failed the physical examination to enter the military, he consoled his brother. "Mother told me about you not passing your physical. Now Hen don't feel too darn bad. I think if I get out there, I can do enough damage to do both of us."[33]

Hobbs hit the dating jackpot on May 23, when he met a girl named Page Du Pre. Captivated by the vivacious female, he spent every possible moment with her. "I had a lovely evening with Page Du Pre," he recorded in his diary on that first night. "I never enjoyed myself more in all my life." Hobbs could not be certain, but he had met the girl who might one day become a major part of his life. "Perhaps I will realize more."[34]

THEIR RELATIONSHIP WOULD have to be from long distance, though. The next month the Navy sent Hobbs to Naval Station Great Lakes near Chicago, where he and other ensigns would qualify for carrier landings. The Navy had converted two Great Lakes sidewheel passenger vessels into modified aircraft carriers, the USS *Sable* (IX-81) and the USS *Wolverine* (IX-64), solely to train officers like Hobbs in conducting their first landings aboard a carrier. Hobbs had to make eight landings aboard the *Sable* to qualify, and in the unnerving initial run, from above the *Sable* appeared to Hobbs as small as a postage stamp. Other ensigns washed out because they could never master the delicate art of setting a plane down on a carrier deck, but Hobbs successfully completed his eight landings to earn his qualification on June 15, 1944.

Now a qualified carrier pilot, Hobbs received a fifteen-day leave to visit family. He had left his hometown as a civilian on his way to training, but returned to Kokomo an ensign, replete in shiny uniform bearing the wings of a naval aviator. He had to pack as much fun as possible into his two weeks, as a new air group was about to form that would take Billy Hobbs, Eugene Mandeberg, and other aviators to war.

CHAPTER 2

"Kids Jerked Right Out of High School"
Air Group 88 Takes Form, 1944

TO DATE HOBBS and Mandeberg had only been training for war, gaining the skills and confidence in an aircraft, but as part of an air group it was now time to put into action all the information they had absorbed over the last year or more.

The naval air group to which the pair would be assigned differed greatly from those that existed during the early portions of the war. In 1942 and 1943, when the United States had no choice but to slow the Axis advances in Europe and in the Pacific, the typical carrier air group featured four squadrons—fighter, bomber, and torpedo squadrons—comprising upward of one hundred planes. By the middle of 1944, the configuration changed as conditions, especially in the Pacific, altered. Naval air enthusiasts claimed that faster, newer enemy aircraft had made obsolete the older and slower Helldiver dive-bombers and Avenger torpedo planes, and that an aircraft carrier could be better utilized if it bore mostly fighters and fighter-bombers. With the advent of the kamikaze aircraft in October 1944, the United States reduced the number of dive-bombers and torpedo planes to make room for more of the superb F6F Hellcat fighters and F4U Corsair fighter-bombers.

Unlike the carrier's day-to-day crew, which remained with the vessel as long as she was operational, air groups typically spent about six months in combat before being reassigned home, where they would become the nuclei of newer squadrons then forming for war. The mixture of experienced and untested fliers, such as Hobbs and Mandeberg, avoided the calamities that occurred earlier in the war when, by necessity, the United States had to send squadrons of inexperienced pilots against war-honed enemy fliers. In 1944, Hobbs and Mandeberg would benefit from the wisdom of men who had already encountered enemy aircraft and could impart lessons more valuable than training-manual dictates.

Air Group 88, the unit to which Hobbs and Mandeberg were assigned, was formed and commissioned at the Naval Air Station, Atlantic City, New Jersey, on August 15, 1944, Hobbs's twenty-second birthday. "What a birthday!" he wrote in his aviation log that day, expressing excitement that he had joined a unit that would within half a year, after completing advanced training as an air group, be on its way to combat.[1] While he had no preference whether he would wind up in Europe or the Pacific—he simply wanted to put his flying talents against those of a foe—Hattie implored the heavens that the Navy would send her son to Europe, where the naval forces played a less prominent role than their Army brethren and where her son would be less likely to suffer injury or death. She followed the war's progress in her hometown newspaper, the *Kokomo Tribune,* and knew of the rape of Nanking, the Bataan Death March, and other Japanese atrocities. The last place she wished for her son to serve was in the Pacific against what everyone on the home front considered a merciless enemy. She prayed that his training, which had been conducted primarily in the eastern half of the United States, indicated that his unit would be earmarked for Europe instead of the more distant and seemingly more brutal Pacific.

Hobbs stood at attention with the other aviators of Air Group 88 as the commissioning ceremony unfolded. Their chief officer, Commander S. S. Searcy Jr., was, according to naval custom, a fighter pilot. In the coming months he would direct the unit's actions and, hopefully, create an *esprit de corps* that would turn disparate elements into a cohesive air group capable of handling anything that came its way, both in training and in combat. Three squadron leaders—one each for the fighter, bomber, and torpedo squadrons—would execute his commands and begin the process of transforming the men into a skilled, confident group of aviators.

In his talk to the fliers, Commodore Gordon Rowe, Commander Fleet Air, emphasized that their success in war depended on the effort they now expended during air group training. He stressed that if they came together now and learned to function as a coordinated air group, not only would they become a well-oiled war machine whose effectiveness in combat would be assured, but they would also heighten their chances of returning to loved ones.

In his brief talk, Commander Searcy ended all debate as to their final destination by emphasizing "the size of the task that had yet to be accomplished in the Pacific in war against the Japanese."[2] Hattie's prayers would go unanswered, but Billy had to stifle his excitement because in the Pacific, where aircraft carriers had emerged as the nation's principal naval weapon, he was all but certain to engage enemy pilots. Hobbs was first posted to the bomber squadron, but when within two weeks that unit was slashed from thirty-six planes to twenty-four so that the fighting squadron could be expanded, included among the aviators shifted to the fighting squadron was Billy Hobbs.

He related to the fighting squadron's demeanor. The other aviators possessed the same confidence in their skills as he did, and wanted nothing more than to finish their training and join other fighter pilots in the combat zone. They exuded that spirit when the fighting squadron gathered at Atlantic City's Claridge Hotel on September 1 for the commissioning party, when Hobbs and his companions boasted that Fighting Squadron 88 (VF-88) was the top unit around and that the Japanese had best be wary when VF-88 arrived in the Pacific.

"THOSE POOR YOUNG GUYS"

It was easy to strut around and show their feathers while still in the United States, though. They had to earn their stripes in combat, something that more than 80 percent of the Air Group had yet to accomplish. Mostly naval reserves instead of regular Navy, the aviators and the aircrewmen of Air Group 88 painted a cross-section of America. The torpedo squadron's (VT-88) history claimed that their members came from every walk of life and were "for the most part kids jerked right out of high school, not old enough to vote, yet old enough to fly a torpedo plane right into the heart of the Japanese Empire."[3] The same could be said of Hobbs's fighting squadron (VF-88) and of the bomber unit (VB-88).

The newcomers had every reason to be confident in a squadron that purposely mixed the inexperienced pilots with combat-tested men. Hobbs could turn to the squadron's executive officer, Lieutenant Malcolm W. Cagle, a 1941 graduate of the Naval Academy who served for two years in destroyers before becoming a flight instructor back in the States. Many called Cagle the best pilot of the bunch.

Lieutenant (jg) Marvin R. Odom, called "Odie" by his squadron members, loved to share humorous anecdotes, especially when accompanied by his close friend, Ensign Leonard Komisarek, called "Komo." The two could go on endlessly about their exploits ashore or while in the air, but Odom had already scraped with fifteen Japanese planes in the South Pacific, shooting down one aircraft moments before his own Hellcat coughed and sputtered smoke from an enemy's guns. He safely landed in the water—one of the two times he had to make an emergency landing in the ocean, before a destroyer picked him up.

He could consult with Lieutenant (jg) William T. Watkinson, who entered the Navy immediately after the attack on Pearl Harbor because he wanted to avenge what the Japanese had done to his country. After being trained in North Carolina by Gerald Ford, a future United States president, Watkinson served as a test pilot, checking out new aircraft before they were handed over for active service. The prototype image of a maverick flier, Watkinson "did a lot of things I wasn't supposed to. I flew under every New York bridge on the East River." By 1944 Watkinson had so proved his skill with an airplane that he had been selected to fly night fighters, usually reserved for the premier pilots as the task required them to take off and land on aircraft carriers in total darkness. Before he went into action with Air Group 88, Watkinson had amassed more than three times the hours in the air as had Hobbs and the other inexperienced aviators, whom Watkinson called "those poor young guys." Despite being surrounded by novices, "I didn't worry about having inexperienced pilots along with me on my missions because I focused on my job, not them."[4]

Hobbs tried to emulate the movements of Lieutenant John P. Adams, a gifted combat pilot from Richmond, Virginia, who had already been awarded one Distinguished Flying Cross for actions against Japanese installations in the Marshall and Gilbert Islands in January 1942, and two Navy Crosses—after the Medal of Honor the highest recognition for valor in the Navy. In the May 1942 Battle of the Coral Sea, Adams ignored thick antiaircraft fire and dove low to charge an enemy gunboat and destroyer, both of which he damaged, and to attack a Japanese aircraft carrier. A month later during the Battle of Midway Adams ignored his own carrier's five-inch shells to defend the vessel from Japanese attack, shooting down one torpedo plane and damaging a second.

Chicago, Illinois, native Lieutenant (jg) Robert S. Willaman had earned a Distinguished Flying Cross for flying forty-six missions over enemy territory in the Solomons; Lieutenant Robert L. De Veer of the torpedo squadron (VT-88) had sunk a Japanese transport while operating out of Munda in the Solomons; and Aviation Machinist's Mate 1/c Enoch P. Tarsilia had received an Air Medal for strafing the conning tower of a German U-boat off North Africa. The bombing squadron boasted Lieutenant Edward T. La Roe, Lieutenant James P. Young, and Lieutenant (jg) Vincent B. Tibbals, the recipients of Air Medals for actions over Rabaul.

The aviators had supreme confidence in the Air Group leader, Commander Searcy, a man of unquestioned fearlessness who had already skippered a squadron in Pacific combat aboard the escort carrier USS *Natoma Bay* (CVE-62). The men assigned to command the Air Group's three squadrons brought solid, even spectacular, resumes. Lieutenant Commander Joseph E. Hart of VB-88 was reputed to be a hard-nosed officer of immense flying ability, and the torpedo squadron's Lieutenant Commander James C. Huddleston, who preferred to lead without fanfare, was labeled by the unit's official report for the early training period "the hottest glide bomber in the squadron." The report added, "We all consider ourselves extremely fortunate to have such a completely sound fellow out in front."[5]

One man, though, towered above the rest. He made an indelible impression the first time he addressed his pilots. The officer walked into the room where he had asked the members of VF-88 to gather, stepped confidently to the front with a swagger stick under one arm, and began to speak. "My name is Richard Crommelin," said the Naval Academy graduate. "You can call me Skipper." His natural ease in talking to the men cut any tension that may have existed and made the young aviators like Hobbs, who realized that they could approach their new commander without hesitation, understand that they had someone special. "I knew he'd be fine to work with," said Lieutenant (jg) Bernard I. Hamilton Jr. of VF-88's commander.[6]

Crommelin came by it naturally. He and his four brothers, Navy all, had so often distinguished themselves in Pacific encounters that newspaper articles had spread their names across the nation. "Oh, yes, we know the five Crommelin brothers," said one official at the naval hospital in Bethesda, Maryland, to *Time* magazine in January 1944. "One or the other of them always seems to be getting shot up."[7]

Four of the five Alabama brothers became naval aviators, while the fifth commanded a destroyer squadron. Richard and his siblings—John, Henry, Charles, and Quentin—had all graduated from Annapolis, and their exploits garnered praise not only in *Time* magazine, which had labeled the quintet "The Indestructibles," and in hundreds of newspapers, but also in comic books. In a piece titled "The Dixie Demons," one comic book mentioned, "Whether it's a stick of bombs smearing the Japs at Rabaul—or a trim-winged Grumman riddling a Zero—or a destroyer laying down a pre-invasion barrage—you can be certain that at least one of the Crommelin brothers had a hand in it! Virtually a 'One-Family Navy,' these five fighting officers have blasted their way through every major battle in the Pacific—vying with each other in piling up both wounded and decorations!"[8]

The oldest, John G. Crommelin Jr., born in 1902, graduated from the Naval Academy in 1923. As the ship's executive officer aboard the USS *Enterprise* (CV-6), John saw action in the June 1942 Battle of Midway. He later participated in the brutal naval slugfests in the waters about Guadalcanal, earning the appellation "Bomb Run John" for his aggressive tactics in commanding carrier-based dive-bombers. While serving as the chief of staff aboard the escort carrier USS *Liscome Bay* (CVE-56), John was badly burned when a Japanese submarine torpedoed and sank the ship off Makin Island in November 1943, during the invasion of the Gilbert Islands. The injured officer made his way through the blazing carrier to the flight deck, jumped overboard, and was rescued by a destroyer.

Henry C. Crommelin graduated from the Naval Academy two years after John. As commander of a destroyer division during the November 1943 invasion of Tarawa, Henry was awarded the Silver Star when he moved his ships dangerously close to Betio islet to knock out enemy shore batteries. He later participated in the October 1944 Battle of Leyte Gulf.

The third brother, Charles, Naval Academy Class of 1931, gained fame as a fighter pilot in the Pacific. He earned a Distinguished Flying Cross for action over the Japanese-held Marcus Island in August 1943, and was severely wounded in November near the Marshall Islands when, while leading a strafing attack, antiaircraft fire ripped into his plane and propelled hundreds of tiny glass and metal particles into his face and body. Blinded in one eye and covered with blood, Charles miraculously made it back to his carrier and eventual evacuation to a naval hospital. When he arrived in Pearl Harbor, Charles convinced the ambulance attendants to stop at the officers' club, where the injured officer walked to the bar and ordered a drink. "I just wanted to show those kids that it's not so tough to be shot up," he later said.[9]

From the Academy's Class of 1941, Richard's fourth sibling, Quentin, served aboard the USS *Saratoga* (CV-3), off Guadalcanal in August 1942. Later in the war he led Corsair squadrons against the Japanese.

The VF-88 skipper had tough acts to follow, but he stamped his mark on the service with the same firm imprint as his brothers. A graduate of the Naval Academy Class of 1938, Crommelin served aboard the USS *Yorktown* (CV-5) in 1942. While with that carrier, he shot down two Japanese Zeros in the May 1942 Battle of the Coral Sea, before Japanese bullets damaged his plane and forced him to ditch in the sea. With his brother John not far away, Crommelin also fought in the Battle of Midway, an action that resulted in his *Yorktown* being sunk but which saw Crommelin help disrupt an attack by eighteen enemy aircraft. For his valor in both battles, Crommelin was awarded a pair of Navy Crosses, becoming one of a few men so honored and an officer marked for fast advancement up the chain of command.

They had an apt teacher in Lieutenant Commander Richard G. Crommelin. He had been through what they were about to experience.

He had faced the fears, the doubts, and the exhilaration they were about to encounter, exuding bravery, charisma, decency, and leadership in the process. He could impart to them the lessons he picked up in the South Pacific and at Midway. The newcomers had much to learn, information that could help save their lives, but with Crommelin as their guide, Hobbs and the other young aviators figured their chances for survival had improved.

"ANY TIME YOU GO UP, IT'S A RISK"

After being transferred from the bombing squadron to Crommelin's VF-88, Hobbs began flying the fighter that he would take into battle, the F6F Hellcat. He took a Hellcat up with the squadron for the first time near the end of August, and fell in love with the ease with which the sleek fighter handled and turned. Flying a dive-bomber accompanied by a rear seat gunner was fine, but he preferred to operate alone, and in a Hellcat he controlled everything, from the speed of the plane to the firing of its machine guns.

From the middle of August to mid-November, Hobbs and the fighting squadron trained at an airfield near Atlantic City, while the bombing squadron did the same at Wildwood, New Jersey, and VT-88 operated off Martha's Vineyard, Massachusetts. Prior to this, Hobbs and Mandeberg had focused on the skills required to operate aircraft. At these locations, each squadron would learn how to conduct war operations as a cohesive unit before eventually joining the other squadrons to practice and develop air group activities.

This phase of training offered two parts: instructions in ground school and execution in the air. They learned to develop squadron tactics; sharpen gunnery, strafing, and bombing skills; drop torpedoes; navigation; field carrier landings; and night flying, during what men in the torpedo squadron called "the inky black nights which nobody likes."[10]

Before the end of August, Hobbs and every inexperienced aviator who thought the war stood thousands of miles distant learned how wrong they were. In an August 25 ceremony at Martha's Vineyard Lieutenant Willaman received the Distinguished Flying Cross he had been awarded for his actions in the Solomons, including attacking and helping sink a large Japanese transport. A high-ranking officer praised the pilot, and then reminded the assembled aviators that even though they were still in the United States preparing for combat, their training presented risks they could not ignore.

Thirty minutes after receiving his medal, Willaman hopped in his torpedo plane for a routine exercise. While conducting a dive over the airfield, the rear section and both wings of his Avenger aircraft ripped off, sending the decorated hero to a fiery death as he crashed west of the field. The skill and courage Willaman had exhibited in the Solomons could not help him avoid a tragic end in a training run.

The death of a decorated combat pilot rattled the younger aviators and offered a harsh lesson. The war they had always viewed as distant, the one they studied on maps and in reports or watched on movie reels, had suddenly planted itself at their feet. The dangers were no longer confined to the war zone; they existed above the fields of New England and in the waters off the eastern United States coast. August 25 proved to be a sobering moment for the neophytes in Air Group 88.

Other incidents underscored those lessons. One day before Willaman's death, Hobbs's squadron mate, Ensign Vincent Dacey, had to make a water landing in his Hellcat near Strathmere, New Jersey, when his motor quit at 5,000 feet. The next month a defective master rod forced another VF-88 pilot, Ensign E. J. Loftus, to make an emergency landing south of Barnegat, New Jersey.

In the bombing squadron, Aviation Radioman 3/c (often referred to as the gunner) Arthur C. Briggs suffered the only injury of his wartime service when he smashed his head during training. "My seat rested on a ring so that I could swing around and protect the rear," said Briggs. "My seat belt ring broke and I hit my head and cut it. Blood was running down my face. I went right to the hospital and they sewed it up. It was more embarrassing than anything."[11] His buddies in VB-88 had fun with Briggs, calling him Dimwit after a popular cartoon character, Denny Dimwit, from the *Winnie Winkle* comic strip that appeared in newspapers.

Other incidents lacked the humor of Briggs's injury. On September 7 at Wildwood, Lieutenant (jg) George E. Tobey Jr. of VB-88, flying in an SB2C Helldiver, "failed to pull out of a dive, and crashed." An investigation concluded "that the forward sliding cockpit enclosure became disengaged during the dive, striking the pilot, and apparently rendering him incapable of controlling the aircraft. Lieutenant (jg) Tobey was killed instantly and the plane was completely demolished."[12]

The next month, again at Wildwood, Ensign Robert A. Kinker crashed and died in the Delaware Bay four miles west of Green Creek, New Jersey, while making a routine dive. The report stated that "the crash appears to have been the direct result of an error on the part of the pilot as to his altitude. A slight haze may have been a contributing factor."[13]

Air Group 88, and the torpedo squadron specifically, suffered its worst day on October 16 when four men—Lieutenant A. William Dorney Jr., piloting one plane with Aviation Radioman 3/c Lewis E. Jones Jr., and Ensign Wallace Brinkley, flying a second plane with Aviation Radioman 3/c Dean D. Shaffer—failed to return from a routine night flight over the sea. Superiors attributed their disappearances without a trace to poor weather or vertigo.

"Once more the chill blast of tragedy iced the squadron's spirits," Lieutenant Commander Huddleston wrote in his official report. "Their loss was a shock and has been keenly felt over the life of the squadron," summed the squadron's history. However, the incident stressed a lesson that everyone, particularly those on the home front, needed to hear. "This tragedy emphasized a fact which is little understood by laymen, that training exercises are difficult and hazardous. Readying for combat is almost part of combat itself. These men died fighting for their country as surely as though they had been shot down over the heart of Tokyo."[14]

Aviation Radioman 3/c Briggs knew Ensign Kinker, and tried to balance his feelings toward Kinker with the realities of war. "We lost some guys in training," said Briggs. "We were around twenty years old, and felt bad that it happened, but you were busy and moved on. That was the way it was. Accidents, engine failure, happened. Sometimes, the pilot concentrated so much on the target that they lost track of how low they were, and the gunner didn't warn them in time. Robert Kinker's death, when you're younger, you don't dwell on those things long."[15]

Aviation Machinist's Mate 1/c Merald R. Woods agreed, but added that the deaths, no matter how hard one tried to forget them, affected the Air Group. "We were very close to our pilots. We were like members of a family, and it really hurt when they didn't come back. The longer you were together, the more fellowship you had. Some probably didn't realize that there could be dangers in training, but any time you go up, it's a risk."[16]

The trying months ended with night field carrier landings and gunnery exercises. By then, confidence had been so developed that the squadrons hosted competitions to see which unit hit target sleeves with more efficiency. "The squadron began to function smoothly, to operate as a unit, to gain confidence in itself," wrote the torpedo squadron's history.[17]

Having trained as individual squadrons, the time had come for the aviators to prove they could fly with the same cohesion as an air group.

"I WILL STICK WITH THE GRUMMAN ALL THE TIME"

The Air Group began arriving at Otis Field, a part of Camp Edwards on Cape Cod, Massachusetts, on November 15, and by early the next month had settled in to start their training. The fliers of the torpedo squadron were especially interested in the hotshot aviators of VF-88, as those fighter pilots would be the ones who would protect them in the air while they launched their payloads in the heat of combat. "These were the lads that would be covering us and protecting us from the enemy," wrote Lieutenant Commander Huddleston in the Air Group's history (edited by Commander S. S. Searcy Jr.) after the war. "What we saw pleased us. They were a snappy alert outfit and the reputation that had preceded them from Atlantic City was plenty good."[18]

The weather off the New England coast in November and December posed a formidable obstacle. "Here conditions were very different," Lieutenant Commander Joseph Hart wrote in VB-88's unit history. Huddleston's conclusion in the torpedo squadron history called their new destination "grim, grisly, winterful Otis Field" and added that while the weather and airplane availability had been less than desirable at their previous location, "here they became a veritable plague."[19]

Billy Hobbs had flown in some rough Indiana weather, but Cape Cod's combination of arctic temperatures, snow, rain, sleet, rough winds, low ceilings, and poor visibility hampered operations in trying ways. Blizzards and high winds prevented the torpedo squadron from flying for almost half of one month, and VB-88 was grounded for more than half the time at Otis Field.

"Doggone, that weather was rough!" said Merald Woods. "That weather is a worry to the pilot."[20] Aviators joked that they could pour defroster on one wing, only to have it freeze before they walked to the other wing. Plane wheels froze to the ground and engines coughed and sputtered without igniting. Those fortunate to lift off feared that before their flight ended, their engines would ice up and cause a malfunction. Hobbs sometimes had to wait before climbing into his fighter because of a line of other aviators waiting for engine preheaters to thaw out their aircraft.

Issues with inadequate buildings magnified their problems. "Seaters, caps, overcoats and gloves were needed as much inside as out," one VT-88 report stated.[21] Men washed and shaved in ice water and often slept in their flight gear in antiquated buildings heated by pot-bellied stoves. Pilots had to be scratched from flying because their nasal passages were clogged from the colds they suffered in the wintry conditions.

Searcy had less than three months to perfect group tactics, meld the squadrons into a cohesive unit, and prepare them for battle, but the gales and howls of the New England weather seemed aligned to deny him his opportunity.

SEARCY WOULD NEED every available day, for by the time the Air Group left Otis Field, men would have to be able to fly their aircraft without thinking and the different squadrons would have to integrate their tactics and learn to operate as a single unit.

Air Group 88 had the latest and, in some cases, the best aircraft with which to go into battle. Huddleston's torpedo pilots flew the TBM Avenger, the Navy's standard torpedo bomber in the war. The advent of enhanced Japanese antiaircraft batteries exploited the Avenger's main vulnerability—its lack of speed—and altered its main function from a torpedo plane to a glide-bombing aircraft. Forty feet long and featuring a wingspan of fifty-four feet, the lumbering Avenger flew at speeds up to 276 miles per hour.

An officer and two enlisted operated the Avenger. The officer flew the aircraft, while a gunner sat in the ball turret at the plane's tail end, facing aft, to be on the lookout for enemy planes. Meanwhile, a radioman worked in a cramped compartment ten feet from the pilot in the plane's belly, where he was blind to outside events.

The plane, which everyone called "torpeckers" (because, as Aviation Machinist's Mate 1/c Woods said, when the bomb bay doors opened to drop its load, "it looked like a pecker hanging down"[22]), featured two .50-caliber forward-firing machine guns, another in the rear rotating turret, and a .30-caliber gun in the belly. The Avenger could carry one ton of demolition bombs, incendiaries, or fragmentation bombs.

Although slow, the sturdily constructed Avenger could absorb tremendous punishment while carrying out its assignments, making it extremely popular to the men who flew them. "It is with reverence in our voices and affection in our hearts that we speak about 'the plane,'" the torpedo squadron's history stated. The Avenger was "dependable, sturdy, fast, and able to come back under the most adverse conditions." The aviators boasted that they could do almost anything in the Avenger, including operating as "glide bomber supreme, long range scout, low level attack plane, and scavenger of enemy subs on the high seas."[23]

The Curtiss SB2C Helldiver dive-bomber made Aviation Radioman 3/c Arthur C. Briggs of the bomber squadron happy that the Navy finally got it right. Almost thirty-seven feet long, the Helldiver carried a pilot and a rear gunner—Briggs's spot—who operated the radio and the twin .30-caliber machine guns. The Helldiver carried four fixed .50-caliber machine guns in the wings, which the pilot fired, and two flexible .30-caliber machine guns in the rear, which gunners like Briggs operated. The plane could carry over a ton of bombs in its bay, or 500 pounds of bombs under each wing. In attacking, the pilot aimed his Helldiver at the objective, aligned the bombsight with the target, and released his bombs.

Numerous problems at first plagued the Helldiver. A faulty electrical system might suddenly lower the wheels, and during landings the plane's tailhook sometimes failed. Earlier in the war carrier pilots had labeled the Helldiver "The Beast" or called them flying coffins because of the inordinate number of men killed in the plane. Happily for Briggs and the other members of VB-88, the Navy had ironed out those early-war issues, and the Helldiver became one of the most dependable dive-bombers to operate in the war. "They got those things corrected," said Briggs. "The SB2Cs had more bombs, were faster and bigger. It was good after they got those kinks worked out."[24]

ENSIGN HOBBS HAD no doubt that he and the third aircraft, the Grumman F6F Hellcat fighter, were made for each other. Some fliers preferred the Chance Vought F4U Corsair, but Hobbs never swayed. "They are a wee bit faster," Hobbs wrote of the Corsair to his brother Henry from Otis Field, "but the old Hellcat is a lot better all the way around. Much more dependable. I will stick with the Grumman all the time."[25]

The Hellcat had to be good if it were to compete with the Japanese Mitsubishi A6M Zero, until then considered by military experts to be the premier fighting aircraft in the war. After the Battle of Midway in June 1942, three of the Navy's top fighter pilots—Lieutenants Butch O'Hare, Jimmy Thach, and James Flatley—told President Roosevelt that the Navy needed a plane that could climb faster than the Zero and possess enhanced maneuverability. Grumman Aircraft Engineering Corporation produced the answer. The thirty-three-foot-long plane had a wingspan of forty-two feet and flew at top speeds over 375 miles per hour. Since it could carry bombs and rockets, it allowed the Navy to reduce the numbers of torpedo and dive-bomber aircraft assigned to each carrier air group. After making its first appearance in the August 31, 1943, attack on Marcus Island, the Hellcat became the Navy's standard carrier-based fighter.

The plane effectively combined ease of handling with superb weaponry. In battle, a Hellcat pilot could employ a 2,000-pound bomb latched to the belly, four .50-caliber machine guns in the wings, each pumping more than 1,000 armor-piercing rounds per minute, two 20mm cannon, and attachments under each wing for launching rockets. Unlike earlier in the war, when fighter guns were aligned to produce a horizontal pattern, a newer bore-sight pattern angled the gun directions toward a midpoint that allowed the pilot to place almost 95 percent of the shells within a three-foot diameter circle from 1,000 feet. Hobbs and Mandeberg could track their firing by loading the Hellcat guns with three different bullets fired repetitively—a tracer bullet, followed by an armor-piercing bullet, and then an incendiary. The tracer bullets let him know how close to the target his firing was. This concentration of firepower made the Hellcat a deadlier machine in attacking Japanese Zeros in the air or strafing them and other targets on the ground.

The Hellcat also handed Hobbs and Mandeberg other advantages. The Zero maintained its edge in maneuverability, but the Hellcat bested the Zero with an extra thirty miles per hour, an engine that enabled it to operate at higher altitudes, armor that protected the pilot and his fuel tanks (self-sealing gas tanks that prevented leaking or igniting after being hit by enemy fire), enhanced vision over the nose, and the ability to carry a drop tank for greater range. These benefits produced an astonishing 19:1 kill ratio for the Hellcat in aerial skirmishes.

Ace Japanese fighter pilot Masatake Okumiya wrote after the war, "There is no doubt that the new Hellcat was superior" in most respects. "Of the many American fighter planes we encountered in the Pacific, the Hellcat was the only aircraft which could acquit itself with distinction in a fighter-vs.-fighter dogfight."[26] David McCampbell, the U.S. Navy's premier ace, topped Okumiya by calling the Hellcat the greatest plane of the Pacific War.

As good as the machines were, victory demanded that the pilots who flew the Hellcat be the best, and here the United States Navy held its biggest advantage. Slow in the beginning to send skilled aviators to the Pacific, shortly afterward naval air training programs, such as the one Hobbs and Mandeberg had recently completed, produced an ongoing stream of capable fliers to man its fighters, dive-bombers, and torpedo planes. As the United States expanded, the Japanese suffered the reverse. They had lost hundreds of talented pilots flying in China and in a host of dogfights across the Pacific, but they failed to create an adequate training program to replace those losses. While the United States stacked its air groups with gifted aviators, the Japanese waged war with depleted air groups.

"ABOUT ALL THAT WAS LEFT WAS THE COCKPIT AND ME"

At Otis Field Air Group 88 expanded to four squadrons. Under the command of Lieutenant Commander Hart, who shifted over from

VB-88, the bombing-fighting squadron (VBF-88) flew the F4U Corsair, a plane with an inverted gull-wing design. The aircraft's powerful engine produced speeds of more than 400 miles per hour, but the long nose required for the larger engine reduced the pilot's visibility during carrier landings, and the plane had a tendency to bounce upon landings. However, those shortcomings were offset by the plane's outstanding performance in battle, as Marine aviators in the Solomons earlier in the war had proven in hundreds of aerial encounters with Japanese pilots. Its faster speed allowed it to climb quicker than most fighters, and the Corsair's longer range and increased fuel capacity permitted the pilot to fly farther and remain in the sky longer. Since the Corsair was able to carry 1,000 pounds of bombs and wield eight five-inch rockets, Hart planned to train his men in dive-bombing and glide-bombing as well as in the customary duties reserved for the fighting squadron.

Lieutenant Commander Hart had to bring his men up to speed in a little more than one month. "We had only a few weeks to check out for the first time on the Corsair and to qualify with CV [carrier] landings," wrote Lieutenant Hennesy, one of those shifted from the fighting to the bombing-fighting squadron. After earning his wings in late 1942, Hennesy was assigned to be a flight instructor, but "I didn't want training. I wanted combat. I spent a year at Barin Field [as an instructor] and I hated it. I wanted to get into action. I don't know why I was so eager to get over there, but I was!"[27]

The elements hampered the training of all four squadrons, who now more frequently operated over water conducting carrier landings. The Air Group focused on integrating all four squadrons into a unified group to simulate actual combat conditions, with Hobbs and fellow VF-88 aviators in the van, clearing the way for the bomber and torpedo planes to follow. They practiced high- and low-altitude gunnery, glide-bombing, day and night field carrier landings, group tactics, and strafing.

Experienced fliers talked to the newcomers about the qualities exhibited by capable, and less able, pilots. They emphasized thorough preparation, marksmanship, composure under stress, thinking of the team before the individual, and above all, that while training taught them how to fly as a unit, it did not teach them combat. "What makes a poor pilot," said Lieutenant (jg) Watkinson, "is being lackadaisical in gathering information, flying alone, and not focusing on their job. You don't want an individualist. You want a team player. A few guys seemed more interested in sightseeing than they were being a pilot, and some were transferred out."[28]

Hennesy and other pilots of VBF-88 debated VF-88 pilots over which airplane, the Hellcat or the Corsair, was better, and soon a friendly rivalry arose between the two squadrons. "We knew we were in the same air group," said Merald Woods, "but there was always competition between VF and VBF, right on through the end of the war. We mechanics did the same with other mechanics to see which squadron did the best."[29]

Hobbs and Mandeberg had to be at their best, especially when it came to what the torpedo squadron history called qualification exercises aboard carriers "in the wild and turbulent North Atlantic," the scene of their first attempt to land aboard a carrier on one of the oceans.[30] Using the escort carriers USS *Prince William* (CVE-31) and USS *Core* (CVE-13), the pilots took turns fulfilling the required twenty day and two night landings at sea. One false move could cause a fiery crash aboard the swaying carrier or send the pilot and plane careening over the side into the frigid waters off New England.

"It is raining, cloudy, and black as hell. I really dread it," Hobbs wrote to his brother, Henry, on January 7, ninety minutes before he had to take off to make a carrier landing in deteriorating weather. He said that he flew out to the carrier two days earlier to make four day landings and a night landing, but matters turned sour in his initial attempt. "On my first pass at the old tub, I hit and my hook didn't catch. I bounced back in the air. The old Hellcat hit the island and #2 and #3 barrier. About all that was left was the cockpit and me. All I got out of the deal was a skinned thumb." He added, "When I was pulled out of the 'heap' everybody on the flight deck started shaking hands and congratulating me on my luck." Although rattled by the mishap, the young aviator immediately switched to another aircraft. "Just as I got out of the wreck they were bringing another plane up on the aft elevator and I took off and made three more landings, all good ones."[31] Hobbs's pluck in swiftly returning to the air earned the admiration of his squadron that day.

At Otis Field, flight activities amassed an alarming list of accident deaths, injuries, and lost planes. Hardest hit was the fighting squadron, which lost three aviators and recorded nine of the ten Air Group crashes. In November and December, one ensign had to parachute from his plane due to mechanical problems, another jumped out over South Dennis, Massachusetts, when his engine caught fire and suffered a sprained ankle, while a third crashed into the carrier barrier while qualifying aboard the USS *Core*. January added five more forced landings or barrier crashes, including Hobbs's January 5 crash, another by Howdy Harrison the same day, and a third when Lieutenant (jg) Joseph H. Sahloff struck a tree during night field carrier landings. The only serious injury during the landings occurred in a freak accident aboard the USS *Core* when Ensign O. W. Johnson of the bombing squadron, according to the unit war diary, was severely injured "as the result of a blow received from a propeller in motion. It is believed that Ensign Johnson, while manning his plane, tripped on a battery cart and was thrown into the propeller by the roll of the ship." Johnson suffered a compound fracture of the skull and was taken to the Naval Hospital, Newport, Rhode Island, and although he suffered "from loss of speech and paralysis of the right side, it is believed his condition will improve and speech regained."[32]

Johnson was fortunate compared to three of his companions. On November 18 Lieutenant Robert S. Travers and his wingman, Ensign Herbert Wood, took off for a flight over the Atlantic. At 3,000 feet, Travers's Hellcat suddenly flipped upside down and, as the Hellcat started its plunge, struck and put a gash in the wing of Woods's Hellcat. Woods feared he would have to jump from his damaged aircraft, but he regained enough control to turn back toward the field. As he did, Woods watched Travers's plane spin toward land and crash on Nashawena Island in a fiery explosion. Travers, with a wife and a nine-day-old baby at home, managed to jump out of the damaged plane before impact, but died when his parachute failed to open.

With Travers's loss, death became personal for Billy Hobbs and Eugene Mandeberg. The earlier deaths had occurred to other squadrons, but they now had lost one of their own, a young aviator who had conducted the same exercises as they did. It could just as easily have happened to Hobbs or Mandeberg, who faced a stark example that nothing was a given during a time of war. Those feelings deepened the next month when Lieutenant J. I. Drew and Ensign J. D. Cassidy, according to the unit war diary, "failed to return from a routine night training flight. Pilots and planes are listed as missing."[33] The men were assumed to have crashed in the ocean, possibly from vertigo or collision.

"I SINCERELY HOPE HE WILL NEVER GO TO THE PACIFIC"

After a long day's work, most aviators headed to the officers' club one hundred yards from the field's hangars, which offered a bar, slot machines, a jukebox, a ping-pong table, and a room for dancing. Called Duffy's Tavern after the officer who managed it, the club served turkey, shrimp, oysters, and other tempting dishes, but for those who preferred to find their fun off-base, many pilots frequented the "Seven Seas" dance club in Oak Bluffs to drink and meet the nurses and secretaries from the area.

Continuing the spirit of competition, and a youthful tendency to laugh at death, the four squadrons designed squadron patches, which the aviators proudly sewed to their uniforms. All featured the Dead Man's Hand, a full house of three aces and two eights that, according to legend, Wild Bill Hickok held when Jack McCall killed the lawman and gunfighter in 1876. The fighting squadron added the name "Gamecocks," the bombing-fighting squadron a cowboy clutching a six-shooter, and the bombing squadron a pair of skeletal hands, while the torpedo squadron inserted a pilot riding a torpedo as it plunged toward the ground, clasping a spear in one hand and two bombs in the other, with the appellation "The Tormentors" inscribed at the patch's bottom.

Most often, their fun entailed girls. "There were parties, moonlight drives to Gay Head, and a million soft words spoken to attentive ears," boasted the torpedo squadron history.[34] Billy Hobbs took full advantage of being away from Kokomo, as a diary he kept during the war listed the names and addresses of thirty-eight females. While some were hometown girls from Kokomo, others included females he met in Miami, Corpus Christi, Chicago, North Dakota, and eventually, a nurse at the Navy Base Hospital in Guam.

"So you like my taste in the way of women," Billy Hobbs wrote to his brother Henry in January, concerning a girl Billy had met. "Well the little gal up the road is really O.K. The picture didn't do her justice. She is really a knockout when she has on a low-neck strapless, backless, (skirtless and frontless) evening gown. I will pause to drool!"[35]

WHILE HOBBS PLAYED the field, the serious-minded Eugene Mande-berg settled on a girl he had met while on leave in New York City in mid-1944. Eugene's cousin, Ruth Rochlin, who lived in Manhattan and worked at USO shows, wanted to fix Eugene up with a redhead named Marie Marsicano. A devout Catholic, Marie worried about the propriety of meeting someone from another religion, in this case, Eugene's Jewish faith. She confided her fears to her priest, who advised that Marie could meet Eugene, but only if she took along another friend from the USO, who turned out to be the beautiful and popular twenty-three-year-old Sonya Levien. The trio met at a coffee shop in Times Square, but feeling uncomfortable, after a few minutes Marie excused herself and left Eugene and Sonya, both feeling somewhat awkward, alone at the table.

"Marie had this plan, and I didn't know anything about it," said Sonya years later. "She said she had this friend coming in, and as soon as she introduced us, she took a deep breath and said, 'Oh, my goodness! I have to go.' And without so much as a by-your-leave, she got up and left. She left me to tango with this guy."[36]

The pair became more acquainted as they sipped coffee. Eugene learned that Sonya had helped organize New York's Stage Door Canteen, a popular place where servicemen could dance and meet girls, and Sonya was attracted to Eugene's intellectual side. After dating a number of men she found to be shallow, Sonya had at last met someone who held aspirations—in Eugene's case, of being a writer. Eugene asked if Sonya would have dinner with him, the first in a series of dates that, within a few months, resulted in Eugene asking for Sonya's hand in marriage. She accepted, but the two agreed that they would wait until after the war to become husband and wife.

Eugene relayed the happy news to his parents in Detroit, Zelda and Nathan. Even though the parents had yet to meet Sonya, Eugene's description of his prospective bride, and a subsequent letter from Sonya to the parents, won them over. In a November 1944 letter to Sonya, Eugene's mother explained that her son had broken the happy news to them over the telephone, and they knew "that our son has chosen the right companion for life's journey, which we sincerely hope will be full of happiness and joy." Zelda added a few more sentences before turning to her son. "There is one thing darling you and I will not argue about and that is the merits of Eugene. He certainly is, even if his mother says so, a very fine and upright young man and it is with all my heart and soul that I wish you both a long life full of harmony and joy." She ended her introductory letter by writing, "I hope to God that it will not be very long when we can meet you and Eugene together."[37]

With additional time to let the news sink in, the next month Zelda wrote Sonya, "I know how happy you are to have Eugene with you; may it always be so." In the same letter Nathan Mandeberg added his thoughts, writing, "We only hope that Eugene completes his services for his country in perfect shape and returns in good health to all of us to continue his life with you in great happiness and accord."[38]

The news of Eugene's engagement spread to other Mandeberg family members, who started calling Sonya by the nickname Sunnie, after what Gene described as her warm disposition. One of Eugene's aunts wrote to his parents that Sonya had written her a letter "telling of her joy at being loved by Genie, and a delightful note from our pilot [Eugene], confirming that they love each other, and that he had told you all about it." She added that "Morty and I are very [underline hers] happy over this. You know how much we love Genie; he is a rare person, and as Sunnie so aptly wrote, we could write a book called 'The Merits of Mandy.' Well, Sunnie is quite a special person, too—her name fits her perfectly. She is bright and sunny and gay, besides being a most capable girl, courageous and resourceful."[39]

The future mother-in-law mailed repeated missives to her future daughter-in-law in which she expressed her joy over Sonya's match with her son. "I hope this war will be over soon and when the boys come back, please God they will be married," she wrote in January 1945. She added three days later, "Just think of all the happy occasions that are in store for you. Life is like that and we must all be patient and have courage." Later the same month she added, "I hope that all your life you will be as happy as you look on the picture [sent by Sonya]" and that "we must be patient and hope and pray that God will be good to him and us."

Turning her attention toward her son's future role in the fighting against Japan, Zelda expressed the fear that simmered barely beneath the surface. "I can hardly think of Eugene leaving," she wrote Sonya. "I get numb all over. Darling, let us hope and pray that God will bring them back safe and very soon." She added in a subsequent January letter, "I sincerely hope he will never go to the Pacific."[40]

ZELDA UNDERSTOOD THE futility of her hope. Sooner or later her son would join Billy Hobbs, Gerald Hennesy, and the other fliers of Air Group 88 and begin their journey to the Pacific. By the time she wrote that last January letter to Sonya, the moment for her son's departure had all but arrived.

CHAPTER 3

"Moved, Always West, Toward the Combat Zone"

To the Pacific, February to June 1945

WITH THEIR TRAINING in the United States completed by the end of January 1945, it was time for Air Group 88 to depart for the combat zone. "Finally we received the magic word that we were leaving the States," stated the torpedo squadron's history.[1]

The aviators received ten days to travel from New England to Alameda, California, east of San Francisco. While the enlisted members of the squadron crossed the country by special train, officers were permitted to make their own travel arrangements, leaving Hobbs enough time for a detour to Kokomo for a last visit with family.

"SHE WANTED TO GIVE HIM SOMETHING TO KEEP HIM SAFE"

Each squadron held separate parties at Otis Field before saying goodbye to New England and joining the fleet. At the VF-88 bash, Lieutenant (jg) Sahloff relayed a vow to Lieutenant Commander Crommelin's wife. Crommelin had selected Sahloff to be his wingman, the pilot who was paired with the squadron leader to protect his flank. Sahloff, honored that Crommelin placed such trust in a relatively untested pilot, assured Mrs. Crommelin that her husband would be in good hands. "Sahloff flew as Crommelin's wingman," said Aviation Machinist's Mate 1/c Woods, "and Crommelin had his pick of any of the sixty pilots. He chose Sahloff, who was a terrific pilot."[2] In a brief conversation over-heard by Woods and others, Sahloff vowed that he would either bring her husband home safe to her, or that the young aviator would perish in the effort.

Billy Hobbs enjoyed his brief stay in Kokomo, splitting his time be-tween his family and his high school buddies. He had no idea when he might return to Indiana and again share in the joys of being a civilian at home, but he was confident of one thing—when he did come back, he would bring victory with him and, hopefully, a record that included a few downed Japanese aircraft.

His training had not only made him more experienced in the air, but a wiser individual as well. He looked forward to reaching the Pacific and taking his place alongside the other aviators as they winged toward com-bat, but his excitement did not blind him to the hazards that awaited. At the end of his ten-day leave in Kokomo, Billy Hobbs handed a box con-taining his few valuables to his brother, Henry. Inscribed on the modest container were words he never would have selected had this moment occurred before the war. "Property of Henry Hobbs if I don't make it. Ensign Wright C. Hobbs."[3]

The family then piled into the car for the sixty-mile ride to the In-dianapolis airport, where an emotional scene unfolded when Hobbs turned to his parents, siblings, and a cousin to say his goodbyes. "My cousin, Joe, and I stood back with my dad," said Nancy Exmeyer of her older brother's departure. "Joe shook his hand. Dad grabbed Billy a little bit and hugged him. That was a big display for him to even do." Billy hugged Nancy before turning to Hattie, standing alone a few feet away, for his last goodbye. She embraced her oldest son, then with her right hand slipped off the wedding ring she always wore on her left finger and handed it to Billy. Surprised with the gesture, and reluctant to accept it, Billy added the ring to the dog tags that dangled from his neck. "She wanted to give him something to keep him safe," said Nancy in 2017, who witnessed the emotional moment. "To this day it still affects me."

Billy stepped toward the airplane that would whisk him to California as his family turned away. Before they reached the car Wright Hobbs, a man of few words, whispered to Nancy, "I'll never see him again." She later recalled, "I don't know what made him say that. He said it after Billy had left. I never told my mom what Dad said. I realized then that my dad hurt, and how much my dad really cared. The drive back home was real quiet. Going down to the airport, we probably talked about everything but his leaving, but it was very quiet on the way back."[4]

Eugene Mandeberg's family in Michigan, less than 300 miles north of Kokomo, experienced the same anguish of parents and siblings sending their loved one off to war. In a February letter to Sonya, Zelda Mandeberg wrote of saying goodbye to her son and Sonya after enjoying a visit to New York to meet the prospective bride. "It was so hard leaving you and Eugene Monday," she wrote of their departure three days earlier. "I tried to be brave but like all mothers I just couldn't hold the tears back." She asked Sonya to let her know any time she received a letter from Eugene, and promised to do the same in reverse. "I just can't think of him leaving," she added. "Let us hope dear that Eugene will be back soon and all our hopes realized."[5]

IN THE WORDS of the Air Group history, after ten months of training, the aviators "moved, always west, toward the combat zone." They were confident, as one Air Group 88 report put it at the time, "that Air Group 88 will take its place among the other CV [carrier] groups which are gradually slipping the pants off the stumped legs of the sons of Nippon."[6]

The men spent only a few days in Alameda before gathering their gear and boarding the USS *Intrepid* (CV-11) for the trip to their next stop, Hawaii. The first large carrier most of the men had seen, the *Intrepid* had participated in many of the 1944 clashes against the Japanese, including the Gilbert and Marshall Island campaigns and the invasion of the Philippines, where she launched her air group against the main enemy surface force during the key Battle of Leyte Gulf in October 1944. The *Intrepid* would not take Air Group 88 into battle—that carrier would be determined after further training in Hawaii and Saipan—but she gave Hobbs and the rest a foreshadowing of what carrier operations would be like.

On February 20 *Intrepid* lifted anchor and steamed under the Golden Gate Bridge, their final glimpse of the mainland United States for the indeterminate future. As the landmark slipped farther out of sight, they had to wonder when they might again see home and family. Leaving Kokomo or Detroit for flight training at US airfields was one matter, but seeing the ocean mists swallow your homeland as the *Intrepid* steamed farther from the California coast proved to be a jarring moment. Each mile the *Intrepid* steamed toward Hawaii was another mile distancing sons from fathers and mothers. "I hope Eugene was able to write to you before he sailed," Zelda wrote to Sonya the day after *Intrepid* slipped out of Alameda. "God be with him and bring him back safe to us. I tried so hard not to cry, but as you said in your letter dear, I am a mother, and when you asked me not to cry it's because you are a sweet daughter."[7]

THE FOUR-DAY VOYAGE gave the Air Group time to decompress and to prepare for additional training in Hawaii before facing combat. "We had a lot of time on our hands as we were just passengers," said Aviation Machinist's Mate 1/c Merald Woods. "The only thing we worried about was a Japanese submarine catching us, but we had good destroyers escorting us."[8] Most men caught up on their reading or letter writing, and many attempted to squeeze in extra sleep they feared would be nonexistent during their training, but the hustle and bustle of the *Intrepid*'s crew, plus the military equipment seemingly packed into every crevice and corner, reminded them that they were not sailing on a pleasure cruise.

On February 24 the *Intrepid* pulled into Pearl Harbor, Hawaii, where a large "WELCOME AIR GROUP 88" sign greeted them.[9] That same morning the pilots boarded transports for a ride to NAS Hilo, Hawaii, whose fully stocked officers' club and tempting swimming pool, all in the midst of some of the most breathtaking scenery in the world, was a welcome contrast to what they had experienced at Otis Field and other New England locales. The USS *Swan* (AM-34), a minesweeper that operated in Hawaiian waters to convey men and supplies from base to base, took their gear from Pearl Harbor to Hilo Airfield, including a few sets of golf clubs that optimistic officers brought in case they could escape to one of Hawaii's luxurious layouts.

Hobbs and others basked in the daily sunshine and different conditions that bathed their exercises. Whereas Otis offered poor weather and lacked spare parts for aircraft, the personnel at Hilo had anticipated the needs of the squadron and had stocked additional items, including extra aircraft. "After the bitter cold of Otis Field," concluded Lieutenant Commander Huddleston of VT-88, "it was a distinct pleasure to come to N.A.S. Hilo where neither ice nor snow hung from props, and flight gear did not include red flannels, sweater, winter flight jackets and pants, scarves, boots and heavy gloves."[10]

"THERE WAS A WAR ON AND EVERYONE WANTED TO GET STARTED"

As soon as everyone was settled at Hilo, according to the VF-88 history, the Air Group "immediately plunged into an active training program." While they still conducted many of the same exercises they had begun in earlier training, such as dive-bombing, strafing, and tactics, they mostly focused on coordinated attacks involving all four squadrons and on carrier exercises. Beautiful conditions at Hilo left the men with few objections, but they found one minor irritant—that the tower at the airfield was controlled by Army personnel, "the only fly in an otherwise pleasant ointment."[11]

"Had group hop, made attack on base," Billy Hobbs wrote in his diary on March 9. He frequently referred to tactics and simulated attacks on Hilo Airfield, with occasional flights to Oahu to strike Barbers Point. "I had a lot of fun this morning on a strike we had," he wrote to his sister, Nancy. "We went out and strafed and bombed a target. While we were doing this some other fighters jumped us. We really had some [underline his] dogfight." Hobbs performed so well that Lieutenant Howard M. "Howdy" Harrison, a veteran pilot for whom Billy flew as wingman, praised Hobbs's skill one evening at the officers' club. They also turned night flying—which, according to the VF-88 history, "almost to a man the pilots hated"—into a more exciting exercise by "attacking" Hawaiian towns. "The good citizens of Hilo were often awakened at sunrise by the sound of Hellcats being put through a vigorous tail chase."[12]

The principal thrust of Hawaiian training was to familiarize the aviators with aircraft carrier operations and to solidify unit cohesion. Aided by the cooperative weather that enabled them to fly almost every day, the Air Group lifted off for two-hour exercises in conducting coordinated attacks, which, according to the torpedo squadron's history, "knit the squadrons together into a smoothly operating group."[13]

New England carrier training occurred aboard smaller escort carriers such as the USS *Prince William* and USS *Core*, but in Hawaii, the Air Group enjoyed its first taste of conducting strikes from one of the newer, larger *Essex*-class aircraft carriers, the USS *Shangri-La* (CV-38). Part of the group of vessels that provided the main offensive striking power of the US Fleet since the middle of 1943, the *Essex*-class carriers looked every bit like the masters of the seas that they were. The carriers with which Hobbs had worked off New England were impressive in their 500-foot length, but *Shangri-La* and the other *Essex*-class carriers, with almost double the length and carrying crews of more than 2,500 officers and enlisted, awed the young aviators.

The reputation of these carriers was already established before Air Group 88 reached Hawaii. USS *Essex* (CV-9) had participated in many of the 1943 and 1944 Pacific strikes, including the attack against the Gilbert and Marshall Islands, Rabaul, Truk, and the Battle of Leyte Gulf. She was host for one of the most heralded naval air units in the war, Air Group 15, nicknamed the "Fabled Fifteen," commanded by the Navy's leading ace and Medal of Honor recipient Commander David McCampbell. USS *Intrepid* had raided Japanese installations at Kwajalein and the naval bastion at Truk, and joined in the momentous October 1944 Battle of Leyte Gulf. Aviators from the USS *Hornet* (CV-12) engaged enemy pilots in the Battle of the Philippine Sea, where they and other units splashed so many Japanese aircraft that the aerial slaughter became known as "The Marianas Turkey Shoot." And the new USS *Yorktown* (CV-10), the successor to her predecessor sunk at Midway, had fought at the Marshall Islands and struck Japanese-controlled bases off the coast of New Guinea, in the Philippines, and at Okinawa.

Most enticing to Hobbs and his companions in VF-88 was that the fliers from these previous air groups enjoyed multiple opportunities to engage Japanese pilots in combat. They did what VF-88 men so badly longed to do—match wits and talents against a skilled enemy aviator intent on killing them.

Hawaii happened to be a layover for *Shangri-La*. Commissioned in September 1944 while Hobbs trained with the fighter squadron off Atlantic City, *Shangri-La* stopped in the islands to conduct operations with the Air Group before continuing to her April 1945 date off Okinawa, where the ship would support the massive invasion of that crucial island to Japan's south. For three days in early March the squadrons boarded *Shangri-La* to practice rendezvousing with other squadrons, mounting coordinated attacks on decoy ships, and landing and approach patterns. "There were many kinks to be ironed out but fortunately we had no glaring weaknesses," concluded the VF-88 report for that period.[14]

The Air Group maintained the same pace into late April, when the squadrons left for exercises aboard the USS *Bon Homme Richard* (CV-31), another *Essex*-class carrier recently arrived in Hawaii after being commissioned in late 1944. "Hilo to U.S.S. *Bon Homme Richard*," Hobbs recorded in his flight log for April 26.[15] The group further practiced carrier procedure, what to do if the aircraft became separated, how to properly rendezvous before and after a mission, and takeoffs and landings. The carrier crew's efficiency in moving the many aircraft from their storage areas in the hangar deck to the flight deck above impressed some of the newer aviators.

As polished as the Air Group was becoming, it could not escape tragedy. In late March Crommelin's brother, Charles, disappeared in his plane off Okinawa. The VF-88 commander had lost a brother only weeks before taking his fighter pilots into battle. The next month Ensign Elmer B. Krause, a VBF-88 aviator flying a Corsair, crashed into the sea twenty-five miles east of Hilo while in the midst of a routine training flight from Hilo to Upolu Point. After pulling out from two unsuccessful dips toward the ocean, on the third attempt Krause tried to level the plane, but according to the squadron report, his "propeller hit the water on the third [dip] and was torn from the engine. The pilot maintained flight for several seconds, the plane then hit the water hard and fast and disappeared below the surface at its point of contact. The plane sank in 5 seconds. Krause apparently did not get clear. Search revealed no trace of plane or pilot."[16]

On weekends the Air Group dispersed to visit the island's famous attractions. They enjoyed nightly movies on the base, squadrons organized softball and baseball teams, and avid golfers took advantage of the island's many layouts. Lieutenant Hennesy and others started the "Twirlers," a group of aviators who grew long handlebar mustaches, and another group donned western-style handkerchiefs and cowboy boots and called their Hilo barracks "The Bunkhouse."

Billy Hobbs sent his family periodic reports. He informed sister Nancy that he enjoyed watching *The Doughgirls*, a 1944 comedy featuring Ann Sheridan, Eve Arden, and Jane Wyman, and thought *Tall in the Saddle*, a 1944 western starring John Wayne and Ward Bond, "was swell." In his diary, he recorded visits to the officers' club, where he "got pretty high," that he danced with local females on St. Patrick's Day, that he went for a swim one afternoon where he "met two chicks," and that he had "a very nice swim" at the beaches of the famed Royal Hawaiian Hotel.[17]

Billy's references to Page Du Pre throughout his correspondence and in his diary appeared more frequently. "Got a real nice letter from Page," he recorded on March 18. In a letter to Nancy Hobbs two weeks later, he wondered what Hattie thought of her son so often mentioning a girl she had yet to meet. "I just got through writing Page a few lines. What does mother say about Page or does she ever say? Page writes me nearly every day." Hobbs was relieved to learn that Hattie, who had received a letter from Page informing the family that she was planning to visit Kokomo, was pleased with the possibility. "Things are shaping up very nicely," he confided to his diary of his prospects with Page after the war.[18]

While the son pointedly omitted any references in letters home that he feared might alarm his mother, Hattie also refused to drop hints to her son of the torments she experienced while he was at war. "I have been feeling pretty good," she wrote him on February 27, "better than I thought I would, but Bill I just made myself not feel too bad. I just want you to take care of yourself." She ended the letter by asking Billy to "Write often and be careful. We are thinking of you every minute & hoping & praying for it to end and all be back, safe & sound—lots of love from all of us." However, she was not above referring to the enemy in less than flattering words. In that same letter she informed Billy that she had collected seventy-five jars of grease to be collected for the next war drive, and wrote that "I hope it gets 7500 Japs & Germans. It's a shame to waste the grease on them rats."[19]

In Detroit, Zelda kept matters lighthearted in her letters to Eugene, but poured out her emotions to Sonya. "No word from Eugene," she wrote the same day Hattie sent her letter to Billy, unaware that Eugene and Billy had only recently arrived in Hawaii. "Mickey called me Sunday, he told me it will be several weeks before we hear from Eugene. I guess we will just have to be patient." She added that working at the Red Cross helped take her mind off her son's welfare, while both she and Nathan tilled a small Victory Garden in their yard. To her relief, the letters resumed once Eugene was in the islands. "Received a letter from Eugene yesterday. He really doesn't give us any clue as to where he is, or what he is doing. Has he told you anything about his work or his whereabouts? I guess he thinks the less we know the better. I hope he stays well."

Zelda viewed the islands as her son's last sanctuary before heading into battle and hoped Eugene would remain in that Pacific paradise forever. "Received a v-mail from Eugene today," she wrote Sonya on March 20, "says he is doing a lot of flying. God watch over him. I hope he is still in Honolulu, at least this is where I hope he is." The next month she wrote that Eugene "still enjoys his sunbaths on the beach. I hope it doesn't change for the duration." In another letter Zelda told Sonya, "Received a nice letter from Eugene yesterday" before repeating the phrase, "I hope and pray he stays on the Island for the duration."

Zelda frequently implored God to protect Eugene. "We had a letter from Eugene. Everything is fine, so he says. Yes, dear, we are being bulldozed but he wants to make it easy for us. God bless him and love him as we do." In another missive, she asked Sonya, "Have you heard from Eugene? We haven't had any mail from him since last week. I have a feeling that he has been moved and is now on active duty. God watch over him."[20]

Eugene sounded cheerful because, along with his squadron mates, he loved Hawaii. Once they reached the combat zone, fun and relaxation would be at a premium, so they took advantage of Hawaii's bounties. "At this point in our career," stated one VBF-88 report, "morale was no problem. Lots of work and lots of play does the trick!"[21]

With their time in Hawaii coming to a conclusion, the Air Group hosted parties marking the end of another phase that brought them closer to combat. Officers attended a lavish affair hosted by the Rocke-feller family. Hobbs, a regular at the officers' club with "Howdy" Harrison, enjoyed the festivities at the VF-88 party where, according to the unit's historical report, "girls of different sizes, colors and shapes appeared from out of nowhere but not insufficient numbers."[22]

Despite enjoying the fun, the aviators in the Air Group, especially the younger pilots, were eager to end their training and get into the thick of things. Over a period of many months, from cadet pilot training to New England flying and on to Hawaiian exercises, they had worked hard to be ready for the opportunity to meet an enemy pilot in battle. "This flying in Hawaii was fun," they wrote in the Air Group history, "but there was a war on and everyone wanted to get started." The VF-88 report concluded that the squadron was at the "peak of efficiency," claimed that "many of the pilots felt that if the Air Group did not get into combat soon, everyone would go stale," and added that "everyone was anxious to shove off. Hawaii had its charms but there was still a war to be considered."[23]

The Air Group had one more stop before attaining its wish and joining what all hoped would be one of those sleek *Essex*-class carriers. Saipan, in the Marianas Islands, awaited.

"THE WAR AGAINST JAPAN STILL APPEARED TO BE A HARD AND COSTLY CONFLICT"

In late April the aviators flew their planes to the *Bon Homme Richard* for last-minute exercises while the ground officers and enlisted said goodbye and departed Hilo aboard the USS *Curtiss* (AV-4), a seaplane tender that transported them to Pearl Harbor. Two days later Hobbs and the other aviators boarded *Curtiss*, now anchored alongside Ford Island, and made final preparations to leave Hawaii on the last day of the month. "Shoved off at 0800, destination unknown," Hobbs wrote in his diary on April 30. "Had gunnery in the afternoon." Of *Curtiss*, he added, "Ship very nice, quarters rather poor."[24]

The additional Air Group officers and men strained the tender's facilities, but the twelve-day voyage to Saipan, which the Air Group learned was their destination once the *Curtiss* was out at sea, was hardly painful. It certainly beat going to war in a jammed troop transport, by which most of their Army cohorts traveled across the Atlantic or Pacific. "Our pilots had the run of the ship, the food was excellent, and the gold braid remained clear of the many harmless little games of Whist which sprang up."

Men devoured the few copies of the ship's daily newspaper, sunbathed, and wrote letters. "Weather superb. Saw many flying fish," Hobbs recorded on May 1. "Odie and a few of the other boys sang in eve." He mentioned playing hearts with other officers, skipping a day when the *Curtiss* passed the International Date Line on May 3, and winning $8 playing craps. Calisthenics and lectures filled the afternoons, with an ocean-going school teaching code and with veteran aviators meeting on the aft boat dock so the men could "be regaled with horror stories by the combat-experienced pilots."[25]

In the dark about her son's location, Zelda poured out her emotions in her letters to Sonya as *Curtiss* steamed westward across the Pacific toward the enemy. Zelda wrote that she was "thrilled because God gave me such a lovely daughter who is so thoughtful, in fact very thoughtful," but anxious because she had not received a letter from Eugene in more than a week. "Honey, still no mail from Eugene. I hope we hear from him soon. I get weak all over when I think of him. God be with him, my baby." Nathan Mandeberg ended the letter by adding a happy note to what Zelda had penned. "The mailman just delivered two letters from Eugene, one dated April 4 and the other May 9. Evidently the letters between these dates will arrive sometime. He feels fine and is at sea somewhere. He doesn't say whether it is just maneuvers, or actual fighting."[26]

On May 10, with *Curtiss* still two days from Saipan, rumors that the European fighting would soon end materialized with the announcement of the German surrender. Unlike back home, where citizens celebrated VE-Day, Air Group 88's muted reaction pointed to the continued necessity that they still had to risk their lives before victory could be announced in the Pacific. Billy Hobbs, who hoped the news would nudge the Japanese to halt fighting, wondered "why we are steaming for the Empire" if peace in the Pacific was at hand. If anything, they were happy that the termination of hostilities on the other side of the world increased the chances that the nation would divert additional resources to their theater. "Everyone aboard was jubilant but there were no wild demonstrations," stated the fighting squadron history. "We still had a war to win in the Pacific. There could be no relaxing until the Japs lay beaten and helpless too."[27]

Close to one million people jammed New York's downtown area to celebrate the moment. Lights illuminated Broadway and Times Square, and the Statue of Liberty's torch again glowed. Politicians celebrated the event, but cautioned that hard times lay ahead. Speaker of the United States House of Representatives Sam Rayburn said, "I am happy and also sad, because I cannot help but think of those thousands of our boys who are yet to die in the far-flung Pacific islands and the Far East in order that victory may come to our armies and that the glory of America may be upheld and peace and an ordered world may come to us again." Noted military correspondent Hanson W. Baldwin wrote in the *New York Times*, "Judged solely by the battlefronts the war against Japan still appeared to be a hard and costly conflict with no end in sight."[28]

The Hobbs and Mandeberg households could not wholeheartedly celebrate the end in Europe, for as long as the Japanese continued to fight—some military experts claimed the war might last well into 1947—their sons remained in peril. They shared the joys of friends and neighbors whose sons would be returning from European combat, but the unknown dangers looming for Billy and Eugene dwarfed their elation. Zelda Mandeberg expressed how both she and Hattie Hobbs felt when she wrote Sonya, "Oh, darling, I wish we were as close to victory in the Pacific, as we are in Europe."[29]

VE-Day was especially hard for Hattie. From the time Billy entered pilot training, she prayed that he would be sent to Europe. Even though the odds pointed to the Pacific, where aircraft carriers and naval aviation played such a prominent role, she maintained hope that he would be dispatched to the war against Hitler. Had that been the case, he might then be on his way to Kokomo, but because he had been posted to the

Pacific, he would remain a part of the bitter combat that each day's edition of the *Kokomo Tribune* reflected with its stories of bloody fighting in the Philippines, Iwo Jima, and Okinawa.

WHILE PEOPLE IN the United States welcomed the collapse of Germany, *Curtiss* and Air Group 88 steamed into Tinian, an island in the Marianas chain 4,000 miles west of Hawaii and 2,400 miles south of Tokyo. The green-clad island was a welcome relief for men who had seen nothing but water since leaving Pearl Harbor ten days earlier, but they remained only a brief time before continuing to the nearby island of Saipan.

Commander Bernard Talbot, the commanding officer at Marpi Point, greeted the Air Group. Known throughout the Navy as "Black Barnie," Talbot wore a short-sleeved shirt that barely covered his enormous belly, shorts, and a baseball cap. When he saw officers passing gear over the side, including tennis racquets, he shouted, "Well, by God, now I've seen everything. I suppose the next thing will be a bag of golf clubs."[30] At the sound of Talbot's barking one of the Air Group officers, lugging a set of golf clubs, hurried out of sight.

"NO ONE CAN SAY WHAT CAUSES ONE MAN TO ESCAPE DEATH AND ANOTHER NOT"

The officers of Air Group 88 may have brought reminders of home front leisure activities with them, but Saipan offered grim confirmation of what they might face. Signs of the recent land battle lay everywhere, underscoring with their presence that this trans-Pacific journey would not end in pleasant conditions. "The Jap defeat on Saipan was a year old when we landed but evidence of the terrific battle was plentiful," stated the VF-88 history. "Many of the palms were shredded stumps; rusty tanks and bullet-riddled, burned-out trucks lay by the side of the road. Shattered pill-boxes and shell-torn buildings stood out against the green vegetation."[31]

They witnessed the remnants of the American assault of Saipan in June 1944, a savage affair in which Marines and Army infantry battled at close quarters with the Japanese. The Japanese defended every yard and hill on Saipan, forcing the Marines and their Army cohorts to pry enemy soldiers from trenches and hillside caves with mortars, flame-throwing tanks, machine guns, and bayonets. More haunting, however, was the spectacle of watching up to 8,000 civilians, including mothers holding small children, retreat to a cliff above Marpi Point and leap to their deaths rather than face what they had been told would be inhumane treatment from the Americans. The place was later renamed Suicide Cliff because of the heart-rending incident.

Air Group 88, the first group to train at Marpi Point, operated in the shadows of Suicide Cliff at a half-completed camp offering primitive conditions and equipment. Aging Hellcat fighters reduced their flying time, and coral dust kicked up by airplane propellers damaged the engines of those that did work. Aviators lived in Quonset huts and drank vile-tasting water, and bathroom and shower facilities stood one-quarter mile away from the huts. "After being pampered at Hilo," said the torpedo squadron history, "this was life in the raw, although a Marine would probably snicker at our luxuries."[32]

Instead of allowing the inadequate conditions to lower morale, the men constructed makeshift devices to catch rainwater and built attachments to a small mill for washing clothes. With the examples of sacrifice at the hands of their Marine and Army counterparts daily staring at them, they could hardly do otherwise. "The confinement of this base brought all hands even closer together," added the bomber squadron history of that time.[33]

Another difference between Saipan and their previous training locations was that the aviators had to be wary of the estimated 1,000 Japanese soldiers living in the adjoining caves and cliffs. Commander Searcy posted armed guards about the camp in case the enemy attacked, and on more than one occasion aviators heard shots ring out from the cliffs as the Japanese tried to evade Army patrols.

Training again focused on gunnery, glide-bombing, rocket-firing, squadron and group tactics, and carrier landings. To gain experience flying in active zones, pilots ferried supplies to Guam, Iwo Jima, Okinawa, and the Philippines, and participated in mock dogfights with Army P-47 pilots stationed on the island.

For the first time in the young aviators' naval careers, their training at Saipan offered combat exercises. Twice each week the Air Group flew combat air patrol over Saipan, but more beneficial were the strikes against nearby Japanese-held islands. They hit Rota's airstrip eighty miles southwest of Saipan, and Medinilla, a tiny rock seventy-five miles to the north. Neither was heavily defended, as American B-29 bombers had been blasting them for months, and according to the fighter squadron history, during its June 7 attack, "If there was AA [antiaircraft fire] nobody saw it. The Japs were probably holed up good waiting for the war to end." Hobbs and other fighter pilots each carried two 500-pound bombs and 2,400 rounds of ammunition in the attacks, giving them their first opportunity to fire at something beyond a towed sleeve. The fighter squadron history reported that each aviator graded well, "and each one felt that he had personally accounted for several Japs. When last seen the island was in a sinking condition."[34]

Though far from the coast of Japan, the danger was real enough. Lieutenant (jg) Bernard I. Hamilton Jr. of VBF-88 barely avoided death during a May 25 outing. "It was one of those days you went out to see how fast you can get your group off, circle, and land. It was a timing thing," said Hamilton. He had successfully completed two landings, but as he headed down the deck for his third takeoff and released the brakes, "I knew that the plane was not jumping like it should. I thought, 'Oh shoot, something's wrong here!'" Hamilton dipped off the end of the deck about twenty to thirty yards ahead of the oncoming carrier. "I didn't want my wheels down when I hit the water, and as soon as I hit the end of the carrier, I pulled the switch for wheels up. If my wheels had been down, it probably would have tipped the plane over, and that would be a different story!"[35]

Hamilton hurried out of his plane, inflated his rubber raft, and pulled himself in. After a destroyer retrieved him and took him back to the carrier, he received a request to see the captain. His superior told Hamilton that when the aviator started down the deck, Hamilton shook his head as if he were in distress. The captain, who had witnessed a similar occurrence before, knew Hamilton was about to splash in front of the carrier and immediately ordered an emergency stop. The lumbering vessel barely missed Hamilton, who credited the captain with saving his life.

Others were not as fortunate. During a scheduled training dive on May 31, Lieutenant (jg) Alvin F. Levenson and Aviation Radioman 2/c Kenneth Boyd in their SB2C dive-bomber collided in midair with a similar plane flown by Lieutenant (jg) Walter M. Leonard and Aviation Radioman 2/c Rowland C. Draudt. The pilots, Levenson and Leonard, landed safely in the ocean and exited their planes, but an extended search uncovered no trace of either aircrewman. "No one can say what causes one man to escape death and another not in an accident such as this," concluded the Air Group history.[36]

Saipan offered few of the attractions that Hawaii provided, with movies and playing with their mascot, Elmer the Saipan Hound, filling their free time. Each night the men gathered to watch the sleek B-29 bombers lift off the Saipan runway on their missions against the Home Islands. "It was a stirring sight to watch their navigation lights as plane after plane climbed into the darkness and disappeared toward Tokyo," said the Air Group history.[37] However, watching some of those same bombers return to the airfield after completing their mission, trailing smoke from a damaged wing and their fuselages peppered from shell bursts, were stark reminders of how close they were to the combat zone.

ZELDA MANDEBERG NEEDED no reminders that her son leapfrogged across the Pacific toward combat. Twice during May she expressed her fears for Eugene's safety and beseeched God to protect him. "God, watch over him wherever he is," she remarked in one letter to Sonya. When she learned that he was in the Marianas, a quick glance at a map confirmed that her son was closer to the Japanese Home Islands than she was in Detroit to Corpus Christi, where many of the aviators had trained. "He is in the Marianas and in combat," she wrote Sonya. "I get sick at the pit of my stomach when I think of him. Oh, God, help us and watch over him."[38]

Eugene did not share Zelda's fears. Like the rest of the Air Group, he was weary of waiting to be assigned to an aircraft carrier. "Life on Saipan was unusual," recorded Eugene's fighter squadron history on June 5. "No one would deny that. However, the men in the squadron still chafed their hawsers waiting for a chance at combat."[39]

Finally, the men were told to pack their gear and be ready within twelve hours to board the USS *Makassar Strait* (CVE-91) to join the fleet. They were happy to leave Saipan, where many believed the Air Group's effectiveness had diminished since leaving Hawaii. "The squadron unquestionably lost the sharp edge it had when it left Hilo," concluded the torpedo squadron history.[40]

With men muttering a firm good riddance, the Air Group left Saipan June 12. Hobbs and the other young aviators were soon to learn the identity of their new home. The USS *Yorktown* waited to receive her new air group.

CHAPTER 4

"An Aircraft Carrier Is a Noble Thing"
Air Group 88 Joins the Yorktown,
June–July 1945

A N UNEVENTFUL FOUR-DAY passage brought the Air Group into San Pedro Bay in the northwest portion of Leyte Gulf, Philippines, on June 16, where the *Makassar Strait* anchored a few hundred yards from the USS *Yorktown* (CV-10), Air Group 88's home for the next four months. The next day, the aviators boarded the gleaming carrier, a proud ship boasting a stellar record since her commissioning in 1943. The warm welcome provided by *Yorktown*'s officers and crew led the VF-88 history to state, "We were made to feel at home. This ship had a splendid record which our Air Group was determined to uphold."[1]

Yorktown's expansive flight deck—872 feet long and 148 feet wide—was a welcome sight to Commander Searcy and his aviators, who appreciated every inch of deck space given to operate the warplanes on hand. They inherited the 103 aircraft from Air Group 9, whose place they would now take—Crommelin's thirty-six F6F-5 Hellcats, Lieutenant Commander James S. Elkins Jr.'s fifteen SB2C-4 Helldiver bombers, Huddleston's fifteen TBM-3 Avenger torpedo planes, and Hart's thirty-seven Corsairs.

The friendly reception continued into the Air Group's first meeting with *Yorktown*'s air operations officer, Lieutenant Commander Cooper Bright. Hobbs and the other new arrivals stifled the urge to laugh at Bright's noticeably ill-fitting toupee as the officer, a veteran fixture and trusted officer on the carrier, strode into the stifling wardroom. Sweat coursed down everyone's face, including Bright's, making some of the new arrivals fear that Bright's hairpiece might slip down his face. "We're here to support the air group; that's what this ship is all about!" bellowed Bright. The air operations officer surveyed the quiet crowd a few seconds before adding, "Man, it's getting hot in here."[2] He then brought out his handkerchief and, rather than dabbing his brow, as most of the Air Group expected, lifted his toupee and wiped his forehead. The aviators erupted in laughter at the unexpected move, which endeared Bright, nicknamed Coop, to the Air Group.

With their arrival on *Yorktown*, Air Group 88 pilots were now part of an offensive weapon that had become the scourge of Japan—the task force. A collection of aircraft carriers and their supporting battleships, cruisers, and destroyers, task forces had been in the vanguard of the American thrust across the Pacific for the past two years, spearheading island assaults, blasting enemy airfields, and pursuing the Japanese surface fleet. Fueled by American home front industries and shipyards that maintained a continuous flow of ships and aircraft to the front lines, task forces were able to remain at sea for indefinite periods, whittling away at Japanese naval strength that Tokyo struggled to replace.

Assigned to Task Group 38.4 (TG 38.4) under Rear Admiral A. W. Radford aboard *Yorktown*, the Air Group was a vital cog of the Third Fleet, commanded by one of the war's foremost Pacific heroes—Admiral William F. Halsey. Along with Task Group 38.1 under Rear Admiral T. L. Sprague and Task Group 38.3 commanded by Rear Admiral G. F. Bogan, Radford's group was one of three (a fourth, British Task Group 37.2 under Vice Admiral Sir Philip Van, would soon join) that prowled the seas together. Like its sister task groups, by itself Radford's TG 38.4 presented a formidable array of naval might, with five aircraft carriers ringed by three battleships—including Halsey flying his flag in the nearby "Mighty Mo," the USS *Missouri* (BB-63)—four cruisers, and twenty-two destroyers. Steaming in the midst of this floating arsenal along with *Yorktown* were two other *Essex*-class carriers, the USS *Shangri-La* (CV-38), with Vice Admiral John S. McCain aboard as commander of the task force, and the night carrier, USS *Bon Homme*

Richard (CV-31), a recent arrival that the *Yorktown* men quickly nick-named "the Big Dick," as well as the light carriers USS *Independence* (CVL-22) and USS *Cowpens* (CVL-25), nicknamed the "Mighty Moo." A supporting group of thirty-one tankers, oilers, and tugs escorted by six escort carriers, thirteen destroyers, and nineteen destroyer escorts fueled and supplied the task force.

"The *Yorktown* was a ship justifiably proud of her fighting name and gallant reputation," proclaimed the Air Group history of its new home.[3] One of nine *Essex*-class carriers commissioned in a six-month stretch in early 1943, including *Independence* and *Cowpens, Yorktown* was the fourth ship to bear a name honoring the deciding battle of the American Revolution.

She had amassed a stellar record, earning eleven battle stars and a Presidential Unit Citation for her participation in numerous operations, including the 1943–1944 assaults of the Gilbert and Marshall Islands, the 1944 operations off New Guinea, the June attack against the Marianas (where her Air Group claimed thirty-seven enemy planes shot down), and the April 1945 sinking of a Japanese supership, the battleship *Yamato*. Two naval luminaries had previously served aboard the carrier, including the brilliant Commander James H. Flatley Jr., universally recognized as one of the Navy's foremost aviators and thinkers, and Lieutenant Commander Crommelin's brother, Charles, who commanded the fighter squadron of a previous air group.

Hollywood enhanced the ship's reputation with the 1944 documentary *The Fighting Lady*, which profiled the life of an aircraft carrier in the Pacific. Directed by Edward Steichen and William Wyler, and narrated by popular movie star Robert Taylor, the film received the Academy Award for best documentary feature at the March 1945 ceremonies.

The members of Air Group 88 were thus honored to be assigned to such a worthy ship, which the unit history described as "the realization of dreams."[4] Since Japanese fliers had risen to meet the carrier's previous air groups, every flier assumed that future dogfights awaited, a tantalizing prospect to which these young American aviators looked forward.

"YOUR SHIP IS BEING RUN BY AND FOR A BUNCH OF BARNSTORMING YOUNGSTERS"

"An aircraft carrier is a noble thing," wrote the popular World War II newspaper correspondent Ernie Pyle, shortly before his 1945 death covering the Armed Forces in the Pacific. "It lacks almost everything that seems to denote nobility, yet deep nobility is there. A carrier has no poise. It has no grace. It is top-heavy and lopsided. It had the lines of a well-fed cow. It doesn't cut through the water like a cruiser, knifing romantically along. It doesn't dance and cavort like a destroyer. It just plows. You feel it should be carrying a hod. Yet a carrier is a ferocious thing, and out of its heritage of action has grown its nobility."[5]

Whereas the battleship was king in World War I, the aircraft carrier dominated this conflict. "Today the carrier is the kingpin of the fleet," wrote *New York Times* correspondent George E. Jones the same month Hobbs and his comrades made their first strike against the Japanese. He added that Task Force 38, the appellation for the vast collection of carrier task groups and air units such as Air Group 88, was "the most lethal seagoing weapon of all time," and that "the war is fought aboard a carrier with a terrible, practical and incessant state of urgency. It is a floating runway, capable of hurling air power into the remotest corner of Japan. But it is also a floating powder keg, on which all of its more than two thousand officers and men sit uneasily on tons and tons of combustibles—powder, oil and gasoline."[6]

The aircraft carrier was the perfect answer to counter Japanese aggression and take the war to Japan's shores. Manned by 150 officers and 2,550 enlisted, *Yorktown* hosted an air group featuring just over 300 men, plus another 100 staff working for Admiral Radford, who flew his flag aboard *Yorktown* and directed the task group from the ship. More than 3,100 officers and enlisted, a small town in itself, worked aboard "The Fighting Lady" at the time Hobbs first set foot on the carrier.

Captain Walter F. Boone had assumed command only two months earlier, running his ship from the captain's bridge located forward on the island. From the signal and flag bridge one level below Boone, Radford directed the task force and the air officer supervised flight operations for Air Group 88. The Combat Information Center (CIC), a small room located below the flight deck, collected the crucial information about weather, targets, and other pertinent material that Boone, Radford, and the air officer needed to perform their tasks.

One year earlier, the standard carrier air group featured fifty-four fighters, twenty-four dive-bombers, and eighteen torpedo planes. By the end of 1944, revised tactics designed to counter the kamikaze threat altered those numbers. With the need for additional combat air patrols, and with concern over the reliability of the Helldiver dive-bomber, focus shifted to the Hellcat fighter. As many as seventy-three Hellcat and Corsair fighters operated in a single air group, while dive-bombers and torpedo planes shrank to fifteen each. The Hellcat could double as a dive-bomber, and its enhanced speed, additional armor to protect the pilots, and racks for two 500-pound bombs or six five-inch air-to-ground rockets made the fighter more desirable.

Yorktown's officers and enlisted faced one main task—keep the Air Group running. The carrier, a floating airstrip atop a hull, was not designed to attack surface targets or to pursue enemy submarines; *Yorktown*'s value lasted as long as she maintained her air group. "Her prime mission was to place against the enemy the greatest air power possible and anything which did not contribute to that end was secondary," stated the ship's history for *Shangri-La,* one of the carriers operating with *Yorktown* in the task group. "Every battle station aboard ship—from the towering gun director in sky forward to the keel-deep radar screens in CIC—was structurally designed and specifically manned to get her squadrons off in time, to keep them flying, and to be there—safe and sound—when they got back."[7]

Without the aviators of Air Group 88, *Yorktown* served little purpose. Remove that element and the immense carrier lacked the impact of one of those escorting destroyers that circled her. On an aircraft carrier, wrote Lieutenant Commander J. Bryan III, who was aboard *Yorktown* shortly before Air Group 88 arrived, "your ship is being run by and for a bunch of barnstorming youngsters who don't tie their shoes at all, if they don't feel like it, and who would just as soon address Admiral King as 'Ernie,' unless it meant that he'd ground them and keep them out of the next scrap."[8]

Rarely older than their midtwenties, according to correspondent Morris Markey, "in the half-forgotten world of peace they would surely have been called boys," but in the deep reaches of the Pacific, sitting in the ready rooms waiting for the call that sent them into battle, they were anything but that. Little rivaled flying for their attention. "They eat it, they sleep it," wrote Lieutenant Oliver Jensen, USNR, when he studied task force operations in 1945. "If a flier and his girl meet another flier and his girl, they will adjourn to the bar on the roof of San Francisco's Mark Hopkins Hotel and start talking about it."[9]

The Air Group resided in its own world, a part of *Yorktown* yet apart in purpose. While the carrier's officers and crew remained aboard the *Yorktown*, like the US Cavalry dashing into battle during the previous century, the Air Group left the main force to attack an enemy operating far from its home base.

"A MOBILE FIGHTER AIR BASE"

Billy Hobbs and Eugene Mandeberg were joining one of the military phenomena of the war—the fast carrier task force. After the attack on Pearl Harbor had all but eliminated battleships as a principal weapon, naval strategists switched to aircraft carriers and the air groups operating from them. In 1943 the strategists developed the task group, with rings of battleships, cruisers, and destroyers capable of erecting a potent curtain of antiaircraft fire to shield aircraft carriers ensconced in the center.

From these task groups emerged the task force, a formidable array of three to five task groups that could operate either independently or in conjunction with the other groups. Normally positioned within ten to twenty miles of each other, the multiple-unit task forces, manned by 28,000 personnel, spread out over hundreds of square miles of ocean. With its ability to refuel at sea, the fast carrier task force could operate at one location one week, and race to a second spot hundreds of miles away to strike at enemy positions the next, thereby keeping the Japanese guessing as to where the next strike would fall. The stream of oilers and supply vessels that transported fuel, ammunition, and food to the task force enabled it to operate at sea for six to eight weeks at a time.

This assemblage of ships and firepower was fashioned to bring the striking power of air group fighters, dive-bombers, and torpedo planes directly against enemy bases, anchorages, and industrial locales. The "carrier-based aircraft is its supreme striking weapon," explained one naval historian at the time, enabling the task force to strike hundreds of miles from the main unit. The fast carrier task force "is in net effect a mobile fighter air base" that could ferry as many as 1,500 aircraft anywhere in the Pacific. "By means of this force, the United States can concentrate enormous fighter or bomber power at any desired point at any chosen time, always being able thereby to focus more air power at the critical place than can the enemy, whose airfields are spread over a vast area of islands and mainland." This effective combination of air power and gun batteries was, according to the historian, "a veritable revolution in the long history of sea warfare." He added that "it is immensely impressive, this Fast Carrier Task Force, as it steams through the blue waters of the Western Pacific at 25 knots, spread out over 75 miles of sea—although it is hard to see all at once, except from the air."[10]

THE PERSPECTIVE DIFFERED below, where Hobbs and Mandeberg tried to adjust to the tighter, yet comfortable, conditions offered by their pilot quarters and the different ready rooms made available for Air Group 88's four units. Commander Searcy and his squadron commanders enjoyed private cabins, but aviators like Hobbs occupied what the Navy called the Junior Officers' Bunk Room, and what sailors aboard *Yorktown* referred to as "Boys Town" after the youthful visages of the aviators that passed through the carrier. Housing up to four pilots, the fifteen-foot-square and eight-foot-high quarters offered few luxuries. Beams and pipes—like everything else aboard the carrier painted white or gray—lined the outboard bulkhead, while overhead a mess of cables snaked through the piping. One electric light provided illumination, while a basin offered water for shaving and cleaning. In addition to his own bed, each officer enjoyed a metal clothes locker, desk and chair, bookshelf, and small safe for valuables.

If they were not in their pilot quarters, Hobbs and Mandeberg spent almost all of their non-flying time in the fighter pilot ready room. Each squadron, as well as the gunners of VB-88 and VT-88, had its own, where squadron officers could meet with their pilots to discuss upcoming operations, and while the four ready rooms stood directly below the flight deck for faster access to their planes—"We only had to go straight out and up from the ready room to reach the flight deck," said Lieutenant (jg) Watkinson[11]—they were dispersed to separate locations so that a single bomb could not take out the entire Air Group.

Comfort was important as the aviators, dressed in full flying gear, spent long hours in the ready rooms, waiting for the order to rush to their planes to counter an enemy air attack or to join the other aviators for an Air Group strike against enemy shipping or airfields. To pass the time they read updates and listened to information relayed by squadron commanders. Consequently, the air-conditioned rooms featured spacious leather reclining chairs with a connecting tray for writing. Flying apparel hung from hooks or rested over the backs of chairs. When off duty, they used the cooler ready rooms to play cards and write letters home, but mostly they engaged in lively banter about battle tactics, boasted of past feats, or teased Sahloff about the cigar that always seemed to be wedged between his lips. They especially looked forward to hearing Mandeberg's most recent anecdote ribbing someone in the Air Group, which he culled from his observational skills. The aspiring writer rarely failed to disappoint his audience, whether he poked fun at Billy Hobbs's amiable nature or a senior commander's penchant for issuing bewildering orders.

"If you walked into the wardroom at two a.m., it was like walking into a casino," said Lieutenant Hennesy. "Guys playing poker, smoking, everybody smoked. We all thought we were pretty hot shots, but the guys on the *Yorktown* had been playing for a couple of years, and they took the pants off all us!" The only interruptions came with the call to battle stations due to a potential threat, at which time the fliers rushed out of their ready rooms to their post. "My battle station was the stateroom," said Hennesy, "because they didn't want us all in the ready room if it got hit."[12]

According to Ernie Pyle, aviators fit into one of three groups aboard the *Yorktown*. He added that fliers like Hobbs "do nothing but fly, and study, and prepare to fly," and while officers and sailors respected them, "hardly a man on the crew would trade places with them. They've seen enough crash landings on deck to know what the fliers go through."[13] A second group maintained the planes and ensured that engines ran smoothly and the planes operated correctly. The ship's crew, the largest group, had little to do with the Air Group except to keep the carrier running so that those pilots could perform their tasks. Unlike air groups, who operated aboard the carrier for six-month periods before leaving, the *Yorktown*'s crew remained aboard for the duration of the war.

Unlike sailors who were assigned to the smaller destroyers and destroyer escorts, the Air Group's home, according to Pyle, "had all the facilities of a small city, and all the gossip and small talk too. Latest news and rumors reached the farthest cranny of the ship a few minutes after the captain himself knew about them."[14] Barbers clipped sailors' hair, and two chaplains and doctors looked after their physical and spiritual health. By scooping water from twenty feet below the surface and running it through evaporators, *Yorktown* provided 60,000 gallons of fresh water each day for drinking, showering, laundering clothes, and cooking meals. Enlisted ate in their own dining areas called messes, while officers consumed their meals in separate wardrooms.

During the eight days the Air Group had to familiarize themselves with the aircraft carrier, they also enjoyed some free time ashore. According to the Air Group history, at Leyte their time was "devoted to five activities: sleeping, eating, drinking, briefing, and watching the movies."[15] During their visits ashore, they flocked to the Fleet Recreation Center at Jinomac, looked for hometown friends aboard other ships, and bartered with Filipinos for bracelets, reed baskets, and other souvenirs. On one occasion Father Joseph N. Moody, the *Yorktown*'s respected Catholic chaplain, organized an outing to a native church where more than one hundred men, splendid in their dress whites despite the mud kicked up by a rainstorm, supped on a native feast after a Filipino bishop had administered Confirmation to a group of youngsters. Eugene Mandeberg located a friend from home then assigned to the Philippines, and the two attended a wedding reception, where Eugene could not help but admire the beauty of the island's females.

The fun ended on June 26, when *Yorktown* took the Air Group to sea for exercises that would familiarize the aviators with flight and deck procedures. The next day the Air Group launched simulated air strikes, giving Hobbs and the others the opportunity to lift off the carrier, rendezvous with their respective squadrons, and return for a landing. The only mishap occurred when the VB-88 commander, Lieutenant Commander Elkins, and his gunner, Aviation Radioman 1/c Charles J. McBride, splashed during a takeoff. Elkins might have died, as he had difficulty getting out of his harness, but the muscular McBride pulled Elkins to safety seconds before the plane disappeared beneath the surface.

BACK HOME, AS mothers of sons about to go into harm's way, both Zelda Mandeberg and Hattie Hobbs felt an anxiety they knew would never abate until their sons returned to them. Unable to telephone Eugene or Billy, only the postal system could relay information to and from their sons. Sketchy in details as was every letter in those days of military censorship, whenever a letter arrived, the mothers at least knew that as of the date of the missive, their boys were safe. A solitary letter brought to their homes by the mailman made their days; a morning without a letter deepened their fears.

"I feel like a millionaire this morning," Zelda wrote to Sonya three days after Eugene and Billy had begun flying off *Yorktown.* "That's why this very beautiful stationery. A letter from Eugene and two from you, my darling. Eugene writes about being on a very fine ship and meeting some boys from Detroit. He seems to be in good spirits."[16]

Hattie had not heard from Billy since he left Saipan. She baked cakes and cookies, carefully packed them in bags with the farm term "Hybrid" stamped across the middle, and inserted a letter imparting hometown news and prayers for his speedy return. Among Air Group fliers, the farm boy from Kokomo was thereafter labeled "Hybrid," both due to Hattie's bag and to the word being used as reference to strains of corn.

The day after a destroyer plucked Elkins from the ocean, *Yorktown* returned to harbor to load supplies for the upcoming mission against the Japanese. A few days later they learned that some of their operations would be in the Tokyo area. "This caused quite a stir although it had been expected," stated the fighting squadron history. "The squadron was as ready for combat as any ever had been. It had ten months of training behind it."[17]

Billy Hobbs, Eugene Mandeberg, and the rest of Air Group 88 were about to go to war.

"THE IGNOMINY OF PEARL HARBOR WOULD NEVER BE WIPED OFF THE SLATE UNTIL THEY HAD BEEN REPAID IN FULL"

When Air Group 88 arrived in the Philippines, almost no one believed the war would soon end. They figured they would be aboard *Yorktown* for six months or so, and then be relieved for other duty before being reassigned to another carrier.

By June 1945, American forces had destroyed or neutralized practically every Pacific bastion the Japanese had seized and fortified since Pearl Harbor. After conducting a holding pattern in 1942 to hand the nation's military time to regroup after the initial blows in Hawaii and elsewhere, and to give home front industries time to develop the system that eventually poured a continuous supply of war materiel to the front, American forces chipped away at Japan's defenses. Built around a rapidly increasing Army, an effective land-based air arm, and an ever-expanding fleet of aircraft carriers, cruisers, and destroyers, the United States swept thousands of miles across the Pacific in breathtaking fashion. They smashed Japanese-held airfields and installations in the Gilberts and Marshalls in late 1943 and early 1944, and within six months had leaped 1,500 miles westward with their successful landings in the Marianas, a lynchpin of Japan's second line of defense protecting the Home Islands. Operations in late 1944 planted General Douglas MacArthur's infantry in the Philippines, while Marine and Army units swept northward to seize Iwo Jima and Okinawa in bitter combat over the ensuing five months to batter the final layer of defense shielding Japan proper.

The fighting was marked by pitiless land combat in which no quarter was given, fast-paced naval surface engagements that included ships firing at point-blank range, and, of most interest to Hobbs and the other members of VF-88, dogfights that painted broad skyward panoramas as opposing fighter pilots attempted to swat one another from the heavens. Navy scuttlebutt quickly relayed the exploits of Pacific aviators who notched kills as if they were shooting stationary targets. Commander David McCampbell and his "Fabled Fifteen"—Air Group 15 aboard USS *Essex* (CV-9)—amassed an astounding record, with McCampbell alone shooting down seven Japanese aircraft on June 19 during the Marianas Turkey Shoot, only to top it four months later by recording nine kills in the wide-ranging Battle of Leyte Gulf on October 24. The aviators of Hobbs's VF-88 and Hennesy's VBF-88—the men who flew the fastest aircraft, and as protectors of the bomber and torpedo squadrons would be the first fliers to engage enemy pilots— anticipated that they would experience more of the same.

However, by June 1945 aerial warfare in the Pacific had changed. Rather than sending their pilots and planes into battle with American air groups, where they would be wasted in foolish endeavors to halt an enemy already on its way to their shores, the Japanese retained them in the Home Islands, waiting to rebuff the expected American invasion of Japan.

Principal among the 11,000 aircraft dispersed and camouflaged about various airfields or hidden in underground shelters were 6,500 kamikaze planes. Beyond that, more than 3,000 suicide boats, plus whatever remained of their submarine and destroyer units, would assail and disrupt the landing force on the surface and below while kamikazes battered it from above. If they failed to turn back the landings, the Japanese had stockpiled seven million chemical munitions in the Home Islands.

Japan made little attempt to keep their preparations secret. According to *Time* magazine, Radio Tokyo boasted that suicide aircraft had been stationed throughout the Home Islands, and claimed that they had amassed secret weapons in such large quantities that they almost equaled the total number of tanks and guns used in the European war. Japanese leaders praised a defense system they claimed would force the United States to destroy it one district at a time, thereby dragging out the conflict and wearying the American public into clamoring for peace terms. Home Minister Genki Abe called upon the nation's population to abandon "all thoughts of self and life," and Radio Tokyo taunted, "The sooner the enemy comes, the better for us, for our battle array is complete."[18]

The enemy was coming, and in numbers that would stagger Japanese leaders. On May 25, 1945, the Joint Chiefs of Staff ordered that the landings on Kyushu, code-named Olympic, would occur November 1. More than forty aircraft carriers, escorted by hundreds of battleships, destroyers, and destroyer escorts, would support landings by thirteen divisions and two regimental combat teams. From the air, carrier aircraft, as well as the planes of the Fifth, Seventh, Thirteenth, and Twentieth Air Forces, would assault enemy air bases, disrupt lines of communications, and smash industrial locations. Coronet, the landings on the Honshu coast near Tokyo, would follow on March 1, 1946, with an end to the fighting hopefully occurring near the end of 1946.

In an effort to reduce Japan's defenses before the American invasion commenced, Third Fleet commander Halsey received the task of attacking Japanese naval and air forces, shipping, shipyards, steel and munitions factories, and any other target he believed vital to Japan's defense. Halsey commanded the task force as it steamed toward Japan, and Air Group 88 would execute Halsey's orders in what was the initial step of the American assault of Japan proper. Halsey's vengeance for Pearl Harbor would be administered by Billy Hobbs and his fellow aviators.

The Americans faced an arduous task, as no one in Washington expected the Japanese to yield easily. A blunt assessment in the *New York Times* cautioned against "any ideas that may be held that bringing Japan to unconditional surrender is something we can do with our left hand and without further great sacrifice." With an army of four million, larger than Germany fielded, defending a contracted area in which they could concentrate forces in massive numbers, the Navy "will need every fighter and bomber plane suitable for Pacific operations that can be built."[19]

In mid-May the military correspondent for the *Los Angeles Times*, Kyle Palmer, who had recently spent time in the Pacific and seen the devastation at Iwo Jima and Okinawa, estimated that the invasion of Japan would cost between 500,000 and one million American casualties. Prominent news magazines leaned toward the higher figure, while

General MacArthur pinned the figure at 720,000. Admiral Halsey's chief of staff, Rear Admiral Robert B. Carney, stated that in July 1945 "the only thing that remained, that unnerved people, was the prospect of having to land in Japan, and probably killing every man, woman, child and dog, to overcome their fanatical resistance."[20]

Admiral Halsey appeared to be the perfect commander to run the show. Since the war's first day, aggressiveness marked Halsey's every move and utterance. The carrier commander became the nation's first major naval war hero of the Pacific fighting by orchestrating attacks against Japanese-held islands in early 1942 and by taking Army Lieutenant General James Doolittle's bombers within flying range of Tokyo for their famous raid against the enemy capital. As commander of South Pacific forces, he helped turn the tide in the Solomon Islands and knock the Japanese on the defensive in the Pacific. Newspaper headlines heaped praise on the pugnacious admiral, who asserted that his only motive every day was to find a fight.

The American public loved his bombastic statements, which Halsey used in the early stages of the war to boost morale at a time when the American military was rebuilding from the war's opening trauma. "Before we're through with 'em, the Japanese language will be spoken only in hell!" he muttered upon seeing the damage at Pearl Harbor.[21] During his tenure as commander of the South Pacific, a large sign at the fleet landing at Tulagi, across from Guadalcanal, exhorted each officer and enlisted to "Kill Japs, Kill Japs, Kill More Japs," and he vowed to ride Hirohito's white stallion through the streets of Tokyo. The home front loved him; the military adored him. They nicknamed him "Bull" and compared him to a storm sweeping toward the Japanese. During those first two years of the war in the Pacific, Halsey was the dominant naval commander, the one the home front counted on to make the Japanese pay for their treacherous attack against Pearl Harbor and the man naval officers most wanted to serve under. Halsey's only regret during that time was his absence during the two key carrier battles—the May 1942 Battle of the Coral Sea and the following month's Battle of Midway. It was an omission he intended to rectify, either by finding and destroying any remaining Japanese aircraft carriers, or by gaining impressive victories in some other fashion.

In part goaded by this passion, Halsey stumbled into three disasters in the war's latter half. Knowing his penchant for a carrier battle, the Japanese dangled four carriers devoid of their air groups to lure Halsey from his post off the San Bernardino Strait in the Philippines in October 1944. By taking his powerful fleet northward in pursuit of what turned out to be a Japanese decoy, the admiral left open a door through which a potent Japanese surface force barreled, intent on disrupting General MacArthur's beachhead inside Leyte Gulf. Only a miraculous interposition by Taffy 3, a unit of escort carriers and their stout-hearted destroyers and destroyer escorts, deflected the Japanese from their goal.

Two months later Halsey led his Third Fleet into the first of two typhoons. The December storm sank three ships, damaged several others, destroyed nearly 200 aircraft, and drowned almost 800 men in what became one of the Navy's most damaging losses since the 1942 battles off Guadalcanal. In June 1945, only a few weeks before Air Group 88 joined *Yorktown*, Halsey again stumbled into a typhoon that buffeted the fleet with seventy-foot waves and gusts approaching 127 knots. While no ship was sunk, fifty aircraft were swept overboard or damaged beyond repair, and six men lost their lives. Courts of inquiry reluctantly absolved Halsey of blame for both encounters, partly because naval superiors in Washington knew that the American public would never accept a public shaming of their hero. Halsey remained in command, but the warrior knew he had lost some of the trust and respect of fellow admirals and of his superiors.

He could reclaim his reputation by notching another victory. An encounter with enemy carriers was out of the picture, as they were no longer a factor in the war, but he could stamp his imprint on the Japanese homeland with his carrier air groups. Halsey could never forgive the Japanese for what he termed their cowardly attack on Pearl Harbor, so he planned to park his ships off the Japanese coast and so thoroughly lay waste to every naval base, airfield, and industrial concern that the Japanese faced no alternative but to surrender. He would provide the brains; aviators like Hobbs and Mandeberg would supply the brawn to finish this war and help return the admiral to the lofty perch he had once occupied.

Earlier that year, in a radio interview with the National Broadcasting Company (NBC) and in an article published in *Collier's* magazine,

Halsey argued that Japan was "not fit to live in a civilized world." He urged that the country should be reduced to the status of a fourth-rate nation so it could no longer threaten the peace, that traces of Japanese militarism should be eliminated, and that a Japanese officer should be executed for every American prisoner of war killed. "If we go easy on these rats now," he said to the NBC audience, "they'll use the next twenty years just like the Nazis used the last twenty-five." That mind-set carried over to his staff. As the war neared its end, the U.S. Navy "set about the business of completely destroying every vestige of major naval power in Japan," said Halsey's chief of staff, Rear Admiral Carney. "Call this what you will, it was a deep-seated feeling in the minds of all of us that the ignominy of Pearl Harbor would never be wiped off the slate until they had been repaid in full, and until they were utterly destroyed."[22]

Halsey's personal motives blended perfectly with what his superiors ordered. An unrelenting campaign against the Japanese people might nudge that nation closer to the peace table, thereby saving American lives, and it would aptly be the culminating piece of that vengeance that had so fueled much of Halsey's ambitions. However, it would demand that the admiral play a delicate balancing act as July opened. He had to know when to risk his aviators' lives and when to rein in those impulses. Standing at the military end of that balancing act with Halsey were Watkinson, Hennesy, and every other aviator in Air Group 88. Their survival depended, in part, on the whims of an admiral who considered their well-being subordinate to his wishes.

In the early days of July, Halsey would find few critics in Air Group 88. Hobbs and most of his squadron mates loved the admiral's aggressiveness, and believed that by operating under Halsey, they were certain to find those aerial battles they longed for. However, doubts had filtered down to some of Yorktown's officers and crew who had been at sea long before Air Group 88's arrival. After Halsey stumbled into the second typhoon in June 1945, Admiral Radford sent an angry dispatch to naval headquarters in Washington, D.C., criticizing his associate.

One of the carrier's previous commanders, Captain Joseph J. "Jocko" Clark, believed the war had become too complex for Halsey, whose bombastic nature better suited the first half of the war, when bold words and daring deeds substituted for a military organization that was gearing up for war. Since Leyte Gulf the responsibilities of a task force commander had magnified to the point where he had to juggle a myriad of duties, including managing multiple task groups, defending against kamikaze aircraft, and remaining offshore in support of island assaults.

Some of the *Yorktown* crew chimed in. A group of sailors expressed their ire at the headline-loving Halsey with a biting poem titled "Ode to the BIG [capitals theirs] Wind" that, in part, said:

> *Bull his name and Bull his nature*
> *Bull his talk will always be.*
> *But for me and many like me,*
> *He's a perfect S.O.B.*
> *Typhoons never worry this guy,*
> *Though they come from north or south.*
> *Typhoons, Bah, he has one every*
> *Time he opens his big mouth.*
> *What if he should lose some pilots?*
> *War is war—the time is ripe!*
> *Fifty more he'll sacrifice to*
> *Gain another inch of type.*
> *He has uttered one desire to*
> *Mount Hirohito's steed,*
> *And the peace parade in Nippon*
> *This bold warrior wants to lead.*
> *He should be a mighty rider,*
> *For I tell you from my heart—*
> *I consider him part equine,*
> *And I think you know which part.*[23]

"THERE WAS ONLY ONE REMAINING TARGET, THE JAPANESE HOMELAND"

The departure from the Philippines to Japan must have been a spectacle to witness for Hobbs and the other young aviators of Air Group 88.

They had worked with carriers before, but always in maneuvers, and mostly with a single carrier. This journey to war, however, was special. In three days the Hobbs family in Kokomo and the Mandebergs in Detroit would celebrate July 4 with parades and fireworks, but nothing could match the seagoing pageant formed by the ships of Task Force 38 as they eased out of the islands and headed toward what most certainly would be a different form of fireworks.

"Slipped from Leyte harbor early in the morning 'for colder climate,'" turret gunner Aviation Ordnanceman 3/c Ralph Morlan of VT-88 wrote in his diary on July 1. At 6:45 a.m. on July 1, a "rather dismal and overcast"[24] day according to Hobbs, *Yorktown*'s anchor lifted off the bottom of San Pedro Bay and the carrier was underway along with the other ships of Task Force 38. *Yorktown* had Rear Admiral Radford aboard as commander of Task Group 38.4, while Vice Admiral John McCain broke out his flag aboard *Shangri-La* and Admiral Halsey his aboard the battleship *Missouri*. In an impressive array of splendor and power, one by one the ships slipped from their anchorages toward the bay's exit, where one hour later they morphed from the long, thin columns into their circular task groups.

Admiral Radford did not expect major opposition from the Japanese surface fleet, which was already depleted from disastrous encounters in the Central Pacific and the Philippines. He figured his main threats came from enemy submarines and kamikazes, but he trusted his conglomeration of power—both aerial and ships' gun batteries—to handle those perils.

"On the first of July," Commander Searcy wrote in a combat summary of the operation, "we left the islands for new adventure. We had reached the stage in the war where there was only one remaining target, the Japanese Homeland."[25] Along with the rest of the task force, Air Group 88 and *Yorktown* embarked upon the first steps of the invasion of Japan.

As the task force steamed northeast toward Japan, Fighting Squadron 88 shared combat air patrol with the air groups of the other carriers. From above, the VF-88 aviators obtained a majestic view of a military panorama that stretched beyond the horizon. The trio of task groups

looked like giant wheels breaking the waves, with the lumbering carriers, moving platforms that the air groups called home, churning in
the middle. About them steamed the surface punch of the task groups,
the potent battleships and cruisers with their batteries of big guns, while
farther out, manning the outer ring, smaller destroyers sliced through
the water searching for enemy submarines or aircraft.

The pilots in Air Group 88 understood the lethal implications of their
mission. "It was going to fight a deadly but unheroic war against Jap AA
and planes on the ground," stated the Air Group history. "The job of
naval aviation was now to hit Jap ships at anchor and Jap planes reveted
on the airfields. The fighting was as deadly—probably more deadly—
than any the Navy Task Forces had engaged in."[26]

"Cowering in the bays and harbors of Japan remained the last little
remnants of Japan's once proud Imperial Navy," stated one of Halsey's
reports at the time. The US Fleet had deflected the Japanese at Coral
Sea, Midway, and in the Solomons. American naval power had decimated enemy air units in the Battle of the Philippine Sea and annihi-
lated her surface forces at the Battle of Leyte Gulf. "For two years, like
twin nemeses, the US Third Fleet and the US Fifth Fleet, with their
fast carrier forces, had battered and then pursued them until only their
home harbors offered the thinnest anchorages of safety. Now the United
States Navy was closing in on them even there for the final kill."[27]

And Halsey, who noted historian Samuel Eliot Morison described
as leaving Leyte for the Japanese Home Islands with "blood in the eye,"
intended to make that final kill as decisive and fearsome as possible. He
wrote, "Our planes would strike inland; our big guns would bombard
coastal targets; together they would literally bring the war home to the
average Japanese citizen."[28]

"WE ARE ALL VERY EAGER TO GET AT SOMETHING"

The first day or two of the journey resembled a vacation cruise. Aviators
still flew CAP (combat air patrol), sharing it with the air groups of other
carriers in the task group, and participated in training exercises, but the
sense of operating in an active combat zone had yet to settle over the

Air Group. Men had time to sunbathe or play deck tennis, gathered at night to watch movies, or on those crystal clear days when they could see the other ships of the task force, marvel at the assembled might of which they were a part. The affable Catholic chaplain, Father Joseph N. Moody, delighted the crew—and Admiral Radford, who believed that Moody's broadcasts boosted morale—with his frequent announcements over the ship's public address system. He relayed information from intelligence officers and read news dispatches from home.

Most of the time, though, the Air Group conducted training exercises to familiarize the aviators with *Yorktown*'s flight system and to give their gunners a chance to sharpen their skills against towed targets. Mandeberg participated in simulated attacks on the carrier, Hennesy patrolled the skies for enemy aircraft, and Hobbs joined fliers from other air groups to rehearse group tactics to, as a VF-88 report said, hone the skills the aviators needed for combat and to give them "a keen edge for the coming combat operations."[29]

"We are being briefed every minute," Hobbs wrote in his diary of the meetings in which the pilots discussed air tactics and enemy maneuvers. He flew nearly every day, even in threatening skies, for each day they steamed north brought them twenty-four hours closer to enemy pilots and guns. "It is very bad this morning," he wrote of the weather on July 2. "We took off at 0845 for a practice strike. It was poor for such work. I did the bomb spotting with Ken Neyer [Lieutenant (jg) Kenneth T. Neyer]." Hobbs mentioned his pleasure over the flying he had just done in the rough weather—"Came aboard very nicely and received several nice comments on it"—but added that while the Air Group aviators looked ahead to grappling with the Japanese, "We are all very anxious."

The next day offered more of the same, but this time instead of taking off in the normal manner, he was launched by catapult. "I had a catapult shot in the dark this morning. Led the endeavor right well. Stayed up for 3 hrs. and 50 min. Was very tired. Got several vectors. Came aboard very good, so some said." Being out of touch with family back in Kokomo started to weigh on the young aviator, though. "I did start to get low. Would like some mail."[30]

Word from families held a deeper meaning on July 4, when everyone's minds were on the parades and festivities that marked hometown celebrations honoring the nation's birthday. They would have preferred joining the fun in Kokomo or Detroit, but the aviators going to war had to settle for sharing their thoughts in letters to loved ones and in diaries. "We're at sea right now, so the mail delivery will again be slowed down," Mandeberg wrote his parents on July 4. "Just be calm and patient—and eventually or sooner, my mail will arrive—and so will yours." He added that "personally, my health is fine and so is everything else. The food continues to be good, the ship friendly, and the quarters clean," and ended the letter with words intended to assuage Nathan's and Zelda's fears for their son's safety. "Don't worry about me. I'm okay now, and will continue to be so."[31]

Although he was thousands of miles from his parents in Kokomo, Billy Hobbs "had a nice day today." He was on standby all afternoon in case enemy aircraft or submarines attacked, but "we had a band concert at dinner tonite. Had fresh peas, steak with ice cream, etc."[32]

Hobbs had been following the war's progress through the pages of the *Kokomo Tribune*. Most of the headlines for early July centered on mundane items, such as Indiana factories preparing to switch from war production into peacetime items, and the Ford Motor Company expanding the assembly of passenger cars. The stories for July 4, however, were different. On one hand, a page one article featured the area's plans for the holiday, and stated, "Although not unmindful that Japan remains unconquered the state's residents seemed to feel more relaxed than during the last three war years and many made preparations for taking a day off from routine tasks." Some plants "which had been working at top speed since Pearl Harbor day were closed," and town stores and businesses shut their doors for the holiday for the first time since 1941. In the same July 4 issue, though, Hattie scanned reminders that while many of Kokomo's residents were confident that they would soon be putting the war behind them, Billy steamed closer to a Japan that had vowed to wage a bloody fight to the death. "500 Superfortresses Hammer Jap Plants," read the main headline.[33] Until the war terminated, Hattie and every other parent of those Air Group aviators struggled with the knowledge that their sons advanced toward Japan as the tip of America's fighting might. Further deaths would occur to those groups in the forefront, precisely where their sons and the *Yorktown* would soon be.

A July 5 accident reemphasized the dangers when Lieutenant (jg) Fred C. Satterthwaite of VB-88, piloting a Helldiver and accompanied by gunner Aviation Radioman 3/c Arthur C. Briggs, crashed into the barrier stretched across the flight deck to stop malfunctioning aircraft in errant landings. "We hit the barrier once," said Briggs. "Satterthwaite was a hell of a pilot, but we hit the barrier, and the tail went way up and we damaged the propeller. There was a series of barriers chest high, three or four of them. If you went through those, that's where planes are that already landed, and that could be messy."[34]

As they neared the Home Islands, Hobbs and the Air Group attended classes in the fighter ready room to discuss the different types of aircraft and shipping they would encounter over Japan. Every carrier participated in task force simulations of strike procedures, during which Watkinson and the handful of night fighter pilots posed as Japanese aviators. "Got up at 1100 today," Hobbs entered in his diary. After obtaining the information in the ready room briefing, Hobbs joined his team leader, Howdy Harrison, as well as Eugene Mandeberg and Joe Sahloff. That quartet operated as Howdy's team and became the men with whom Hobbs would most frequently fly into combat, to fly CAP. Hobbs wrote that while they had "a very enjoyable hop" and that "Howdy was quite pleased," the four wanted to experience the real thing. "We are all very anxious."[35]

By July 7, three days before their first strike into Japan, a line of seven submarines had taken station off the enemy coastline to cover the task force's approach to launch positions for a July 10 strike. It proved to be a wise precaution since the Japanese were already aware of the American armada. "There are signs of a powerful force coming out from Ulithi and Leyte," wrote Vice Admiral Matome Ugaki of the Imperial Navy's General Staff on the same day.[36]

Sailors can be a superstitious lot, and some of *Yorktown's* crew saw the accident that occurred on July 7 as a bad omen. Instead of lifting Lieutenant C. D. Hughes's Hellcat skyward, a catapult malfunctioned and careened the fighter into the water close to the carrier. A sailor dropped a smoke bomb to mark Hughes's location, but it ignited the fuel from Hughes's aircraft and further harmed the flier. A nearby destroyer plucked him out of the water, but Hughes was so badly injured that he had to be sent to the hospital ship USS *Rescue*.

After refueling and taking aboard fresh provisions east of Iwo Jima the next day, Task Force 38 began its high-speed run toward Point Option, 200 miles from Tokyo, from where they would commence operations against the Home Islands. A favorable weather front helped mask their approach from what Halsey and everyone aboard *Yorktown* expected—a massive Japanese air strike, including kamikaze aircraft.

Other than CAP—"Had a standby hop and was shot off," Hobbs recorded in his diary—all flight operations halted on July 8 in preparation for the task force's opening strike. Daily briefings intensified now that, according to the VT-88 history, the "first great venture was now just around the corner."[37] Lieutenant Hennesy made mental notes he hoped might yield an edge in the fighting, while the ever-studious Eugene Mandeberg collected new information to what he had already gathered for his first mission.

The mood on July 9, the day before the Air Group's first strike, differed dramatically from the eight prior days. Laughter and joking diminished, and men felt a tension that had been absent. Briefings in the ready rooms became more detailed as to the nature of the targets, the opposition the aviators could expect, and the weather. Meanwhile, *Yorktown*'s crew broke out their cold-weather gear: blue Navy sweaters, blue stocking caps, rain capes with parkas to cover the head, and long underwear.

As aviators listened in their ready rooms, Captain Boone announced that the Air Group's goal—attacking the enemy's homeland—was now in sight, and that from this point on the carrier could expect stiff resistance. He assured them that if they carried out their duties, they would emerge victorious and bring peace closer.

The next day, Howdy Harrison and the other three aviators of his team, the tip of the military spear pointed at Tokyo, would plunge into Japan. Talk was over; drills and exercises had ended. A combat strike, which asked each young man in the ready room to fly directly into Japanese antiaircraft fire to deliver their bombs and rockets, loomed. As Aviation Ordnanceman 3/c Morlan of the torpedo squadron wrote in his diary that day, "Everyone talking about it, a few writing letters. Tomorrow is the big day—God help us."[38]

Billy Hobbs was ready. "This is [the] day before strike day," he entered in his diary on July 9. "We are all very eager to get at something. We still have very little idea where we shall hit. We are to be briefed tonite."[39]

The war that had been so distant during training at Otis Field had suddenly arrived.

PART II

THE JULY 1945 BATTLES

CHAPTER 5

"Today Our Group 88 Starts Raising Hell with the Japs"
Preparation for Battle, July 10, 1945

THE MONTHS OF practice and preparation were over. Combat, with real bullets and antiaircraft shells, loomed only hours away for Air Group 88. They would have plenty of company in attacking Japan, as aircraft from the other task groups, now stationed twelve miles apart 150 miles off the Japanese coast, would join Radford's Task Group 38.4 in striking enemy airfields, industrial locations, and shipping. While Halsey's planes lashed Japanese installations and shipping from his offshore perch, B-29 bombers from Marianas airfields and Army and Marine fighters and medium bombers from Iwo Jima and Okinawa continued their onslaught from the sky. Every Japanese plane or antiaircraft position destroyed now, made the task a little easier for the planned American assault of the Home Islands. Every factory hit diminished the enemy's capability to supply rifles and mortars to its soldiers or aircraft to its pilots. And every bomb exploding on Japanese soil affected the morale of men, women, and children who had been told that their nation would never be attacked.

The pilots filed into their ready rooms one level below the flight deck, one each for the four squadrons, to receive the final details for their initial strike into the heart of the Japanese Empire. One by one they entered—Howdy Harrison and Ted Hansen, who had already been through so much combat; Komisarek the jokester, whose quick wit eased the tension; Adams, the Navy Cross recipient whom everyone admired; and Crommelin, whose presence as one member of the famed family of aviators instilled confidence in the entire squadron. Hobbs and Sahloff sat as full members of the fighting squadron, every bit as much as Crommelin or Adams, but they knew that complete acceptance and respect would come only after they had proven themselves in the crucible of combat. Until then, they dealt with a self-imposed isolation from their more experienced comrades, a feeling that would only end when they, too, could think of themselves as combat veterans.

The men remarked that the letters "CIC," standing for *Yorktown*'s Combat Information Center, the source through which all the information passed to conduct air strikes or to defend the carrier from enemy attack, actually meant, "Christ, I'm Confused," but the joking ended as Crommelin and the intelligence officer walked into the ready room. The pilots either stood off to the sides or sat in one of the comfortable reclining chairs. Some aviators sitting in the seats or leaning against the bulkheads took notes, while the veterans relied on their experience to separate the newer information from what they had culled from prior missions. A mounted chalkboard filled with information spread across the front wall, while piping crisscrossed above. Equipment hanging from the ceiling or along the walls gave the room the appearance of a cluttered military closet, but every pilot knew the exact location of each item. Crommelin, as well as his three fellow squadron commanders in separate ready rooms, informed their aviators that the next day, July 10, they would destroy area airfields arcing along the northern sector of Tokyo, and the aircraft operating out of those airfields. Konoike, Kashiwa, and Kasumigaura Airfields northeast of the capital; Tokorozawa and Irumagawa Airfields to the northwest; Katori Airfield along the eastern coast; and others would become frequent targets for Hobbs and the men of Air Group 88 in the coming weeks.

The speakers emphasized that the aviators needed to concentrate on the assigned targets instead of chasing after something that, while it might look appealing, would distract them from the main mission. They claimed that it was crucial to destroy the enemy's air arm, both to protect the task force and to further impair Japan's ability to wage war. The briefing officers cautioned the fliers that they could expect heavy resistance, in the air and from the ground, from an enemy who would now be fighting to defend its homeland.

The officers reviewed information from the Air Intelligence Group Division detailing the enemy's antiaircraft tactics. They reminded the pilots that should they attack a target more than once, the pilot should vary his approach in the second dive to confound Japanese gunners waiting for them to repeat their patterns. They emphasized that they should be alert to Japanese guns positioned along and at both ends of the airstrips, as well as artillery embedded on the slopes or crests of hills. Hobbs and Sahloff had listened to many air briefings during their New England training, but those prior affairs seemed like children's games compared to this moment. Nowhere while flying off the Massachusetts coastline did they need to worry about antiaircraft positions, and enemy fighters intent on shooting them down never rose from Rhode Island airfields.

As if that were not enough new information for Hobbs and Sahloff, the intelligence officer explained that the Japanese sometimes used tracerless ammunition and flashless cordite, making it harder to locate antiaircraft positions or to see the fire coming toward them. They admonished them not to forget the words from carrier aviators who had attacked the Home Islands earlier in the year. "AA [antiaircraft] fire over Tokyo area proved to be the most intense and accurate yet encountered by the Air Group," said one pilot of those strikes. "All types of fire were directed at the planes with the result that it was necessary to make all attacks at high speeds and with radical maneuvers, preventing deliberate attacks and complete observation of results."

The briefing officers recommended that when attacking at treetop level, pilots should avoid evasive action and frequent course changes, as that only decreased their speed and increased the risk. "Once committed to the carefully selected avenue of approach, the cardinal rule of thumb is 'low, fast and straight [underline theirs],'" stated one intelligence bulletin shared with the men. Aviators had died because they pulled up to observe the damage their bombs caused, handing the Japanese antiaircraft gunners an easy target. The bulletin added, "And it is at this point that the plane may well be caught in a deadly cone of fire. Remember—stay

<u>on the deck until well past the outermost fringe of the target area</u> [underline theirs]."[1]

The officers then distributed charts of the target area, predicted the expected weather, gave rough estimates of the anticipated opposition, and released the position of rescue submarines stationed along the coast that would rush to their aid should their plane be damaged by antiaircraft fire. Crommelin cautioned his fighter pilots to use as much of the deck as they could before lifting off from *Yorktown*, and to join up on the man ahead and begin forming their divisions as fast as possible. He explained that they faced one principal task—to clear the way for the ensuing bombing and torpedo squadrons by eliminating any air opposition and by strafing airfields and antiaircraft positions. He ended by handing out mimeographed sheets containing the *Yorktown*'s position at their return, wind speed and direction, miles to the target, the post-attack rendezvous point ten miles out to sea, and other crucial information.

Flying his flag in the USS *Missouri*, one of the three battleships accompanying Radford's task group, Halsey looked forward to launching his planes against the enemy's homeland. The Japanese had dragged the United States into war by what Halsey considered its cowardly attack against Hawaii—and it seemed appropriate that he now returned the favor. He intended to punish the Japanese, and the instrument of his retribution—Harrison, Hobbs, and the other aviators of Air Group 88 combined with the air groups of the other carriers—sat aboard those *Essex*-class carriers and light carriers he commanded.

"EACH MAN WAS CHALLENGING HIS OWN SOUL"

Reveille awoke Hobbs at 2:30 a.m. *Yorktown*'s executive officer, Commander Myron T. Evans, issued a Plan of the Day which started with the rousing call, "Today our Group 88 starts raising hell with the Japs." "They are plenty good and we have to 'hump' to keep up with them; however we can do it by being on our toes all the time," stated Evans. "Let's help them by keeping all planes flying—no dud bombs and all guns talking." He admonished the crew to keep a close watch on the sky, as "there is a possibility that a few Indians (Kamikaze-Zoot Suiters) may be running loose so it behooves us to *keep alert* and scalp 'em as soon as they get within gun range. Remember that we have room for more scalps up on our score board." He added, *"Don't let the sleeper sneak in on us—nail him!!!* [italics his]" He included a special word for Harrison, Hobbs, and the other aviators by stating, "To Air Group 88 goes our very best wishes and may their bag of Jap planes be the biggest bag of any Air Group."[2]

The first handful of Hellcat pilots to take off comprised the dawn Combat Air Patrol over *Yorktown* and other vessels. They catapulted into the still-darkened sky to begin their vigilance over the task group, while the aviators included in the day's morning missions prepared for their actions to come.

With CAP on station, the other aviators sat down to the usual strike-day breakfast of steak, fried eggs, fried potatoes, and coffee. Those who talked spoke faster than normal, and invariably about any topic other than the strike, but most, especially Hobbs and the others facing their first trials in combat, picked at their food as they quietly battled emotions they had never before faced. They had been trained to fight; they even wanted to fight, but here, off the coast of Japan, a hint of self-doubt dented the cockiness that marked most combat pilots as they asked themselves if they would conduct themselves honorably under the strain of combat. Some barely held down their food, and others declined to eat anything at all. As one veteran of an earlier mission said, "Each man was challenging his own soul to tell him how he would measure up in battle. No man ever lived who got the answer in advance."[3]

AFTER BREAKFAST, THE aviators prepared for battle. Complete with their war gear of coveralls, helmets, parachute harness, shoulder holsters, knives, and life jackets, every pilot, like modern day versions of gladiators about to do battle in the arena, once more walked to their appropriate ready room for last-minute details. They sat in the reclining leather chairs and watched as ticker tapes provided updated weather information and other flight details. They made certain that their canteens had water and cleaned their goggles, and tried to settle nerves they knew would not ease until the heat of combat obliterated conscious emotion. Unanswered questions persisted: Would Japanese fighters rise to meet them? How thick would the flak be? Would they shoot down a plane? Would they act honorably? Would they return?

Howdy Harrison, a veteran of the war, had already confronted those questions, but he had a deeper motivation for sitting in that chair. He could have accepted a safer post after his first tour, but he instead chose to return to combat. "He had been in the war and came back," said Lieutenant (jg) Bernard Hamilton of VBF-88. "I think he had the feeling that he hadn't done enough for the war. He came back and seemed to be trying to make up for that."[4]

To relieve the tension, some joined in the macabre teasing that often marks men about to enter battle. They told their buddies that if their friend was killed in action, that they would take care of their personal effects as well as their girlfriend. Others lay claim to a fellow pilot's scotch or his poker winnings. No one took offense. Everyone acknowledged the good-natured ribbing for what it was—a harmless way of relieving the pressure by laughing at what would very quickly transform into a deadly situation.

A few rubbed a rabbit's foot for good luck or clutched other items reminding them of home and loved ones. Ensign Herbert Wood of VF-88 had sewn one of his infant daughter's booties onto his leather flight helmet, while others pinned religious medals to their coveralls or dropped good luck coins or small photos of wives or girlfriends in their pockets. Hobbs had his mother's wedding ring securely attached to his dog tag. The items may have had little financial value, but one could not put a price on the connections with loved ones back home that those charms represented.

On the other hand, Lieutenant (jg) Watkinson preferred to let fate deal its hand. He never "had religious medals or anything in the plane for good luck." Besides, as he explained, he had another motive. "If I had to splash, I didn't want to be too attached to something."[5]

Hansen and Sahloff checked the weather one final time, hoping to enjoy what the meteorologists called CAVU—ceiling and visibility unlimited. In those conditions they could spot targets from twenty miles distant, but clear skies also made it easier for the enemy to see them coming. On the other hand, a cloud cover might mask their approach, but it could be treacherous for large numbers of aircraft flying in a small sector. It would also force them to attack through holes in the clouds, which allowed Japanese antiaircraft gunners, knowing that the planes would charge through those openings, to concentrate their guns on those few gateways.

Ensign John J. Willis decided that the somber mood in the fighting squadron ready room was an inappropriate beginning for men soon to fly into the most crucial tests of their lives. "The first day we were to go into combat, after briefing in the ready room, all pilots were sitting around with thoughts of their own," said Willis. "Tension and anxiety were everybody's attitude." Willis slowly rose from his leather chair, looked at the men with whom he would fly into combat, and said, "I don't know about the rest of you guys but I'm scared shitless."[6] At Willis's unexpected remark, the other young pilots erupted in wild laughter and the tension eased.

"PILOTS, MAN YOUR PLANES!"

"The launching of planes is the main event of the carrier show," wrote *New York Times* correspondent George E. Jones when he joined one of Task Force 38's aircraft carriers that month, "rich in sounds and smells and sights which a man always will carry in his memory." Jones noticed that everything about a takeoff was planned to the smallest detail, "for in carrier warfare speed is of the essence."[7]

Contrasting with the stillness of the wardroom was the activity elsewhere on the *Yorktown*. One level below the flight deck, mechanics on the vast hangar deck checked each plane to ensure they were at the peak of readiness, realizing that a mistake made now could have fatal consequences for the pilot later. Some installed replacement parts while others checked the tires and engines. Ordnance men shuttled bombs and torpedoes from *Yorktown*'s magazines to the bomber and torpedo planes, where they hoisted them onto bomb racks and into torpedo bays for delivery to enemy targets. As a final step, other men fueled each aircraft, and then ferried them to elevators that lifted them to the men waiting on the flight deck one level above.

The aviators assigned to participate in this first Air Group 88 assault against the Japanese trusted the head mechanic of the bombing-fighting squadron, Aviation Machinist's Mate 1/c Merald Woods, and the men who worked for him on the flight deck to have their planes at peak performance. His eyes adjusting to the darkness, Woods supervised the spotting of aircraft to takeoff positions, placing the fighters forward, ahead of the larger bombers and torpedo planes that required more of the flight deck to gain the speed they required for liftoff. Woods sent back to the hangar deck any aircraft he assessed needed further work, but when he was satisfied that each Corsair checked out, he nodded his approval for the plane to be launched, a sign that sent small jeep-like vehicles darting about the deck to haul the planes to their positions.

A cluster of aircraft earmarked for later missions occupied the aft portion of the flight deck, their wings folded to preserve space. Since aircraft launched and landed from the stern to the bow, idle planes had to be shuttled from one end of the carrier to the other to keep the deck open for air operations, and once the launchings were complete, the crew would move them forward on the deck to create a landing area for the returning aircraft.

Strike days never employed the full complement of Hellcats and Corsairs, as *Yorktown* needed to retain some to fly CAP over the task group. Twenty-seven of the thirty-six available Hellcats and eighteen of the thirty-seven Corsairs were involved in the morning and afternoon sweeps and strikes on July 10, while all thirty bombers and torpedo planes participated in the two large-scale strikes. That pattern persisted in varying degrees for the duration of their stay off Japan.

IN THE READY rooms below, the aviators continued their preparations until they heard the command, "Pilots, man your planes!" Before the phrase was complete, they grabbed helmets, navigational chartboards, notepads, and other gear and rushed from the ready rooms. Harrison and his wingman, Hobbs, climbed the ladder to the flight deck, where red-helmeted firemen holding extinguishers provided the first hint that this was no ordinary training exercise. Plane handlers stood ready to release the wheel chocks, while each plane captain, the man in charge of that aircraft's maintenance, polished the glass canopy of his assigned aircraft.

Harrison and Hobbs carefully wound their way through the packed flight deck to their planes and climbed into Hellcats with wings still folded. The plane captain greeted each pilot and helped lower him into the cockpit. The captain assisted Hobbs in attaching his oxygen mask and speaking tube, made certain Hobbs's goggles were clear, and checked that his chin guard and helmet were in place. Before leaving, Hobbs's plane captain informed him that everything with his Hellcat functioned properly, and finally wished the Indiana aviator good luck. Now waiting for the command to start his engine, Hobbs ran through a final check of his instruments and reviewed the information listed on his chartboard and notepad. He had conducted checks like this a hundred times, but never before embarking on an actual combat mission. Accuracy and clear thinking were now required more than ever.

While Harrison and Hobbs checked their gauges, in the bomber and torpedo planes the aircrewmen secured their hatches and swung out the guns they would use to fend off enemy aircraft or to strafe ground targets. The assistant air officer's voice boomed from the loudspeaker and interrupted everyone with the order, "Check all lines, chocks, and loose gear about the deck." After half a minute, he followed with "Prepare to start engines," and waited another half minute while the plane captains checked the cartridges that ignited the Hellcat motors into action. Finally, when all was in order, the officer shouted to every maintenance man on the flight deck, "Stand clear of the propellers," at which Merald Woods with the VBF-88 Corsairs and every other mechanic stepped carefully away from their planes.[8]

Elation muted everyone's anxiety, though, as Air Group 88 was about to embark on a mission for which it had long trained. Hobbs's dream of flying into battle against an equally determined enemy pilot, and Hennesy's desire to display the courage and skills of Eddie Rickenbacker and those World War I aces he had long admired, were about to materialize. "This was the day for which the squadron had been waiting for over ten months," stated the fighting squadron's account of the day.[9]

WITH NERVES OVER making their first combat launch mounting, Hobbs and Sahloff sat in their planes packed tightly on the deck's aft portion and waited for the final commands. "Stand by to start engines" first bellowed from the carrier's public address system, followed a few seconds later with, "Start engines!" While the bomber and torpedo plane engines instantly flared to life with a press of a button, mechanics had to insert a small explosive charge into a firing mechanism under the engine of each Hellcat, as no man was strong enough to turn the propellers by hand. When Hobbs pressed an electric button inside the cockpit, the cartridge ignited a charge that rotated the propellers. Amid noise that reached deafening levels, bursts of blue flame emitted from every plane, bathing Yorktown's deck in a soothing light that belied the violent nature of the endeavor they were about to start.

The engines of every aircraft sparked with energy, creating an initial low hum that suddenly exploded into a roaring thunder that reverberated off Yorktown's island and made verbal communication between pilot and deck crew impossible. Aviation Machinist's Mate 1/c Woods noticed that the engine blasts pressed dungarees to mechanics' bodies and hurled loose items bounding along the deck.

Hobbs smelled gasoline fumes and Harrison felt his plane shake as the propellers rotated and their engines sputtered and coughed to life. Hobbs exchanged hand signals with his plane captain and mechanics indicating that everything functioned correctly, and then waited for the signal to move forward. Sunk low in the cockpit, Hobbs taxied down the deck with the help of signalmen holding red and green flashlights— green meant to continue; a red flashlight indicated the pilot should stop because of a malfunction—who lined up along the deck to guide him to his takeoff position.

The plane captains and mechanics move cautiously, as a misstep could send them into the propellers that whirled within inches or a wind stream could knock them off balance. Should they stumble, they were trained to swing onto their bellies and dig their fingers into the deck's narrow gratings normally used for lashing down planes. "At such a time, you can almost taste the danger that saturates the deck," wrote a naval officer who observed Yorktown takeoffs. "Tolerances on a live flight deck are always small, but now they are infinitesimal. An instant's inattention, a slip or even a lurch, an extravagant gesture, a languid response, and a man loses a limb or his life to those murderous propellers. No actuary on earth could list all the ways that you can get killed or maimed on a live flight deck."[10]

Those words proved prophetic when a plane captain, Seaman 1/c Robert Miller, was blown into a whirling prop and died from his injuries two hours later. The day's first casualty occurred before Hobbs had even lifted off *Yorktown*'s deck.

"THICKLY STUDDED WITH AIRFIELDS"

The waiting finally ended when the head signalman shook a green-tipped baton at the lead plane, which Lieutenant Adams piloted for the morning sweep and Howdy Harrison flew for the strike to follow. As deck handlers pushed his wings into flying position, Adams ran through a list of items to ensure he did not take off with malfunctioning gauges or any other problematic issues. He and the pilots of every aircraft made certain their canopies were open in case a problem forced them to quickly exit the plane, and checked that the straps holding themselves in place were sufficiently secure to avoid being thrust against the stick or instrument board during any crash. After a few moments the signalman stopped shaking his baton, swept it in a wide circle a few revolutions, and pointed the baton forward, at which mechanics yanked away the chocks that anchored the wheels to the deck before scurrying to the side.

Captain Walter F. Boone, *Yorktown*'s commanding officer, turned the carrier into the wind for the launching, trying to keep the wind slightly on the port [left] bow for best effect. Taking off boiled down to a simple equation. An aircraft could not lift off the deck until enough air had passed beneath its wings. If a plane's weight needed 70 knots (80 miles per hour) to take off, a combination of a 10-knot wind (11 miles per hour) and a carrier speed of 20 knots (23 miles per hour) required that the pilot attain 40 knots (46 miles per hour) while still on the deck to force enough air under the wings for liftoff.

AT 3:55 A.M. twelve *Yorktown* Hellcats, three teams of four planes each, led by Navy Cross recipient Lieutenant John Adams, left the carrier and turned toward a rendezvous with fourteen fighters from *Shangri-La*. They were the first in what would become a familiar pattern employed throughout Air Group 88's time off Japan's coast for every attack day— two morning sweeps preceding the more comprehensive morning strike, with a repeat performance of the two sweeps and one strike in the afternoon. Fighter sweeps, in which eight to twelve Hellcats and/or Corsairs attacked enemy airfields, would approach the target area before the main force to clear away enemy aircraft and to neutralize Japanese antiaircraft locations. Their actions opened the path for the larger bomber and torpedo strikes to follow, which on July 10 consisted of forty *Yorktown* fighters, including Harrison and Hobbs, escorting in their Hellcats, as well as thirty bombers and torpedo planes joined by an equal number from *Shangri-La*.

From the yardarm a red-and-white flag signaled that takeoff was moments away, while twin rows of dim, white stud lights illuminated the outlines of the deck ahead for Harrison and his squadron mates. Once he received the signal, the pilot of the center Hellcat in the front row taxied out a few feet and the deck crew unfolded the wings. The pilot put down his flaps, held on to his brakes while he revved his engine, and waited for the launching signal officer, the man in complete control of every plane's movements until each pilot lifted off the carrier, to signal his assent to start down the deck. The officer stood abreast the island structure at the starboard [right] wing-tip of the first Hellcat, holding a black-and-white checkered flag with which he relayed his signals to Harrison, Hobbs, and the other pilots. Behind those Hellcats waited, in order, the TBM-3 Avenger torpedo planes and the SB2C-4 Helldiver bombers. Harrison felt his Hellcat shake amid the mounting noise as multiple engines operated in close proximity. When the officer lifted his left arm upward and twirled his flag, Harrison revved his engine for additional speed, released the brakes, swerved slightly to starboard so his slipstream did not hit the plane behind, and headed down the deck.

During the morning strike launch, less than one minute elapsed from the time when Howdy Harrison lifted off to the moment Hobbs, his wingman, started down the deck. As they had done for Harrison, deck crew with their lighted wands signaled Hobbs to taxi clear of the other aircraft, at which time other sailors, careful to avoid the propellers or slipping on the deck, unfolded and locked his wings. Hobbs gunned his engine, checked his gauges, nodded that all was in order, and released his brakes at the LSO's signal. His plane jolted and lurched forward, streaming halos of vapor from the propeller blades and curling from his wing-tips as Hobbs maintained a straight path down the carrier. Men on deck covered their ears as Hobbs's plane raced by, and from practice launches, Hobbs knew he would not have a clear view forward until his Hellcat tail lifted a few feet off the deck and he straightened out his plane. Once that occurred, he eased off on the stick and felt another jolt as his Hellcat left *Yorktown*'s deck. Due to the added weight of the bombs he carried, the aircraft momentarily dipped below the flight deck after leaving the carrier. "The first time I flew with a thousand-pound bomb attached, I almost splashed because the bomb weighs you down so much," said Lieutenant (jg) Watkinson of a moment that normally caught aviators by surprise. "We had no practice for this, either."[11]

Now in the air, Hobbs retracted the flaps and the wheels, which could flip his plane upside down should he have to make a hurried landing in the water, turned on his running lights to aid the next pilot in rendez-vousing with him, and looked for the tiny light indicating Harrison's Hellcat. Once Hobbs joined Harrison at the rendezvous point, they flew in a circular path and awaited the other two pilots of their team, Lieu-tenant (jg) Laverne F. Nabours and Ensign Ronald J. Hardesty.

Takeoffs were scarier for rear seat gunners in the torpedo planes. With their backs to the pilot, and with the bomb-laden Avenger mo-mentarily dipping toward the water, they looked up at the bow before their aircraft gained altitude and *Yorktown* receded. For the entire mis-sion, while the pilot saw the target, enemy aircraft, and everything else forward, the rear gunners' views were restricted aft. They, not the pilots who fired the guns and launched the torpedoes, saw the explosions and noted the accuracy, or waywardness, of the bullets and torpedoes that came from their plane. These missions reminded some rear gunners of riding in the end cab of a rollercoaster while facing backward.

Destroyers steamed close to the carrier in case Hobbs or any other pilot experienced problems during takeoff and had to splash. *Yorktown* could not slow down or turn to rescue the aviator, as the carrier had to maintain its speed for the following planes to take off, so these escorting ships were welcome sights to every airman, lending comfort simply with their presence. Most destroyers kept a record of the aviators they rescued, just as *Yorktown* did of planes shot down or locations bombed, and boasted that they could pick up an aviator within three to seven minutes after he hit the surface. After they returned the man to the *Yorktown* by way of the bosun's chair, in gratitude for saving his aviator Captain Boone sent twenty gallons of ice cream to the destroyer. Only one man that day, Lieutenant (jg) Ilario F. Del Maso, suffered a mishap during launching, but he managed to land his Corsair aboard the *Shangri-La* when his engine cut out.

While Harrison and Hobbs circled at their rendezvous point, elevators on the *Yorktown* had already hoisted additional planes from the hangar deck to the flight deck, complete with pilots inside, engines humming, and propellers spinning so the planes could take off as soon as they reached the flight deck. One by one the Hellcats lifted off, followed by the torpedo planes and bombers, all on their way to the rendezvous point, where they would arrange in attack formation and start toward the Tokyo region 150 miles from the *Yorktown*.

At the rendezvous point, all Hellcats formed into multiple inverted "V" units, with the pilots aligning in four-plane sections—Harrison at the point; Hobbs, as Harrison's wingman given the task of protecting his leader's flank, flying slightly behind and to Howdy's right; and Nabours and Hardesty comprising the left arm. The quartet would remain in that V throughout the mission, attacking in unison and firing at the same targets. The bomber and torpedo planes gathered in units of three or four aircraft, but aligned horizontally rather than in the V formation. While the bombers and torpedo planes flew at the same altitude as they winged toward Japan, Harrison and the other escorting Hellcat pilots took station 2,000 to 4,000 feet above, weaving to reduce their speed to match that of their slower companions below. At the same time, the air groups from three other carriers in the task group—*Shangri-La*,

Cowpens, and *Independence*—rendezvoused in their own sections before all four groups joined and headed toward the coast in a combined strike led by Commander W. A. Sherrill, Searcy's counterpart on the *Shangri-La*.

BACK AT THE *Yorktown*, a sudden silence replaced the noise that had enveloped the carrier since the first engine turned over. A klaxon interrupted the momentary calm, sending deck crews and mechanics into action once again to tow the parked planes forward and re-spot them for the next strike or to make room for when the combat flights returned for landing.

The men aboard *Yorktown* could do nothing now but wait for the strike group to return. Most of the ship's crew had little contact with the pilots, but for Merald Woods and the other Air Group 88 mechanics who closely operated with Hobbs, Sahloff, and the Air Group aviators, and for those pilots held back from the mission to be available for CAP or to counterstrike attacking Japanese aircraft, the minutes passed slowly until the planes reappeared. As he would do for every sweep or strike, Aviation Machinist's Mate 1/c Woods took a moment to mutter a hasty prayer for those fliers now on their way to attack airfields in the Tokyo area. "Religion meant a lot to us out there," said Woods. "It means a lot when you are in combat. I always said a prayer before every flight."[12] Woods feared that his compatriots would need the extra help, as those forty planes had been asked to attack one of the most heavily defended sectors of the Japanese Home Islands.

Men aboard *Yorktown* felt almost as if a family member had departed. During strike days, the crew devoured cartons of fresh donuts washed down by double the amount of coffee consumed on non-strike days. Pilots sat in ready rooms, listening to their comrades over the loudspeaker as the planes turned into their dives. Officers in Air Plot could sometimes hear commanders assigning targets, and even eavesdrop on pilots and rear seat gunners as they shouted jubilantly when their bombs exploded, but it was not the same as being in the air with the aviators. "We knew our boys were there," wrote Ernie Pyle of one such attack. "After that, for us on the ship, it was just a matter of waiting, and hoping."[13]

TAKING OFF AND circling in the rendezvous area consumed two-thirds of the two hours required for the morning sweep to arrive over Tokyo, but once on their way, the force reached the coast within thirty minutes. Hobbs checked his fuel gauge to ensure that he had a sufficient amount of fuel beyond what he needed for the return flight in case Japanese fighters attacked him, while a lifeguard submarine below steamed on station to rescue any aviators forced to ditch in the ocean. The odds favored any aviator whose plane was hit while diving on a Japanese airfield as long as he reached the water.

The massive air strike crossed the Japanese coast sixty-five miles east of Tokyo. The route to and from the airfields had been carefully planned and marked on the pilots' charts to avoid the heaviest known antiaircraft positions, but air intelligence, while accurate in many instances, could not possibly locate and identify every gun that might fire on them along the way. Now over enemy territory for the first time, Hobbs focused on two actions that instructors had repeatedly emphasized—he monitored his gauges and scrutinized the sky for enemy aircraft. The Japanese had earned a reputation as fierce warriors in bloody island campaigns, capped by the terrifying kamikazes that plunged into scores of American destroyers and other vessels in the Philippines and off Okinawa. Air Group 88 aviators could expect no less now that the Japanese were fighting for their homeland.

They had reason to be wary, as the Japanese had ringed Tokyo with airfields and had placed others lining the path to the metropolitan area. Major airfields at Chosi, Konoike, and Kashima guarded the coast, Katori Airfield waited only five miles inland, and at least nine other fields operated anywhere from five to twenty miles apart, with smaller secondary strips standing in between. "The great Tokyo plain was so thickly studded with airfields that ten or a dozen were visible from almost any point at 5000 feet altitude," wrote Lieutenant (jg) Henry J. O'Meara, one of the fighter pilots who accompanied Hobbs.[14]

With the bombers and torpedo planes flying at 12,000 feet and Harrison's Hellcats escorting from 3,000 feet above, the planes encountered thick antiaircraft fire from enemy coastal batteries as they approached the Japanese mainland. One gun at Chosi, south of their intended targets and due east of Tokyo, opened fire when the air groups were still twenty miles out at sea. For the first time, enemy shells whistled by Hobbs and Sahloff, confirming the deadly nature of their mission. Until they reached Japan proper, the aviators still felt mentally connected to their carrier, but once those enemy guns opened up and the planes passed over the Japanese coast, that connection was severed and they were on their own. Hobbs and everyone else now navigated over an enemy's homeland sporting thousands of guns and aircraft eager to kill them, and *Yorktown*, as mammoth and powerful as she was, could not come to their aid.

Now facing the opening salvos of battle, Harrison's team changed course and altitude every thirty to sixty seconds and dropped thin pieces of aluminum, called window, which filled the sky with decoy targets to confuse enemy antiaircraft shells, which ignited when nearing metallic surfaces. Most aviators had expected enemy aircraft to rise from those airfields, but surprisingly none challenged them. Rather than throw their dwindling air arm at these attacks, the Japanese opted to hold it in reserve to counter the expected American landing force when it appeared off the coast. They camouflaged aircraft at every field and hid others in revetments constructed as much as a mile or two from the landing strips. "Our pilots discovered that the Japs were playing it very cagey with their Air Force," stated the fighting squadron history; "planes were cunningly hidden in covered revetments" in adjoining fields and woods. "The pilots were a little disappointed over not seeing any Jap planes in the air."[15]

The aviators might have been disappointed at the lack of opposition, but antiaircraft bursts captured their attention as the group turned to begin Air Group 88's first major strike against the Japanese homeland.

THE TWO SWEEPS attacked while Harrison and the subsequent morning strike neared Japan. Lieutenant Adams's sweep approached Katori Airfield, a few miles inland and fifty miles east of Tokyo, from the northwest. From an altitude of 10,000 feet the planes turned into dives to strafe the airfield as withering antiaircraft fire streamed toward them. Antiaircraft bursts peppered the sky, and smoke that smelled like a burning cloth penetrated the Hellcats and momentarily hampered the aviators' views. While Lieutenant Hoke Sisk's and Lieutenant (jg) Verne

Hongola's teams dropped bombs on airplane revetments at the northern edge, Adams took his team down to strafe other locations along Katori's airfield.

"I did not like diving into antiaircraft fire," said Lieutenant Hennesy. "You had to block it out and focus on your job. You concentrate on getting yourself lined up with whatever target you've been assigned. I was aware the antiaircraft fire was there, but there's no way to duck it. You're trying to get yourself lined up with the target."[16]

After making their runs, the teams turned eastward to blast Konoike Airfield along the coast eight miles east of Katori. While they encountered additional antiaircraft fire between the two locations, again to their astonishment, enemy fighters declined to challenge them. Except for a few dummy planes, they saw few aircraft on either airfield, for the Japanese, again intent on saving their air arm for the expected land invasion of the Home Islands, had camouflaged every plane or removed them to sites a few miles from the airfields. At Konoike, Adams and Hongola strafed installations and camouflaged aircraft, while Sisk bombed and strafed a smaller airfield nearby. Japanese fire hit Ensign Ray Silvia's Hellcat during his strafing run, but he was able to nurse his damaged plane back to the carrier.

One hour later a second sweep of twenty-four Corsairs, half each from *Yorktown* and *Shangri-La*, plunged deeper into Japan. They crossed the plain east of Tokyo, flew a few miles south of Ryugasaki, thirty-two miles to Tokyo's northeast, swung west around Tokyo to avoid the hundreds of antiaircraft guns that shielded the city, and attacked Narimasu Airfield to Tokyo's northwest. Diving into heavy antiaircraft fire, they dropped bombs and fired rockets on aircraft located on the northern edge of the field before returning to their carriers.

In the four-hour-long sweeps, Adams and his fellow VF-88 aviators strafed and bombed revetments, hangars, and antiaircraft positions to soften the targets for the following strike. Even before Adams set his Hellcat down on *Yorktown*'s deck the thirty bombers and torpedo planes of the morning strike, escorted by ten Hellcats, including those flown by Howdy Harrison and Billy Hobbs, were over their targets.

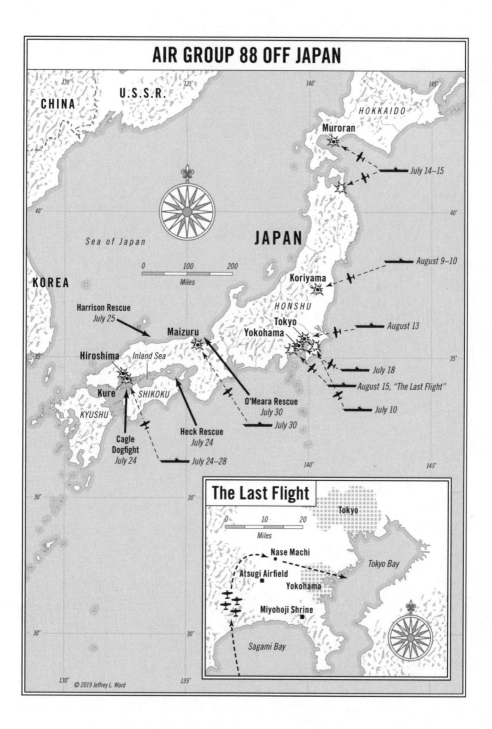

AIR GROUP 88 OFF JAPAN

CHINA

U.S.S.R.

HOKKAIDO

Muroran

July 14–15

Sea of Japan

JAPAN

KOREA

Koriyama

August 9–10

HONSHU

Harrison Rescue
July 25

Maizuru

Tokyo
Yokohama

August 13

Hiroshima

Inland Sea

July 18

Kure

SHIKOKU

O'Meara Rescue
July 30

August 15, "The Last Flight"

July 30

July 10

KYUSHU

Cagle
Dogfight
July 24

Heck Rescue
July 24

July 24–28

0   100   200
Miles

The Last Flight

Tokyo

0   10   20
Miles

Nase Machi

Atsugi Airfield

Yokohama

Tokyo Bay

Miyohoji Shrine

Sagami Bay

© 2019 Jeffrey L. Ward

CHAPTER 6

"Carrier Pilots Were the Best in the World"
The First Attack, July 10, 1945

AIR GROUP 88 and the other aircraft from Task Group 38.4 formed part of a large-scale strike involving the two companion task groups of Halsey's Third Fleet, as well as Army bombers from three island bases. While Admiral Radford's air units, including Air Group 88, attacked airfields in the Tokyo region, the other forces would hit similar targets elsewhere on the Japanese homeland.

Good fortune, in the form of favorable weather, greeted them. The four air groups from Task Group 38.4 approached Chosi and the mouth of the Tone River, one of Japan's major inland waterways dissecting the massive Kanto Plain, where the aircraft changed course and proceeded north along the coastline. At the southern edge of Lake Kitaura, twenty miles northwest of Chosi, the planes turned southwest over gentle hills, raced inland across fertile farmland south of Lake Kasumigaura, and followed the Tone River westward until they reached a point ten miles south of their target, Kasumigaura Airfield. Maps provided by intelligence officers familiarized the aviators with the generally flat terrain, but that same intelligence had also made Harrison and Hobbs aware of the hundreds of guns and aircraft that dotted the Tokyo region.

Around 9:15, two hours after they had lifted off from the *Yorktown*, the strike turned north for a few miles before making a west-to-east run in to Kasumigaura. From his station above the groups of planes, purposely selected to give him a better vantage from which to observe the action and to issue commands, Commander Sherrill shouted "Seminole!

Seminole!"[1] At his signal, the fighters descended into their strafing runs to keep the Japanese pinned down, while the Corsairs, Helldivers, and Avengers peeled off at steep angles to bomb their assigned targets. If all unfolded as planned, the attack would end within three to four minutes.

Every Hellcat aviator raced down to strafe the airfield and fire at the antiaircraft guns. Hobbs's first combat dive was nothing like those he had conducted during training. Japanese antiaircraft guns pumped volumes of shells his way, but he blocked those from his mind while he concentrated on his tasks. Now helpless to control his fate until his dive ended, he plunged directly into those shells and hoped his mother's wedding ring protected him. Howdy Harrison's presence nearby, more sensed than seen, was comforting, but for the next few minutes Hobbs was on his own, his survival now dependent to some degree on his talent as an aviator, but largely on fate.

Hobbs had learned by now to aim above the target to allow for the slight gravity pull, and watched his tracer shells light a tiny curvature toward his targets. In a high-speed run like this, he only had a few seconds to aim and fire before pulling out, all the time being careful to avoid colliding into another plane.

As he descended, red balls arced toward Hobbs and antiaircraft fire burst on his flanks, emitting the familiar burnt cloth odor that permeated Hobbs's Hellcat. He had handily executed dives during his training, but none prepared the Hoosier for seeing tracers zipping by only feet from his Hellcat. Instead of racing straight at his Hellcat as he expected, they converged on him in wavy lines, like red worms meandering skyward from antiaircraft positions. To Hobbs, as well as the other untested aviators, it seemed as if every gun on the airfield had chosen him as their target. As he closed the distance to the airfield, Hobbs's instinct was to pull back on the stick and scramble away, but he kept his hand steady and continued his dive. Hobbs observed enemy planes on the field, but many, he learned later, rested undetected in cleverly camouflaged and dispersed areas. Still fighting the tendency to pull out before a Japanese shell shredded their planes, Hobbs and the other three pilots in his team blasted antiaircraft positions and planes while the Corsairs, according to the torpedo squadron's report, "harried

Jap gunners. Attack was superbly coordinated, and, as a result, AA fire was quickly quenched."[2]

Hobbs's plane shook from the speed of the dive and the nearby AA fire as he triggered short bursts at revetments and planes. In an instant, he and Harrison had swept by the airfield and, with their guns now silent but Japanese fire still pursuing them, raced to a higher altitude and continued westward along the northern shore of Lake Kasumigaura for the rendezvous point over the water. Along the way, Harrison led his four Hellcats in a rocket run on Kashima Airfield on the Japanese coast, releasing their rockets at 2,000 feet in an attack he later concluded had demolished a small building on the field's southern side and damaged five planes.

The danger for Hobbs would not end until he had safely landed aboard the *Yorktown,* but now over the ocean and on his way to the post-battle rendezvous point, he only had to circle and wait for the bombers and torpedo planes to join them after their attack, at which Harrison would signal his Hellcats to begin escorting their companions back to *Yorktown* for the landing.

RED TRACERS RACED toward Aviation Radioman 3/c Arthur C. Briggs and antiaircraft bursts came uncomfortably close to his bomber as the formation drew near the coast, but the untouched aircraft droned toward their target airfield. Planes from *Shangri-La* and *Cowpens* attacked first, followed by the *Yorktown* and *Independence* groups a few moments later. Briggs stared out from his rear seat of the Helldiver as his pilot turned into a steep dive from 8,000 feet, his straps and the force of the dive cementing him to his seat. Briggs saw nothing of Hobbs's Hellcats, which had already begun to strafe the airfield, or of the Avenger torpedo planes, which would conduct their attacks from a lower altitude.

One by one, the Helldivers peeled away from the formation and entered their approaches. They employed a step-down formation, in which the first man turned downward and dove, followed by the next in line, until all fourteen bombers dropped toward Kasumigaura in a line fanning out to 1,500 feet. Some men screamed to relieve the pain to the eardrums caused by air pressure as their planes plummeted downward, and Briggs tried to ignore one obvious thought—that if his Helldiver was hit during such a steep dive, his parachute would be useless.

Briggs scrutinized the sky for enemy aircraft as his pilot dropped window to confuse the enemy's fire. With Briggs keeping watch, the pilot stared into the tiny crosshairs of his sight and kept his plane on a steady course against a wind trying to knock the Helldiver slightly off line. With the pilot's attention completely on the target ahead, Briggs kept track of the altitude and alerted the pilot as they descended toward the cutoff line. If they dipped lower than 1,800 feet, they risked being unable to pull out and avoiding a fiery impact with the ground.

When within range, the pilot fired his rockets, throttled back, and extended his wing flaps to slow the Helldiver. When they reached 4,000 feet, he released the new fused fragmentation bombs, which contained ground-sensing radar that triggered an explosion shortly before the bomb impacted the terrain. Briggs felt a violent jump as the Helldiver lost its payload, and almost regurgitated his breakfast when the Helldiver veered sharply upward and rammed him into his seat.

With his Helldiver gaining altitude and putting distance between the plane and the enemy's guns, Briggs scoured the sky. Continued anti-aircraft bursts forced his pilot to take evasive action and to again drop window as a countermeasure, but fortunately no enemy aircraft attacked. Briggs was surprised that more Japanese planes had not crowded an airfield that protected the approaches to Japan's major city, but concluded that the clouds of dust and smoke created by VB-88's exploding bombs had hit their intended targets.

FROM THE MOMENT they had lifted off from the *Yorktown*, the rear seat gunners in the torpedo planes had seen nothing of what lay ahead, for they faced aft, their backs to the pilot, and watched for enemy aircraft that might attack. The New England training helped them adjust to that awkward view, but some had never quite settled in as comfortably as they would have liked. The takeoff a short while ago tested their nerves, especially when their aircraft dipped toward the ocean as they left *Yorktown*'s deck before leveling off and gaining altitude, squeezing the gunners between the rushing ocean below and the carrier deck above. For the entire flight, they had to trust their pilots, do their best to ignore enemy fire they could not see closing in on them and their Avengers from ahead, and concentrate on their tasks. Their fate rested with the skills of the pilots only feet away, their talent as gunners, and providence.

The Hellcats' and Helldivers' attacks were precursors to their torpedo squadron comrades. Dispersing his fifteen Avengers over the target to make it more difficult for ground fire to hit his planes, Lieutenant Commander Huddleston dove toward one end of the airfield while the other fourteen planes approached in a line abreast to bomb the airfield from end to end. Huddleston chose such a low altitude—4,000 feet—from which to make his attack, that some of the fighter pilots flying over the field to provide protection feared that the enemy's antiaircraft guns would handily destroy them. Since they were the final aircraft of the group to strike the enemy, torpedo pilots and crews faced greater risks than their predecessors, as every Japanese gun would be shooting at those tail-end planes.

Accurate fire ripped through the formation. A shell smacked into Lieutenant (jg) Thomas D. Quinn's Avenger as he pulled out of his dive, creating a three-foot hole in the right wing-tip, but he was able to nurse the plane back to the *Yorktown*. Two other pilots had to turn away with mechanical problems, but despite the issues, on their way out turret gunners and radiomen in Huddleston's planes observed hits against revetments, buildings, and a few aircraft.

While the fighters, dive-bombers, and torpedo planes blasted the airfield, a quintet of Hellcats took photographs of Kasumigaura and the antiaircraft positions. The images would later be developed and circulated to the men tasked with mounting the day's afternoon strike. After snapping their photographs, the five conducted three strafing runs against a lugger, leaving the fishing boat in flames and settling rapidly at the stern.

"BURNING IN GRAND STYLE"

While Hobbs and the morning strike dove on Kasumigaura Airfield, the first sweep clearing the way for the afternoon attack left *Yorktown* to hit Kashiwa, Imba, and Shiroi Airfields southwest of Kasumigaura. The three airfields stood five to ten miles apart northeast of Tokyo, stationed there to repel American aircraft that eluded the coastal airfields and antiaircraft fire while on their way to strike at the nation's capital.

Like every ensuing strike day, Aviation Machinist's Mate 1/c Merald Woods and the Air Group 88 mechanics operated a wartime shuttle service from *Yorktown*, launching and landing aircraft in such dizzying fashion that from 3:55 a.m. to 5:00 p.m.—a little more than thirteen hours—they serviced six launchings and six landings comprising four sweeps and two strikes. Three hours after Adams's first plane took off, every aircraft for the morning mission was either winging toward Kasumigaura, attacking the airfield, or on their way back to the carrier. In the following hours Woods and his companions, faced with servicing both the morning and afternoon missions, juggled morning landings with afternoon launchings.

Strike days taxed the mechanics and deck crew, who faced long hours and near-nonstop work in preparing and tending the planes. Hurried coffee breaks and quick lunches interrupted the mayhem, but until the final aircraft returned from battle and landed on the carrier, rest would be a scarce commodity. No one complained, for how could someone bicker about shifting plane locations on deck while their aviators dove into enemy fire?

In the first afternoon sweep, twelve *Yorktown* Hellcats joined with sixteen Corsairs from *Shangri-La* to hit three airfields. Lieutenant Commander Crommelin made his first appearance in combat with Air Group 88 by leading the twenty-eight planes to their first target, Kashiwa Airfield. Ten miles from Kashiwa, Crommelin ordered a high-speed approach using radical turns and weaving to evade antiaircraft fire. Crommelin instructed his pilots to maintain speeds from 400 to 460 miles per hour, which, while consuming more fuel, according to his subsequent report, "deals the Jap AA gunner a weak hand and saves planes and naval aviators for another day. Slow down and the law of diminishing returns will take effect."

In the first Hellcat, Crommelin dropped below 5,000 feet before releasing his fragmentation bomb. One by one the other fighters followed suit, pulling out at 1,000 feet and maintaining high speed for their retirement to the northeast. After a brief moment "to look over the target,"[3] they turned to Imba and Shiroi Airfields a few miles away to conduct coordinated strafing and rocket attacks before returning to the *Yorktown*.

As Crommelin's sweep headed back to the carrier, the second sweep winged toward Tokorozawa and Irumagawa Airfields twenty-five miles northeast of Tokyo. After crossing the coast, the *Yorktown* and *Shangri-La* pilots traversed eighty-five miles of the Tokyo Plain—a risky endeavor as the path took them over hundreds of antiaircraft guns—skirted east and north of Tokyo, and against heavy antiaircraft fire, bombed, strafed, and fired rockets that damaged a handful of hangars at the two fields.

As had occurred in the morning, the more potent afternoon strike followed closely on the heels of the two afternoon fighter sweeps. Commander Searcy, the strike leader, guided almost one hundred aircraft from four carriers in attacking Konoike Airfield along the Japanese coast, less than thirty miles southeast of the morning's target, Kasumigaura. Searcy took a predetermined route to avoid known antiaircraft defenses. As they approached Konoike, according to the bombing squadron report, aviators noticed that Kasumigaura was "burning in grand style as a result of the morning strikes. The pilots who flew both strikes were happy to see their morning's efforts still visible."[4]

Before the attack, Searcy descended and circled the airfield at 4,000 feet to locate enemy aircraft. He found a cluster of wrecked planes littering the south side of the field, empty dispersal area and revetments in front of the hangars, and painted decoy aircraft standing in the center of the airfield. However, he also unearthed ten to fifteen intact planes hidden in a second dispersal area to the north. Searcy directed every pilot to focus on those intact planes. With a few Corsairs accompanying him, Searcy remained above to direct the attack, and waited until the other fighters had completed their runs before taking his team down to strafe the now smoking revetments and airfield.

The Helldivers and Avengers followed so closely behind the Corsairs that one torpedo pilot explained, "The whole strike seemed to be diving at the same time."[5] Dive-bombers raced toward their targets from a forty-five-degree angle, while below, the torpedo plane pilots droned straight at the airfield, ignoring shell bursts and tracers to land their bombs on Japanese aircraft and hangars. The bombers saturated their assigned revetment area with fragmentation bombs before pulling out and heading for the rendezvous area, while their compatriots in the torpedo squadron pockmarked the airfield. Thick antiaircraft fire claimed the first Air Group 88 fatality when Ensign Charles E. Emhoff's Corsair exploded 3,000 feet over Konoike. Emhoff's plane crashed in flames, but as no other pilot saw the ensign parachute from his Corsair, it was assumed that Emhoff went down with his aircraft.

Four other Hellcat pilots were more fortunate than Emhoff. Low on gas, three landed aboard the first carrier they spotted, the *Bon Homme Richard,* and Lieutenant (jg) Raymond Gonzalez splashed his damaged Hellcat into the water near the formation. During combat, antiaircraft fire had jammed Gonzalez's belly tank release, leaving the fuel tank dangling perilously beneath his Hellcat. With the possibility that the extra fuel tank might explode when it hit the water, he landed between the picket destroyers and the carriers. After collecting his life raft and other gear, the unharmed pilot walked onto his wing, leaped into the water, and swam as far away as he could to avoid being sucked beneath the surface by his disappearing Hellcat. The USS *Wedderburn* (DD-684) retrieved Gonzalez as he sat in his tiny raft and delivered him to the *Yorktown* the next morning, just in time for Gonzalez to hop into another Hellcat for morning CAP.

"ANYTHING CAN HAPPEN IN THOSE LAST FEW SECONDS"

Throughout the long day, once their sweeps or strikes had ended, each squadron rendezvoused fifteen miles out to sea before proceeding to the *Yorktown.* The carrier would by then be in a different position than she was for the launching, but the aviators had updated information and only had to fly in the general direction to pick up her signal and follow it straight to the *Yorktown.* Once the planes arrived over the carrier, Merald Woods and others on deck counted to see if the numbers of aircraft returning matched the number that took off. "We had our favorites among the pilots," said Woods. "I used to sweat them in until they were safely aboard."[6]

Tiers of landing groups circled until *Yorktown* turned into the wind and signaled that the carrier was ready to receive them. If any plane had significant damage, or if the pilot was wounded, the pilot circled closer to the carrier so that flight officers aboard *Yorktown* could assess the aircraft's condition and relay information to the flight surgeon. When ready to touch down, the aviators dumped any extra fuel to reduce the plane's weight and make their landing safer, lowered their wheels and flaps, and dropped behind their leader. To sailors on the carrier's deck, the oncoming streams of Hellcats, Corsairs, Helldivers, and Avengers looked like ducklings following the mother duck.

"The first time you see a plane land on a carrier you almost die," wrote Ernie Pyle about the spectacle. Pyle tensed as he watched plane after plane descend, writing afterward that "it is so fast, timing is so split-second, space is so small." He added, "Somebody said that carrier pilots were the best in the world, and they must be or there wouldn't be any of them left alive."[7]

One by one the pilots broke out of their formation and entered what they called the landing circle. Rather than approach in a long, straight glide, the planes commenced a counterclockwise route that paralleled the *Yorktown's* starboard side, cut across the carrier's bow, and turned parallel to the port [left] side, almost as if, as Pyle remarked, the planes were sneaking up on the carrier. Coming in from the port quarter, the pilots spaced themselves so that the plane ahead had landed and cleared the crash barrier just as they entered "the groove," the path leading to *Yorktown* from dead astern.

Yorktown's deck came alive with various yellow, green, blue, and red hues as three hundred men rushed to their stations. Red-shaded firefighters and white-clothed men wearing asbestos masks, tasked with dousing fires and pulling the pilot out to safety, stood ready at their posts, while carpenters waited to patch any holes gouged in the deck by propellers. The aviators had risked their lives to deliver *Yorktown's* military might to enemy installations. Their task was over. It was now time for the deck crew to do theirs.

When the pilot drew within a half mile of the *Yorktown*, the landing signal officer (designated the LSO) took over. A pilot himself, he directed Hobbs and every other plane into their landings, and until each plane's wheels touched the deck, he had complete control over the aircraft. The LSO had to know everything he could about each aviator so that he could identify the pilot simply by the plane's movements. Some aviators flew a steady course to the deck, while others had a tendency to swerve slightly from side to side. Some had difficulty landing in foul weather, while other aviators alighted smoothly under any conditions. The individual pilot's mannerisms and skill level guided him in relaying his signals as the plane came in.

Wearing a bright yellow sweater and yellow helmet, the LSO was easy for pilots to spot amidst the swirl of activity on deck. Positioned on a platform just off the stern, with rope netting beneath in case he fell, he stood in front of a huge canvas backdrop to help him stand out and make it simpler for the fliers to see his directions, which he relayed with the bright yellow paddles clutched in each hand.

"The LSO is actually flying the plane by remote control, and the pilot is only a robot who does what the LSO orders," explained Pyle, who added that every pilot had to obey the LSO or risk being grounded.[8] The LSO informed the pilot if he was out of the groove or flying in any errant manner. He arranged his arms in a "V" if the aircraft came in too high, an inverted "V" if too low, horizontally if the plane was in a correct, level position, and crisscrossed to wave off the pilot, who veered away for a second attempt. Once the LSO was satisfied with the aviator's approach, he gave the "cut" sign by drawing his right hand across his throat or by whipping his flags back and forth below his waist.

"Anything can happen in those last few seconds," wrote Pyle. The carrier's island creates air currents that can buffet the plane and can knock it off course, or the plane might lose speed and either spin into the water or smash into the stern. "For landing on the deck of a small carrier in a rough sea," wrote Pyle, "is just about like landing on half a block of Main Street while a combination hurricane and earthquake is going on."[9] The pilot hoped to simultaneously touch down both wheels on the deck's center as the plane dropped into the arresting cables stretched across the deck to slow his movement. If he landed too hard, he could blow a tire and send his aircraft swerving out of control. A touchdown too close to the deck's edge risked careening the plane over the side into the catwalk or into the sea, and if the pilot approached too high and missed the arresting gear, he had to hope the backup steel cables stretched across mid-deck, called the "barrier," would envelop him with its tentacle-like cables before he crashed into the island or into other planes parked on the deck. If all went well, his tailhook caught one of the cables stretched across the deck to halt the planes, slightly lifting his plane before it settled. Once the flier landed safely, the steel cables momentarily dropped to allow him to taxi by, when the cables again rose for the next plane. A signalman motioned for the pilot to move forward to the elevator, which would take his fighter to the hangar deck.

Once the pilot hit the deck and moved by, the LSO directed the next plane in line and relied on his assistant to make certain the previous aviator had landed safely and cleared the barrier. If so, the assistant shouted, "Clear," but if the flier experienced problems, the assistant yelled, "Foul, foul!" and the LSO waved off the next plane. After each plane landed, the LSO described to another assistant that pilot's techniques. The assistant recorded these observations in a notebook so that once the landings ended, the LSO could talk to each flier about what went right or wrong.

Wave-offs occurred more frequently in heavy seas, when *Yorktown's* stern rose and dipped as much as thirty feet with each sway, forcing the LSO to match the pilot's touchdown with the deck's movements. If he ordered the aviator to cut his engine too soon, a rising deck could smash his landing gear, but if the order came too late, the deck might fall away and leave a drop of fifty feet for the pilot to navigate. The LSO thus waited until the carrier rose to the crest of its upward swing, where it steadied for a moment before descending.

Hobbs and the other fliers put unquestioned trust in the LSO. Aviators can be an independent bunch. They hate yielding control of their aircraft to anyone and prefer to rely on their skills to bring them home, but at this moment, weary from battle and possibly wounded, they willingly handed the reins to an officer bedecked in bright colors. "So all in all a landing signal officer, in his yellow sweater and yellow cloth helmet, may look gaudy out there next to the fantail, and he may look funny waving those colored paddles around his head," wrote one observer of a 1944 carrier landing, Lieutenant Max Miller. "But above him there may be as many as sixty pilots and their gunners who would like very much to be able to eat that night. He wants to see to it that they are able."[10]

As he taxied by the bridge, every pilot relayed information to Air Group personnel. A thumbs-down signal indicated issues with his equipment, such as a jammed machine gun or a faulty radio, while a thumbs-up gesture meant a hassle-free mission and landing. The favorite gesture was a broad grin accompanied by a raised index finger, which signaled that the aviator had shot down a Japanese plane.

The flight surgeon and his pharmacist's mates, already on deck with medical supplies, removed any wounded pilot or aircrewman by stretcher and rushed him to the sick bay. Tractors shuttled away damaged aircraft to be repaired, but if beyond salvaging, the deck crew shoved the plane over the side to clear the way for ensuing aircraft. Time was of the essence, as Captain Boone knew that his *Yorktown* was most vulnerable from an air attack while launching or landing planes, those times when he had to slow the carrier and maintain a steady course for the Air Group.

After the last plane had landed and a klaxon had sounded, the deck crew rushed out to re-spot the planes aft to be ready for the next launch. Following the final landing of the day, small tractors pulled the aircraft into place for the night and with heavy rope fastened them to gratings in the flight deck. In rougher seas, men stood duty until dawn to make certain none of the ropes had broken, which could send the aircraft bumping into others or into the sea.

"THE BLOW WAS DELIVERED IN THE HALSEY MANNER"

After the Air Group returned, the squadron leaders first walked to the bridge to make their reports to Captain Boone, Commander Searcy, and, at rarer moments, Admiral Radford. In the meantime, aviators of all four squadrons hurried to the wardroom to grab sandwiches and coffee, and then stepped to their respective ready rooms to compare notes, boast about the accuracy of their firing and bombing, and answer the intelligence officer's questions, which were a part of every sweep or strike. Four intelligence officers, one for each squadron, quizzed each pilot on what he saw and did on the mission. Typically lawyers or newspaper reporters in civilian life, these officers knew how to ask the right questions and, more importantly, how to listen to the answers. They learned which targets might have been destroyed so as to eliminate them from future strikes, and which required additional runs. They distilled this information and, along with any photographs taken, handed it to the squadron leaders to aid them in planning and conducting future missions.

Buoyed by the mission they had just concluded, and still pumped with adrenalin, the aviators rambled about the hangar they destroyed or the Japanese planes they strafed. Each cast furtive glances about the ready room to see if anyone was missing, for everyone judged the success of their operation according to the number of pilots who returned. An empty chair might indicate the loss of a man, as the fliers of VBF-88 noticed with the absence of Ensign Emhoff.

Hobbs shared the disappointment felt by the other Hellcat and Corsair pilots of VF-88 and VBF-88 that the Japanese declined to send a squadron of fighters to oppose them. Aviators involved in the great aerial encounters of 1944 had claimed multiple kills, but for this mission, he returned with an empty hand. "Strike Tokyo," was all he entered in his flight log for that day.[11]

The fighter squadron's report more candidly assessed the aviators' disappointment. They had thought that enemy aircraft would surely rise to challenge their intrusion so near to their capital city, Tokyo, and to Emperor Hirohito's palace, but no pilot could claim "with certainty that he destroyed a single operational aircraft or killed a single Jap." The report added, "We had lain awake at nights thinking of spectacular air battles over Japan."[12]

ACCORDING TO THE *Yorktown* war diary, on July 10 the Air Group fired more than 200 high-velocity aircraft rockets, dropped 322 bombs, and fired 34,000 rounds of .50-caliber bullets. Aviators claimed to have sunk one freighter, destroyed twelve aircraft on the ground, left Kasumigaura and Konoike Airfields "saturated by bombs and strafing, and damaged hangars at four other airfields.[13]

Exaggeration, unintended or otherwise, often marred wartime reports. Multiple pilots simultaneously strafed airfields and dropped bombs, leading the pilot of one aircraft to mistakenly think his bomb destroyed an enemy plane, while another aviator's bomb actually inflicted the damage. In the frantic pace of action pilots catch only glimpses of targets, planes, and bombs. Adding to the day's confusion was the enemy's skill at camouflaging and dispersing their aircraft, while others were parked at village street intersections with their tails backed into alleys. Some supposed aircraft detected by Air Group 88 pilots proved to be wooden dummy planes rather than the real item, leading Lieutenant Commander Hart of VBF-88 to conclude in his action report that more treetop strafing was required if they were to locate the dispersed planes. Lieutenant Commander Crommelin added in his report that enhanced photography of the airfields and the areas surrounding them would aid his pilots by giving them precise points of aim rather than a general target area. He explained that some of his fighter pilots wasted valuable minutes surveying the whole airfield seeking targets, which left a smaller portion of time for them to mount attacks, while others simply strafed the first object sighted, which often turned out to be a decoy plane.

As Air Group commander, Searcy mentioned Emhoff's loss, but focused on lessons and conclusions. Like Halsey, he believed that "the enemy was much less aggressive than he had been on previous occasions," something he attributed to their catastrophic losses sustained during the protracted Okinawa campaign.[14] He and the other Air Group senior officers urged that each strike maintain a high cover of at least four Hellcats or Corsairs to protect against a possible enemy air attack and to assist in locating and calling out the enemy's antiaircraft locations.

The Air Group gauged July 10 a success, but the newcomers to combat learned something that the veterans already understood—success came with a price. The Air Group lost Ensign Emhoff in his Corsair and Lieutenant Gonzalez's Hellcat to flak, plus six other aircraft damaged. July 10 illustrated that any aviator in the squadron, flying the best plane, could still fall prey to enemy guns. An antiaircraft shell could just as easily bring down Searcy or Crommelin—or Hobbs.

Halsey was delighted that the enemy had failed to mount an aerial counterattack, either against his task forces steaming off the Japanese coast or against his aviators delivering the bullets and bombs, especially as Air Group 88 and the air groups of three other carriers roamed the greater Tokyo region rather than an outlying area. "I was so surprised at the almost utter lack of defense of this area so vital to the Japanese Empire," Halsey wrote of the July 10 attack.[15]

While Halsey and most American commanders considered the July 10 operations a success, opinions elsewhere varied. Naval Commander Masatake Okumiya wrote that "July became a nightmare of carrier-plane attacks," and Vice Admiral Matome Ugaki of the Imperial Navy's General Staff, when alerted to the day's morning sweeps and strike, expressed his chagrin at the boldness of Halsey's attacks. "At noon the enemy broadcasted to the states from on board ship that they were attacking the Tokyo district with one thousand planes. They even mentioned the names of some ships. What insolence!"[16]

People on the home front welcomed news of Halsey's strikes. "For the first time, Japan's home islands saw a U.S. fleet and felt the lightning strokes of its big guns," bragged *Time* magazine in an issue bearing Halsey's image on its cover. "The Third Fleet that swung up & down the east coast of Japan was the mightiest the world had ever seen," led by "the tough, stubby seadog whom the Japanese mortally hate & fear. 'Bull' Halsey was on the prowl." Calling Halsey "the Annapolis-trained Dead End Kid who calls the Japs monkeys, whose battle cry is 'Kill Japs, kill Japs, and then kill more Japs'" and is "the calculating, chance-taking seaman," the raids showed what was in store for the enemy. "The blow was delivered in the Halsey manner that they had learned to expect. It was daring, powerful, crushing. The Third Fleet's battleships could have run into serious trouble, standing off Japan for a shore bombardment. Halsey took the chance." The magazine continued that there was "no telling to what lengths Halsey might go in succeeding days. His love of spectacular improvisation knew no limits," a longing ignited on the war's first day. "Ever since Dec. 7, 1941, he had been obsessed with the desire to hit Japan."[17]

While the general public overwhelmingly reacted favorably to Halsey's assault of Japan, muted responses came from Hattie Hobbs in

Kokomo and Sonya Levien in New York. Both women followed the news to keep track of their son or future husband, usually relying on the daily newspaper—the *Kokomo Tribune* for Hattie and the *New York Times* for Sonya—and radio broadcasts. When Hattie read that day in the *Kokomo Tribune* that "more than 1,000 fighters, dive-bombers and torpedo planes from Adm. William F. 'Bull' Halsey's Third Fleet smashed at Tokyo's 72 to 80 airfields hour after hour," her first thoughts were not excitement over Halsey's exploits, but concern that Billy might have flown over their enemy's capital city. When the article explained that "the carrier fleet hurled its first Hellcats into the air in the crisp dawn and they swept in to catch the enemy capital napping," she knew from previous letters that Billy flew that type of aircraft. In reading that "Admiral Halsey, who returned to the Western Pacific with his powerful Third Fleet to 'knock hell out of the Japs,' was doing just that today," she again bemoaned the fact that her son was assigned to the Pacific instead of the European Theater, where his wartime service would now already be at an end.[18]

To Hattie's east, when Sonya read in the *New York Times* that "more than 1,000 carrier-based planes of Admiral William F. Halsey's Third Fleet struck today against airfields in the Tokyo area," she was pleased because each strike against Japan brought the end of the war closer, but frightened because Eugene was most likely involved. The odds alone indicated that he must have participated in such a mammoth employment of carrier aircraft, and while she erred in thinking so, as Eugene flew CAP over the task group carriers that day, she arrived at a logical conclusion. She must have felt almost as if she accompanied Eugene in his Hellcat when she read in that day's edition, "As this is being written, waves of naval planes are continuing the blows against the enemy's bases surrounding his capital without retaliation," and that "carriers of Admiral William F. Halsey's powerful Third Fleet" caught the enemy by surprise by hitting "the Kanto Plains district around Tokyo in wave after wave."[19]

That day's *New York Times* editorials bolstered everybody's belief that the United States had Japan on the ropes. The paper contended that the enemy's boasts of inflicting horrifying casualties on the United States "must have a hollow sound to a Japanese hearing the whine of carrier fighter planes in his own sky." They praised both the commander and his aviators by adding, "The return to the wars of Admiral Halsey and his fliers marks a great acceleration in the war of attrition against the Japanese Air Force and against isolated targets that cannot be attacked successfully by the big four-motored bombers."[20] Hattie and Sonya understood that Billy and Eugene bore dangerous responsibilities, but that they flew directly into the heart of the Japanese Empire, straight at a heavily defended capital city, was an image the women wished they could avoid. They felt isolated from their son or future husband, and utterly incapable of assisting them, now more than 6,000 miles from Kokomo and New York, flying against an enemy that vowed never to surrender.

Across the Pacific, Billy had neither the time nor the inclination to worry. He wrote tersely in his diary that day, "We hit Kasamgura [*sic*] air field and hit Kashima & Konoike on way out. This was my first real combat hop and I was certainly scared. Saw plenty of ack ack. Expended rockets. Saw first Jap plane in the air."[21]

Billy could not afford to let one mission affect him, for he faced many others before he returned to Kokomo. He was at least satisfied that he had his initial combat experience behind him and, though frightened, had controlled his emotions and carried out his assignments.

Still anxious to grapple with Japanese aircraft, he hoped that the next strike would include a dogfight with those enemy pilots who refused to show themselves on July 10. The ensuing mission offered plenty of exciting moments, indeed, and one horrible consequence.

CHAPTER 7

"Somebody Said We Are to Hit Hokkaido"
North to Hokkaido, July 14–15, 1945

THE DAY AFTER the first strike, Halsey pulled the task force farther from the Japanese coast so his ships, now low on fuel, could replenish. Once complete the next day, Halsey directed the three task groups to set a course northeast for Hokkaido to conduct the next offensive strike on July 13. The targets for Air Group 88's second mission differed from the airfields that protected Tokyo. Rather than assaulting military installations, Air Group 88 would hit Hokkaido's coal mines, a vital cog near the city of Muroran in southwest Hokkaido fueling Japan's war machine. Successful attacks against those locations would impair the enemy's ability to mount a viable defense and hopefully reduce the number of casualties predicted for the land assault of the Home Islands.

In unison, the three collections of carriers, cruisers, and destroyers turned toward Muroran and northern Honshu 470 miles to the north, presenting a glorious pageant as the seagoing arsenal, reaching to the horizon and beyond, sliced through the waves. "We are refueling today and hope to get mail," Hobbs wrote in his diary on July 11. "We are steaming north. I never did imagine what a strong force we can assemble. Sure makes a fellow feel good."[1]

A group of Halsey's officers, which his staff affectionately labeled Halsey's Dirty Tricks Department, hoped to fool the Japanese into moving aircraft out of Hokkaido and relaxing their vigilance to the north by broadcasting messages indicating that Halsey planned to strike airfields far to the south. The department transferred a transmitter from

Halsey's flagship, *Missouri,* to a cruiser, and ordered the ship to steam south of the task force and relay messages as if they came from the flagship. With luck, they might fool the enemy into weakening the defenses on Hokkaido.

The four-day break from sweeps and strikes gave Air Group aviators a chance to unwind from their first combat mission while Halsey moved the task force north toward a station off Hokkaido, the northernmost of the Japanese Home Islands. Hellcat and Corsair pilots took turns flying CAP and searching for enemy submarines, but mostly the men remained in their cabins or ready rooms, chatting with their buddies or writing letters to family.

Hobbs and the other aviators who participated in the July 10 strike talked animatedly about that day. They discussed enemy antiaircraft shells, which looked surprisingly like fiery eels wriggling toward their planes, and agreed that chance had as much to do with their returning safely as did their aviation skills. Eugene Mandeberg and the others who missed out on July 10 listened with a touch of envy and hoped that their names would be called for the next sweep or strike. No fighter pilot could be assigned to every offensive mission, as CAP and submarine hunting also had to be conducted, but they figured they would be selected when Halsey halted his northward movement and ordered the second massive strike against the enemy homeland.

The Air Group flew multiple air patrol missions each day as the force moved steadily northward toward Muroran, and men were surprised at how quickly the air temperature cooled compared to their southern post off Tokyo. "Had a very cold day today," Hobbs entered on July 12. "Temperature was about 60°. Slept very nice last nite. Everybody put on heavy clothes today. We are in very bad weather right now." Despite the deteriorating weather, Hobbs was eager to hop back in his Hellcat for another crack at the enemy's airfields. "Somebody said we are to hit Hokkaido. I hope," he wrote in his diary.[2]

Halsey shifted the task force to an area of Japan previously untouched by carrier aircraft. He and his staff had little idea what the aviators might face once they approached their targets near Muroran and in northern Honshu, but the worsening weather—cold, rain, and most ominously, fog—hinted that these attacks would offer different challenges from the July 10 assault. Thick fog so reduced visibility that Halsey delayed the planned July 13 sweeps and strikes in hopes that the weather improved sufficiently to enable him to bring his ships closer to the coast for an attack.

IN INDIANA, HATTIE would not have been pleased with one of the *Kokomo Tribune*'s headlines for July 13, which declared in a subheading, "Enemy Believed Hoarding Planes to Repel Allied Land Invasion."[3] She would have been more upset with an American admiral claiming in the article that the enemy might have amassed as many as 9,000 aircraft to counter any assault of the homeland. Since Billy was likely to fly one of those Hellcats tasked with suppressing Japanese opposition, she preferred to ignore the fact that the enemy was stockpiling aircraft. Hattie would not have been reassured by her son's entry for July 13 either. "Today was supposed to be strike day but weather was very bad," Billy wrote. "Cagle's element was scheduled for first sweep. Weather was very cold. Was about 48° at 0300. God may [*sic*] give us courage."[4]

"THE WORST WEATHER IN WHICH THE SQUADRON HAS FLOWN"

Dismal weather greeted the July 14 dawn, but when the cloud cover lifted slightly to 1,200 feet, the two morning sweeps and the ensuing strike took off as scheduled from only eighty miles offshore. Their objective was to hit factories, coke ovens, shipping, railroad lines leading from Muroran's coal mines, as well as airfields in southern Hokkaido and northern Honshu. Halsey hoped to severely restrict the movement of coal from Muroran to Honshu, which needed that coal to keep her factories producing the materials of war. Halsey planned to accomplish his goal by bombing the railroad lines and locomotives that moved this coal, and by eliminating the Hokkaido-Honshu ferries connecting ports located on both major islands.

When Lieutenant Commander Crommelin climbed to the flight deck to his plane, he found that due to mechanical difficulties his favorite Hellcat, and the one he most loved flying, had been replaced with another aircraft. Seeing that the replacement was Hellcat #13, and wary of flying an aircraft bearing that number, he asked Merald Woods, "Don't you have any other plane?"[5] When Woods replied that every other Hellcat was either in use or in repair, Crommelin said nothing more, but appeared to Woods to be hesitant as he stepped into the plane.

With heavy seas swaying the deck, the Air Group launched into visibility so limited and winds so strong that veterans of Atlantic Ocean duty compared it to the worst they had encountered off northern Europe. Low ceilings and thick patches of fog impeded every pilot's vision throughout the morning sweeps and strike, forcing them to rely on momentary breaks in the cloud cover and on their instruments to safely guide them through the perilous conditions. As a result, much went haywire in the confusion. Lieutenant Cagle, leading eleven Hellcats in the first morning sweep, which included Howdy Harrison and Billy Hobbs, took them to the rendezvous area to meet a similar group from *Shangri-La,* but according to the action report, they "were never joined despite many attempts after takeoff and enroute."[6]

Four pilots of VB-88 became separated in the fog from their squadron and instead joined up with the torpedo planes from USS *Belleau Wood* (CVL-24). Along the way to their targets, the quartet became so shrouded by the fog that they had to jettison their bombs and turn back. In the process, their bombs triggered dangerously close to other aircraft, "almost blowing them from the sky," and "unable to find the rest of VB-88, and narrowly avoiding collision with a group of VF [Hellcat fighters] the division returned to base."[7]

The torpedo planes, as well, launched "in perhaps the worst weather in which the squadron has flown." The fifteen planes attempted to rendezvous with their fighter escort, but hampered by the fog, only nine succeeded in pairing off with their Hellcats. After searching in vain for the *Shangri-La* planes, the group "proceeded on its own merry way—a Marco Polo jaunt around the southern Hokkaido countryside."[8] With a low ceiling impairing their vision, the group headed in the general direction of Muroran in southwestern Hokkaido.

A trio of mishaps hit the bombing squadron before it reached the coastline. Lieutenant Edward T. La Roe's gyro-horizon failed to work, forcing him to return to *Yorktown* "after getting through the fog on needle and ball." Lieutenant (jg) Alvin F. Levenson lost the group in the fog "and after several narrow escapes from collision he tried to pull out his chart board which was stuck. The chart board broke, came apart and smashed the cockpit canopy and tore off the radio antenna."[9] Levenson joined up with another pilot, and after proceeding halfway to Muroran without sighting any plane or target, both returned to the carrier. Lieutenant Louis J. Miller also turned his Helldiver back to the *Yorktown* when his gauges malfunctioned and he could not find his bearings in the fog.

Completely enveloped by the heavy overcast, Lieutenant Cagle searched for Erimo Saki Point, a prominent land feature jutting from Hokkaido's coast 125 miles southeast of Muroran, but only mountain tops poked through the heavy overcast below. Thus frustrated, Cagle turned west in hopes of spotting familiar landmarks.

The Corsairs of VBF-88, led by Commander Searcy, rendezvoused at 1,500 feet with twelve *Shangri-La* Corsairs for a joint fighter sweep, but they, too, encountered difficulties. Nearing the coast, the fog "formed a solid wall to the ocean surface," permitting only a handful of mountain peaks to protrude.[10] Unable to find their assigned airfields, Searcy ordered the sweep to attack targets of opportunity, meaning whatever the Air Group saw through the overcast.

Ensign Michael F. Hannon Jr. of the bombing squadron was about to join with another Helldiver, "when several fighters came through the fog, passed between them and a mid-air collision was averted by an unbelievably small margin." Hannon pulled up and turned away, but in the process lost the other Helldiver in the fog. After unsuccessfully trying to locate other planes "in the soup," Hannon returned to the *Yorktown*.[11]

"Visibility was so bad on this hop," stated the torpedo squadron report, "that six of the planes taking off failed to rendezvous and after wandering about the task force for an hour, decided to return to base. Their difficulty was a common one throughout the groups in the force. The air was cluttered with transmissions regarding downed pilots, pilots with vertigo, and pilots who wanted to find out just where they were in these gray, baleful, foggy skies of Hokkaido."[12]

THERE WERE SOME successes. Even though Howdy Harrison at times could barely see his wingman, Billy Hobbs, he and the other Hellcats under Lieutenant Cagle had been able to rendezvous and descend through the overcast closer to the water's surface, where they continued westward until they arrived over the town of Shikabe on Hokkaido's southern coast across Uchiura Bay from Muroran. When Harrison detected several small sailboats, a handful of fishing boats, and bridges, he asked permission to attack, but Cagle ordered the unit to maintain their formation until they came upon more enticing targets. Still hugging the coastline, they approached Hakodate, twenty-five miles south of Shikabe, where they spotted a railroad and marshaling yard. "The locomotives were plainly visible chugging along the tracks," Cagle later wrote in his report, "pulling freight cars and coaches, and sending up very noticeable puffs of white smoke."

The eleven Hellcat aviators turned into their dives. Strafing from as low as fifty feet from the ground, they fired rockets and pumped hundreds of bullets from their six .50-caliber machine guns into eight or nine locomotives, creating explosions that sent steam several hundred feet into the air. Lieutenant Cagle and his wingman, Lieutenant (jg) Kenneth T. Neyer, demolished one train traveling along tracks, Lieutenant (jg) Leo J. Kerivan's team of four Hellcats hit two more, while other pilots fired rockets and dropped bombs on railroad bridges close by. When Lieutenant (jg) Henry G. Cleland Jr. and Lieutenant (jg) Gonzalez dropped on their train, Cleland's rocket hit directly in front of the engine, "and exploded with such violence that dust and mud were thrown up on the attacker's [Cleland's] windshield."[13]

NOT LONG AFTER Cagle attacked the trains, Searcy led his fourteen *Yorktown* and *Shangri-La* Corsairs against railroad yards at Oshamanbe on the western side of Uchiura Bay. They charged three locomotives and a sailboat in the harbor before breaking into two units, with the *Shangri-La* Corsairs continuing to Uchiura Bay and Searcy's unit crossing the bay to strafe two wooden vessels and three locomotives. The Corsairs then reunited and followed the coastline southeastward to Muroran to continue their assault in the bay.

Fifty miles to the southwest, Howdy Harrison and his team bombed two trains advancing in a valley leading to Hakodate. For a second time in five days, Billy Hobbs dove straight into enemy antiaircraft shells, his eyes locked on the target, and trusted that luck and Hattie's ring would again pull him through. Dancing lights raced by their Hellcats as Howdy Harrison and Billy Hobbs flew yards apart in their downward descents.

While attacking the trains, Harrison alerted Cagle to a number of vessels that he glimpsed through the fog in Hakodate Harbor. Cagle regrouped the Hellcats north of Hakodate and sent them against what his report summed as a harbor "full of shipping and worthy targets."[14] Each of his three teams selected a large merchant vessel and dove from 10,000 feet, strafing as they drew closer. Cagle and Hobbs planted four rockets in one vessel, and Cleland and Gonzalez destroyed a fishing boat. While Lieutenant (jg) Nabours and Ensign Hardesty attacked Hakodate train ferries, Harrison and Hobbs turned toward a six-story building near the waterfront, which they damaged with two rocket hits.

As they exited, Cagle spotted a destroyer or destroyer escort trying to flee the harbor. His fighter pilots had accomplished their objectives and were running low on fuel, but the naval vessel proved too tempting to ignore. Cagle's Hellcats first dove on and silenced the heavy antiaircraft fire in the area, then reformed to conduct two passes on the ship, with one team concentrating on the bow, another on the fantail, and the third amidships. They strafed the hapless vessel so thoroughly that before it sank, an ear-shattering explosion rifled metal fragments and flame dangerously close to Hobbs and the others. After this successful run, Cagle led his Corsairs from the Muroran area and set a course for their carrier.

When Cagle landed his Hellcat, a voice over the loudspeaker called him to the flag bridge. Expecting a cool welcome for making the additional run on the enemy warship, he climbed several ladders to Radford's cabin, where the admiral asked him why he had been tardy in returning to the carrier. When Cagle explained that the delay had occurred when he had interrupted his homeward flight to attack a destroyer, Radford remained silent for a few seconds and drummed his fingers on a small desk. Finally, he said, "Okay, I guess I can hold Admiral Halsey's fleet into the wind to sink a destroyer." He paused again and added, "But don't you be late again!"[15]

A FEW HOURS later, the morning strike finished the job. The heavy overcast enabled only five of the fifteen Helldiver pilots to find their assigned targets, but the torpedo squadron enjoyed better luck. Through the clouds and haze, nine Avenger pilots attacked a 2,000-foot-long highway bridge at Ogifushi, east across the water from Muroran. Since the bridge connected the highways between the region's coal mines and the vital iron factory and coke ovens at Muroran, the pilots swarmed on the bridge and damaged the structure sufficiently to put it temporarily out of operation.

When torpedo pilot Lieutenant William R. Thurston became separated from his unit in the heavy overcast, rather than turning back to the carrier, he continued toward Hokkaido unescorted. Taking advantage of the few breaks in the cloud cover, Thurston bombed and strafed a locomotive and a railroad station before rejoining the carrier. "To some degree," stated the torpedo squadron report, "the progress of the war can be measured in terms of such a hop—one TBM, unescorted, flying over the Japanese homeland looking for a target!"[16]

THE MORNING'S MISSIONS had been marred by heavy seas and pilots lost in the fog, but the most catastrophic part involved the Fighting Squadron's respected commander, Crommelin, and his wingman, Lieutenant (jg) Sahloff. Flying by instrument in the thick cloud cover sixty miles east of Muroran, Crommelin unexpectedly swerved toward Sahloff. Crommelin's left wing-tip nipped Sahloff's Hellcat, sending the veteran commander careening out of control and disappearing into the mist. A shaken Sahloff, the man who had promised Mrs. Crommelin to bring the commander back from the war, hoped that when he returned to the *Yorktown*, he would find Crommelin safely aboard the carrier, but the commander was never again seen. Taking over as the acting commander of VF-88, Lieutenant Cagle listed Crommelin as missing in action since no crash or body had been sighted.

Crommelin's was a devastating loss to Hobbs and the other aviators of the squadron. Since his arrival as commander in New England, he had injected confidence into the untested pilots. With Crommelin at the helm, the pilots believed that they would perform better. Under his

tutelage, Hobbs and Mandeberg concluded that their chances of returning to Kokomo and Detroit were better than if some other commander
took them into battle. While everyone trusted Lieutenant Cagle, some
wondered about their futures. If Crommelin, the most capable flier in
the squadron, didn't make it back, how could they expect to survive?

THE WEATHER FOR the afternoon sweeps and strike improved around
noon, providing a clearer opening for *Yorktown* aircraft to hit their assigned targets in the Muroran area. However, the fog again thickened
once they neared Muroran and forced the pilots to switch from inland
objectives to shipping in Uchiura Bay. Enough holes punctured the
overcast to permit masthead-level and shallow gliding attacks on destroyers, luggers, and other vessels, and even runs on iron factories and
locomotives operating along the bay's coast.

Muroran's antiaircraft fire, which protected the extensive steel and
iron factories near that important city, was far more intense than the
attack four days earlier. The Japanese placed guns in the hills surrounding the harbor, which, combined with the antiaircraft batteries of their
warships, created a deadly crossfire that aviators twice had to survive,
once before and while completing their dives, and a second time while
retiring westward from the bay directly over those hillside guns.

With Hennesy's VBF-88 Corsairs providing intermediate and
close cover, *Yorktown* Helldiver pilots dove out of the northeast, racing through the antiaircraft fire with what their action report called "a
combination of good luck plus an application of the standard evasive
tactics of 'zig and zag and go like mad.'"[17] They bombed and strafed
the Wanishi Iron Works and coke ovens, as well as the railroad yards
leading into the factory. Rear seat gunners had clear views as their planes
sped away of explosions that crumbled smokestacks and destroyed coke
ovens. Shells hit two planes, but both pilots managed to retain control
and return to the carrier.

While keeping an eye out for enemy aircraft, Hennesy observed the
attack from above with his team. According to the action report, when
the Helldivers and Avengers completed their runs Hennesy and the other
Corsair aviators, eager to expend their bombs, "felt safe in indulging for

the next 30 minutes in the sport of pilots, namely attacking Sugar Dogs [merchant shipping]. Next to locomotives, they are wonderful meat."[18]

Enemy fire danced by Hennesy's quartet as they released their bombs on a steel factory. After pulling out of their dives, they spotted an anchored Japanese transport, "and immediately dove down on it with us firing our machine guns at its upper deck. I noticed greenish balls in the air around us, and was at first fascinated by them, until I realized that they were from their guns firing at us." With their bombs and rockets expended and with only a few machine gun bullets remaining, "I also figured any further attack would be an uneven fight. I broke off and continued on out to sea, rendezvoused and returned to our ship."[19]

"RIGHT INTO THE ENEMY'S JAWS"

Back at the carrier, gunner Aviation Ordnanceman 3/c Ralph Morlan of the torpedo squadron looked forward to the next day's strikes, as he believed the Air Group had some unfinished business. "We go on another strike tomorrow," he wrote. "Boy, I hope the weather is clear. I want to get those ships, coke ovens and steel plants. G. Whitehurst said he was strafing a town. He must be getting bloody thirsty. Ha!"[20]

However, the impediment that hampered operations for much of their time off Japan again intruded. "Once again soupy weather closed in target areas and made searches for targets of opportunity a nerve wrecking [sic] experience," summed the July 15 report submitted by Morlan's torpedo squadron.[21]

Almost one hundred Hellcats and Corsairs from *Yorktown* and *Shangri-La* swept airfields eighty-five miles north of Muroran near Sapporo on Hokkaido and shipping in adjoining Otaru Bay to clear the way for the strike against the Otaru area. The low ceiling—in some places barely five hundred feet above the sharp mountain peaks—forced the planes to attack below the clouds, which brought them closer to the antiaircraft and ground fire they had hoped to evade. Otaru Bay, according to one action report, "proved to be a flak trap, the flak coming from shore batteries and also, with great accuracy, from frigates and other armed vessels in the harbor. Flak batteries took full advantage of the restricted course and limited altitude imposed on planes by the low overcast and encroaching fog bank."[22]

Flying in an Avenger piloted by Ensign Richard G. Robinson, Aviation Ordnanceman 3/c Morlan and Robinson circled above the mountains for thirty minutes before finding a break and dropping to the coast at 700 feet altitude. After watching four Corsairs strafe a destroyer in Otaru Bay, they joined *Independence* torpedo planes in dive-bombing the vessel and dropped one of their four 500-pound bombs directly onto the target. "It was sinking, but the blood thirsty pilots kept attacking it," wrote Morlan. "We left it, broken in half and going down. We then strafed survivors in the water and lifeboats. There weren't many left when we left it. We then went along the coast and broke off and attacked houses on the beach, some small fishing boats, railroad bridges, and anything that moved."

Robinson released another bomb that barely missed a fishing boat, and a third on a railroad bridge along a cliff. "Robinson dropped his bomb directly on it. It really made a swell explosion. As we were going in after the bridge I strafed the beach. When we finished we had started three fires on the beach, mostly among the houses. F4Us were strafing the houses under us, they were really raising hell with that place. We had two bombs when we left and dropped them in the drink."[23]

The thick antiaircraft fire brought down two Air Group 88 Corsairs and one Hellcat. Shells punctured Lieutenant (jg) Herman B. Chase's Hellcat while in his run, but he ignored the damage and pressed his attack, landing rocket hits but leaving him little time to bail out of his flaming Hellcat. He leaped from the cockpit at 200 feet, moments before the plane smashed into the water, but when his parachute opened just as Chase hit the bay, the aviator floated motionless in his inflated Mae West. Lieutenant (jg) John Haag, Chase's close friend, saw his buddy hit the surface and circled around, but Chase bobbed lifelessly on the surface. Two other Hellcat pilots strafed Japanese craft speeding out to capture Chase and dropped life rafts to the water, but Chase was either already dead, or so badly injured that he could not swim toward them. With their fuel supply dwindling, and not having observed any motion from Chase, the Hellcats turned away to return to the *Yorktown*.

Ensigns Robert G. Shepherd and Maurice D. Springer of VBF-88 attempted to make emergency landings in Otaru Bay after being hit by antiaircraft fire. Shepherd rode his flaming plane down and died when it impacted with the water, but Springer successfully alighted his fighter in the bay. Corsair pilots Lieutenant (jg) Clifford M. Roberts and his wingman, Ensign Parmer Downing, were circling in their Corsairs three miles outside the harbor when they saw Springer go down. They veered over to the crash site, where Roberts tossed his life raft to Springer, but the raft fell one hundred yards away, too far for the exhausted aviator to reach. Roberts and Downing dropped four dye markers to mark the spot, but with Springer drifting closer to shore and to enemy gun batteries, and with the Corsairs running low on fuel, Roberts and Downing had to leave their fellow aviator and hope that rescue planes came to his aid. Such aircraft were dispatched, but when they mistakenly flew to the wrong harbor, Springer was left on his own, presumably to fall into the hands of the Japanese. "Ens. Springer may, or may not, be a Prisoner of War," stated the VBF-88 history of the incident.[24]

Upon approaching the carrier during his return, Lieutenant Hennesy dropped his landing gear, flaps, and tailhooks, checked that his wingman's landing gear and tailhook were down, and reduced his speed almost to the point of stalling. Now on a downwind leg moving opposite from the course of the ship, Hennesy picked up the LSO and his fluorescent paddles. "If the LSO was not satisfied with your position as you reached the stern of the ship, or if the deck were fouled, you would get a wave off and had to go around again for another approach," wrote Hennesy. "I felt very comfortable landing the Corsair and kind of enjoyed it. I only had one really bad landing. We were in heavy seas and the ship dropped out from under me just as I got a cut. I slammed down hard, caught a wire, but hit so hard that the fuselage and wings were wrinkled. I got out of the plane and they pushed it over the side into the ocean."

When his hook grabbed the landing cable, the impact thrust him forward against his shoulder straps. "With a jolt you are stopped and are sitting on the deck of a rocking ship. It is a strange feeling. Two men ran out to help disengage my hook." A man in a yellow jersey signaled him forward, at which Hennesy raised his tailhook, lifted his flaps, and folded his wings. He moved quickly to pass over the lowered barrier cables before they rose behind him for the next plane, his wingman, Hunter. "I followed the signalman in the yellow jersey who parked me. I filled out a yellow sheet on the conditions of the plane. Climbed out of the plane and reported to the ready room."[25]

ADMIRAL HALSEY HAD a more direct hand in the Hokkaido operation than the prior mission when on July 15 his flagship, *Missouri*, accompanied a force of battleships and cruisers to bombard the Muroran area. For the first time since 1908, when he had visited Japan as part of Theodore Roosevelt's famous round-the-world cruise of the Great White Fleet, he saw the enemy's homeland. Throwing caution to the wind and practically daring the Japanese to employ its air arm, Third Fleet surface ships, according to Halsey's account, in broad daylight steamed "right into the enemy's jaws" despite being landlocked on three sides. During what he termed "the longest six hours I spent in my life"—three hours within sight of land as the unit approached, an hour bombarding land targets, and three hours pulling away—the mammoth guns rained shells on the country that had yanked the United States into war with a surprise attack. They blasted Muroran's steel factories and set coal yards ablaze, the same factories and yards that helped fuel the Japanese war machine that had humbled America's military in the war's first six months. "We opened fire from 28,000 yards and poured in 1,000 tons of shells. It was a magnificent spectacle, but I kept one eye on the target and the other on the sky. Our three-hour approach had been in plain view, as would be our three-hour retirement, and I thought that every minute would bring an air attack. None came; the enemy's only resistance was desultory AA fire against our spotting planes; but those were the longest six hours of my life."

Since Halsey expected to be attacked by aircraft once he pulled within sight of Muroran, he concluded that the lack of any defense was an indication that the Japanese ability to defend their homeland was deteriorating. "This opened an entire new phase in the war against Japan and brought the war intimately to the Jap on the home islands. They could not convince a man an American ship had been sunk when his home had just been bombarded by it, and he had seen both the American ships and the effects of the bombardment."[26]

Halsey's bombardment collected praise in the press. "Halsey Turns Surface Craft Loose on Japan," trumpeted the *Kokomo Tribune* headline in Billy Hobbs's hometown. *Time* magazine placed Halsey on its July 23 cover, glaring outward as a tidal wave behind sweeps over a samurai warrior, and declared that "ever since Dec. 7, 1941, he had been obsessed with the desire to hit Japan." These attacks off Japan restored some of the luster. "For the first time, Japan's home islands saw a U.S. fleet and felt the lightning strokes of its big guns," continued the article. "If the enemy had not already heard the crack of doom, he heard it now. The Third Fleet that swung up & down the east coast of Japan was the mightiest the world had ever seen. The Navy took pains to ensure that Japan should feel its power."[27]

Air Group 88 aviators did not share the home front's enchantment with Halsey. In their opinion, surface bombardments achieved sparse results for the expenditure committed, and they believed that carrier aircraft could achieve more with their sweeps and strikes directed at enemy airfields and installations. As far as they could see, Halsey had wasted a valuable asset.

"THIS HOP PRODUCED NAVIGATORS, NOT HEROES"

During the July 14–15 raids, aviators from Air Group 88 and companion air groups sank a destroyer and thirty-one other vessels, wrecked more than twenty locomotives, and destroyed a collection of bridges and buildings, including warehouses across Uchiura Bay on northern Honshu. More importantly, they succeeded in cutting coal production moving from Muroran to Honshu's vital factories by more than 80 percent, hamstringing the Japanese capability to fuel its war machine and to mount a capable defense of the Home Islands.

In their action reports, Air Group 88 commanders pointed to shortcomings revealed by these and the July 10 operations. They expressed concern about the variable-time-fused bombs prematurely exploding and endangering aircraft flying a few seconds behind, that too many pilots hampered rescue attempts by breaking radio discipline with unnecessary transmissions about probable bomb damage, and that the pressure to return to the carrier on schedule reduced the amount of time they had over the targets.

Cagle complained that the Corsairs of VBF-88 received the bulk of the assignments and that his fighter pilots "were not getting enough of the offensive operations," and almost every commander claimed that an aircraft carrier employing two versions of fighters—the Hellcat and Corsair—"runs into confusion and inefficiency not experienced by groups using only one type." Since Corsair pilots could not pilot a Hellcat, nor could a Hellcat pilot fly a Corsair, deck crews had to constantly reshuffle and re-spot the fighter types on the flight deck, spare parts for both types had to be stocked, and plane captains and mechanics had to be familiar with the workings of both types of aircraft. Once in the air, the faster Corsair accelerated better and consumed less gasoline than the Hellcat, but during operations, the Corsair had to throttle back to allow the Hellcats to keep up, otherwise the Hellcats would run out of fuel trying to maintain pace with the Corsair. "It is not believed that any material advantage is gained by using two different types of fighter aircraft and it is definitely a hardship on the Air Department of a CV," concluded Commander Searcy.[28]

Aviators, from both *Yorktown* and her companion carrier, *Shangri-La*, questioned whether the outcomes of July 14–15 validated the risks of attacking in dangerous fog. They asserted that rather than Japanese fire, pilot losses were "a direct result of the extremely bad weather. It is felt that the risks attendant to operating in weather such as that prevailing on the morning of 14 July are out of proportion to the damage which might be inflicted." Commanders reported that dive-bombing in thick fog was impossible, and glide-bombing was restricted to a shallow approach from low altitudes. "Furthermore, the pilots were faced with the possibility, and even the probability, that fog would develop rapidly, completely closing in on the task force, and [pilots staring at] the prospect of ditching or bailing out over water with a temperature of about 55° in which a person could survive for only a few hours."[29]

One pilot reported that he was catapulted directly from his carrier into the overcast "and became lost when he looked back over his shoulder and could not see the ship." As a result, "this hop produced navigators, not heroes. The take-off was made in the fog, the mission was executed (in its fashion) in the clouds, and return to the base was attributable to a few wings, prayers and what navigation the pilots could marshall for the occasion."[30]

The weather caused the loss of the fighting squadron's most esteemed member, Lieutenant Commander Crommelin. His death, coming less than four months after his brother, Charles, disappeared off Okinawa, impacted the entire unit. "Our stay at Hokkaido had taught us some bitter lessons," concluded the fighting squadron report. "It was hard to face the inevitable fact that our losses would probably not end with Crommelin and Chase."[31]

The disappearance of four pilots, "nearly all of which losses were directly or indirectly attributable to the weather," affected every Hellcat pilot, but Lieutenant (jg) Sahloff, who wondered if he had caused the collision, especially mourned Crommelin's demise. Merald Woods said that "from that day on he was a changed pilot." To assuage his guilt over contributing to Crommelin's death and for inadvertently breaking his vow to Crommelin's widow to bring her husband home safe, Sahloff became "more daring. He tried to go lower, fastest, and tangle with any aircraft." Woods added that Sahloff "almost hoped he wouldn't come back and have to face the skipper's wife."[32]

ASTONISHMENT AND GLOOM marked the reaction in Japan to Halsey's most recent strikes. "They maneuvered as if nobody was standing in their way after making a thorough, precise reconnaissance," Admiral Ugaki entered in his diary of Halsey's Third Fleet.[33] After enjoying the stunning victories of 1942, Japan had been retreating before the ever-burgeoning American military, until now nothing stood between Halsey, who had angered the Japanese by vowing to ride Emperor Hirohito's prize white stallion through the streets of Tokyo, and their shores.

Halsey's progress was good news for Hattie in Kokomo, Zelda in Detroit, and Sonya in New York, as each successful raid would end the war sooner and bring their loved ones home. At the same time, the information heightened their apprehension. Halsey commanded the force, but their sons and fiancé executed his orders, which included diving straight into deadly fields of antiaircraft fire. A *Kokomo Tribune* article on July 11 stated that the Japanese claimed that they had shot down twenty-five American aircraft and damaged many others. Hattie's daughter, Nancy, recalled that her mother followed the war's progress in the paper, and an accompanying map in that edition showed carrier planes striking Tokyo. Could Billy have been in one of those aircraft that the Japanese claimed to have shot down? Hattie had to wonder. The newspaper editors printed the map to help their readers better understand the day's news, but from Hattie's vantage, it was a snapshot of the risks that threatened her son, not just that one day, but every day he served in the Pacific.

An article three days later described how ships and ferries transporting coal across the Tsugaru Strait from southern Hokkaido to northern Honshu had been "hammered throughout the day by the Avengers, Helldivers, Corsairs and Hellcats." Billy had mentioned in his letters how he enjoyed flying a Hellcat. Was he piloting one of these? The article added, "Even as the guns roared, swarms of carrier planes that only five days before had raked Tokyo's airfields, were raining bombs, bullets and rockets on northern Honshu and the northernmost island of Hokkaido—the latter never before touched by American air power," and "American naval power was embarked upon its next to the last job of this war—using its guns and planes to strike at the core of Japan's war industry and paralyzing the enemy's air strength." A line near the article's end had to be most difficult for Hattie to read, however, by putting into words what every American mother dreaded. "The final job will be to support invasion, wherever it may come."[34]

Hattie had read of the fanatical resistance mounted by Japanese defenders on island bastions thousands of miles from the Home Islands. If they battled so tenaciously at those places, fighting even to the death, what lay in wait for Billy as Halsey's ships and planes operated off Japan's shores? Her fears were not exaggerated, as military experts predicted that a planned November 1945 land invasion would lead to months, some said years, of hotly contested fighting.

Her son's calm reaction contrasted with Hattie's. Despite experiencing his first taste of combat nerves, he had mastered his emotions and executed his tasks. Two simple words in his flight log summed the July 14 action—"Sweep Hokadate [sic]."[35]

He was a little more effusive after answering the intelligence officer's queries and checking with his fellow pilots to see how they fared on a day that saw four Air Group 88 aviators lose their lives over Otaru Harbor in Otaru Bay. "Well today we took off for the first sweep," he wrote in his diary later that day. "We hit very thick overcast. Finally let down to deck. Hit mine trains. Howdy spotted shipping up in Hokadate [*sic*] Harbor. We sank about 6,000 tons of shipping and one tin can [destroyer]. I made diving runs on it. Kootz [*sic*, Ensign Ralph M. Koontz] was hit. Today we lost our skipper. It was a very pitiful case. <u>Yes, we sank a tin can</u> [underline his] solely by strafing!" He added that because of the concentration of antiaircraft batteries, the area "was a deathtrap. Weather was very bad. Did little damage. Later VBF hit same and Shephard [*sic*] was killed, Springer captured."[36]

The multiple operations left little free time during which Billy and Eugene could pen letters to Hattie, Zelda, and Sonya. When they were not scheduled to fly a mission, they still faced five-hour combat air patrols. Even off-duty hours were not theirs to control, as the fighter pilots could be called to their planes at any moment to counter threats from enemy aircraft or submarines.

Their lack of time to write meant little to mothers in Kokomo and Detroit, or to a fiancé in New York, who waited for anything—a brief note, a photograph, a few words—that let them know that at least as of the date of the writing, Billy or Eugene were safe. "Did you hear from Eugene this week?" Zelda asked Sonya in a letter written two days after the July 10 sweeps and strikes. "No mail here." Three days later, as Billy and Eugene completed the attacks on Hokkaido, Zelda penned, "No mail from Eugene. I hope to hear from him soon. I am terribly anxious."[37]

Their concerns would only deepen with the next few operations. Halsey, vigilant toward any opportunity to strike at the Japanese, set his sights on a target that had eluded him since December 7, 1941. The remnants of the Japanese Imperial Navy lay hidden and sheltered in Japanese harbors, coves, and bays. He was coming for them.

CHAPTER 8

"Stay Away from Kure"
Finishing the Imperial Japanese Fleet, July 18–30, 1945

THE MOMENT WAS a dream come true for an admiral who had steamed into Pearl Harbor on the afternoon of December 8, 1941, and witnessed the devastation Japan had inflicted on the American fleet. Black smoke, raging fires, and sunken ships had then transfixed the commander, who vowed that afternoon that he would never forget the scene. He held true to his promise, but now, three and one-half years later, those images were replaced by that same admiral come to administer a nation's vengeance.

Halsey relished the irony of the moment, but not nearly as much as he enjoyed the favorable tactical situation. In complete control of the sea about the Home Islands, Halsey could maneuver his Third Fleet from one end of Japan to the other, attacking targets at leisure, with little concern that the Japanese would counter. He most wanted to seek out and destroy the remnants of the Imperial Japanese Navy that had left Pearl Harbor in ruins, and with the floating arsenal he now commanded, he could pursue that dream.

Unlike the early months of his command in the South Pacific in late 1942, when he admitted that he lacked the surface ships and ammunition to mount a powerful offensive, he now supervised a fully stocked flotilla. After the July 14–15 attacks on Hokkaido, his Third Fleet took on another 400,000 barrels of fuel oil, 6,400 tons of ammunition, 1,600 tons of stores and provisions, and 99 replacement aircraft. Halsey not only had the same craving to eradicate the Japanese fleet that he possessed in 1941, but he now commanded the ammunition, aircraft, and aviators to bring it about.

After smashing Muroran's coal mines and factories, Halsey conducted a high-speed return to a launching point near Tokyo to administer his first blow against the Imperial Japanese Navy, but a thick cloud cover forced him to cancel the planned July 17 strikes against the Yokosuka Naval Base, where the battleship *Nagato* and other warships had taken refuge. During the run 470 miles south to the Tokyo region, Eugene Mandeberg, Ted Hansen, and other VF-88 fighter pilots flew CAP, rising thirty minutes before daylight so that they could be in the air by dawn. They remained in the sky for up to five hours as they flew above and near the fleet at assigned altitudes, where they could be directed toward unidentified aircraft that might appear.

Time passed quickly during the sweeps and strikes when a man had little time to ponder his situation, but lulls such as this, when two or three days interrupted the action, invariably brought introspection. In a ready room packed with aviators, Hobbs or Sahloff could boast about looking forward to another mission, but when left alone, in their bunks at night or retreating to a quiet corner of the carrier, less confident thoughts sometimes crept in.

Lieutenant Hennesy's reflection typified almost everyone in the Air Group, especially those with minimal combat experience. "I remember the exact time and place when it dawned on me that it was likely I might be killed," Hennesy recalled. "In the evenings I often strolled up to the open area on the bow of the ship, which was on the same deck as my stateroom. One such evening, after we had lost several of our air group killed in combat, I thought about the fact that when subjected to enemy antiaircraft fire there was little you could do to avoid being hit. It seemed to be only a matter of luck." Hennesy's mind drifted to his father, who had died shortly before the war started. Hennesy did not consider himself very religious at that time, "but I did believe in the possibility of an afterlife, and I recall talking to my father and telling him that I might be joining him soon."[1]

Admiral Halsey struggled with no such concerns, for he had the Japanese exactly where he wanted them. He roamed untouched off the enemy's coast, and although enemy antiaircraft fire had taken a toll in the previous three operations, generally the Japanese had mounted a weak defense against Halsey and his ships. Few enemy aircraft lifted off from airfields. In harbors and bays lay the last few vessels that had survived the mammoth naval clashes that had begun with the May 1942 Battle of the Coral Sea and culminated in the October 1944 Battle of Leyte Gulf, but not a single battleship or cruiser had barreled out of home ports to challenge the intruder.

Halsey's motivation for singling out the Imperial Japanese Navy ran deep. After starting the conflict with its surprise attack at Pearl Harbor, the enemy fleet added insult to injury by eluding him in the aftermath of December 7. An engagement with Japanese carriers had twice been denied the admiral, at the Coral Sea and at Midway, and it was Admiral Isoroku Yamamoto, flying his flag in the battleship *Nagato,* who in 1941 and 1942 had been his victorious counterpart. Halsey now had only to bide his time, maneuver his carriers into position, and in a series of blows let the air groups dismantle the feeble remnants of the Imperial Japanese Navy Yamamoto once commanded, aptly in the same fashion with which the Japanese had begun the war—with carrier air group attacks.

The Japanese may have retreated to their Home Islands, but they could still inflict severe damage, especially at the bases and harbors in which *Nagato* and the other warships took refuge. While *Nagato* rested at Yokosuka, thirty miles south of Tokyo, the bulk of the enemy's fleet lay at anchor at Kure Naval Base 420 air miles southwest of the capital. Three aircraft carriers, three battleships, and three cruisers, the final pieces of a once-dominant fleet, waited with destroyers and other vessels for the inevitable United States land invasion of their homeland. The undermanned ships lacked the fuel to stage more than brief forays, and even if they could steam out to engage Halsey, they were all but stripped of air cover to shield them from Halsey's air groups.

Vice Admiral McCain, the commander of Task Force 38 flying his flag in *Shangri-La,* dismissed the Japanese ships at Kure as minor threats and disputed Halsey's argument that they should be targeted. Halsey, however, claimed that people in the United States, eager for vengeance, would not be satisfied until the navy that attacked Pearl Harbor rested on the ocean floor. Enjoying the support of the Joint Chiefs of Staff in Washington, D.C., he also argued that he needed to eliminate any potential hazard to Russian supply lines once that nation entered the war against Japan, and that if he allowed those ships at Yokosuka and Kure to remain afloat, the Japanese could use them as bargaining chips in peace talks with the United States. Furthermore, countered Halsey, he had been ordered by Admiral Chester Nimitz to conduct an unrelenting campaign against the Japanese.

In his book *Whirlwind: The Air War Against Japan, 1942–1945*, historian Barrett Tillman rebuffed Halsey's claims. Tillman agreed that Halsey had received those orders, but weary from four hard years of bloodshed, the American public only wanted the war to end. Any vengeance that existed rested with Halsey, not the public. Tillman contended that the United States Navy that now controlled the Pacific could have easily handled any threat to Russian supply lines by a handful of Japanese warships, and that with President Harry Truman insisting on unconditional surrender, those Japanese ships were removed as a factor in negotiations.

Tillman added that a partial reason for the July and August attacks had more to do with interservice rivalry than they did with winning the war. Sensing a postwar battle with proponents of an independent air force, which might eliminate carrier aircraft from the Navy, Admiral Ernest J. King in Washington and Nimitz in the Pacific wanted an impressive campaign that highlighted the contributions to victory made by naval aviation. Every ship sunk, every airfield ravaged by the Third Fleet buttressed the arguments in support of keeping a naval air arm. Yamamoto's flagship, *Nagato*, and the ships inside Kure Naval Base perfectly suited those needs.

Halsey had his detractors in 1945. Lieutenant Richard W. DeMott, a member of *Shangri-La*'s Bomber Fighting Squadron, VBF-85, wrote in his diary July 14, "Halsey is going wild on publicity and we are all fed [up] to the teeth listening to all the crap he is putting out. . . . Halsey is a big disappointment to me as he is to most of us." Aboard the *Yorktown*, Corsair aviator Lieutenant Hennesy also wondered about the wisdom of these attacks. "The decision to again attack Kure Harbor in July was strongly questioned whether the loss of our planes was worth it, in view of the limited ability of the Japanese fleet to emerge and interfere with the planned invasion. However Admiral Halsey and Admiral King favored it, in large part as revenge for the Japanese attack on Pearl Harbor."[2]

Intelligence officers on *Yorktown* agreed. They contended that the Japanese ships would never again leave their anchorages, and that because Kure Naval Base was so heavily guarded by flak, possibly the worst Air Group 88 would face, that lives would be lost in needless attacks. They attributed the decision to the same aggressive behavior that compelled Halsey to leave his post off the Philippines in October 1944 to pursue carriers sent to lure him away, and to later barrel into two typhoons. They feared that the same belligerence would now unnecessarily threaten Billy Hobbs and the other fliers aboard *Yorktown*.

"PRIZE AMONG THEM WAS THE PONDEROUS *NAGATO*"

Halsey and his naval planners outlined five major strikes against the Japanese fleet to occur in the coming twelve days, commencing with the prize target, *Nagato,* at anchor in Yokosuka near Tokyo. Three raids against a major Japanese naval concentration at Kure Naval Base, the first carrier attacks sent to that distant portion of the Inland Sea, would follow. The final set of sweeps and strikes would put the finishing touches on Tokyo-area airfields and shipping. If all went according to script, the relics of what had once been the dominant naval force in the Pacific would be junkyard fodder, and Halsey would have his vengeance.

In conducting the five operations, the aviators of Air Group 88 would face the deadliest collection of enemy antiaircraft fire of their stay off Japan. "Undoubtedly the toughest target ever attacked by the Air Group was the *Nagato,* at Yokosuka," stated the Air Group's history. Intelligence officers painted a gloomy image to the aviators sitting in their ready rooms. The opening raid would demand that the fliers seek out a heavily camouflaged battleship that the Japanese had cleverly nestled along the shore. Nearby mountains bristling with antiaircraft positions cradled *Nagato* on three sides and so shielded the battleship that the Air

Group could only approach on the ship's port side. Antiaircraft batteries on other vessels in Yokosuka would be able to weave a deadly crossfire to hammer intruders from every angle. Each aviator would have no option but to attack directly into that frightening semicircle of fire and hope that they eluded the shells screaming at them from three sides. Intelligence officers made it clear to the hushed aviators that casualties were expected to be high from what they called a "flak trap."[3]

The picture at Kure Naval Base was as dismal, even though its collection of shipping offered equally attractive targets as *Nagato* at Yokosuka. Twenty-two antiaircraft positions, supported by additional guns at Hiroshima only twelve miles to the northwest, covered every approach to the surface vessels anchored at Kure and left no safe avenue for the Air Group. One glance at a map filled with circles marking the antiaircraft locations indicated that a flier might avoid one enemy gun position, but in doing so would maneuver into the firing lanes of other antiaircraft guns. Intelligence officers again stressed that, especially in the latter two strikes against Kure, the aviators would have to vary their paths of attack to confound antiaircraft gunners who would lie in wait expecting a repeat approach. They warned that continued poor weather conditions might squeeze the squadrons toward holes in the overcast, and while the openings would provide a path toward their targets, skilled Japanese gunners below would have already fixed their antiaircraft guns at those same breaks because they knew the American fliers would burst through them. After listening to the intelligence information, one flier aboard another carrier participating in the attacks whispered to his buddy, "Back in the shooting gallery as one of the ducks."[4] They hoped that the practice of posting one division of fighters as top cover to spot and report the locations of the heaviest antiaircraft fire, first begun by *Shangri-La* aviators, would aid them in avoiding the thickest resistance.

Enticing targets offered bounties that every aviator would love to claim. Mighty *Haruna*—the battleship that had participated in many of the most crucial actions of the Pacific War, including Midway, Guadalcanal, the Philippine Sea, and Leyte Gulf, and the ship inaccurately reported as sunk in December 1941 by one of the early heroes of the Pacific, Captain Colin P. Kelly—lay at anchor inside Kure. The Imperial Japanese Naval Academy at Eta Jima, termed the "Japanese Annapolis," sat directly across the harbor from Kure, where for almost sixty years the school turned out generations of naval commanders. Howdy Harrison and Hobbs would not lack for attractive targets, but in quiet moments in their cabins, a few aviators questioned the wisdom of risking their lives in unnecessary operations.

THE QUINTET OF carrier attacks opened July 18 with sweeps against Tokyo-area airfields, paving the way for the strike against *Nagato*. Pilots awoke shortly before 3:00 a.m. to prepare for the flight and to man their planes. Rain and heavy overcast canceled the morning operations, but improving weather allowed the afternoon mission to lift off as scheduled against ground aircraft and air installations at Kashiwa, Katori, Konoike, and Kasumigaura Airfields. Again finding enemy aircraft dispersed and camouflaged, they destroyed only four aircraft, but in the process lost to flak Corsair pilots Lieutenant Leon G. Christison over Kashiwa and Lieutenant (jg) Theron H. Gleason—whose aircraft, according to Searcy's action report, "disintegrated by a direct hit by heavy AA"—over Katori Airfield, the sixth and seventh Air Group 88 aviators to perish in the unit's first eight days of combat. Searcy added that "the experience of this day and of the 10th made it apparent that in the Tokyo area, and presumably throughout the Japanese home islands, the complete destruction of all aircraft and installations on a given field can no longer be expected to be accomplished without undue losses except by throwing overwhelming power against one field at a time, knocking out its AA defenses and air installations by coordinated, concentrated attack, and thereby enabling VF [Hellcat fighters] to search out and burn hidden planes with minimum altitude strafing."[5]

Two hours later Lieutenant Commander Huddleston, the torpedo squadron skipper, led the *Yorktown* group of eleven Hellcats, fifteen Helldivers, and fifteen Avengers in the first foray against the battleship *Nagato*. Aware of the multiple antiaircraft positions that all but ringed the battleship, Huddleston carefully selected a route he hoped would minimize their exposure.

The strike stumbled at the start. Lieutenant (jg) Raymond Gonzalez had to remain aboard the carrier when the Hellcat directly behind him moved forward too soon and chopped off Gonzalez's tail section.

Again flying wing for Howdy Harrison, Hobbs was slightly delayed by mechanical issues and had to join the bomber squadron when he failed to rendezvous with Cagle and the other Hellcat pilots.

Yorktown and *Shangri-La* fighters swept in to suppress antiaircraft fire and clear the way. They dove so fast, up to 550 miles per hour, that they were out of their dives and away from the *Nagato* before the first torpedo planes reached their release point. Close on their heels raced *Shangri-La* and *Cowpens* bombers a few minutes before Huddleston, now joined by planes from the carrier *Randolph* (CV-15), led *Yorktown*'s bomber and torpedo planes down. "Then the fifteen big bellied, supposedly antiquated Avengers converged on the heart of the once great 29-yr-old BB," Huddleston wrote after the attack, "now slunk under the musty veil of her inadequate camouflage. Antiquity reigns—antiquity dies—we hope!" Starting their attack from 12,000 feet, the planes veered into steep dives through what Huddleston described as "the thickly clustered nests of AA which spat all types of flak into the diving hordes of carrier planes."[6] Fortunately, the enemy gunners' errant aims permitted Huddleston and his aircraft to swoop down on the heavily camouflaged *Nagato*'s port bow and drop a pair of bombs that damaged the battleship's bridge and ripped a fifteen-foot hole in her deck.

Lieutenant (jg) Herbert D. Hoyt Jr. of the torpedo squadron piloted the final plane, which gave him a perfect vantage for observing the devastation. Before he released his bomb, he spotted one hit on *Nagato*'s stern, another on the starboard side amidships, and two near the bow. Hoyt's bomb plunged straight into the *Nagato* and ignited a new burst of flame.

Task Force 38 aircraft from multiple carriers flew hundreds of sorties that day against the once-mighty *Nagato*, raining bombs and rockets on the smoldering vessel and on adjoining ships. "Prize among them was the ponderous *Nagato*, one of the last proud remnants of a decimated fleet," stated the *Shangri-La*'s report. "Like a clumsy mastodon tracked to its lair, she stood at bay under a swarming attack of Corsairs, Avengers and Helldivers, trying to swat them down with the full fury of her combined batteries."[7] Water geysers and smoke enshrouded *Nagato* in an attack that, at a minimum, canceled her as a future threat.

The July 18 attack neutered *Nagato,* but additional quarry lay hidden in other harbors and bays. Next on the list was another flak trap—the Kure Naval Base.

"HERE'S HOPING WE COME THROUGH OKAY"

The July 18 attack convinced Admiral Halsey that his aviators had boxed the Japanese into a corner from which he intended to make certain they would not escape. He later wrote that by July 19 "it had become very apparent to me that Japan was little more than a hollow shell. We were operating outside their front door at will, hitting them with bombs and shells, and meeting only light opposition from antiaircraft and a few planes." Believing that the time was ripe to crush a demoralized enemy, he planned to be even more aggressive than the already bellicose admiral had been. Consequently, "we stepped up our sweeps and bombardments by light forces."[8]

He first needed to replenish his carriers and air groups. For three days beginning on July 20, Halsey pulled his carriers farther to sea to refuel and bring aboard replacement aircraft, ammunition, butter, beef, bacon, milk, eggs, coffee, beans, potatoes, and other supplies. During the lull, carrier crews relaxed in the evenings, watching Hollywood films, writing letters, and resting their muscles and minds from the wearying missions.

Lieutenant (jg) Watkinson could not as easily unwind. As one of the few night fighter pilots aboard the carrier, frequently assigned to night-time combat air patrol missions, his catapult launchings and subsequent landings in the dark raised the hairs on more than a few observers. Each night that Watkinson took off, cables secured the front of his plane to the catapult trolley beneath the deck. When the carrier's bow rose, the flight officer released the catapult trolley while the pilot brought the engine to full throttle and placed his head firmly against the headrest. The trolley yanked Watkinson's plane down the deck, and within one hundred feet his plane had accelerated enough to lift off the deck in an exercise some compared to being propelled by a slingshot.

"We took our hats off to those night fighters!" said Aviation Radioman 3/c Arthur Briggs. "That was scary. We'd go to the bridge to watch them take off and land, almost like an accident waiting to happen." Watkinson had to launch and alight on the *Yorktown* in near complete darkness, for even a sliver of light could impair the night vision he gained from the dark red goggles worn by every night fighter pilot. "In night fighters, the gauges were red hued because it was easier on the eyes," explained Watkinson. "Doctors told us to look at the lights peripherally. I liked night flying because I was by myself."[9]

Mandeberg or Sahloff were more than happy to let Watkinson assume those duties. Catapulted launchings were not unusual, but the night landings in which Watkinson had to set down on a darkened carrier moving away from him at twenty-five knots offered their own set of perils. When he drew close to the carrier, a radio signal helped guide him through the darkness, but he most welcomed those nights when the moon and stars created a shadow of the *Yorktown* or allowed him to discern the ship's wake.

"Landings were my biggest worry," he said. "The takeoffs were short because we were catapulted so there would not be the flame, but the landings were more of a worry as they were longer and more roundabout." Approaching downwind on the port side, Watkinson looked for two red lights on the carrier, one posted forward and the other aft. When one of the lights disappeared, he knew he was on a parallel course between the two lights and had to begin his landing. "You then see the ship's wake, and that takes you right to the carrier." Donned in a phosphorescent suit with phosphorescent paddles so Watkinson could see him, the landing signal officer directed Watkinson in to the deck. "I never had a wave-off at night," said Watkinson. "They make day landings seem like a piece of cake."[10]

THE CATHOLIC CHAPLAIN, Father Moody, used the interval to relay news to the *Yorktown* crew and to make certain he was available for religious consultation, hearing confessions, celebrating Mass, and distributing Holy Communion. Aboard such a massive vessel as the *Yorktown*, he could not possibly tend to each man, but he intended to do what he could to prepare those young sailors and aviators to enter combat with clear consciences.

In one afternoon announcement over the ship's public address system, Father Moody explained what to expect once the refueling and replenishing ended. "We are making preparations to strike Kyushu, Kobe & Osaka," he said. "Our targets will mainly be the bulk of the Jap Navy. The battleship *Haruna,* many others along with cruisers, carriers, destroyers, drydocks, airfields, factories and other vital war interests. We expect some enemy opposition. Here's hoping we come through okay."[11]

Mandeberg and Hansen might not have noticed the slight drop in enthusiasm of those final words, where Father Moody avoided saying that they *would* come through, favoring instead to end with the *hope* that they would emerge intact. The Air Group had formed in New England with an eagerness to go to war, but after the first four July missions, a touch of brutal reality had seeped through.

Father Moody reinforced those thoughts with his July 22 Sunday sermon. "Life out here has a way of stripping a man down to essentials," he said to those in attendance—mostly Catholic but with a few non-Catholics always joining in. "A Marine does not hit the beach loaded down with useless gadgets. An aviator does not burden his plane with the superfluous; nor does a man in a combat area spend his days with the trivial. I find myself giving more consideration to the things that really count in life. There is so little that stands up in time of crisis. When the chips are down, the petty things fade from sight. Basic values emerge in their true worth. That is why home and family and loved ones mean so much more to me after this experience."[12]

Billy Hobbs and Eugene Mandeberg, who mailed and received so many letters to and from parents and loved ones, would not argue with that point. They served aboard an aircraft carrier in the Pacific to defeat an enemy, but equally, if not more important, was their love of people in Kokomo, Detroit, and New York City. Medals for valor and acclaim for splashing an enemy fighter had their place, but those moments paled in comparison to what really counted—an end to this war and a return to their loved ones.

That might prove more difficult in light of their next target, the strategic Kure Naval Base along the Inland Sea. Photo reconnaissance had divulged the presence of multiple enemy warships at Kure, and Sahloff and Hobbs understood that with more Japanese vessels came more anti-aircraft guns. Over drinks in Philippine bars, veterans of the March 1945 strikes against Kure cautioned their Air Group 88 aviators about that base, protected by guns placed on nearby hills and on anchored warships. "Stay away from Kure," they warned.[13]

Little by little, the enthusiasm with which they headed to combat was diminishing.

"THEY SHOT COLORED TRACERS AND EVERYTHING THEY HAD"

The July 24 attack against the Kure Naval Base was the first of three colossal strikes against the vital naval base in four days. In each attack, Air Group 88 aviators charged in, strafing and dropping bombs on their quarry in the same way a boxer who sensed his foe was at the ropes unfurled a deadly combination of punches. Poor weather once more hampered their navigating, and since Kure rested 200 miles from the *Yorktown*, the aviators would have little time over the base before dwindling fuel levels forced them to begin their flight back to the carrier.

Tempting targets took refuge in Kure, but they came with a hefty price. With *Nagato* all but removed from the picture, the Air Group pilots focused on the battleship *Haruna* and the cruiser *Tone*, another veteran of the Battles of Midway, the Philippine Sea, and Leyte Gulf. Both ships spent their final days at Kure, hoping before their demise to land one or two more blows on the encroaching Americans. Buttressed by twenty-two antiaircraft positions that shielded Kure, they were prepared to punish any air squadrons dispatched by Admiral Halsey.

Multicolored antiaircraft bursts greeted the Air Group while it was still five miles from its target. Red, brown, yellow, black, and gray puffs peppered the sky on all sides of the aircraft and lent a pleasant Technicolor hue that sharply contrasted with the deadly streams of fire coming from the harbor below.

When Commander Searcy sighted a battleship through a hole in the clouds, he ordered his three divisions of Corsairs in an immediate attack on what he thought was the *Haruna*. As his eleven Corsairs dove on what turned out to be the battleship *Settsu*, charging through what the action report described as "intense and accurate" antiaircraft fire, *Yorktown*'s bomber and torpedo aircraft, joined by planes from *Independence*, *Shangri-La*, and *Cowpens*, peeled off and followed. Upon commencing his dive, Lieutenant Allyn C. Shefloe collided with a *Shangri-La* Corsair, bending his left wing upward and causing his plane to spiral out of control toward Kure Harbor. "No parachute was observed to open," stated the action report, "and it is assumed he was still in his aircraft when it crashed."[14]

While four fighters remained at higher altitude to keep watch for enemy aircraft, Helldivers and Avengers swept in from the north of Kure to attack the *Oyodo*, at anchor in a small cove on the west side of the harbor. Ensign Clarence A. Hansen, who landed a bomb squarely on the cruiser's stern, narrowly avoided injury when antiaircraft fire hit his Hellcat just behind the cockpit, but the pilot was able to pull away and return to *Yorktown*.

Lieutenant (jg) Henry G. Cleland and his wingman, Lieutenant (jg) Raymond Gonzalez, also ran in on *Oyodo*, firing their machine guns as they dropped lower into the thick crossfire created by antiaircraft guns aboard ships in the harbor and from gun positions on the hills. With puffs of flak and shells erupting uncomfortably close, the aviators pressed their charges and released 500-pound bombs that ripped into the cruiser's starboard side and amidships. "Cleland and Gonzalez were the only two planes attacking at that time and they fully expected to be hit," recorded the fighting squadron's report, in words that could have been said of any aviator in the Air Group for any one of the July strikes and sweeps.[15] Ensign Frank G. Rita was not as fortunate. While conducting his dive not far from Cleland and Gonzalez, flak ripped into his Corsair, sending Rita and his plane flaming into the harbor.

Lieutenant Commander Elkins, leading fourteen Helldivers of VB-88, turned left over Kure Harbor toward Eta Jima Island, where the *Oyodo* and *Tone* sat in their cove. Flying against heavy flak that, according to his report, "was bursting in many various colors," Elkins broke up the squadron at 13,000 feet and started a steep dive at 275 miles per hour.[16] Elkins and ten other Helldivers dove on *Tone*, leaving the cruiser aflame and listing, while the other three Helldiver pilots planted additional bombs on the already damaged *Oyodo*. After rendezvousing, the bombers returned to the *Yorktown*, with one pilot ditching while running out of gas during his third approach on the carrier. The rest landed in the dark with less than forty gallons of fuel remaining.

One by one the Avenger torpedo planes, the final unit to attack, peeled off and followed the Hellcats and Helldivers toward *Oyodo* and *Tone* while intense heavy flak burst beneath them. "They shot colored tracers and everything they had," said torpedo gunner Aviation Ordnanceman 3/c Ralph Morlan. "The heaviest barrage I have ever seen yet. We started doing evasive action and it was a 'free for all' for all pilots." The pilot of Morlan's Avenger selected a warship anchored in the cove and dropped into the steepest dive Morlan could recall. With flak hitting so close that it bounced the plane about, the pilot dropped four 500-pound bombs and immediately pulled up. Morlan saw two of the bombs hit the battleship or cruiser, but when his Avenger pulled away, a Japanese shell punctured the right wing, ripped a hole near the flap, and threw shrapnel that hit Aviation Radioman 3/c Walter E. Stanton in the foot. "He started rolling around on the floor and I got pretty scared," said Morlan. "I got Robby [the pilot] and he said to do what I could for him, and we got the hell out of there. Stan put a leather strap around his leg and laid on the floor of the plane. We started back alone so we could get back faster, and a Jap plane started following us, so we rejoined formation."[17]

In all, the Air Group claimed to have made six hits on *Tone* and eleven on *Oyodo*. Despite the results, Lieutenant Cagle was livid with the poor radio discipline exhibited by his aviators. One pilot shouted, "Look at that bastard burn," and another boasted, "How did you like the show Tojo."[18] Cagle needed those airwaves clear to help any man who had to splash, or in case Cagle had to call for assistance should Japanese aircraft appear. With the airwaves cluttered by unnecessary chatter, endangered aviators would be out of communication precisely when they most needed help. Cagle made a mental note to reprimand his fliers once he had them assembled back at the carrier, and to add a stern entry into the record so that other squadrons and air groups might take notice.

Some pilots thought that at least part of the unapproved chatter came from the Japanese in an attempt to gain information on the Americans. They became suspicious when a voice asked, in excellent English, what ship an aviator belonged to. Another American pilot, certain that no carrier aviator would ask such a question, quickly interrupted with a warning to his fellow pilots that the unwelcome participant was Japanese.

"ADMINISTERED THE *COUP DE GRACE*"

Halsey asked for a repeat performance the next day, but heavy rains and overcast allowed only two planes to punch through and drop what were described as near misses on a vessel. Rather than allow the day to be a complete washout, the Air Group shifted its objective and attacked distant Miho and Yonago Airfield, resting 250 miles from the task group on the Sea of Japan on Honshu's west side. Since the Japanese would hardly suspect the American pilots to fly straight across the Japanese Home Islands to attack targets along the Sea of Japan while ignoring airfields closer to the task force, they hoped to surprise the Japanese and find aircraft parked in the open.

Pilots were understandably nervous as the planes lifted off *Yorktown* and headed toward Japan. No carrier aviator had plunged so deeply into the Home Islands, and should they be forced to make an emergency landing in the Sea of Japan, the chances of being rescued at such a distance from their carrier were slim at best.

On the way to Yonago, the *Shangri-La* fighter squadron leader spotted two vessels and asked Cagle for permission to attack. Cagle told him to focus on the northern merchant ship while he and VF-88 strafed and bombed the other, a 2,700-ton merchant ship. Then, in a spirit of fun, Cagle added a challenge. "We'll race you to see which squadron can sink their ship first."

Cagle and his Hellcats strafed and rocketed the ship from bow to stern, and then made a second attack across the beam. Cagle hit the bridge three times, "leaving it mangled and battered" and dead in the water. When other VF-88 fighter pilots flew low over the ship, they were "appalled at the damage of some 15 rocket hits and repeated strafing.

Many dead Japanese were seen on deck and in the water alongside, and there were fires, debris and damage everywhere."[19] Cagle reported this ship as sunk, since a rescue plane which flew over the area ninety hours later saw nothing but an oil slick and wreckage.

The attack on Miho and Yonago Airfield caught the Japanese, who had assumed they were safe from Halsey's planes and failed to camouflage or disperse their aircraft, completely unprepared. A group of Corsairs from *Yorktown* and *Shangri-La* selected forty to fifty aircraft parked on the open airfield, with *Yorktown* aviators targeting the aircraft parked along the side and *Shangri-La* taking those sitting on the airfield. The Corsairs swept down "at altitudes of 50 feet or less with all guns firing and pieces of Bettys [Mitsubishi bomber] and Helens [Nakajima bomber] and other types of aircraft filling the air" in what Lieutenant Commander Hart called "the most productive sweep to date for VBF-88." Later, the Air Group history added, of the chance to attack exposed aircraft while facing minimal antiaircraft opposition: "It was here that our boys had some of their best 'sitting duck' hunting."[20]

YOKOSUKA, AND ESPECIALLY Kure, had been tastier alternatives than their earlier missions. *Nagato* and *Haruna* personalized the war for Hobbs and his fellow Hellcat flier, Lieutenant (jg) Maurice Proctor, more than did a parked Zero, for those ships had already played significant roles in battles that inflicted harm on United States personnel. *Nagato* had been home to Yamamoto, who had been until his death in 1943 an arch villain of the war since Pearl Harbor. Landing a bomb or a rocket straight into one of these warships, or into any of those vessels floating nearby, was the next best thing to downing a Japanese aviator in a dogfight.

Air Group 88 pilots returned to Kure on July 28 to mop up what the previous two strikes had missed. Sweeps attacked airfields, factories, and railroad facilities, and according to the bomber fighter squadron report, "put the fear of Democracy into 10 little Nips making hasty attempts to camouflage their locomotive parked in the mouth of a tunnel."[21]

During their mission against Hanshin Airdrome near Osaka, eleven Hellcats led by Lieutenant (jg) Robert P. Hall hugged the ground to avoid the antiaircraft fire streaming above. When the eleven arrived, they found most aircraft well camouflaged, but Hall countered with a deft move. As he wrote in his report, "I took the boys in low, firing into the revetments and burning off the camouflage. If we found a plane inside, we'd come back for a second pass and blow it to bits. We took the nets off all the bunkers, and found a lot of them had only dummy planes inside, but that some had real planes."

Hall was surprised that, as he and his group crisscrossed the field, many Japanese civilians watched the action from a nearby highway. Some, Hall observed, fled in their vehicles, but most stopped along the highway to stare at the American planes. "I guess they got a damned good look at a Hellcat," Hall said.[22]

Meanwhile, Commander Searcy led the strike in to put the final touches on *Haruna* and *Oyodo* at Kure Harbor. After taking off and heading to the rendezvous point, the *Yorktown* planes proceeded to the target alone when they were unable to join with the other four carrier units of the task group. The planes approached Kure cautiously, planning to make their dives from the west into Kure rather than from the north side, where antiaircraft positions had punished the Air Group in previous strikes. However, when USS *Wasp* (CV-18) aircraft arrived first and consumed so much time circling for their dives, Searcy had to hold his bombers and torpedo planes from attacking. As a result, Japanese gunners, as Lieutenant Commander Huddleston later wrote, "had plenty of chance to anticipate *Yorktown* planes' course. Predicted concentrations of heavy flak, intense and accurate, rocked the attacking planes."[23] Many of the Helldiver and Avenger aviators avoided damage during their dives, but Lieutenant (jg) Perry L. Mitchell and his gunner, Aviation Radioman 1/c Louis L. Fenton, became the eleventh and twelfth Air Group 88 casualties when flak from shore positions and gunships in the harbor brought down their Helldiver. Lieutenant (jg) Herbert D. Hoyt Jr. in his Avenger also limped back to *Yorktown* after a shell smashed into the aircraft's engine wall.

Searcy's pilots landed nine hits or near misses on *Oyodo* and seven on *Haruna*. *Oyodo* capsized, and photographs later showed *Haruna* enveloped in smoke, with her main deck and hull damaged at the bow, sixty-five feet of her deck ripped off from one side to the other, and her superstructure, according to Searcy, "a mass of wreckage." Because of the destruction to the pair of warships, Searcy added that his aviators "may well claim to have administered the *coup de grace*."[24]

NOW A VETERAN of several sweeps and strikes, Eugene Mandeberg climbed into his Hellcat on July 30 to join the other aviators for the eighth and final Air Group 88 attack of the month. After Admiral Radford took the task group northward toward Tokyo, Mandeberg lifted off the *Yorktown* and joined other Hellcats for the brief flight to Tokyo. Some of the pilots carried napalm bombs, a terrifying weapon which engulfed planes, ships, and people in flames. Aviators preferred to drop conventional bombs rather than napalm, out of concern that the Japanese would seek a horrible retribution on any pilot shot down and captured, but orders dictated otherwise.

When poor weather obscured the objectives near Tokyo, Mandeberg's morning mission swerved south against shipping and submarines in Sagami Wan, where they strafed and bombed merchant ships, a supply depot, four vessels, and a railroad station. An afternoon strike subsequently crossed Japan and hit similar targets in Maizuru Harbor, damaging ships and sinking a freighter before pulling away and strafing small boats.

"THE PACIFIC FLEET IS STRIKING AND WILL CONTINUE TO STRIKE"

Air Group 88 aviators were pleased with the results of their recent missions. The Air Group started with the attack on *Nagato*, of which Cagle wrote in his report, "The extremely well-coordinated and expertly timed attack by this force on the *Nagato* on 18 July is evidence that large groups of naval carrier aircraft can be effectively used against pin point targets. The above plan is offered as a means of effectively using that force and destroying hidden enemy air strength." They conducted their strikes on the Japanese battleship despite facing such withering antiaircraft fire that veteran pilots on their second tour of duty declared that "the A/A equaled <u>ALL</u> [capitals and underline theirs] the A/A they had ever seen in prior combat experience."[25]

Cagle waffled on the issue of whether to allow his fighter pilots to strafe from low altitudes, which enhanced their accuracy on the camouflaged Japanese aircraft but exposed his aviators to deadlier antiaircraft fire as well as to dangerous automatic weapons. He explained that the normal tactic for fighter attacks since 1943 had been to "dive fast, steep, and be in level flight by 1,000 feet," but many aviators chose to drop lower than that to ensure better results.[26]

He urged that whenever possible, strikes should avoid mixing aircraft from different carrier groups, as each air group had been briefed separately and had its own rendezvous point, altitudes of attack, and approaches. "In other words, the many months of careful group training, the familiarity thus gained between pilots within a group, is largely lost, when planes of many squadrons from two carriers are assembled to make one strike group. It is believed that more is lost than gained by this system."[27]

Because Air Group 88 pilots continued to be disappointed with the lack of air opposition, some had become overly aggressive, at times even leaving the Helldivers and Avengers they escorted to strafe tempting targets of opportunity. "It is believed that lack of fighter opposition has made flight leaders and individual pilots somewhat careless," wrote Lieutenant Commander Huddleston of VT-88. He cautioned that there were still several thousand Japanese planes in the Home Islands, "most of them fighters capable of picking off many stragglers," and that absent fighter escorts exposed the bombers and torpedo planes to unnecessary risks.[28]

Above all, the increasing combat losses hit home. The seven men killed in these attacks against the Imperial Japanese Navy at Yokosuka and Kure Naval Base—one aviator from VF-88, four from the Corsair squadron, and two from VB-88—brought the total battle casualties to twelve in only three weeks of action, a toll that left no man unblemished. When, after completing his July 24 mission against Kure, Lieutenant Hennesy learned that Lieutenant Allyn C. Shefloe and Ensign Frank G. Rita had been killed in the same attack, Hennesy could no longer celebrate his achievements, as "two of my shipmates who I had lived with, talked with, drank with, and flew with for many months had ceased to exist on this day."[29]

THE AIR GROUP 88 feats mattered more to family in Kokomo and New York City who, separated by thousands of miles from the war front, were insulated from the death and danger that Billy Hobbs and Eugene Mandeberg encountered. Home front news was generally positive, as the American military had knocked the Japanese back to their Home Islands. Rear Admiral DeWitt C. Ramsey, chief of staff to Admiral Raymond A. Spruance, claimed in a radio broadcast that the Air Group's bombing of Japan was the beginning of the invasion of Japan itself, and Admiral Halsey said from his flagship near *Yorktown* that "the Pacific fleet has opened a new phase of naval warfare. It cannot be interpreted by our own people or the Japanese as anything but the beginning of the final plunge into the heart of the Japanese Empire." He promised that "what is left of the Japanese Navy is helpless, but just for good luck we will hunt them out of their holes," and assured listeners, in words that Hattie and Sonya must have found disconcerting, "The Pacific Fleet is striking and will continue to strike with every weapon it has. . . . The Third Fleet's job is to hit the empire hard and often. This superb fighting outfit is doing just that and my only regret is that the ships do not have wheels so as to chase them inland after we drive them from the coast."[30]

Hattie, Sonya, and Zelda could follow the progress of the war through the *Kokomo Tribune,* the *New York Times,* or the Detroit newspapers, all of which reprinted similar articles posted by Associated Press reporters. Each story painted a positive picture about the war's progress, but they skirted any mention of hazards, enemy antiaircraft guns, and downed American aviators.

Without knowing specific details, they read of Billy and Eugene's involvement in Halsey's wide-ranging strikes against the Home Islands, especially the attacks against *Nagato* and the Kure Naval Base. A July 17 Associated Press article in the *Kokomo Tribune* and other publications around the nation explained that "in a week, Admiral William F. 'Bull'

Halsey's Third Fleet has ranged from Tokyo to the northern end of Japan and back again, smashing with bombs and shells vitally important steel, munitions, and oil plants, shipping and rail transportation and airdromes. Japan has taken it all helplessly without offering more than token resistance." While the aircraft "caught hundreds of ships and surface craft scurrying out of harbors like ants," it also "cost the attacking forces 16 airmen and 24 planes."[31] Might Billy be one of those sixteen airmen? Hattie had to ask. Was Eugene still back at the carrier safe and whole? Zelda and Sonya had to wonder.

Two days later news reports relayed that Halsey's aircraft had struck "the Yokosuka naval base, just inside Tokyo bay on its west shore and only 18 miles south of Tokyo." Family did not know until the end of August that Billy had participated in this strike against *Nagato*, when the *Kokomo Tribune* listed Hattie and Wright's address and stated that their son was "one of the fliers who pounded the Jap battleship *Nagato*," and when their son wrote that during this action, his "engine died twice, quite a scare."[32]

Hattie was not reassured with a July 28 account that carrier aviators had struck "the great Japanese naval base of Kure, where the remnants of the Mikado's fleet took futile refuge under extensive camouflage." The article added, "Despite the accuracy of the flak, the attackers pressed home the attack, bent on carrying out Halsey's orders to erase the enemy's fleet as a factor to be counted upon when invasion comes."[33] As Nancy Exmeyer explained, Hattie started connecting the dangers faced by her son with Admiral Halsey's orders. The article described a Japanese fleet in disarray, yet Halsey continued to order her son out against that lethal flak.

Billy kept his letters upbeat and positive. "Have been pretty busy lately. Right now, I am in the ready room now playing a mess of records. They all sound pretty good, mostly the old popular ones that bring back good times." He asked his sister Joyce to thank Hattie for sending a batch of photographs of family and friends, and expressed his hopes for more. "Say Joyce, Mother sent those swell pictures out a while back and they are really swell. Nothing hits the spot like a few good snapshots to pep a fellow up."[34]

In Detroit, Zelda worried the entire month of July because she had not heard from Eugene. "No mail from Eugene," Zelda wrote to Sonya on July 18. "I am getting very anxious. I hope all is well." Two days later, after learning that Sonya had received a letter, she added, "So glad you heard from Eugene. We haven't heard in over two weeks." She waited eight more days, which must have seemed eight years to the anxious mother, before again sending another missive to Sonya, this one shaded with anger. "No mail from Eugene. I do hope all is well. I am frozen to the radio. Hoping for good news. Those rats won't give up so quick."

Zelda finally received word of her son when an aviator who had seen Eugene six weeks earlier, most likely in the Philippines, telephoned her. "He told us Eugene is well. The ship he is on is one of the finest, the food is good, the service excellent. He too said that Eugene should be home for Christmas." While the pilot most likely added those last sentiments for Zelda's benefit, she at least knew that as of six weeks before, her son was safe.

She finally heard from Eugene when two letters arrived on July's final day. The letters conveyed little factual material, but clutching a piece of paper that her son had held a short time ago temporarily calmed her. "Yes, I too received two letters from Eugene," she wrote Sonya. "As usual he doesn't tell us a thing, but it's swell to see his handwriting. He sounds good." Taking heart from the aviator's words, Zelda added, "The war news is good and I hope it won't be long now."[35]

BY THE END of July, Billy Hobbs, Eugene Mandeberg, and Air Group 88 had helped Admiral Halsey achieve an ambition that had driven the commander since the war's opening day—the destruction of the Japanese surface fleet. In the five missions from July 18 to 30, the four squadrons had, according to Commander Searcy, smashed *Nagato* "into useless debris"; sunk destroyers, submarines, and other escort vessels; and destroyed numerous aircraft on the ground and locomotives at railroad stations. They had damaged or sunk the battleships *Ise* and *Hyuga* and watched *Tone, Oyodo,* and *Haruna* settle on the bottom. The cost had been high, but they had achieved enough that the carrier's war diary could claim that their work had "just about completed the job of destroying the heavy units of the Japanese Navy."[36]

The Japanese had been so stripped of their naval might that the situation handed Halsey the opportunity to strut. In his autobiography, he boasted, "The commander in chief of the Combined Japanese Fleet could reach his cabin in his flagship, the light cruiser *Oyodo,* only in a diving suit." The results were so satisfying that Halsey also concluded, "By sunset that evening [July 30], the Japanese Navy had ceased to exist."[37]

Despite the achievements, Halsey wanted more. As August dawned, he planned to continue strangling the enemy until the Japanese begged for mercy. His aviators, including Billy Hobbs, Eugene Mandeberg, Joe Sahloff, and others, would make certain that happened.

PART III
TO WAR'S END

CHAPTER 9

"The Navy Would Be in to Get You"
The July 1945 Air Sea Rescues

OVER EIGHT JULY days of sweeps and strikes, Air Group 88 had attacked airfields, railroad stations, small vessels, and what remained of the Japanese surface fleet. Missions against Japanese airfields and other locations did not compose Air Group 88's entire story, however. Spread out over their final five July strike days, the period during which Air Group 88 applied the finishing touches to the Japanese fleet, were a trio of impressive rescue operations as well as that elusive dogfight every fighter pilot had sought.

"START WEAVING!"

In his aerial engagement, Lieutenant Cagle could not have encountered worthier opponents, as the battle involved some of Japan's most revered fighter pilots. Captain Minoru Genda, who had helped plan the attack on Pearl Harbor, believed that with proper training, Japanese fliers could challenge the Hellcats and Corsairs that had recently claimed the skies. Hoping to create an alternative to the kamikaze units that sacrificed so many young men, in December 1944 Genda formed the 343 *Kokutai* (Fighter Group), a unit of veteran pilots that included Ensign Kaneyoshi Muto, who was credited with shooting down four B-29 bombers among his nearly thirty kills. Saburo Sakai, Japan's renowned ace with sixty-four downed aircraft to his credit, claimed that Muto was "brilliant in the air, already an ace, willing to fight at any time, anywhere," a man who "confounded the enemy pilots with brilliant aerobatics."[1]

Genda and his fellow aviators carefully planned their July 24 attack against the American planes that hit Kure. Without facing opposition since their arrival two weeks earlier, those carrier pilots had relaxed their vigilance. They appeared to fly toward Kure and return in almost leisurely fashion, as if they had not a worry in the world. Genda instructed his pilots to select one of those enemy groups as it left Kure, hit it hard, and then retreat before a second group of American planes charged in. Genda chose to strike after the American pilots had already hit Kure, since their carrier planes would be low on fuel and ammunition and the aviators would be weary from striking Kure Naval Base, further diminishing their vigilance as they winged back to their carriers.

Ensign Muto pounced on two Corsair pilots from the USS *Bennington* (CV-20), Lieutenant (jg) Robert M. Applegate and Ensign Robert J. Speckmann, as they flew through the Bungo Channel south of Kure. "We hadn't seen any aerial opposition and I think we let our guards down," said Lieutenant Applegate. "I put my plane on maximum lean so that I could conserve fuel. We weren't in a hurry to get to the carriers anyway because you never landed immediately."[2]

Applegate spotted four aircraft flying ahead and crossing him at a higher altitude. He at first assumed they were Hellcats, but suddenly the four unidentified planes split, bracketed Applegate and Speckmann, and charged the pair of Corsair pilots. Boxed in on both sides, the two Americans started to weave, but bullets tore into Speckmann's plane, which exploded and corkscrewed in flames to the water.

Lieutenant Cagle, leading the *Yorktown* fighters, and his wingman, Lieutenant (jg) Kenneth T. Neyer, had just finished attacking the cruiser *Tone* in Kure. They had retired to the rendezvous point through Bungo Channel when Cagle saw Speckmann's Corsair explode. Moments later twelve enemy fighters jumped Cagle and Neyer, who immediately started weaving in an attempt to shake their pursuers. While Cagle maneuvered into position and put several long bursts into a fighter, one of the Japanese pilots, Ensign Minoru Honda, approached Neyer's Hellcat from behind. He closed the distance until he could clearly see Neyer's head, and pumped twenty rounds into the fighter that severed Neyer's right wing and sent the American spiraling to his death.

Now alone, Cagle turned to help Applegate, who was frantically trying to shake a Japanese fighter on his tail. As the Japanese aviator maneuvered into firing position a short distance behind Applegate, Cagle "did a wingover and got on the Jack's tail." He fired several long bursts into the Japanese plane, which exploded and sprouted a burst of flame before veering downward and smacking into the water. "Thank you!" Applegate shouted to Cagle, who had just saved his life. "Start weaving!" answered the VF-88 skipper.[3]

Cagle joined up with Applegate, intending to fly back to their carriers together, but within moments six Japanese fighters dove at them. Outnumbered three to one, Cagle called over his radio for assistance, but none of the *Yorktown* Hellcats heard his plea because the airways were cluttered with unnecessary transmissions from pilots celebrating their successes at Kure. The pair again weaved as they raced for the open sea, but Ensign Muto crossed above the two and dropped into position for a head-on run on Applegate. Muto and Applegate pumped bullets at each other, hoping to destroy their adversary before the pair collided in a ferocious explosion. Applegate felt some of Muto's bullets smack into his engine as his own appeared to hit their mark, but neither of the two swerved from their paths. Finally, with hardly ten feet separating them, Muto's plane slipped slightly to the side and passed by Applegate, barely missing the Corsair. As the plane sped by, Applegate noticed that the Japanese pilot was slumped forward in the cockpit, apparently dead or dying.

Applegate nursed his smoking Corsair as far as he could in an effort to reach the nearest carrier, but was forced to splash when his engine quit. With Cagle watching, the plane veered downward, making what Cagle said in his report "appeared to be more of a crash than a landing."[4] Hoping to find evidence that Applegate had survived, Cagle circled for a few moments, but had to abandon the search and take shelter in a nearby cloud cover when a group of Japanese fighters materialized. Protected by the haze, Cagle evaded his pursuers and returned to the *Yorktown*. Meanwhile, Applegate bailed out before he hit the water and was rescued the next morning by an American submarine. Muto, who had accumulated a national reputation as one of Japan's best aviators, either died from his wounds or drowned after his plane smashed into the water.

The fighting squadron mourned the loss of Lieutenant (jg) Neyer, but celebrated Cagle's feats. In the only dogfight for Air Group 88 in the unit's first two weeks of combat, Lieutenant Cagle was credited with downing two enemy planes, which the fighter squadron history proudly labeled "the first 'kills' for VF-88."[5] For his accomplishments, the Navy awarded Cagle with its highest honor—the Navy Cross.

"A PROMISE OF HOME, AND FAMILY AND A GOOD LIFE"

"Today in the Pacific, Dumbo is synonymous with life-saving."[6] Those words, which appeared in the October 1944 issue of *Flying* magazine, did not refer to the popular Walt Disney cartoon elephant sporting oversized ears, but to the PBY-Catalina rescue aircraft, dubbed Dumbo due to its large dimensions.

Air rescues at sea had existed since the war's beginning, but a special unit designed specifically for that purpose was not created until June 1945, when Admiral Nimitz ordered its formation to prepare for the increased numbers of aviators he expected would be shot down and forced to the sea during the upcoming invasion of Japan. Based out of Okinawa, Air Sea Rescue, Ryukyus plucked numerous aviators from the waters off the Home Islands, and often flew deep into Japan to retrieve Americans sitting in life rafts floating on inland bays and seas, frequently under heavy fire from Japanese artillery. Those lumbering Dumbos provided reassurance to the young pilots of Air Group 88, for each time they lifted off the *Yorktown* to fly into enemy antiaircraft fire, they knew that if they had to parachute from a burning aircraft or ride it to the seas, they had an excellent chance of surviving due to those Catalinas.

"Our fleet had operated, from the very start, on the theory that the men who risked their lives to rocket, bomb and strafe the enemy wherever and whenever possible should, under no circumstances, be left to fend for themselves when disaster struck them," stated the commander of the Air Sea Rescue unit, Captain William L. Erdmann. "Admiral Halsey and Admiral Spruance made it clear that those airmen who were downed were to be rescued at all costs. This attitude on the part of the Fleet Commanders was a tremendous factor for the amazingly high morale of the pilots."[7]

Four rescue squadrons serviced the Third Fleet and other American units during the war's latter stages. They risked their lives, often in dangerous seas and usually under intense fire from shore batteries, and in the process saved more than 200 American fliers in 108 sea landings.

According to the August 6, 1945, issue of *Time* magazine, Japanese officials wondered why the United States exerted so much effort and expense, often tying up ships, submarines, and rescue aircraft, into saving one man. But, the magazine continued, the country and the military had always placed a premium on coming to the aid of those in dire straits. Of those Dumbo aircraft, *Flying* magazine added, "to pilots facing constant death over the unfriendly Pacific wastes they are a promise of home, and family and a good life after the war." As one pilot said, "I sometimes forget things I've learned down here, but I never forget how to call Dumbo."[8]

Every naval aviator appreciated that they were not considered disposable. They accepted that their occupation placed them in dangerous situations, many from which they might not return, but they flew into combat buttressed by the thought that their military would do whatever possible to bring them back. As one pilot said, "It's a mighty good feeling to know that even if you were shot down in Tokyo harbor the Navy would be in to get you."[9]

DUMBO AIRCRAFT CONDUCTED three rescue attempts for Air Group 88 aviators during their stay off Japan. On July 24 flak hit Ensign Edward Heck's Corsair while he attacked Himeji Airfield near Osaka, on the Inland Sea 200 miles northwest of the carrier. Unable to clear Osaka Bay, Heck safely ditched three miles west of Awaji Island in the Inland Sea, but was unable to release his life raft. With the bay's waters gushing into his Corsair, Heck inflated his Mae West and kicked away from the aircraft, which sank within twenty-five seconds of hitting the surface.

Heck glanced above to see three Corsairs circling his position. The pilots had already sent a rescue transmission, and the trio remained over Heck for forty-five minutes before their fuel supply forced them to depart. Alone in the waters, Heck prayed that the fighters would return or that a Dumbo would reach him before the Japanese did. "The water seemed to run in patches that were alternately warm and cold. There was land all the way around me," he said afterward. "I just kept hoping the fighters would get back before the Japs came along."[10]

Lieutenant Hennesy piloted one of those fighters. Back at the carrier after participating in that morning's fighter sweep, when Heck went down, Hennesy learned that a flying boat based out of Okinawa was on its way to save Heck. The commander of Air Sea Rescue in that area, Captain Erdmann, had never before ordered one of his Dumbo crews to take a Catalina this far into the Inland Sea between Shikoku and Honshu, where the plane could easily be attacked by the Japanese, so he ordered eight *Yorktown* Corsairs, including Hennesy, to rendezvous with another eight from *Shangri-La* and return to Heck's position to the northwest to provide cover while the Dumbo pilot landed and picked up the aviator.

While Hennesy and the Corsair group winged away from their carriers, Lieutenant (jg) Robert H. MacGill circled his Dumbo at his rescue station one hundred miles south of the entrance to the Inland Sea. His radio suddenly cracked to life with orders to join the Corsairs dispatched as escorts and to retrieve Ensign Heck. The sixteen Corsairs rendezvoused with MacGill's Dumbo in gray misty rain squalls, which, according to Hennesy, was "making it difficult to keep the flying boat in sight."[11] They broke into the clear as they neared the Japanese coast, and at the entrance to the Kii Suido Strait fifty miles south of Heck, eight Corsairs under *Yorktown* pilot Lieutenant David C. Steele Jr. dropped low to search for Heck while the other eight, including Hennesy, remained with MacGill.

When they entered the entrance to the Inland Sea, Lieutenant Steele located Heck one mile offshore, floating in the middle of green dye he had released onto the water, and, according to the action report, "very much alive, attested by his violent gestures."[12] Held afloat by the Mae

West, only Heck's shoulders and head showed above the water, making it more difficult to locate him from higher altitudes.

Before the Dumbo and her escorts reached Heck, a Japanese picket boat and a lugger emerged from shore and steamed toward the aviator. "The ship was within a quarter of a mile from me and I was getting pretty worried," Heck said later. "Then four Corsairs roared in from the channel. What a beautiful sight! Two circled over me while the other two peeled off to take care of the Sugar Dog [ships]."[13] The two Corsair pilots strafed and turned away the enemy vessels.

With the area now clear, Steele radioed MacGill to commence his landing. Vectored to Heck's location by Steele, the only angle for a safe landing required MacGill to fly directly over nearby Kobe, in plain sight of the city's civilians and within easy range of antiaircraft guns. He dropped lower as he approached Kobe and the water, expecting antiaircraft shells to rattle the Catalina and shrapnel to pepper the fuselage. "We were so close to Kobe that we could see people walking around on the streets," said MacGill. "We were surprised not to encounter ground fire from the city. I guess we worked a little too fast for the Japs to get organized."[14] MacGill landed alongside Heck, and within seventy-seven seconds of the time MacGill cut his engines, the crew had pulled the exhausted aviator aboard and MacGill had lifted off the water, all while under the noses of enemy soldiers and civilians.

With antiaircraft shells buffeting his Catalina, MacGill circled around the edge of Shikoku on his way out and flew through the channel between that island and Honshu. Hennesy, orbiting at 5,000 feet near Osaka at the time, dropped lower to protect the flying boat as it climbed. "Looking back down behind my left wing, I saw a plane flying level with big orange red circles on each wing moving towards the flying boat." Another pilot shouted over the radio, "Meatballs below!" When Hennesy saw the red dots grow larger, he "pulled the trigger and saw my tracers stabbing a little in front of the Jap's right wing. I kicked a little left rudder and saw them move into his cockpit. Fearing I would overrun him and come in front of his guns, I pulled up and around in a quick wing over and began firing at his fuselage again. He began letting out a white vapor and began diving down in spiral turns toward the ground. I followed him and saw him crash on his belly on the beach at the entrance to the Inland Sea." In the process of defending the Dumbo, Hennesy shot down a Nakajima Ki-43 fighter, nicknamed "Oscar" by American aviators.

With Heck safely in his plane, MacGill set a course for his tender, USS *Pine Island* (AV-12). Hennesy and the other aircraft escorted Mac-Gill until he was safely out to sea and then veered into the rain and darkness for an uncomfortable trip back to *Yorktown* and *Shangri-La*. Hennesy had not executed a night landing in these conditions in some time, but as he approached *Yorktown* he "picked up Willy, our landing signal officer, in his green and orange fluorescent suit and paddles," and landed safely. One by one, the others followed suit.

Hennesy returned to a jubilant welcome from his squadron. "The news of my shoot down had already been flashed on the teletype in front of our crowded ready room full of pilots still in flight gear, and as I walked in they all shouted congratulations to me. I had a feeling of great satisfaction that my long time ambition to become a real fighter pilot had been achieved."[15] Hennesy received an Air Medal for escorting the Dumbo and for shooting down the Oscar.

Home front newspapers praised the operation, not merely for rescuing Heck, but for flying deep over Japan to the Inland Sea to pick him up within eyesight of Japanese civilians. "Perhaps the most daring and the most spectacular of all Pacific air-sea rescue missions was the first mission into the Inland Sea to bring out a downed Corsair pilot within the very sight of Japs walking the streets of Kobe," reported Leo Litz in the *Indianapolis News*. He praised the aviators for "braving the hazards of Japan's defense" and for "thumbing their noses at the enemy." He added that "air-sea rescue is doing much to bolster the morale of combat airmen" as the pilots knew that even if they were downed hundreds of miles from their carrier, someone would come to their rescue.[16]

"MIRACULOUS ESCAPE"

Six days later, the air-sea rescue unit again came to the rescue of an Air Group 88 aviator when Lieutenant (jg) Donald R. Penn of VBF-88 ditched his flak-damaged plane in the Sea of Japan close to the Maizuru

Ensign Wright C. "Billy" Hobbs, Jr. before leaving Kokomo for duty off Japan. *(Cary Hobbs Collection)*

This photo was taken on February 11, 1945, during Billy Hobbs's brief visit home before departing for California and duty overseas. The inscription on the back of the photo reads, "Taken Feb. 11, 1945. Departure for naval duty in Pacific area." *(Cary Hobbs Collection)*

Billy Hobbs (right) with Kitty Davis, the owner of a popular Miami Beach nightclub, and an unidentified friend in April 1944. *(Denny Clelland Collection)*

Billy Hobbs in the cockpit of his fighter aircraft. *(Cary Hobbs Collection)*

Nancy Exmeyer, the sister of Billy Hobbs, stands before the photograph of her brother that has for decades occupied a prominent place in her Kokomo home. *(Author's Collection)*

In June 2018 three members of the Hobbs family visited Patriots Point to see the USS *Yorktown* (CV-10) and to meet William Watkinson, one of the survivors of VF-88. They were able to talk to Watkinson about Billy Hobbs and war service off Japan. Watkinson often meets with visitors to the carrier, and can often be found sitting at a bench bearing his name situated near a Hellcat. From left to right in front of a Hellcat fighter aboard the *Yorktown* are Cary Hobbs, William Watkinson, Greg Hobbs, and Troy Hobbs. *(Cary Hobbs Collection)*

Sonya Levien in 1945, posing with the engagement ring Eugene Mandeberg gave her. *(Sonya Levien Collection)*

Eugene Mandeberg with his mother, Zelda, one year before the war started. *(Sonya Levien Collection)*

Eugene Mandeberg in the Pacific before Air Group 88 joined the *Yorktown*. *(Jean Mandeberg Collection)*

Sonya Levien Kamsky (sitting) poses for a photograph taken when the Mandeberg family visited Sonya in New York for a reunion. On the left is Jean Mandeberg, Eugene Mandeberg's niece and namesake, while Sonya's daughter, Susan Kamsky Sussman, is on the right. *(Jean Mandeberg Collection)*

Sonya Levien Kamsky in her New York apartment in 2018. *(Author's Collection)*

VF88 At NAS Hilo with Names

Chase
Haag Sahloff
Rodgers
Welch Mandeburg
Koontz
T Hansen

C Hansen
Hobbs Komisarek
Godfrey
Martin
Bloski

O'Meara

Caravan
Proctor Harrison Hall Cagle Sisk Adams Odom
Joyce Crommelin Thompson

VF-88 gathered for this photograph taken in Hawaii shortly before the aviators departed to join the USS *Yorktown* (CV-10). The thick lines point to aviators most frequently mentioned in the book. *(John Haag Collection)*

The F6F Hellcat, the fighter used by Harrison, Hobbs, Mandeberg, Sahloff, and the other members of VF-88, became one of the best fighter aircraft of the war. *(National Archives)*

VBF-88, the bombing-fighting squadron, employed the F4U Corsair aircraft, a versatile aircraft flown by Lieutenant (jg) Gerald C. Hennesy and his fellow aviators of VBF-88. *(National Archives)*

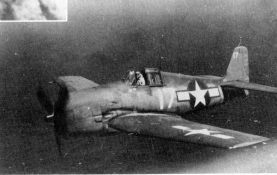

The bombing squadron, VB-88, flew the Curtiss SB2C Helldiver bomber. A rear gunner, such as Aviation Radioman 3/c Arthur C. Briggs, occupied the seat behind the aviator. *(National Archives)*

Members of the VT-88, the torpedo squadron, flew the TBM Avenger torpedo plane. An aviator, a gunner, and a radioman manned this aircraft. *(National Archives)*

Air crews manning this plane rescued numerous downed aviators in the Pacific. The men they saved included Lieutenant Howard M. "Howdy" Harrison, Ensign Edward Heck, Lieutenant (jg) Henry J. O'Meara, and Lieutenant (jg) Donald R. Penn. *(National Archives)*

The USS *Yorktown* (CV-10), nicknamed "The Fighting Lady" because of her prowess in battling the Japanese, housed Air Group 88 for its entire stay off Japan. *(National Archives)*

After the war, the venerable USS *Yorktown* (CV-10) found a permanent home at Patriots Point Naval & Maritime Museum in Mount Pleasant, South Carolina. Here she is pictured in 2018. *(Author's Collection)*

The hangar deck, one level below the flight deck from which the planes took off, was where ordnancemen, seen here working on bombs, serviced the aircraft. In the background, other crewmen are watching a movie flashed on a screen. *(National Archives)*

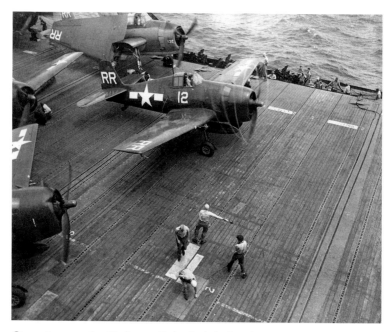

Operations on the *Yorktown* flight deck had to be organized to the tiniest detail to ensure a steady flow of aircraft to the air. In this photograph, a signalman gestures for the first Hellcat to proceed down the deck, while a second Hellcat (left) prepares to follow. Behind, some with wings still folded, other Hellcats await their turn. *(John Haag Collection)*

Lieutenant (jg) William T. Watkinson in his Hellcat fighter aircraft in 1945. *(Connie Reynolds/William Watkinson Collection)*

In 2018 aboard the USS *Yorktown* at Patriots Point Naval & Maritime Museum, Bill Watkinson sits on the bench provided for him on the carrier's hangar deck. He enjoys chatting with visitors to the *Yorktown*. *(Author's Collection)*

Lieutenant Gerald C. Hennesy in the cockpit of his F4U Corsair fighter aircraft while off the Japan coast in mid-1945. *(Gerald C. Hennesy Collection)*

On the *Yorktown*'s flight deck, Lieutenant Gerald C. Hennesy (second from left) stands with the other three members of his team. From left to right are Hennesy's wingman, Ensign Richard F. Hunter, Hennesy, Lieutenant (jg) Henry H. Moyers, and Ensign James K. Murphy. *(Gerald C. Hennesy Collection)*

Lieutenant Howard M. "Howdy" Harrison was one of the most popular aviators in Air Group 88. Here a group of fellow aviators warmly greet him after a PBY Catalina aircraft rescued him from the Sea of Japan. *(John Haag Collection)*

From left to right, Lieutenant Malcolm Cagle greets Lieutenant (jg) George Smith, who piloted his PBY Catalina aircraft across Japan through treacherous weather to rescue Lieutenant Howard M. "Howdy" Harrison from the Sea of Japan. Lieutenant (jg) Maurice Proctor (second from right) and Lieutenant (jg) Joseph Sahloff escorted Smith's Dumbo. *(Connie Reynolds/William Watkinson Collection)*

Welcoming Lieutenant Howard M. "Howdy" Harrison (middle) after his incredible rescue from the Sea of Japan are Lieutenant (jg) Maurice Proctor (left) and Lieutenant (jg) Joseph Sahloff (right) with a cigar that always seemed to accompany him. *(Connie Reynolds/William Watkinson Collection)*

Standing on the USS *Yorktown* flight deck, three aviators check information before taking off for another mission. From left to right are Lieutenant (jg) Herman B. Chase, Lieutenant Hoke Sisk, and Lieutenant (jg) John Haag. On July 15 Haag watched antiaircraft fire hit the Hellcat of his close friend, Herman Chase, who died in the incident. *(John Haag Collection)*

Lieutenant (jg) Kenneth T. Neyer (left) and Lieutenant Malcolm Cagle (second from left) talk to two unidentified aviators on the USS *Yorktown*'s flight deck. Neyer and Cagle participated in the only dogfight involving Air Group 88 until the war's last day. Lieutenant Neyer was killed in the July 24 action. *(John Haag Collection)*

In March 1945 four of Air Group 88's top commanders enjoy light banter at a party in the Officers' Club in Hilo, Hawaii. From left to right are Lieutenant Commander Joseph Hart of VB-88; Commander S. S. Searcy, Air Group 88 commander; two unidentified officers; Lieutenant Commander Richard G. Crommelin of VF-88; and Lieutenant Commander James C. Huddleston of VT-88. *(John Haag Collection)*

Lieutenant Commander Richard G. Crommelin, seen here in his fighter aircraft, was the beloved commander of VF-88. A part of an esteemed Navy family, he gained fame before taking the helm of the fighter squadron, where he used his experience to help fashion aviators out of the raw recruits. *(National Archives)*

Admiral William F. Halsey became one of the Pacific War's home front heroes with his aggressive style of command and headline-grabbing quotes in 1942-1944. Halsey's hard-hitting style off the Japanese coast in July and August 1945 kept Air Group 88 aviators in action until the very final moments of the war. Here he is depicted in a wartime poster. *(National Archives)*

Admiral William F. Halsey's bellicose attitude toward the Japanese is featured in this sign erected by one of his commanders at Tulagi Harbor across from Guadalcanal in the Solomons Islands. The large sign, intended to motivate the crew of every ship that steamed into the harbor, perfectly expressed Halsey's intent to wage unrelenting warfare until the Japanese surrendered. *(National Archives)*

Lieutenant (jg) Theodore W. Hansen led the flight team that accompanied Lieutenant Howard M. "Howdy" Harrison's team for the final dogfight on August 15, 1945. Hansen and Lieutenant (jg) Maurice Proctor survived, while all four aviators on Harrison's team perished. *(Kathleen Hansen Collection)*

Lieutenant (jg) Laverne F. Nabours (left) and Ensign Ronald J. Hardesty flew on the same team with Lieutenant (jg) Theodore W. Hansen and Lieutenant (jg) Maurice Proctor for the final flight on August 15, 1945. Nabours and Hardesty were detached to relay messages to and from the USS *Yorktown* (CV-10), while Hansen and Proctor survived the last dogfight near Tokyo. *(John Haag Collection)*

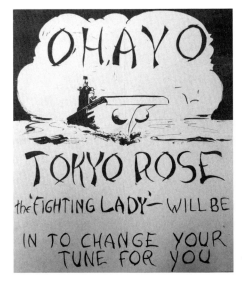

This cartoon displays the spirit aboard the USS *Yorktown* (CV-10) as she transported Air Group 88 toward the Japanese coastline in July 1945. *(Patriots Point Collection, Miscellaneous Folder)*

Dangerous flak greeted any aircraft that approached the heavily defended Kure Naval Base. This photograph shows some of the air bursts from Japanese antiaircraft guns during one raid. *(National Archives)*

On July 14, 1945, Air Group 88 attacked railway ferries and other targets on Hokkaido. Here a series of bomb bursts surrounds a ferry operating between Honshu and Hokkaido. *(National Archives)*

Third Fleet aircraft, including those from Air Group 88, attacked Kure Naval Base in late July. Here aircraft concentrated their bombs on the battleship, *Hyuga* during a July 24, 1945 attack. *(National Archives)*

Air Group 88 returned to Kure Naval Base on July 28, 1945. In this photograph, carrier aircraft bomb the Japanese battleship, *Haruna*. *(National Archives)*

While operating off the coast of Japan, Admiral William F. Halsey's massive Third Fleet brought its formidable air power directly to the Japanese homeland. Here a portion of that fleet spreads to the horizon. *(National Archives)*

As part of the September 2, 1945 surrender ceremonies, Admiral William F. Halsey arranged an impressive flyover in Tokyo Bay by five hundred carrier aircraft as well as by Army bombers. Here a portion of the planes pass above the USS *Missouri* (BB-63), where the ceremonies occurred. *(National Archives)*

V-J DAY

ABOARD

The U.S.S. Yorktown

The USS *Yorktown* (CV-10) marked the end of the war with another cartoon, this time depicting Japanese emperor, Hirohito. *(Patriots Point Collection)*

Naval Base, 275 miles from the *Yorktown*. Fellow pilots maintained cover over Penn and radioed for a Dumbo, but low on fuel and facing a rough landing in the dark, they could not remain until the Catalina arrived. "It was getting late. I was really worried," Penn said. "It's one thing to be shot down in the morning and another thing in the late afternoon. When the Corsairs with me pulled out it was a sad sight indeed. A Jap showed and I pulled a blue poncho over the raft and hid. With the fleet pulling out in the dark I didn't have much hope."[17]

In the meantime, a Dumbo flown by the U.S. Army Air Forces Lieutenant John Rairich, a veteran who had already whisked forty aviators from the sea, lifted off from its base in Iwo Jima and joined with four *Yorktown* night fighters, including twenty-one-year-old Lieutenant (jg) Henry J. O'Meara and Lieutenant Edward M. Chamberlain of VF-88. Rairich accepted the mission even though it was already late in the afternoon, and with Penn downed so far from friendly forces, Rairich would lack the fuel needed to return to his base. He faced a nighttime water landing, hopefully near a task group that could dispatch a destroyer to his rescue.

Thirty minutes into their flight, the five aircraft received a call from the fighters orbiting Penn that they had to leave due to their fuel. O'Meara and Chamberlain raced ahead of the slower Catalina to reach Penn sooner, but when they arrived over Penn's reported location, they had difficulty locating the aviator, who had covered himself in his raft with the blue poncho to hide from an enemy float plane. After Rairich's Dumbo arrived, O'Meara and Chamberlain spotted Penn when they noticed a reflection from a mirror Penn held.

As Rairich swung around to land, a Japanese destroyer raced out of Maizuru Naval Base toward Penn. With shells splashing near the aviator and darkness closing in, another Hellcat pilot, Lieutenant Fred C. Sueyres, turned toward the warship to draw attention from Penn. The destroyer opened fire on Sueyres, the father of a five-month-old son he had not seen, who dove on and strafed the destroyer while Rairich landed his Catalina near Penn.

Rairich's problem doubled when the oil pressure in O'Meara's Hellcat dropped after being hit by a shell. Forced to ditch, O'Meara hit the water as far as possible from the oncoming destroyer while Rairich gunned his engines and lifted off with the newly rescued Penn in hand. "We had no trouble locating Penn," said Rairich, "but we also spotted a Japanese destroyer about 12 miles off. It saw us too and headed our way. We made a quick landing and picked up Penn and just had got off the water when we received word that O'Meara was down."[18]

Sueyres and two other Hellcats continued to strafe the destroyer while Rairich took off amid a torrent of enemy shells splashing uncomfortably close. The three Hellcat pilots saw their shells strike the destroyer's forward guns and spark an explosion, but were almost out of ammunition when Rairich turned back to get O'Meara.

Rairich, fearing he might fall prey to Japanese fire if he cut his engines, instead kept them running. "We set down near O'Meara and taxied toward him, with shells hitting around us," said Rairich. "We tossed him a rope and damned if it didn't break. We threw him another one, which he grabbed, and we started taxiing at once, dragging him behind us like a surfboard."[19]

Now flying in the dark, Rairich and his escorts crossed Honshu toward the carrier, a course that took him directly over the guns at the Maizuru Naval Base. "I didn't know anything about the place," said Rairich. "All I wanted to do was get out of range of that can [destroyer] and find some cloud cover. So I headed right for a cloud layer. Unfortunately, it happened to be in the direction of the naval base."[20] Rairich navigated through a curtain of flak, which bounced the Catalina as if it were a toy, while Penn and O'Meara muttered quick prayers for a safe exit they assumed had been theirs when they left the water.

Rairich eluded the errant Japanese fire and proceeded across the island to the *Yorktown*, which was then 150 miles south of Tokyo. One destroyer escorting the carrier illuminated her searchlights to designate where Rairich should land, permitting the Dumbo pilot to execute a safe water landing nearby. The destroyer picked up the Dumbo crew and two aviators before executing orders to sink the Dumbo, which could not be taken aboard the carrier.

Yorktown's report of the rescue praised Rairich's valor for accepting the mission despite knowing that at the end, after operating under fire to rescue Penn, and then returning to retrieve O'Meara through the thick enemy fire, he faced a water landing because he lacked enough fuel to return to his base in Iwo Jima. Newspaper accounts called the mission a "miraculous escape" for Rairich, who rescued the pair of aviators from "under the nose of a pursuing enemy destroyer."[21]

"DEAD RECKONING AND THE GRACE OF GOD"

The third rescue involved one of the most popular members of the Air Group. "Everybody on the carrier liked him, for he was a personable fellow, a good shipmate, and a first-rate flier. So when news came that Lt. 'Howdy' Harrison was down in the Sea of Japan, there was deep gloom on the ship."

So wrote the Catholic chaplain aboard *Yorktown*, Father Joseph Moody, about Howdy Harrison. As impressive as were the Heck, Penn, and O'Meara rescues, they lacked the drama and emotions of Howdy Harrison's retrieval. The story appeared in hundreds of home front newspapers and so impressed the Air Group and entire crew of the *Yorktown* that Father Moody wrote a lengthy account to supplement the action report of the incident.

Accompanied by his wingman, Billy Hobbs, Howdy Harrison led a July 25 morning sweep against Miho Airfield resting on Japan's northern coast 270 miles from *Yorktown*. Intelligence officers briefed the pair that they would face horrible weather, a base that Father Moody wrote was surrounded "with powerful AA positions," and a flight that demanded they fly across Shikoku and the Inland Sea before navigating the breadth of Honshu to reach their target.[22]

Once they had traversed Honshu's thick overcast, Howdy led the Hellcats down into thick antiaircraft fire in a glide-bombing attack, dropping bombs on the Miho hangar area and strafing two planes parked on the east side of the airfield before pulling out at 500 feet. Ignoring the flak bursting close by, Hobbs destroyed one aircraft with his bullets, while Joe Sahloff and Maury Proctor planted bombs in hangars. As they pulled out of their strafing runs, Japanese guns seemed to zero in on Harrison. "There were so many tracers sailing up past him that he could've lit a cigarette just by sticking it out of the cockpit," said Maury

Proctor. "Then they connected. They hit the underside of his engine, and it put out a long black streamer of smoke and oil."

Harrison felt a familiar crunching jolt, the same as the previous four times he had been hit by Japanese fire. This time, flak had hit the underside of his engine, which spouted smoke and oil. Hobbs dropped underneath Harrison to inspect the damage, and informed Howdy that his Hellcat bled oil from two large holes. Harrison turned north toward the Sea of Japan to put as many miles as possible between himself and the Japanese guns and ships, every second keeping an eye on his oil pressure gauge. When it reached zero, Harrison jettisoned his hood, pulled back on the stick, and brought his Hellcat down safely, fifteen miles off the coast in the Sea of Japan. The plane bounced a few times as Harrison skimmed the surface of the water before coming to a halt. "Howdy's a wonderful pilot," Sahloff said. "He ditched about as smoothly as I could land on La Guardia Field."[23]

Harrison stepped out of the cockpit with all his gear, walked off the port wing, and inflated his raft. A few of his fellow fighter pilots circled while Proctor led the rest back to *Yorktown*. Before he departed, Proctor radioed Harrison's position to the carrier, figuring that *Yorktown* would then arrange for a Dumbo to rescue the pilot, but because of the weather and Harrison's extreme distance from *Yorktown*, the message never went through. Proctor did not learn that his transmission failed until after he landed on the carrier.

As his Hellcat plane disappeared beneath the waves, Harrison inflated his life raft, climbed into it, and spread green coloring from his dye marker that surrounded the yellow raft and identified his position. The fighters circled above until a dwindling gas supply forced them to leave, at which time the pilots dipped their wings and turned away. On their way out, they spotted a Japanese destroyer escort ten miles from Harrison, but when the ship did not alter its course and steam toward the pilot, they concluded the Japanese had failed to detect their buddy and resumed their course to the *Yorktown*. Harrison, now alone in the Sea of Japan, was not only far from his carrier, but had all of mainland Honshu standing between him and *Yorktown*. "That was a sad sight," Harrison said of seeing his comrades leave. "I hope I never feel that lonely again."[24]

Harrison figured that unless the Japanese reached him first, he had sufficient equipment and food to last until a rescue craft appeared overhead. A quick inspection revealed he had a whistle for signaling, a metal reflector for visual signaling, a combination compass and waterproof match container, a jackknife, a fishing kit, sail fabric, a first-aid kit, rations and water, and two smoke grenades. He had already used the dye, which only lasted a few hours before dissipating, but he assumed a Dumbo would arrive before that occurred. He hoped never to employ the suggestion about one of nature's predators offered by the manual he and every other aviator studied during their training in the United States: "Treat sharks with plenty of respect," and if "you do happen to go overboard or if the raft capsizes—splash and kick as much as you can while getting back aboard."[25]

BACK AT *YORKTOWN*, instead of the usual post-mission excitement that filled the ready room, Proctor, Sahloff, and the others who returned entered silently before informing fellow aviators that enemy fire had forced Harrison down in the distant Sea of Japan. Everyone understood what the news meant, as several pilots had been forced to ditch on the Asiatic side of Japan, and none had been saved. "It is not easy to operate on one side of Japan, and send a rescue mission across the enemy territory to pick up a pilot close to the other shore," wrote Father Moody. They had tried it several times, "but weather, the approach of darkness and the inherent difficulty of finding a man drifting at sea had thwarted each attempt." The chaplain added, "There are some cases which appear hopeless, and Howdy appeared to be in just such a pass."[26]

When a ready room teletype alerted the group that eight aviators from another carrier had been assigned to escort a Dumbo to Howdy's location, Proctor and Sahloff angrily reacted. "Like hell they will," shouted Proctor. "They'll never find Howdy. But we saw right where he went down."

He and Sahloff hurried up the ladders to Flag Plot. When they burst in, Proctor approached the chief of staff, Captain F. M. Trapnell, and asked permission to return to the site of Harrison's ditching. Trapnell explained that planes from another carrier had already been launched, but Proctor would not back down. "But, sir, we saw where he went down—and, well, we just wouldn't come back without him." Trapnell paused, at which Proctor again asked if he and Sahloff could head out. "All right. Be ready in five minutes."[27]

Proctor and Sahloff donned their flight gear and ran to the flight deck. The maintenance crew informed Proctor that the gyro, a device that helped ensure his Hellcat maintained a proper course, was not working properly, but Proctor dismissed it. For his good friend, he was willing to again fly into that heavy overcast near Miho, even in a substandard plane.

WHILE EVENTS UNFOLDED in the Sea of Japan and aboard *Yorktown*, Lieutenant (jg) George B. Smith orbited his position near the Home Islands in his Dumbo, ready to fly to the aid of a downed aviator. Since he, along with his eleven-man crew, had been in the air for several hours, they looked forward to the arrival of their relief and the prospect of returning to their base on Okinawa, where much needed food and rest awaited.

His thoughts were interrupted by an alert to rescue another pilot in trouble, this time not close by, but in the remote Sea of Japan. Smith immediately checked his fuel supply, most of which he had consumed flying those circles on station. A quick mental calculation brought the sobering conclusion that he lacked fuel to fly to the downed aviator, land in what could be choppy waters, and return to Okinawa. In addition, the mixture control for his starboard engine had jammed at automatic lean. He could still fly, but he would be unable to climb to the altitude needed to avoid a nasty weather front that had moved in.

Smith turned his PBM-Mariner toward the Sea of Japan. Only three weeks earlier, he and his crew had crashed in the East China Sea, 200 miles off Korea, while picking up an Army pilot. The twelve had bobbed in life rafts for almost forty hours before an American submarine arrived and took them aboard. The last thing Smith wanted was a repeat of that exhausting experience, especially on the far side of Japan. As Father Moody described of the Dumbo, "With all these handicaps, it had to make a 300 mile trip to effect the rescue in weather conditions that were as wretched as conceivable."[28]

Smith rendezvoused with Sahloff, Proctor, and six other escorts thirty miles from the task force. Deteriorating weather engulfed the planes in a thick overcast as they neared the coast of Shikoku, limiting their visibility to fifteen feet and all but blinding the pilots. "It wasn't a pleasant prospect to fly over flaming and exploding Japanese naval bases in a big slow Mariner with a low gas supply," said Smith of the terrifying flight.[29]

Sahloff, flying off one side of the Dumbo, could barely discern the Mariner through the overcast, and often lost sight of Proctor, who was stationed off the other wing, but the aircraft lumbered ahead, hoping for a break in the clouds. The pair had to slow their Hellcats to remain on the Dumbo's sides, mostly to help with navigating through the harsh weather, but partly to make sure Smith would not change his mind and turn back. "We were a funny sight," Proctor said. "It was kind of like a big old St. Bernard plodding along through the snow with a couple toy bulldogs beside him."

Smith had perfect radio communication with Sahloff, but interference prevented him from reaching Proctor, the other Hellcat pilot. As a result, for the remainder of the flight, Sahloff communicated with Smith, and then relayed the information to Proctor on a channel not available to Smith.

"We'll navigate if you want us to," Sahloff told Smith at one point. "We can find Miho easy."

"O.K.," Smith replied, "but you'd better be right on the nose." Smith explained that if they had been off course by even a few degrees when they entered the cloud cover, they would be far from Miho when they subsequently emerged.

"Just follow us, pal," Sahloff said with a trace of false bravado.[30]

Smith accepted Sahloff's words, but was not entirely convinced the young aviator knew what he was doing. "We flew through a heavy overcast," said the Dumbo pilot. "I didn't know where we were going and I wasn't entirely convinced that Sahloff and Proctor did either."[31]

Dependent on Sahloff and Proctor for navigation and for the location of the downed pilot, Smith ordered every unnecessary item to be tossed overboard to help maintain the Dumbo's altitude and airspeed. "By this time the crew became increasingly alarmed and urged Smith to turn back," said Ensign Lyman Hellman, one of the crew. "Smith, with all his problems, would not listen, and kept forging ahead with our two escorts."[32]

Sahloff asked Proctor if he thought they were on the proper course, but Proctor countered that he had no idea. After thirty minutes, Smith checked in, telling Sahloff, "I don't like the looks of this. Is our heading correct?" Sahloff reassured him that it was and that the weather was certain to clear, even though Sahloff wondered the same thing.

Another half hour later, Smith informed Sahloff that his faulty engine would prevent him from climbing higher to break out of the clouds. Sahloff told Smith that he expected to reach clear skies soon, but refrained from informing him that the top had risen another 8,000 feet since they started the journey. He figured that under these conditions, there was no sense in relaying what was now irrelevant information.

The lull lasted only another thirty minutes, when Smith relayed news that no one wanted to hear. "If my engine keeps on detonating, I'm going to have to turn back. I hate to say that, but I mean it." Smith had to consider the fate of his eleven-man crew; if, in his opinion, he risked losing them in an effort to save one aviator, he had the authority to turn back and leave Howdy Harrison adrift.

When Sahloff informed Proctor that Smith might have to turn away from Harrison, Proctor snapped, "Tell him, that if he turns back now, so help me God, I'll shoot him down." Sahloff wisely decided to keep this request to himself, and instead Sahloff told Smith that they should reach Miho in ten minutes. "All three of us were so Goddam scared we didn't know our names. If we'd known how scared the others were, we'd all have turned back."[33]

IN THE SEA of Japan, an uneasy Harrison wondered why the Dumbo had failed to arrive. He was certain that the Dumbo would have landed and picked him up by now, but nothing had come over the horizon. If he were not rescued soon, *Yorktown* and the rest of the task force would pull away for the night, leaving him to the whims of the sea, weather, and Japanese. "If that had happened," Harrison said, "I'd've started paddling. I don't know where I could've gone—China, Korea or Siberia—but that didn't matter. The point was to get away from Japan."

To avoid drifting too far from his original position, the location to which any rescue effort would go, he dragged his parachute in the water and paddled against the tides. "I was glad to have something to keep me busy," he says. "I didn't want too much time just to think."

Harrison's mind drifted to his wife, his two-year-old son, and a six-month-old daughter whom, except for photographs, he had never seen. He thought of his exploits in high school football games, fishing trips with his family and friends, and anything else to keep his mind off his predicament. "I was really all right," he said, "except for that silence. Once, when I couldn't stand it any longer, I sang 'God Bless America' as loud as I could. I'm a terrible singer, but it seemed like a fine idea at the time."[34]

HARRISON'S RESCUERS FACED their own problems. With the moments ticking away and his fuel supply dipping lower, Smith developed an attack of vertigo. Losing a sense of balance can affect any pilot, veteran or neophyte, especially when he has flown into thick overcast. Proctor and Sahloff guessed what was happening when first one and then the other of the Dumbo's mammoth wings suddenly dipped. Sahloff alerted Smith to the issue, and to keep him on course suggested that whenever Smith's wing dropped, either he or Proctor would dip their wing as a signal.

Smith's faulty engine continued to backfire. When he asked Sahloff if he feared they had overshot Miho, Sahloff assured him they should sight their destination any minute. The aviator then told Proctor, "We've got to do something to keep this guy from turning back. Any ideas?"

Proctor took out his plotting board and pencil. As Smith in his Dumbo watched through the haze, Proctor made a show of figuring out calculations with his compass and charts, nodded, looked at Smith, and gave him a thumbs-up to signal all was fine. Proctor had actually done nothing but doodle, and admitted "I was so nervous I couldn't have added two and two," but the ruse worked.[35]

Sahloff had another trick up his sleeve. The next time he saw Smith looking in his direction, he smiled and pulled out one of those big cigars that had become Sahloff's trademark. With a free hand he stuck the cigar in his mouth, lit a match, and puffed away as if he had no care in the world. "Later," according to Father Moody, "Dumbo [Smith] acknowledged that this bravado banished his doubts."[36]

Worried that they had indeed overshot Miho and were now flying over the open sea, Proctor suggested to Sahloff that they continue on course for another fifteen minutes before turning back. The decision became moot a few moments later when the aircraft burst from the overcast into clear skies. "When we broke out of the overcast," said Proctor, "Yonato [Miho] airfield was directly below and flak was bursting close around us." As Father Moody described it, after more than two hours flying in the thick cloud cover, "with nothing but dead reckoning and the grace of God, they came out of the 200 mile black-out right over the Miho airfield, which was the precise point they sought."[37]

Sahloff and Proctor could weave to avoid the Japanese shell bursts, which came from guns so close that one newspaper account in Sahloff's New York home town described the pair as maneuvering "within 'BB range' of a Jap emplacement," but Smith could only maintain a straight, slow course as he flew into the heavy flak.[38] Sahloff and Proctor were surprised that not only could they see Howdy floating in his raft, but a second downed aviator several miles north of Harrison. Ensign John H. Moore, a Corsair pilot from the *Shangri-La,* also had to ditch shortly before the rescue group arrived. Smith now faced a second taxi run over the water to pick up Moore, burning up its few extra gallons of gasoline.

As Proctor and the accompanying fighters led Smith down for his landing, Sahloff zoomed over Harrison to let him know he would soon be picked up and dropped a smoke light to mark Howdy's position for the Dumbo. Smith safely landed, taxied over to Harrison, and approached close enough for the Dumbo crew to toss a lifeline and life ring to the pilot. Realizing he flew a faulty plane, Smith opted against cutting the troublesome engine to preclude the chance that he might not be able to take off, but in doing so he complicated the crew's job in pulling Harrison aboard. "They yanked me over the waves like an aquaplane," said Harrison.[39] The crew struggled to lift Howdy into the Mariner, but after a few moments Harrison, wet, tired, but grateful, flopped into the plane. Once he regained his bearings, one by one Harrison gave each crew member, including Smith, a big hug.

With Howdy safely aboard the Dumbo, Proctor radioed, "If you just taxi over here, you can pick up this other guy." Wet from Harrison's hug, Smith taxied his Dumbo near Moore, "almost drowning the poor guy before bringing him aboard."[40] After forty-five minutes on the water, using precious fuel with each minute but bearing two grateful pilots in the hold, Smith lifted off, now facing a second trip through the fog across Japan and another water landing once he reached the task force. The outlook brightened once Smith broke out of a front east of Shikoku. Now in the clear and away from Japanese antiaircraft fire, he informed a rescue submarine that he thought he could make it to the carrier.

In the waters east of Japan, *Yorktown* and the task force circled and waited for the Dumbo's appearance. The ships had been scheduled to retire after the day's last strike, but Halsey delayed their departure in hopes that Sahloff and Proctor would shepherd the Dumbo in before dark. Hundreds of officers and men aboard *Yorktown* crowded the flight deck and catwalks, squinting into the sunset for any sign of the planes. Finally, Sahloff, Proctor, and the other escorts appeared. Dangerously low on fuel, they had been ordered to leave the slower Dumbo and return to their carriers at normal speed.

After the fighters landed, the tension mounted as men scanned the sky for the Dumbo. Rougher seas, whose waves would only exacerbate Smith's landing, heightened their nervousness. Finally, *Yorktown*'s crew cheered when they spotted the Dumbo lumbering in toward the carrier.

Smith's first attempt to land petrified Howdy Harrison. Smith brought the Dumbo in slow, barely above the ten-to-fifteen-foot-high swells and white caps kicked up by the twenty-knot wind. "We hit hard, bounced in the air, hit again and we must have been fifty feet in the air," said Hellman. Officers and sailors aboard *Yorktown* hushed, especially when a large swell rolled toward the Dumbo and pounded tons of water against the plane's hull. Smith gunned the engine and hoped he had enough power to lift up for another try. "For a moment there," Harrison said, "I wished I was back in the raft."[41]

Halsey's flagship, the battleship *Missouri,* veered out of position to create a wake in which Smith could better land his Mariner. Smith, now only fifty feet above the surface, approached the smoother water fashioned by the *Missouri*, hit the surface and bounced twenty-five feet, rose slightly once again, and hit and bounced a second time before skimming along the surface to a successful stop. "When the PBM made a beautiful landing, a cheer went up from the carrier," wrote Father Moody.[42]

The destroyer USS *Wren* (DD-568) moved alongside to remove the pilots and crew. The ship took Harrison, Moore, and Smith to *Yorktown*, where the three boarded the carrier to give a report to Admiral Radford and receive congratulations on the successful rescue.

Air crews would normally have made an effort to save the Dumbo, now floating on the surface, but with sunset fast approaching, and with Halsey hesitating to remain close to Japan's coast any longer than necessary, the *Wren* sank the Dumbo with a few well-placed shots. The Dumbo was lost, but the Air Group had its pilot back. "What the hell?" Proctor said to Sahloff. "We got Howdy back, and that was the only thing that mattered."[43]

It mattered to Smith, who had now lost his second plane. During a June 29 rescue of an Army flier, Smith had knocked off a wing float upon landing, causing the plane to sink. Happy to be safe from this second incident, Smith nonetheless mused about his future in the military. "It's the second plane I've lost in a little more than a month," he said. "I hope the Navy doesn't take it out of my pay."[44]

Newspaper accounts of the dramatic rescue thrilled home front readers. "Airmen from 'Fighting Lady' Take 1,000 to 1 Chance, Span Japan in Solid Fog to Save Pal," read a headline in the *Plainfield Courier-News* in New Jersey. The *Los Angeles Times* related that strafing planes held off the Japanese while a Dumbo retrieved two aviators "from the Japan Sea practically under the nose of the enemy and got them safely back aboard their 3rd Fleet carrier yesterday," and an article by noted correspondent Richard W. Johnston praised Smith: "A gull-winged Martin Mariner air-sea rescue plane—nearly out of gas and with one engine sputtering—flew across Honshu island to pull two carrier pilots out of the Sea of Japan yesterday."[45]

Lieutenant (jg) Sahloff's hometown newspaper heralded the area's most recent hero. "Lt. (jg) Joseph G. Sahloff, son of Mr. and Mrs. J. F.

Sahloff of Selkirk, recently took part in the rescue of one of his buddies who was forced down in the Japan Sea," began the account. When Sahloff and Proctor landed on their carrier, they convinced their superiors that they be allowed to immediately return to the scene. They hopped back into fighters, and "flew their Hellcats back across Japan leading the rescue plane to the scene of the crash. This was the first rescue ever made from the Japan Sea which has always been boasted by the Nips as their 'private sea.'"[46]

FATHER MOODY TYPIFIED the reaction aboard *Yorktown* to the incredible rescue of their downed Air Group aviator. Some had already begun grumbling that Admiral Halsey was more interested in his reputation than in the welfare of his pilots, but this operation momentarily stifled those outbursts. "We learned a great deal that day," wrote the chaplain. "We found out once more to what extent the Navy would go to save one of its pilots. And we had a glimpse of what game men will do to save a friend."[47]

Smith's piloting skill and bravery, combined with Sahloff and Proctor's courageous escorting, brought Howdy back to the carrier in one piece. Because Smith persisted, risking himself and his eleven crew members, Hobbs's friend and the man for whom he flew wing, Howdy Harrison, was retrieved from a situation that otherwise would have meant, at best, a stint in a Japanese prisoner of war camp, and at worst, death and never again seeing that home and family to whom he so longed to return.

When they learned of their son's rescue, Howdy Harrison's parents wrote a letter to Smith and his crew expressing their gratefulness for the feat. "The annals of this war are full of the accounts of deeds of courageous men," the parents wrote. "But the one that will stand out in our memories was the rescue of our son, Lt. Howard Harrison out of the sea on July 25. And, so we wish to convey to you, the pilots and crew of the rescue plane our deep and heartfelt gratitude.

"We know that you risked your own lives that he might live," the couple continued. "'Greater love hath no man.' We would like to grab each of you by the hand and thank you personally. May God bless you all and richly reward you for your skill and courage in performing this gallant deed." They ended the letter, "Yours Sincerely, Mr. and Mrs. M. H. Harrison, Father and Mother of Lt. Harrison VF 88."[48]

THE MONTH OF July had been costly for Air Group 88. Twelve pilots or aircrewmen had been killed during the eight strikes, and no one knew how much longer this bloody conflict would continue. A few men predicted they would be home by Christmas, but most believed that the strife would persist into 1946 or 1947. The newcomers to war, like Hobbs and Mandeberg, had arrived in the Pacific from training camp, eager to enter the fray. Their veteran comrades, however, knew that the rigors and realities of combat would grind away at that enthusiasm. It was only a matter of when and how soon.

August would provide answers.

CHAPTER 10

"Fighting a War That Had Already Been Won"
August 1–14, 1945

THE FIRST WEEK of August was not at all what everyone in the Air Group expected. Instead of more missions, the Third Fleet pulled farther from the Japanese coast. Halsey had done this on a regular basis to refuel and replenish his ships, but whereas those breaks typically lasted a day or two, this lull in the fighting occupied an entire week. After resupplying the fleet, Halsey maintained his position rather than returning closer to Japan. His staff issued the explanation that Halsey wanted to avoid a typhoon forming 400 miles to the northwest—a plausible reason as the admiral had already endured biting criticism for steaming his fleet into two previous typhoons—but added that he planned to use the time to conduct group tactics, an odd statement considering that the fleet had been operating for much of July as a unit. Some men in the task group asked why the normally aggressive Admiral Halsey was "steering clear of the enemy homeland—playing games again—when every precious moment counted?" Even Admiral Radford was perplexed. "Something more than a typhoon seemed to be delaying our operations, but in *Yorktown* we did not know what it could be."[1]

Halsey knew what it could be. On July 22, in the middle of the Kure Naval Base operations, Rear Admiral William R. Purnell arrived with the assistant secretary of the Navy. Behind closed doors Purnell, the Navy liaison on the Military Policy Committee for the Manhattan Project, the code name for the program to develop the atomic bomb,

informed the admiral of the top-secret project, and told him that when
so ordered by Admiral Nimitz, Halsey was to keep his distance from the
Japanese coast until matters in the area cleared. When those orders arrived after the July 30 strike against the Tokyo region, Halsey pulled his
ships back and covered the move by stating that he needed to replenish
his fleet and conduct group tactics.

In an August 1 article that appeared in the *Kokomo Tribune,* Rear
Admiral William P. Blandy, commander of the Pacific's cruisers and
destroyers, provided examples of the varying emotions—encouraged by
the war's progress, yet concerned because of the indeterminate duration of the war—with which Hattie Hobbs and Sonya Levien struggled in the first days of August. Blandy said that while the Japanese
knew they faced certain defeat, no one should expect a quick end to the
fighting. "They hope to beat down our resistance and our will to win.
The current idea that the end of the war is just around the corner is
bad business." The next day's headline, "Sheets of Fire Blanket Japan,"
reinforced the notion that Billy and Eugene remained in the center of
fury and flames.[2]

National publications added fuel to the fire. *Life* magazine's predic-
tion in its July 16 issue of 1 million casualties suffered by American
forces in an invasion of the Home Islands did nothing to calm either
woman's fears. Edgar L. Jones wrote in the *Atlantic Monthly* that the
war in Europe, the conflict to which Hattie had hoped her son would be
sent instead of to the Pacific, was civil compared to the barbaric combat
occurring on the other side of the world. The Pacific War, he wrote,
was a war between two peoples, "a war of extermination between the
Americans and Japanese. The showdown battle is not being fought for
political, economic, or social theories, but for survival."[3]

"We haven't heard from you for quite a spell but I suppose all is as
well as can be expected," wrote Billy's sister, Joyce, on August 1. "I do
worry about you though and we all think about you so much." Joyce
mentioned two of Billy's friends, Danny Bock and Richard Rutan, who
had returned from the European fighting, and their appearance did little
to diminish Joyce's fears for her brother. "I've only seen Danny Bock
once since he has been home. He doesn't look so well either, thin and

nervous. Richard Rutan also is home now. He is in the Navy you re-member. He also is thin and much older looking. But I guess after so much action almost all fellows begin to show wear and tear."[4]

The next day Joyce mailed a birthday card to Billy, who would cele-brate his twenty-third birthday in thirteen days. That same August 15 one year ago, Billy had joined Air Group 88, and since then he had traveled to distant locales and experienced terrifying events that Joyce assumed he would keep to himself after the war. Where might this Au-gust 15 find her brother? On the inside of the card, she wrote, "Bill Dear, As I write this little message, I pray God is keeping you safe from all harm and will bring you back here to all of us who love you so much. Happy Birthday!"[5]

Zelda Mandeberg in Detroit was more optimistic. In an August 2 letter to Sonya, she avoided any mention of the hazards her son must be facing, and instead concentrated on her hopes: "Oh, darling, I feel that every day brings us closer to victory and Eugene's return."[6]

"MAYBE I'LL BE HOME SOON"

At least Hattie and Zelda could take encouragement from the peace ru-mors that appeared with more frequency in the newspapers. "From both Washington and London there has come in recent days an increasing flood of unsubstantiated rumors about an imminent Japanese surrender and even actual peace proposals," stated a July article in the *New York Times*.[7] Although top government officials like Joseph Grew, former U.S. ambassador to Japan, dismissed them, they sustained both mothers and helped them believe that they would once more see their sons.

The stories contained much truth, as both peace and war factions in the Japanese government had been making their moves to direct the future of their nation. Admiral Kantaro Suzuki had risen to power after the April 1945 American invasion of Okinawa, but despite being in the military, he urged peace and led an effort to gain Soviet premier Joseph Stalin's aid in mediating an end to the war. When that failed, and under intense pressure from militarists, on June 8 Suzuki passed a resolution saying that Japan would fight to the end. Alarmed by this statement,

Emperor Hirohito encouraged the military and Suzuki to increase their efforts to find a peaceful way out of the war.

Led by President Truman and British prime minister Winston Churchill, the Allies tried to prod the peace process along with the July 26 Potsdam Proclamation. From a location southwest of Berlin, the leaders said that the military power that converged on the Home Islands handily surpassed the coalition amassed to defeat Hitler, and if Japan did not agree to an unconditional surrender, their complete destruction was inevitable. Truman and Churchill would permit non-military industries and some form of non-military government to remain, but they remained silent about Hirohito's future. Accept the terms or perish was the thrust of their message.

The Japanese quickly rebuffed the Potsdam Proclamation. Foreign Minister Shigenori Togo said that as long as Truman demanded unconditional surrender, "the whole country, as one man, will pit itself against him in accordance with the imperial will," and former foreign minister Mamoru Shigemitsu warned that further bombing would strengthen Japan's resolve. "If the emperor ordained it," he said, "they [the Japanese people] would leap into the flames."[8]

The swift rebuttal mirrored the outlook of most Japanese civilians. "The nation was being torn asunder, our cities lay prostrate and flaming as if trampled by a gigantic foot," wrote Japan's top aviator, Saburo Sakai. "There was no doubt in anyone's mind that the end was near, that soon the fighting would be transferred to our soil. There was no possibility of surrender. We would fight to the last man."[9]

Reaction in the United States matched, if not surpassed, Japan's belligerence. *New York Times* editorials asserted that as Japan had now rejected the terms, "the war in the Pacific must and will go forward to a decision on the field of battle" and any thoughts of a shortened war had to be dismissed. "The contemptuous Japanese rejection of the well-meant Allied ultimatum has made it plain that the war in the Far East, as in Europe, will have to be fought to the end, and that the bitter cup of redeployment and final assault on the Japanese islands will not be spared us." The United States had no choice but to proceed with the "full application of our military power until the complete destruction of the Japanese armed forces and the utter devastation of Japan."[10]

Even though Japan's ability to wage war was steadily collapsing before the American military juggernaut storming toward their shores, the two nations appeared trapped in hardline stances that would permit neither to yield unless forced to by a cataclysmic event. The Japanese rejection convinced Truman and Churchill that Japan had to be totally defeated.

Truman delivered his answer in August's first week. On August 6 Colonel Paul W. Tibbets of the 509th Composite Group of the Army Air Forces piloted the *Enola Gay* over the Japanese city of Hiroshima, which some Air Group 88 aviators had flown near during the Kure strikes, and dropped the world's first atomic bomb, instantly killing an estimated 100,000 civilians. "An atomic bomb, hailed as the most terrible destructive force in history and as the greatest achievement of organized science, has been loosed upon Japan," said an Associated Press article printed in the August 6 edition of Hattie's newspaper, the *Kokomo Tribune*.[11]

In a statement appearing in every newspaper across the land, President Truman warned the Japanese that if they failed to surrender, further destruction lay ahead. "We are now prepared to obliterate more rapidly and completely every productive enterprise the Japanese have above ground in any city. We shall destroy their docks, their factories and their communications. Let there be no mistake: we shall completely destroy Japan's power to make war." He added, "It was to spare the Japanese people from utter destruction that the ultimatum of July 26 was issued at Potsdam. Their leaders promptly rejected that ultimatum. If they do not now accept our terms they may expect a rain of ruin from the air, the like of which has never been seen on this earth."[12]

Admiral Suzuki thought the destruction of Hiroshima would move even diehard militarists toward peace. Emperor Hirohito, upon hearing of Hiroshima, said to his confidant, Marquis Kido, "Under these circumstances, we must bow to the inevitable. No matter what happens to my personal safety, we must put an end to this war as speedily as possible, so that this tragedy will not be repeated."

While Japanese leaders debated whether to surrender, three days later a second atomic bomb ravaged Nagasaki, this time killing 35,000 people. Truman explained that more would follow, and that he had given the order to use the atomic bomb to save lives and to gain vengeance for what the Japanese had done in the Pacific. "We have used it against those who attacked us without warning at Pearl Harbor, against those who have starved and beaten and executed American prisoners of war, against those who have abandoned all pretense of obeying international laws of warfare. We have used it in order to shorten the agony of war, in order to save the lives of thousands and thousands of young Americans."[13]

Suzuki called an emergency meeting to discuss accepting Truman's terms, but the militarists refused to budge. Deadlocked, Suzuki appealed to the emperor, who agreed to call a conference of the cabinets and the Supreme War Leadership Council. When that group failed to arrive at a solution, Suzuki asked Hirohito for guidance. The emperor replied that to continue the war only meant "prolongation of bloodshed and cruelty" and that "I cannot bear to see my innocent people struggle any longer." He added that although surrendering would be difficult, "the time has come when we must endure the unendurable."[14]

News of the bombs slowly filtered to Air Group 88. The day after the destruction of Hiroshima, Admiral McCain informed Admiral Radford what had occurred twenty-four hours earlier. Radford had known so little about the new weapon that McCain had to explain the word "atomic" to him. That same evening, after most of the crew had finished their dinner, the *Yorktown* crew and Air Group 88 learned from a stateside radio broadcast that a single bomb dropped from a solitary aircraft had destroyed a major city. "All hands very much thrilled about it," wrote Ralph Morlan. "It will shorten the war tremendously."[15]

The end to a long-running war that had one day earlier appeared distant now stood at their doorstep. The hopes of going home that everyone harbored during the months and years of combat suddenly flowered into reality. Thoughts of wives and children, parents and siblings overshadowed operational plans.

Those hopes heightened when Father Moody announced that the Soviet Union had entered the war against Japan and had hurled multiple divisions against the Japanese army in Manchuria. With the military might of the Soviet Union joining the Allies, combined with the devastation of the atomic bombs, every member of Air Group 88 was convinced that the war would end within days and that they would never again have to fly into those lethal antiaircraft guns that protected Kure, Tokyo-area airfields, and other locations.

According to the Combat Summary compiled by Commander Searcy, Air Group 88 pilots believed the atomic bomb was so terrifying "that even the tenaciously stubborn Jap could ill afford to carry on a war which could bring nothing but total destruction to his homeland and his race." Hobbs and others gathered around radios to keep track of the fast-moving developments, and when the Soviet Union's entry quickly ensued, "Events followed one another with dizzy speed and we eagerly awaited every news report our radios brought us for some indication of Japan's reaction to these new developments."[16]

That night, Billy Hobbs shared his enthusiasm with his parents that the war might soon end. The brevity of his letter did not surprise them, but the emotions expressed did. "Thank God," Hobbs wrote, "maybe there will be a lot of lives saved and maybe I'll be home soon."[17]

In New York, Sonya's hopes spiked with the welcome news from the Pacific. The *New York Times* reported about the "whispered and spoken prayer that the second and most terrible blood-bath in our generation might indeed be at an end," and mentioned of city residents "that the war would be over in a day, in several days, in a week, they [New Yorkers] did not for a moment doubt."[18]

Sonya even allowed herself to think of an event that both she and Eugene had deferred—their wedding. She shared those thoughts with Zelda, who wrote back that she was equally as pleased, if somewhat cautious. "We are going to talk about the wedding," Zelda wrote Sonya after learning of Hiroshima. "Of course, dear, it's kinda hard to make definite plans not knowing exactly when Eugene will be home." However, "just talking about it makes me very happy."[19]

Eugene's brother, Mitchell, still posted in Europe with the Army's occupation forces, injected a word of caution. He had yet to meet Sonya, but "from all the letters received I take it the family in general likes you not a little." He told her to be elated over the war news, but "there is still a war going on in which men are dying. Yesterday I was overseas three years and I am damned tired of being over here, and just tired in general and there isn't a chance in hell of my getting back nor out in the imme-diate foreseeable future. I am hardly alone in this. The business goes on and on, to the point of exasperation."[20]

Halsey harbored no such thoughts. He told *Time* magazine, "If the Nips do not know they are a doomed nation, then they are stupider than I think they are."[21] Until the enemy yielded, he planned to utilize his for-midable conglomeration of ships and aircraft without mercy. He would continue to order his airmen into Tokyo's antiaircraft fire to destroy every Japanese ship, railroad yard, and industry.

THE ATOMIC BOMBS strengthened the Japanese peace faction, but each day that the Japanese government dragged its heels in arranging peace was another day Air Group 88 pilots faced the prospect of flying into enemy flak. On August 10 Japan reached out to Switzerland and Sweden to convey to the United States that Japan was prepared to talk peace. The news delighted Truman, but the president insisted that until Japan accepted every condition of the Potsdam Proclamation, including unconditional surrender, the attacks off Japan would continue. Mat-ters discussed at the highest levels—in distant Washington, in nearby Tokyo, and aboard Halsey's battleship, *Missouri*, floating within sight of *Yorktown*—now decided whether the Air Group 88 fliers would con-tinue their missions or make plans to go home.

Four days later—four days in which *Yorktown*'s airmen twice lifted off to strike Japanese installations, in the process losing two aviators to Japanese fire, Lieutenant (jg) William B. Tuohima on August 10 and Lieutenant Wilson L. Dozier on August 13—Emperor Hirohito in-formed his leaders that he wanted no more delays. "I appreciate how difficult it will be for the officers and men of the army and navy to sur-render their arms to the enemy and to see their homeland occupied," he said as tears welled. It needed to occur, though, as "I cannot endure the thought of letting my people suffer any longer."[22]

Even the emperor's express wishes did not stifle all opposition from the militarists. Fifteen army and navy officers in the war ministry, who intended to assassinate anyone who counseled peace, isolate Hirohito, and convince him to continue the war, broke into the imperial palace on August 14, killed some officials, and looked for discs containing Hirohito's message of surrender, scheduled to be delivered the next day. The attempt failed, but it illustrated the difficulty of forcing Japan to the peace table. Tokyo now teetered on the brink of peace, and Halsey intended that his aviators would deliver the final nudge toward surrender.

EMOTIONS ABOARD *YORKTOWN* fluctuated as wildly as did the prospects for peace. Each rumor that Japan was about to surrender buoyed hopes for a speedy conclusion to the fighting, while further delays meant one more day risking their lives to strike at the heart of the empire. Celebrations erupted the evening of August 10 when Captain Boone's voice sounded over the loudspeaker. "This is the Captain speaking. Word has just been received that the Japs have notified the Swiss government that they are ready to agree to terms of unconditional surrender as discussed at the Potsdam Conference, provided they be allowed to keep Hirohito as emperor."[23]

"The whole ship went up in a roar," wrote Ralph Morlan. The torpedo squadron history said that "everyone on the ship was practically delirious with joy. Each shouted and smacked his mate on the back and shook hands with him. Parties were started in staterooms, ready rooms, anywhere handy. One forehanded [*sic*] officer walked the passageways in a civilian suit. No one, of course, believed such an offer could be refused."[24]

The premature celebrations ended the next morning, when they learned that the Japanese had not yet accepted Truman's terms. "The war was still on, and plans were being drawn up for further strikes," said the torpedo squadron history. "There followed, for the next few days, as unsettling a period as many of us have ever experienced." For a glorious few hours, Sahloff, Hansen, and everyone else in Air Group 88 believed that their combat had ended, "but alas, not so," wrote Lieutenant Commander Huddleston. "The very next morning the war was on again."[25]

Each day passed in torturously slow fashion. Peace rumors appeared, only to be countered by reports of impending sweeps and strikes. Men in the Air Group wondered how much longer the Japanese could hold on, and how many more strikes Halsey would order. Everyone within Air Group 88 and aboard the other ships of the task group knew that the war was over. Would Japanese and American politicians soon arrive at the same conclusion, or would more men have to die before they reached that point? Would they be asked to continue flying, and dying, for what was most certainly a decided outcome? "Then followed five days of nerve-racking, anxious waiting," wrote Commander Searcy of that difficult time.[26]

One *Yorktown* man called it "a tense, questioning, expectant watch." When orders arrived on the morning of August 11 that Halsey planned additional missions, the ship's history of the aircraft carrier with whom Howdy Harrison and Air Group 88 had most often flown into battle, the *Shangri-La*, candidly expressed the mood, not only for that carrier, but for every ship in Halsey's task force by stating that "the agonizing letdown set in. Forty days at sea had left them in no mood to be taunted by unconfirmed reports or false rumors. When it came to joking about peace, they had no sense of humor. Constant uncertainty of the future and the aggravating fatigue of extended operations against the enemy had left them with raw nerves and quick tempers." The history added, "They knew too that the longer it took to bring the negotiations to a favorable conclusion the longer they would be fighting a war that had already been won."[27] Tensions became so roiled that *Shangri-La* initiated a "Be Kind to One Another Week" to help calm the crew.

Rumors continued to circulate about *Yorktown* on August 12, especially when a call went out asking for volunteers to form naval brigades to occupy Tokyo. Sailors conducted close order drills on *Yorktown*'s flight deck, a space normally reserved for Air Group 88 combat operations, and sailors chatted about going home. Men griped that although the war in Europe had ended three months earlier, the United States had still not diverted those military forces to the Pacific to help end this conflict. "Meanwhile, we are preparing to strike tomorrow if the Japs don't accept our final unconditional surrender offer," said Gunner's Mate 1/c Edward N. Wallace. "We are still hopeful of getting word soon. Otherwise we will blow up their biggest power station tomorrow." Aviation Ordnanceman 3/c Ralph Morlan could have spoken for every member of Air Group 88 when he recorded in his diary on August 12, "We are supposed to strike tomorrow if nothing is settled. I surely hope and pray it is. I never want to fly again, at least in a military aircraft."

Their dismay over the lack of progress toward peace appeared in diaries. "The men are pretty disappointed," wrote Ed Wallace. "But until we get some word about the Japs surrendering, we will keep on fighting, and it promises to be very rugged." On August 14, with rumors that war's end was imminent, Radarman 1/c Edward A. Brand added, "All hands still waiting on Japan. This is terrible; I wish Japan would make up their minds."[28]

Cables shot across the Pacific from Washington, D.C., and Admiral Halsey kept his radioman busy with a torrent of messages to and from Admiral Nimitz and other top naval officials. "The tension mounted as peace rumors reached a new high," said the torpedo squadron history. "However, no slackening in attack pace was noticed. Halsey's 'We strike tomorrow,' flashed across the teletype screen, left no doubt as to our plans."[29]

HALSEY HARBORED NO doubts. He would keep applying the military pressure on the enemy until the political leaders yielded. With diplomatic negotiations in flux, he asked his chief of staff, "Have we got enough fuel to turn around and hit the bastards once more before they quit?" As his report of Third Fleet operations stated, "the Commander Third Fleet saw no reason why the enemy should be spared if he was behaving in a dilatory manner but still in a belligerent status."[30]

"I WISH WE WOULD GET THE HELL OUT OF HERE"

For those reasons, despite the startling employment of the atomic bomb, Air Group 88 aviators continued to fly into danger. On August 9, 10, and 13 they struck enemy bombers in northern Honshu that had reportedly gathered to transport 2,000 suicide troops and crash land in the Marianas; mounted sweeps and strikes against airfields in central Honshu and the region south of Tokyo; and smashed the expansive Tokyo Shibaura electronics plant, supposedly protected by more than 500 antiaircraft guns.

With each mission, Air Group 88 aviators wondered what their small bombs could possibly do to unnerve a nation reeling from the double atomic blasts. They obeyed their orders, but whereas in mid-July they lifted off the *Yorktown* eager for battle, they now took flight believing they embarked on unnecessary missions. The war was certainly over; the major combatants only needed to declare it so. Until their silence ended, however, the pilots risked their lives against antiaircraft guns that guarded targets that were shells of what they had once been.

They had reason to be concerned over being shot down with war's end so tantalizingly close. A low ceiling on August 10 forced aviators to drop into what "proved to be a flak trap." The bomber fighter squadron report claimed, "Next to the Yokosuka area, Kisarizu A/F [*sic,* Kisarazu Airfield] is one of the most heavily defended in the Tokyo area. It was not surprising therefore that heavy flak came up in considerable quantity as the perimeter of Kisarizu was attained." Automatic weapons fire was "put up in layers every 500 feet," and antiaircraft guns followed the planes as they dove and as they retired. As far as Sahloff, Proctor, and Hansen, three pilots who conducted that day's sweep, were concerned, Niigata Airfield near Tokyo also "seemed to have a heavier concentration than observed at Yokosuka naval base."[31]

Other events underscored the risks. During that August 10 sweep against Kisarazu Airfield across from Yokosuka, Lieutenant (jg) Verlyn H. Branham in his Corsair radioed his division leader, Lieutenant Harold F. Greene, that he would have to ditch because he was losing oil pressure from a hit to his plane. After watching Branham make a safe landing two miles from shore, Greene contacted the submarine USS *Perch* (SS-313), on rescue station, which turned toward the coordinates supplied by Greene.

With his Corsair sinking, Branham hastily left the plane, but was unable to inflate his raft. Seeing the predicament from above, Greene pulled out his raft, balanced it on the port rim of the cockpit with the hood fully open, slowed to almost a stall, and shoved out the raft to a waiting Branham. Greene continued flying above the position until Branham signaled by mirror that he had inflated and entered the raft, at which Greene dropped a message telling Branham that a rescue submarine was already underway and that he should row away from the beach.

Greene kept station above Branham until he spotted *Perch* twelve miles out. Greene radioed the submarine Branham's precise location, dipped his wings to alert Branham that help was at hand, and left for the carrier. *Perch* picked up Branham, and one hour later rescued a second Corsair aviator from VBF-88, Lieutenant Leo Horacek Jr.

In a raid that same day against Niigata Harbor, a shell ripped a hole in Ted Hansen's left wing. He turned back toward the carrier, often flying as low as fifty feet above the water, but when he approached *Yorktown,* he was unable to lower his landing wheels into proper position because his Hellcat had lost much of its hydraulics and part of its electrical system. Hansen radioed the carrier to clear the deck for a possible crash landing. After the landing signal officer waved Hansen off in his first two attempts Hansen, fearing he would run out of fuel, alerted the carrier, "Ready or not, here I come."[32] As he drew closer to *Yorktown,* Hansen finally heard the Hellcat's wheels click into position moments before the plane's tail hook grabbed the wires stretched across the deck, but the momentum jarred Hansen's rockets loose from under the wings. Fortunately, they bounced twice and went over the side into the ocean instead of careening into part of the carrier. When mechanics later checked Hansen's plane, they discovered that he had only enough fuel remaining to take Hansen the length of the carrier.

Lieutenant (jg) Bernard Hamilton of VBF-88 avoided injury during the same attack. "We were on one fighter sweep of thirty-two planes to hit Kisarizu and Yokosuka, both in Tokyo Harbor, one on the left and the other on the right," said Hamilton. "There was a lot of antiaircraft fire there, and I picked out my target and got so focused on it that I pulled out the wrong way and was heading toward Tokyo! I went low, turned back, and got out." Running out of fuel, "we then started back, conserving fuel by flying low." When Hamilton and two other Corsairs sighted the *Yorktown,* "we had very, very little gas when we landed," he said. "I was anxious I might have to ditch as I was flying back."[33] Branham, Horacek, Hansen, and Hamilton safely returned to the *Yorktown,* grateful that in what had to be the final few days of the war they had barely avoided serious injuries, capture, or death.

Three days later the Air Group attacked what one squadron report called "the toughest target yet assigned—the Tokyo Shibaura Electric Company #2 in south Tokyo." The report added, "The area fairly bristled with antiaircraft defenses. It is small wonder pilots, having already received several reports of imminent cessation of hostilities, were puzzled at the assignment, but to their credit they intended to carry out the job with the same determination and pride in accomplishment that had become such an integral characteristic of their attacks." Shocked *Yorktown* aviators asked each other why, so close to the termination of hostilities, this attack against such a stoutly defended location—one almost certain to produce casualties—was required. In the hours before the strike, they waited and hoped that a message arrived announcing the war's end, but when none came, they stepped into their aircraft to attack Shibaura, which pilots from previous encounters had labeled "Old Bloody."[34]

Each new rumor brought heightened expectations for an end to the conflict, only to have those hopes shattered by yet another mission deep into Japan. As the rumors about peace moves mounted, the aviators of every air group more insistently questioned the need for that August 13 mission. "This strike was ordered after the Byrnes note [a communication to the Japanese that Hirohito would remain in office, but under the control of the Allied Supreme Commander] had been dispatched to Japan and on what appeared to be possibly the last day of the war," stated an action report of the *Shangri-La*'s torpedo squadron of the August 13 attack against the Shibaura electronics plant. "The target was in what is believed to be the most heavily defended area of the empire—the western shore of Tokyo Bay."[35] In ready rooms across the task group, heated statements and bewilderment at the continued missions nudged aside the usual ready room chatter.

"As the diplomats discussed peace proposals and the whole world celebrated in anticipation of an early cessation of hostilities, the aircraft on this mission were launched on a strike against the Tokyo-Shibaura Electric Company, Plant No. 2," lamented the report of *Shangri-La*'s bomber squadron. "This plant located in the heart of the Kawasaki District of Tokyo had been at the top of the list of high priority strategic targets for attack by carrier based planes since the first of the year. In the intervening months with the task force operating within striking distance on a number of occasions not one strike had been launched against this target, and yet here at what appeared to be the eve of peace, the strike was ordered against this heavily defended strategic [underline theirs] target. Questions were raised in the pilots' minds but they manned their planes determined to perform their mission." The fliers had to mentally prepare themselves for a mission no one wanted. "We strike tomorrow also," Aviation Ordnanceman 3/c Ralph Morlan entered in his diary. "I wish we would get the hell out of here."[36]

During that August 13 attack, Lieutenant Wilson L. Dozier Jr. was shot down and killed. A football and baseball star at the College of William and Mary, in 1939 Dozier joined the Royal Canadian Air Force for eight months before returning to the United States to enter the Navy's aviation program. In the war's dying moments, Dozier, a family man who left behind a wife, eighteen-month-old daughter Patricia, and four-month-old daughter Susan, whom Dozier had never seen, perished before having the chance to see the three again.

The thirteen deaths that had occurred during training, and the twelve men lost in the July operations, had been easier to accept, for those were the risks of combat in what at the time looked to be a drawn-out war. But Tuohima's and Dozier's deaths, killed so near to what had to be the end to the fighting, were more difficult for the Air Group to digest. Men struggled to find answers to multiple questions: Were their deaths really necessary? Had their loss brought the war's end any closer, or prodded politicians in Washington or Tokyo to action? Was Halsey any likelier to cancel further missions? Did Halsey even know about Tuohima and Dozier, or was personal glory all he cared about?

HATTIE HOBBS AND Sonya Levien experienced their own tumultuous weeks back in the United States. In Kokomo, Hattie read of a proposed prayer service to be held in town when peace was formally announced, but without Billy at home, how could she celebrate? "The committee in charge feels there are those who wish to attend such a service to pray for their sons and daughters and thank God for His providence," mentioned the reporter covering the proposed ceremony, but Hattie preferred to give thanks only when her son walked through the door.[37]

Peace rumors filled the front pages one day, while Halsey's strikes occupied the same spot the next. It mattered little to those friends without soldiers or sailors in the Pacific whether peace arrived tomorrow or the next week, but each added day of combat posed a clear threat to the safety of Billy and Eugene. On August 13, while the Air Group struck the dangerous Tokyo electric plant, the *Kokomo Tribune* reported that top White House officials "stuck close to their desks or telephones" waiting for word that the Japanese had accepted President Truman's terms. "Hopeful at first, they became puzzled as the day wore on that the enemy should delay so long in accepting terms which Washington had been confident would be readily taken." Hattie became more frustrated as the hours passed without word of peace, and her fears escalated with the mention of additional air strikes. "The Allies tightened their stranglehold on Japan today while Tokyo struggled to decide whether to surrender now or continue a suicidal war," stated the article about Halsey maintaining his pressure on the Japanese. Instead of announcing peace overtures, the article added, "the fighting in the Pacific and Asia continues full scale."[38]

As if that were not enough for Hattie and Sonya, an August 13 Associated Press article provided further evidence that while much of the world celebrated peace, their son and fiancé continued to fight a war no one doubted was over: "Admiral Halsey's Third Fleet blasted the Yokohama docks and submarine pens in a resumption of the assault on Japan today and stood alert for one last, desperate aerial Banzai charge which the Tokyo radio implied already had begun."[39]

"A TRAGIC WASTE OF MEN IN A WAR ALREADY WON"

As August 15 neared, emotions continued to fluctuate for the aviators of Air Group 88. The war could not last much longer, but until they heard Halsey announce that peace had come, the fighting would continue. "News of Japan's surrender was expected hourly," Commander Searcy wrote in his report.[40] He, too, longed for a cessation of hostilities, but until it arrived, it was his duty to keep preparing the Air Group for war.

The daily news summary culled from radio dispatches and distributed aboard the *Yorktown* on August 14 did nothing to soothe anyone's nerves. The summary raised hopes by reporting that "up to this time, Tokyo radio has had nothing to say directly concerning allied surrender terms. However, the general tenor of broadcasts seems to indicate the Japanese are being prepared for some very bad news. Japanese newspaper editorials for the second day in a row, appeal for unity in this time, described by one editorialist as 'The worst national crisis in all history.'"

The summary quoted a front-page article in *Yomiuri Hochi Shimbun* that said each citizen faced "a national crisis of unprecedented magnitude." It added, "The present national crisis is such that we must know the worst has finally come to worst. We humble subjects of his Imperial Majesty the Emperor are literally filled with trepidation."

According to the report, however, in Washington, D.C., a mood of hopeful suspense reigned. "Since the United States State Department is handling surrender negotiations, all eyes today were turned on Washington." People throughout the country "spent today glued to their radio." Rumors abounded that reporters had been alerted to be ready at any moment to rush to the White House, and that General MacArthur and Admiral Nimitz had already boarded a Japanese battleship to discuss peace terms. "Rumors flew around like flying squirrels all day long," stated the *Yorktown* summary.

On a more pessimistic note, the summary explained that Washington officials had heard nothing yet from Japan, and that presidential secretary Charles G. Ross said "the war is still in progress." Even when Japan surrendered, according to the summary, it would still take eleven hours to transmit the news through diplomatic channels, meaning what was all too obvious to Hobbs and Sahloff—that the war would continue for almost half a day even after the enemy had asked for peace. "Jap silence built up suspense in a peace-hopeful world whose predominant interest was the answer to the question, 'is the end of the war at hand—or will Japan take more beating before she quits?'"

Only one part of the summary reflected the main concern for the pilots—that until official word arrived that the war had indeed ended, Air Group 88 would continue to send its aviators into battle. "Japan shook under new aerial assaults today," stated the summary, "and Allied fleets rode offshore primed to hit again with devastating power if Japan refuses to accept the stern terms of surrender." The summary quashed any hopes that an aviator might be spared further missions by adding, "Admiral Halsey declared his Third Fleet, now plowing the seas off the Japanese home islands, would keep on striking until Japan surrendered."[41]

Aboard *Shangri-La,* a carrier within sight of the *Yorktown,* Corsair pilot and Navy Cross recipient Lieutenant Richard W. DeMott, an aviator who had proven his valor during raids against Kure and other locations, had seen his fill of death. On August 14 he wrote, "Rumors and reports all day that Japan has broadcast and has accepted our peace treaty. We still have not accepted it or acknowledged so we don't know what the hell is going on. . . . I wish to hell we could find out if the Japs are surrendering before we go needlessly groping around over Japan again and lose more pilots needlessly. This routine is getting harder to take each time."[42]

Maurice Proctor, scheduled to fly into action the next day beside Hobbs and Mandeberg, wrote in his diary on August 14 that he preferred to avoid combat. "Aboard the *Yorktown.* If ever I prayed in my life, I am praying tonight that they will end this bloody war tonight . . . Chaplain Moody just came by and said no dice on the news so I guess we will strike."[43]

The plan called for a typical fighter sweep to hit Atsugi Airfield twenty miles southwest of Tokyo while the bomber and torpedo squadrons destroyed the Shibaura electronics plant near Tokyo. One Hellcat pilot aboard the *Ticonderoga* (CV-14), Lieutenant James W. Vernon, called these last missions "a tragic waste of men in a war already won." He added, "We could see no reason for continuing to risk our precious skins by striking more targets in Japan. But that sentiment did not coincide with those of the men who were running the war."[44]

Everyone aboard *Yorktown* had misgivings about the recent sweeps and strikes. No one wanted to push his luck, and as aviators they understood that each mission they participated in increased the odds that something tragic might happen to them. Mechanical failure while over the target, enemy antiaircraft fire, pilot error—any or all could result in the downing of their airplane and in their death. "We didn't know it as yet," Proctor wrote as August 15 dawned, "but this day, the anniversary of our squadron's forming, was to be the happiest day in 126,000,000 people's lives and one of the saddest in mine and the rest of the squadron's."[45]

CHAPTER 11

"Failed to Return with This Flight; Shot Down over Target"
August 15, 1945

O N THE EVE of the last day of the war, the *Yorktown* refueled and replenished her stores. Once that operation ended, Captain Boone ordered a course change to be in position should Halsey follow through with the planned air strikes against installations and shipping in and around the Tokyo area the following day.

That night, Howdy Harrison met with Lieutenant Robert F. Hall, who was scheduled to lead the twelve-plane flight the following morning. Even though the war was winding down and few aviators wanted to again risk Tokyo's guns, Lieutenant Cagle and Harrison had noticed that Hobbs needed one more strike to record the five required for promotion to lieutenant (jg). Although Harrison's team was not scheduled for that strike on August 15, Hobbs's twenty-third birthday, Cagle and Harrison seemed eager that the young aviator receive the boost in rank and pay. Howdy asked Hall if he might be willing to let Harrison take his team up so that Hobbs could gain that fifth strike, because with surrender due at any moment, this might be the final opportunity for Hobbs. Hall readily agreed.

Lieutenant Cagle and Howdy Harrison surprised Hobbs with the news that Harrison was taking his team, including Hobbs, into action the next day, in what had to be the fading moments of the war. Billy Hobbs faced a dilemma. He wanted the promotion, but was it worth the risks? Since he had no say in the matter anyway—orders were orders, after all—Hobbs once more prepared for battle. "We shouldn't need to strike again," Hobbs recorded in his diary. "But CAP [Cagle] says I need one more run to make Lieutenant."[1]

HARRISON AND HIS eleven Hellcat pilots awoke at 2:30 a.m., washed, and slipped on their khaki shirts and pants. Exchanging few words, they stepped to the hangar deck and down the ladder to the officers' wardroom, where they consumed the normal pre-combat breakfast of steak and eggs. After finishing their meal, each man returned to his cabin, donned his flight gear, and slipped his revolver into a condom to keep it dry should he have to set down in the water.

Now ready, the group walked to the hangar deck and meandered through a cluster of planes under repair to the ready room. Once inside, Harrison and an intelligence officer delivered the final preflight briefing. They explained that the twelve Hellcat pilots would conduct a sweep of Atsugi Airfield twenty miles southwest of Tokyo while the bombers and torpedo planes, carrying 2,000-pound bombs, hit the Shibaura electronics plant near Tokyo. They went over the expected weather, the opposition they would encounter, and in what order the three teams of four Hellcats each would dive to the attack. Few listening, including Hansen, Hobbs, and Mandeberg, looked forward to returning to those heavily defended Tokyo-area airfields or to the Shibaura power plant and its guns, for they had their fill of flying into enemy fire and those deadly tracers that sped by.

After the briefing, the aviators put on their Mae Wests and made sure they had their helmets, goggles, oxygen masks, and chartboards on which they had written the day's identification codes and flight headings. Some leaned back in the recliner chairs and puffed on a cigarette, while others absentmindedly chatted with the aviator next to him or gave a hurried thought to home and family. Each glanced at the chalkboard containing their names, the plane assigned to them for this mission, and the order in which they would take off. Finally, the message "Pilots, man your planes" flashed across the teletype screen, sending each pilot hastening to his Hellcat.

Like everyone else, Hansen preferred to avoid the sweep. He had already survived a few close calls. Enemy fire damaged his wing on one mission, a bullet had punctured his cockpit and missed his head by inches on another, and he had witnessed antiaircraft shells knock down Hellcats near him. Those brushes with death had caused a nervous tick—Hansen's hands shook each time he returned from a sweep or strike.

Hansen had plenty of company. No one, not Hobbs nor Mandeberg nor any of the twelve, wanted to fly over Tokyo again. The odds favored their safe return, but they would just as soon remain in their cabins.[2]

"THE WAR IS OVER"

As they scrambled to their Hellcats, the twelve were not alone in having reservations about this strike. Doubts as to the propriety of the August 15 mission extended to the commander of their task force, Admiral Radford, who was so concerned that he sent a message to Admiral McCain urging that he cancel the operation. "I hated to see our planes taking off that morning, feeling that the war would be over within hours," Admiral Radford wrote later. Despite his recommendation, McCain agreed with Halsey that they had to maintain the pressure on the Japanese, "so off went the planes." Radford contended afterward that "I felt I should have been able to convince Admiral McCain to delay offensive operations."[3]

Qualms existed among men on other carriers in *Yorktown*'s task group. Fliers follow orders, but in their opinion this strike made no sense, especially when compared to their July missions. "If the pilots were puzzled on the 13th when they were ordered to attack the Tokyo Shibaura Electric Company #2 they were completely bewildered when at 0530 15 August they found themselves taking off on the same mission," stated the history of Torpedo Squadron 50 aboard the USS *Cowpens*. "Peace was at best a matter of hours away, yet here they were tackling their most dangerous job. It took guts to go on that flight with such a mental hazard, but when those pilots left the Ready Room each one was prepared to do his duty and do it in full measure, regardless of his personal misgivings as to the necessity for it." An officer in one ready room even asked Air Plot, "Is this trip really necessary?"[4]

Sahloff, Proctor, and the other ten Hellcat aviators about to take off from the *Yorktown* shared those lackluster emotions. They were in the

Pacific to defeat the Japanese and would do as told, but as the torpedo squadron history stated, "it would be impossible to describe the nervous uncertainty with which planes were manned. Peace—so near and yet so far."[5]

The twelve walked around their Hellcats for a visual check to make sure that everything worked properly. They greeted their plane captain, the enlisted man who looked after their plane, and climbed up into the cockpit. As each plane captain helped the fliers adjust their parachutes and shoulder straps, they said, "Good luck, Sir," before climbing down. Now alone in the cockpit, Hobbs, Mandeberg, and the other ten went over their takeoff checklists as Boone turned the *Yorktown* into the wind. Upon hearing the air operations officer bellow over his loud speaker, "Gentlemen, start your engines," each flipped the starter switch and felt the vibrations as the engine roared to life.[6]

At 4:15 a.m. Howdy Harrison and his eleven Hellcats took off and rendezvoused with Corsairs from *Shangri-La* and *Wasp* to head for airfields in the Tokyo area. Harrison's unit had only flown fifteen miles westward when they encountered a thick cloud formation spewing lightning, thunder, and showers. They tried to circle over it, but unable to break out, Harrison ordered his planes to descend in the miserable conditions and continue close to the water's surface toward Tokyo. To maintain contact with *Yorktown*, he detached two of the twelve pilots, Ensign Ronald J. Hardesty and Lieutenant (jg) Laverne F. Nabours, and told them to seek a clearing at a higher altitude, and circle there to relay messages to and from the carrier while he maintained course with the rest toward Atsugi southwest of Tokyo.

Still battling remnants of the weather front, Harrison took his planes toward the coast. Lieutenant (jg) Odom's team of four Hellcats somehow became lost in what the action report called a "finger of overcast," leaving Harrison to continue with his unit, now down to the six Hellcats flown by himself, Sahloff, Hobbs, Mandeberg, Hansen, and Proctor, toward Atsugi Airfield.[7]

Harrison's planes crossed the coastline south of Chosi Point due east of Tokyo, where they turned south toward Sagami Bay to approach Atsugi from the south. Those antiaircraft guns that lined their approach to Atsugi now loomed larger, for with peace so close they had become possibly the final barrier to their safe return. If they eluded those guns and returned to the carrier, this mission might be their final action of the war. The six aviators could not dismiss the threat that Japanese fighter pilots might challenge them, but they considered that unlikely. Since the Air Group's arrival off Japan, the enemy had yet to engage them in the air since *Yorktown* arrived off their coast. Why should they now?

With Harrison's Hellcats winging their way toward Atsugi, the word the pilots had been awaiting finally arrived. *Yorktown* had already launched both Howdy Harrison's sweep and Searcy's strike when at 6:30 a.m. a message arrived from Admiral Nimitz to immediately suspend operations. The carrier quickly relayed the news to Searcy, who was then thirty miles from his target flying with the Corsairs escorting the bomber and torpedo units. Searcy was told to have all planes dump their bombs in the ocean and return to the ship because, as Lieutenant Commander Huddleston of the torpedo squadron wrote, "The war is over."[8]

Searcy obtained an authentication on the message and relayed the good news to Harrison and his fighter sweep, adding that they should jettison their ammunition and return to the carrier. When he received an acknowledgment from Harrison, Searcy focused on his unit with the assumption that Harrison would extricate his Hellcats from the attack and turn back toward *Yorktown*.

Harrison's planes had reached Atsugi Airfield by 6:45 and had begun preparing to attack when Searcy's news struck like a bolt of lightning. Harrison led the flight in a quick circle about the airfield and started on the journey back to *Yorktown*, to safety, and to an end to the war. The nervous excitement of battle had been swiftly replaced by the elation of peace and by the thought that each of the six had survived what so many of their fellow aviators had not. Hobbs and Mandeberg had never intended to make the military their careers. They had joined the Navy to defeat the Germans and Japanese, and once that task had been completed, they planned to return to Kokomo and Detroit and resume their civilian lives, which for Billy included pursuing Page and for Eugene meant marrying Sonya. It appeared at long last that those postwar dreams had arrived.

"All pandemonium broke loose," wrote Huddleston. "Men shouted, 'Whoopees,' 'Here go my bombs,' 'Bombs away,' and 'California, here I come.'" Ralph Morlan of the torpedo squadron later wrote, "Hurray! We had to drop our 2000 lb. bomb in the water. The war ended when I was on my way to Japan. We were all very happy."[9]

Hennesy, flying escort in his Corsair for Huddleston's torpedo planes, listened excitedly as his radio "was immediately filled with whoops, hoorays, and silly remarks by the pilots in our formation until Commander Searcy ordered 'Knock off the chatter and prepare to drop bombs.'" The group turned back, and once they reached the open sea Searcy gave them the signal to release their loads. "The bomber planes were flying behind us even lower, just above the waves. Some of the bomber pilots had already armed their bombs and when they dropped them they exploded and sent geysers of water high into the air. Planes following them had trouble keeping from hitting and crashing into the geysers. There was a flurry of yelling on the radio in the nature of 'The war is over and you dumb-ass bastards almost killed us.'"[10] In their excitement, the aviators had forgotten about the formations of planes below.

Odom, still separated from the formation, tried to contact Harrison for instructions, but due to a garbled radio transmission, he was unable to understand Howdy's words. Odom took his team to the rendezvous point over Sagami Bay, but when he found no trace of Harrison or any other American unit, and upon hearing a transmission from *Yorktown* that the war had ended, Odom returned to the carrier. When he landed, Odom informed the intelligence officer that he had no idea what had happened to any other aircraft, including Howdy's team of six Hellcats.

Odom arrived to a jubilant company of officers and sailors as, according to the carrier's war diary, "the word was received that the Japanese Government had agreed to comply with the terms of surrender as specified by the United Nations." Halsey ordered the task force to retire and await further orders, but cautioned that each ship should maintain its vigilance in case any Japanese pilot tried to sneak in and attack. Later that day the combat air patrol shot down nine Japanese aircraft that approached the force, according to the war diary apparently because "at that time the Japanese Emperor had not notified his force that hostilities were to cease."[11]

The war was over, but men aboard *Yorktown* still had to be on guard. The thought of dying after the Japanese government had agreed to surrender was too macabre for them to consider.

"MANY RATS SIX O'CLOCK HIGH, DIVING!"

Meanwhile, back in the Tokyo environs, Howdy Harrison faced one more task—to lead his five aviators back to *Yorktown* where they could join in the jubilation that was sweeping through every corner of the carrier. A controversy occurred over what happened next. Odom, already safely aboard the carrier, later claimed that Harrison suggested to the other five Hellcat pilots that since the war was over, they should take a quick tour of Tokyo and its environs. Supposedly, according to Odom, the quintet wanted nothing to do with an extra excursion but, trusting their leader, followed Harrison's suggestion. In an interview conducted fifty years later, Hansen asserted that his team leader, Proctor, mentioned the idea, which Hansen strongly opposed.

Whoever might have floated the notion, the claim, if true, is hard to fathom. No flight or team leader, especially one as concerned as was Harrison for the welfare of his wingman, Hobbs, and the other pilots, would willingly risk their lives and ignore orders to return to the carrier merely to embark on a risky tour of Tokyo. Not only was the capital heavily protected by antiaircraft fire, but the leaders would be asking them, at a time when Japanese emotions were at their highest, to fly close to those same Tokyo-area airfields they and other air groups had been ravaging since mid-July. Their nation had just surrendered, against the wishes of many in the military, and it was not farfetched to conclude that some of those irate Japanese aviators would have no reluctance to jump into their fighters and attack any American plane that appeared.

When other aviators—from World War II and beyond, including one who flew more than one hundred missions over North Vietnam in an F-4 Phantom fighter—considered this scenario, all agreed that a side jaunt would have been unthinkable under those circumstances. The Vietnam War aviator said if he had received an order to turn back to the carrier, the only thought he would have had was how fast could he have turned his fighter back and scrambled out of enemy air space. Harrison appeared to do precisely the same by veering his group away from Atsugi and heading toward Tokyo Bay, south of the path he would have taken had he decided to lead his planes toward the capital.

They did not maintain that route for long, however. They had only flown five miles from Atsugi Airfield when, between Atsugi and the bay, Sahloff shouted, "Tallyho! Many rats six o'clock high, diving!"[12]

Through the light overcast they spotted fifteen to twenty Japanese army and navy fighters attacking the group from 4,000 feet above. Pilots in Nakajima Ki-84s, Kawanishi N1Ks, and Mitsubishi J2Ms suddenly sliced toward the six Hellcats, intent on taking out their vengeance on the American fliers. Not only were these aircraft some of the newest and best the Japanese had remaining, but the talented pilots who flew them, hoarded by the Japanese to defend their homeland against the expected American land assault, were the most skilled and experienced fliers in the land. Hobbs, Mandeberg, and the other four fliers, who had thought they were safe, suppressed their thoughts of peace while Howdy shifted his planes into a defensive position and prepared to fight it out.

Slowed with the extra weight of the wing tanks and rockets they had intended to drop once over sea, the six not only possessed less maneuverability than their opponents, but faced the disadvantage of flying into a dogfight in which they were outnumbered three to one. "Our planes, burdened with rockets and belly-tanks, which they had no chance to drop, fought at a great disadvantage,"[13] concluded Commander Searcy after the attack. The absence of Odom's four Hellcats, now safely aboard *Yorktown*, was critical.

"A wild fight ensued, the last important air battle of the war,"[14] later wrote Admiral Radford of this August 15 encounter between Harrison's six Hellcats and the fifteen to twenty Japanese fighters. Hobbs and most of the inexperienced aviators had arrived in the Pacific eagerly seeking the same massive dogfights in which their naval brethren had earlier engaged, but that elation had gradually diminished with each combat death, and had all but disappeared with the hints of peace and with the employment of the atomic bombs. Now, when they least desired an engagement, in the skies near Tokyo, the six aviators found themselves in the last dogfight of World War II.

"FROM THEN ON it was a melee with everyone fighting in the same air," described the action report of the battle that spread across the sky. Details of this encounter are sketchy, as each aviator had to concentrate on avoiding enemy bullets rather than on what someone else was doing, but every survivor agreed that a dogfight to match those that had earlier painted the skies over the Solomons and other Pacific isles now unfolded over the Tokyo region.

With multiple enemy fighters winging their way, each aviator selected the first target they spotted. Harrison and Hobbs veered off in pursuit of a pair, while Mandeberg and Sahloff peeled off in their own attacks. Their intensive New England training paid dividends when, in the opening minutes of the dogfight, the group shot down four opponents. Proctor's wingman, Hansen, in a daring head-to-head charge, splashed two Japanese fighters, one which came so close that Hansen feared they would collide head-on, while Proctor's bullets severed the wing of a third plane and sent it plunging toward earth. Japanese fighters made repeated passes at Hansen, but each time he evaded them by exchanging machine gun bursts and escaping into the clouds.

Noticing an enemy fighter on Sahloff's tail, Proctor and Hansen turned to Sahloff's aid. Proctor shredded the enemy fighter with accurate fire from 700 feet, and then informed Sahloff that as his plane was emitting smoke, that he should try to make it to the open sea. Proctor planned to escort Sahloff to safety, but tracers from an enemy plane on his tail forced him to take evasive measures and leave Sahloff on his own. From above, Hansen came to his partner's aid and splashed the plane targeting Proctor, who had started a 180° turn in an effort to shake his pursuer, while Sahloff ducked in and out of clouds and appeared to bail out before his plane rolled twice before tumbling earthward. "It is hoped he is in Tokyo Bay," stated the action report.

He had no sooner pulled out of that close call when Proctor spotted seven Japanese aircraft closing on him. Six veered upward, giving Proctor a belly shot that sent one spiraling downward in flames before, as the action report described, he "high tailed it for the clouds below with all the planes chasing and firing at me."[15] Enemy bullets punctured twenty-eight holes in his fuselage and propeller, but Proctor nursed his

Hellcat to cloud cover, where he remained until he reached the sea and exited for the trek back to *Yorktown*.

The Japanese abandoned their pursuit of Proctor and turned their complete attention on Harrison, Hobbs, Mandeberg, and Hansen. One Hellcat exploded, forcing the unidentified pilot to parachute from 7,000 feet, while two others, outnumbered by the Japanese, quickly plummeted in flames and smashed into the ground. Hansen, who fended off the Japanese and subsequently made it back to the *Yorktown*, was so occupied defending himself that he had no time to identify which of his three companions had parachuted and which two rode their planes to a fiery end. Whether he dangled from the parachute or crashed with his burning Hellcat as it impacted the ground, Billy Hobbs died with his mother's wedding ring still hanging from his dog tags.

They also died knowing that the war was already over. Imagine the thoughts they must have had as their Hellcats plummeted toward the ground or water. Like millions of young Americans, they had been willing to sacrifice their lives to defend their nation, but that urgency had ended with the order to return to the *Yorktown*. Peace had now arrived, a moment for which they had fought and seen squadron members perish, but instead of joining their fellow aviators in celebrating the event, and eventually returning to loved ones back home, Harrison, Hobbs, Mandeberg, and Sahloff enjoyed only a few seconds of peace before once again fighting for, and this time losing, their lives.

The action report credited the six Hellcat aviators with downing nine Japanese planes during the battle, including a pair for Lieutenant (jg) Sahloff, whose flight log recorded, "Sweep Tokyo. Probably shot down one or two planes which they were unable to confirm." Four Americans—Harrison, Hobbs, Sahloff, and Mandeberg—were listed missing in action, while Proctor and Hansen landed aboard *Yorktown* in Hellcats aerated with enemy bullet holes. Admiral Radford, who had hesitated in sending the unit on this mission, later wrote that the four missing fliers were "our last combat casualties. Their loss was a personal tragedy to me on that day of victory."[16]

Yorktown's Catholic chaplain, Father Moody, took it more personally. He reflected on the bitter irony that Howdy Harrison had only recently escaped death during the dramatic Dumbo rescue, only to meet his demise when "he, Sahloff and two other pilots were lost on what I always considered a stupid mission on the day the treaty was signed. Personally, I blame Halsey for sending out this strike when he knew the war would be over momentarily."[17]

Admiral Halsey was less restrained to the news that the war was finally over. "We all let out a cheer," recalled Halsey. "My first reaction, of course, was great joy that the war that had started for us so badly had ended up so successfully. . . . My next thought was, 'Thank God I don't have to send any more men out to die.'"[18]

That peace he so joyously celebrated came minutes too late for Howdy Harrison, Billy Hobbs, Eugene Mandeberg, and Joe Sahloff.

"LET US NOT FORGET THOSE GALLANT COMRADES"

While the other carriers and ships of the task group celebrated the end of the war, muted joy, not exhilaration, engulfed *Yorktown*. "In the ready room there was a great feeling of joy and relief among us that the surrender had finally come," said Lieutenant Hennesy. "It was a kind of party atmosphere. The flight surgeon visited us with the ration of brandy we were entitled to after each mission." Hennesy's joy, and that of everyone's, faded with the news that Howdy Harrison, a father of two children, one of whom he had never seen; the popular Billy Hobbs, who never seemed to have a harsh word for anyone; the intellectual Eugene Mandeberg and his clever wit; and the skilled pilot and cigar-chomping Joseph Sahloff had yet to return from that final dogfight. "While we were enjoying the fact that our combat days were over however, it was tempered by the news of the fate of some of our buddies in the Hellcat flight who had gone out before us that morning."[19]

Commander Searcy had already landed with his Corsairs and the other planes set for the morning strike. After reporting, he waited for the Hellcats to return, and was buoyed when half an hour later "a fighter returned, followed by another, both pretty well shot up, but they got aboard safely. We waited in vain for the other four. I was heartsick," said Searcy.[20]

Each pilot in the ready room knew that their four missing comrades had, as one news article described it the next day, "fired probably the last shots of the war." Ensign Leonard Komisarek said that "after the time of their scheduled landing passed, we prayed every minute that they were delayed somehow and would return before the next minute was up. Our disappointment was bitter when we realized that they would never get back and our only hope was that they were taken prisoners of war."[21]

In expletive-filled tirades, men castigated Halsey for the four missing aviators. Why, they asked, would the admiral send men out to die when the war was all but over? Were their sacrifices necessary to defeat an already beaten foe? What need was there for carrier strikes when the nation possessed an atomic bomb? "The hell with that," scoffed one of the sweep's survivors, Ensign Ronald J. Hardesty, at celebrating the end of the war. "What I want to know is what chance have we got to rescue these pilots?" Lieutenant (jg) Watkinson said that he and others "wanted vengeance. We wanted to go back. I think they had to make the planes inoperable so that we wouldn't go after the Japanese."[22]

BACK IN JAPAN, farmers Iwajiro and Teruo Watanabe were tilling their field near the Japanese village of Nase Machi, twenty-five miles southwest of Tokyo, when, around 7:00 a.m., they stopped to watch two planes in combat directly above their home. The trailing aircraft fired at the plane ahead, which seemed to be unsuccessfully trying to twist and turn out of the path of the bullets. Smoke suddenly trailed from the first plane, which fluttered out of control and veered downward. The farmers never saw anyone parachute from the descending aircraft, which crashed and exploded near a hill one quarter mile from the Watanabes. According to their report, they ran toward the site and "saw a large hole in the lower slope of the hill, smoke pouring from it, and parts of the plane strewn about on both sides."[23] They instantly recognized it as an American aircraft.

Meanwhile Yasushige Kadokura, Assistant Chief Civil Fireman, was notified that a plane had crashed on the Watanabes' land. When he arrived, he saw black smoke and flames coming from the spot, plus aircraft parts scattered about the location. The heat from the flames caused some of the ammunition to explode, forcing the Watanabes to take pre-cautions and Kadokura to rope off the area to protect the ten to fifteen civilians that had gathered.

Soon after, two army officers and three enlisted men arrived with two members of the Kempeitai, the Japanese military police arm of the Imperial Japanese Army. They waited for up to three hours for the fires to cool sufficiently to allow them to examine the site, at which time they found the body of an American flier about three yards to the right of the plane. Amid the pieces of bone and flesh that lay scattered about, they located a male's trunk, but found no traces of the head, hands, and feet. Civilian firemen wrapped the remains in a straw mat and carried them to the Miyohoji Shrine for burial.

Later that afternoon the firemen delivered the remains of this un-identified American flier to Sentai Mochizuki, a Buddhist priest at the shrine. The priest buried the remains without unwrapping and looking at any portion. Since Joseph Sahloff had earlier turned toward the open sea before disappearing, it is probable that these were the remains of either Howdy Harrison, Billy Hobbs, or Eugene Mandeberg. That the body was recovered southwest of Tokyo counters the contention that Howdy Harrison wanted to take his Hellcats on a tour around Tokyo twenty-five miles to the north.

OFF THE JAPANESE coast, once all carriers had recovered their aircraft, Admiral Halsey issued orders to move the bombers and torpedo planes below so that the decks could be cleared for fighter operations, and to in-crease the number of fighters flying CAP. Not trusting that the Japanese would honor the cessation of hostilities, he told the carrier fighter direc-tors to instruct their pilots to "investigate and shoot down all snoopers—not vindictively, but in a friendly sort of way."[24]

At 11:00 a.m. Halsey's flagship, the battleship *Missouri*, and sur-rounding vessels sounded their whistles and sirens for one minute to cel-ebrate the end to the war. Two hours later Halsey delivered his victory address to the Third Fleet, which was simultaneously relayed to a wait-ing audience back home. He proclaimed, "You have brought an impla-cable, treacherous, and barbaric foe to his knees in abject surrender. This is the first time in the recorded history of the misbegotten Japanese race that they as a nation have been forced to submit to this humiliation." Thinking of the officers and enlisted who had served under him—many, like Harrison, Hobbs, Mandeberg, and Sahloff, who had perished—he said, "Your names are writ in golden letters on the pages of history—your fame is and shall be immortal. . . . The forces of righteousness and decency have triumphed."[25]

Later in the afternoon, after his fleet's CAP had shot down eight Japanese aircraft that had drawn alarmingly close, the Third Fleet's guns and aircraft drew silent. "After that minute," Halsey wrote, "the Third Fleet never fired another shot in wrath." The Third Fleet Log aptly summed Admiral Halsey's mood with Japan's capitulation. "So closes the watch we have been looking forward to. Unconditional surrender of Japan—with Admiral Halsey at sea in command of the greatest combined fighting fleet of all history! There is a gleam in his eye that is unmistakable!"[26]

That gleam shone with less luster aboard *Yorktown*, where the ship's company and the Air Group personnel struggled with the thought that victory had brought with it the loss of their four comrades in the few nascent seconds of peace. In his address to the crew, Captain Boone first congratulated them for their impressive accomplishments. "Three and a half years ago, when we heard over our radios that Pearl Harbor was under Jap attack, we said, 'This is it,' and we went to work." He added, "We have won a complete victory over a once powerful enemy who attacked us without warning, who sought to invade and conquer our country, and who has waged war with a cruelty and treachery without parallel in history."

He then reminded them of the cost, referencing the four aviators lost in the war's last moments. "Our victory is a glorious one, in which every individual on board has had a personal and important part. We may be profoundly proud of the role played by our ship—our Fighting Lady—and by the air groups who have flown from her deck. But in our joyous relief that the fighting is over, let us not forget those gallant comrades who made the supreme sacrifice to make this victory possible."[27]

The gleam further dimmed in the fighting squadron, whose members grieved over what they viewed as the unnecessary, almost criminal, loss of four of their members. "This was the crowning loss," stated the fighting squadron history. "The end of the war brought little jubilation among the pilots. The news was accepted quietly. . . . Morale among the pilots was at rock bottom after the last four deaths."[28]

IN ITS NINE weeks of combat, Air Group 88 had lost eighteen pilots or aircrewmen, including nine from the fighting squadron, six from the bombing-fighting squadron, and three from the bombing squadron, but none struck as severe a blow as the loss of those final four aviators who flamed to their deaths at precisely the same moment the world began celebrating peace. In early July Hobbs and the other new aviators had reached the Pacific in hopes of engaging the Japanese in one of those crazed, action-packed dogfights. Poignantly, their craving to match skills with an enemy flier finally materialized, but at a moment they hoped to avoid such an encounter. On his twenty-third birthday, exactly one year after Air Group 88 had formed for war, Hobbs, along with his three companions, flew to their deaths when they might have been celebrating peace.

"Thus, ironically, the air group's numerically greatest air-combat successes and losses took place after the war had supposedly ended," concluded Commander Searcy in his action report. He added, "And thus ended the offensive operations of this air group, one year exactly after the date of its commissioning."[29]

Yorktown's war diary employed simple, but stark, words to express the final losses of World War II:

> F-26, bureau 79592, piloted by Lieut. H. M. Harrison, 1556629, A1, USNR, failed to return with this flight; shot down over target.
>
> F-28, bureau 78065, piloted by Lieut. (jg) J. G. Sahloff, 347463, A1, USNR, failed to return with this flight; shot down over target.
>
> F-23, bureau 78244, piloted by Ensign W. C. Hobbs, Jr., 355123, A1, USNR, failed to return with this flight; shot down over target.

F-18, bureau 77458, piloted by Ensign E. E. Mandeberg, 363034, A1, USNR, failed to return with this flight; shot down over target.[30]

"THE TOWN WAS CELEBRATING, BUT HIS PARENTS COULDN'T BE PART OF IT"

Disbelief and anger marked the Japanese side as well. When Saburo Sakai learned that the military was to lay down its arms, "I myself was incapable of thought or speech. I walked in a fog, crossing the field [Oppama Base] without looking to either side. For some reason I wanted to be near my plane, and I leaned weakly against the Zero."[31]

Shortly before noon on August 15, and only a few hours after Harrison, Hobbs, Mandeberg, and Sahloff were killed, the Japanese national anthem, "Kimigayo," sounded on radios in Japanese homes. Emperor Hirohito spoke slowly, without emotion, and told his people that as the war no longer favored the country, especially with the advent of the atomic bomb, he had decided to accept Truman's peace terms.

Captain Minoru Genda never envisioned such an outcome. "It was my thought we could continue war on the soil of Japan for as long as the Japanese nation existed, even if it took ten, 20, 50 or a 100 years!"[32] He took pride that the country had not lost a war in more than 2,600 years, and the thought of admitting defeat now was almost too much for the famed aviator to consider.

THE CONTRASTING MOOD in Kokomo, where citizens poured out of homes and businesses to celebrate the end to a long, weary war, could not have been more dramatic. Celebrations lasted well into the night as people released emotions they had kept buried inside while the fighting continued. They danced in the streets and honked car horns, and stores and city government offices announced they would shut down the next day. Jubilant citizens hugged every serviceman in uniform.

"Just at sundown when the 'rising sun' was setting, the magic words, 'The War Is Over,' rang across the land and Kokomo citizens generally at their evening meals heard the word over radios tuned with expectant fingers," reported the *Kokomo Tribune* that day. "Knives and forks were dropped as family after family raced for the family cars and long lines of automobiles raced for the public square. In less than ten minutes the all-time record for traffic jams was set in the courthouse square. The bedlam of blaring automobile horns, clanging bells and crashing tin pans was terrific."[33]

Members of the Hobbs family joined in celebrating the end of the war, but their hearts could not be completely in it until they received word from Billy that he was all right. They assumed he was safely aboard his aircraft carrier, as news articles explained that Admiral Halsey had canceled the final day's strikes. The odds seemed favorable, but until Hattie received definitive word from her son, she could not escape the apprehension that had been her daily companion since she had handed Billy her wedding ring as he had left for war. "I remember going home with Mom and Dad, and they were crying," said sister-in-law Carolyn Hobbs of the night Kokomo celebrated. "Billy was still over there in the Pacific. The town was celebrating, but his parents couldn't be part of it."[34]

State government officials reminded people that, in the midst of the revelry, they should not forget the price paid by so many Indiana families. The war was over, but thousands of husbands, fathers, and sons had been lost in gaining victory. In its article covering the town's festivities, the *Kokomo Tribune* included a powerful sentence emphasizing the high cost. "Standing with [her] back against a wall, however, stood one woman, alone. There were tears in her eyes and she seemed to falter a bit as she worked her way out of the crowd into a side street. For her there was no end of pain and tears—she remembered a yellow telegram which said, 'regrets to inform you that—.'"[35] Might the coming days make Hattie a companion to that saddened mother, or would they enable her to at last enjoy the peace she had so long awaited?

Other articles reinforced Hattie's fears. Although she had no idea that these stories described that last dogfight near Tokyo that took her son, the accounts explained that while peace had arrived, its pronouncement came too late to halt Halsey's final strike into the enemy's heartland. As a result, "Crack pilots of Admiral Halsey's great American and British carrier fleet fought on in self defense Wednesday—after they had been told officially to 'cancel all operations and return to base.'" On their way back, they shot down a large number "of the biggest group of intercepting Japanese fighters encountered in weeks," but no one aboard their carrier was "elated over firing what theoretically were the last shots of the war, for several of their friends failed to return from that early-morning, post-surrender scrap with nearly 50 enemy fighters."[36]

The first indication that something had gone wrong occurred when one letter and a birthday card that Billy's sister, Joyce, had mailed to her brother were returned to the family home. The unopened envelopes bore the stamped words, "Return to Sender." Why had these two pieces of mail been returned when every prior letter had reached its destination?

The Mandebergs and Sonya Levien experienced the same tribulations. Eugene's parents could only relax when their son sent a letter informing them that he was fine, and Sonya found it too difficult to join her neighbors in celebrating the arrival of peace. "Mom was planning a life with Gene," said Sonya's daughter, Susan Sussman. "The war had just ended, and all New York was celebrating, but she couldn't."[37]

DESPITE THE END of hostilities, Air Group 88's work was not complete. Halsey's Third Fleet, including *Yorktown*, stood guard southeast of Tokyo, ready to attack any disgruntled group of Japanese military or to shoot down any aircraft that approached.

The carrier's company and Air Group 88 personnel enjoyed the easing of wartime conditions, though. Father Moody celebrated a Mass to honor the arrival of peace, and for the first time since the war's start, each night ships' lights pierced the darkness. Smoking on the upper decks was permitted, and nightly movies on deck entertained the men.

On September 2, more than three hundred correspondents, photographers, and government dignitaries boarded Halsey's flagship, the *Missouri*, for the surrender ceremony. "God, what a great day this is," Halsey said to General Douglas MacArthur. "We have fought a long long time for it." MacArthur opened the proceedings with a few words expressing his hopes for a lasting peace, signed the document, and then stepped back to allow other officials to do the same. At the close of the ceremony, MacArthur walked to Halsey and said, "Start 'em now!"[38]

At his signal almost 500 carrier aircraft, including those from Air Group 88, and Army bombers flew overhead in a display of might that awed onlookers. Back at the carrier afterward, they sat down to a victory dinner of turkey, mashed potatoes and gravy, orange cake, and ice cream, and enjoyed a special performance by the ship's band before watching the film selected for the occasion—*Rhapsody in Blue,* starring Robert Alda.

In peace's aftermath, the *Yorktown* crew and members of the Air Group were permitted to go ashore. Father Moody wrote that the devastation of Japanese cities stunned him. "Men have written of 'fire and sword' in describing war's desolation, but the phrase takes on new meaning from what has happened here. Wide areas have been seared by flame, leaving a mass of rubble and rust, with a few broken spars of metal and an occasional bulky safe standing above the ruin. No living thing could have escaped, and all man's handiwork has been crushed into a desperate pattern of destruction." He added, "I could not help being affected by these sights, and they provided thought for us at Mass today."[39]

While most of *Yorktown*'s crew bartered for souvenirs, Ensign Komisarek and other members of the fighting squadron searched for information about their four missing comrades. Komisarek wrote to the Hobbs family that "we did all that could be done in trying to find out what actually happened that day. We checked all the rosters of the prisoner of war camps and couldn't locate any trace of their names. We also checked with all the rescue ships and submarines that were in the vicinity at the time, but no news was to be had. I promise, however, to send you any information that will be made available to us."[40]

While many in the Air Group continued to blame Halsey for the loss of the four aviators in the war's dying moments, American prisoners of war who had languished in atrocious conditions welcomed his arrival. Before the September 2 surrender ceremony, Halsey had dispatched military units throughout Japan to liberate the thousands of captives, and within two weeks, 19,000 prisoners of war were freed. Air Group 88 aviators participated by flying over prison camps and dropping food and medical treatment to the men, leading one group of ecstatic prisoners at a Yokohama camp to post a huge sign, "YORKTOWN THANKS."[41]

Halsey, the admiral who had gained the nation's admiration for his exploits in the war's first two years but who had earned the approbation of Air Group 88 aviators, handed over command of his fleet and, on September 20, departed for home. He enjoyed a well-deserved retirement, but he never forgot the events of August 15. Although he failed to refer to them by name, Halsey made a point to mention in his autobiography that he hoped history would always remember those VF-88 aviators—Harrison, Hobbs, Mandeberg, and Sahloff—who died during the final wartime mission ordered by the admiral.

Eleven days later the *Yorktown* and Air Group 88 left Japan on its journey to the United States. As the California coast came into sight on October 20, the crew lined up in dress whites about the deck spelling out "YORKTOWN" and "FIGHTING LADY." A Navy blimp circled overhead with "WELCOME HOME" painted on its side, and when the carrier steamed beneath the Golden Gate Bridge, civilians lined the structure, cheering and waving as a band played, while anchored ships blew their sirens and cars honked their horns.

A stanza written by one *Yorktown* aviator summed the emotions of the moment.

The last tallyho has been sounded,
The sea washes thick with the tears;
Remember the ranks of the fallen,
As memory fades with the years.[42]

Air Group 88 brought victory home with them, but it had left behind eighteen aviators killed from July 10 to August 15, including the final four men to die in World War II.

CHAPTER 12

"Two Only of the Six Returned"
The Aftermath

I N ITS SEPTEMBER 1, 1945, issue, the *Kokomo Tribune* summed the feelings of almost every American about the arrival of peace. "This opportunity for rest and relaxation comes to the community with almost ideal timeliness. The stress, rush and anxiety of wartime is over; the harvesting of crops maturing in summer has practically been completed. The long period of high-pressure activity necessitated by the world conflict has ended. There is scarcely any line in which operatives cannot afford a couple of days of leisure. There is in the situation something that impresses all with the blessedness of peace. In the heart of all but the unthinking there is gratitude that mankind has again come upon tranquil times."[1]

The Hobbs family, however, still could not completely relax until they had heard from their son. "As far as we knew, he was still alive," said Billy's sister, Nancy Exmeyer, but they lacked definitive word.[2]

Another troubling moment occurred when a letter that Joyce Hobbs had written Billy shortly after the end of hostilities also came back, unopened, with "Return to Sender" stamped across the envelope. She had asked Billy, "How are you by now. Fine since the Japs have surrendered I bet. How did you spend your birthday Bill? I can imagine." She then inquired about Billy's friend and team leader. "You haven't mentioned Howdy Harrison lately, Bill, is he all right?"[3] Why, she wondered, was this letter returned if Billy was fine?

WHILE STILL OFF the Japanese coast, Air Group 88 aviators had already started the painful process of gathering the personal effects of the four missing pilots and notifying their families. Ensign Komisarek and Ensign Robert N. Kelly inventoried Billy's items, including his uniforms, letters, photographs, wallet, wings, and an "Officer sweetheart pin." Although Hobbs would not officially be promoted until after he completed this final mission, he already had two sets of lieutenant (jg) bars that he looked forward to adding to his uniform. Komisarek and Kelly placed the bars among the other items and packaged everything for shipment to Kokomo.

Lieutenant Cagle, recently promoted to lieutenant commander, faced the unpleasant task of writing to the families. Many officers struggle to find the proper words for families about to receive such wrenching news, but Cagle crafted touching letters that imparted the information he had about their sons' disappearances while offering his sympathies and hope. "It is my unwilling duty to inform you that your son Eugene is listed as 'missing in action.' There is, however, some hope for his life," he opened his letter to the Mandebergs. He provided details of that last dogfight and explained, "On the morning of the official news of the cessation of hostilities, Mandy was among a group of our planes over the Empire. The surrender news was radioed to them, and they were instructed to return to base. Enroute back to our carrier, and in the vicinity of Tokyo, the flight of six planes were attacked by some twenty Japanese fighters, so there was no alternative but to fight. In the ensuing engagement, nine enemy planes were destroyed, but Mandy is one of four of our lads who failed to return."

Since their son was officially listed as missing, and not dead, he tried to include optimism with the stark words. "Nothing was heard or seen of your son during the dogfight. These actions are so intense and furious that it is impossible for all planes to keep track of one another. All we know is that there is hope that Mandy's plane only was damaged, and then he succeeded in landing it or parachuting to safety. A search of the ocean proved fruitless, but it is quite possible he was shot down over Tokyo Bay or the land itself, since the flight occurred above the clouds. The Admiral has been notified and immediate steps will be taken to locate your son by the forces of the occupation."

He followed by conveying his and the squadron's sympathies over the disappearance of the popular aviators. "Mandy's loss at such an ironic moment, has left us bitter and bewildered, and we are fervently hoping that he will be found alive and well. His unbounding and infectious humor was a great morale factor in these past bitter weeks. He was certainly one of the squadron's great assets. I can't begin to convey to you how deep our sorrow is or to say the words that will comfort your anxiety."

Cagle ended by promising to inform the families as soon as he received additional news about their sons. "I will see that any news of your son reaches you with all speed. We are all praying and hoping for the best. If there is anything I may do to assist, any information I can give, please write to me."[4]

Cagle wrote that letter, as well as similar ones to the Harrison, Hobbs, and Sahloff families, the day after the final dogfight. They would not reach the four families until the next month, however, leaving them in a state of consternation. The Mandebergs typified what the other families also experienced in those trying moments. Four days after Eugene's plane went down, and before they received Cagle's letter or official word from the Navy, Zelda poured out her feelings to Sonya. "I feel I owe you an apology for not writing all week. What a week! The strain played havoc with my nerves. I feel all pood [sic] out. I know I'll feel much better as soon as I hear from Eugene. We had a letter yesterday dated July 30, he is fine. Like all his letters he tells you nothing. We are sending him a cable tomorrow. I hope he can send us one in return."

Three days passed without word from the Pacific. "No mail from Eugene," she wrote to Sonya. "I am terribly anxious to hear from him after the proclamation. I hope that will speed his return to the States." By August 26, eleven days after the war's end, the families had still not learned anything about their loved ones. "Still no mail from Eugene," Zelda informed Sonya. "I do hope to hear from him soon. This waiting is getting me down. Of course I did read in the paper that the mail from the Pacific is slow."

Zelda finally received word from her son on August 29, exactly two weeks after he had been shot down near Tokyo, when a group of letters arrived, the last written the day before Eugene climbed into his Hellcat for the last dogfight. "What a relief," she informed Sonya. "Five letters from Eugene, the latest one Aug. 14. Thank God. I worried so that I just didn't care what happens to me. It was an effort to keep going. I felt weak. I went to the Dr. today and after he examined me he says to me there is nothing I can do for you that a letter from Eugene won't do." She added before closing, "Eugene told me not to send him any more packages. I hope that means he will be home soon."

The information from her son bolstered Zelda's optimism. She wrote Sonya that Nathan had already asked contractors to build a bedroom, hall room, and shower that she and Eugene could use whenever they visited Detroit, and added, "Yes, dear I shall welcome the noise of my three children, how wonderful it will be to have you all home."

September arrived, and while Zelda remained upbeat because of those five letters, she noticed that the last one had been written before the August 15 attacks. Why had Eugene not contacted them since? The other three families wondered the same. Neighbors in Detroit, as well as in Kokomo, New York, and other cities, had heard from sons and husbands that they would soon be on their way home, but the four families knew nothing, as if they had been suddenly cut off from their sons. "I hope you heard from Eugene. No mail here," Zelda wrote Sonya on September 3, followed three days later with, "I wish I would get a letter from Eugene. I am anxious to know where he is right now, and what happens now." The renewed angst placed enormous strain on Zelda, who wrote Sonya on September 11, "Still no word from Eugene. I am just about worn out. I find the strain is terrific."[5]

Hattie Hobbs was bewildered when she received a letter from Howdy Harrison's wife, who had been informed by two of her husband's Air Group 88 friends that her husband had not returned from that final flight. Billy had often mentioned Harrison in his letters, and told Hattie how happy he was to be flying as Harrison's wingman. Did this letter mean that her son also was missing?

"THERE IS NO LOSS AS GREAT TO A MOTHER AS THE LOSS OF A SON"

They received their answers in mid-month. From September 19 to September 24, men in uniform delivered to the four families the news they had hoped never to receive. All knew immediately what that knock on their front doors portended. The telegrams contained only two sentences, but the words impacted the families as if a sledgehammer had knocked them senseless. "I deeply regret to inform you that your son Ensign Eugene Esmond Mandeberg USNR is missing in action 15 August 1945 in the service of his country," stated the telegram delivered to Nathan and Zelda Mandeberg, with similar ones handed to the other three families. "Your great anxiety is appreciated and you will be furnished details when received."[6]

These were blunt, stark words for parents who had looked forward to a letter from their sons informing them that they would soon be home. Thousands of mothers and fathers had received the same heartbreaking news over the last four years, but because these were the final four men to disappear in the war, the telegrams from Vice Admiral Louis Denfield, Chief of Naval Personnel, carried greater impact. Families who had only days before watched a nation celebrate the end of the war now received the news that, even though the fighting had ended, their sons might not be returning. One final flight, meaningless in the grand scheme of the war, had ripped their sons away.

Beneath a September 20 headline spread across page one—"Ensign W. C. Hobbs Reported Missing Since August 15; Shot Down As War Ends Over Japan"—the *Kokomo Tribune* informed its readers of Billy Hobbs's disappearance. "The parents of the young man have learned that their son was on a plane which was shot down by Jap planes shortly after word came that the war had ended." The article added that Hobbs had last been seen preparing to parachute from his damaged plane near Atsugi Airfield, and that while subsequent searches had found no trace of the aviator, the military had assured them that they would continue to look for their son. The article explained that Mr. and Mrs. Hobbs "have little hope that favorable news will be forthcoming," mainly because so much time had elapsed since the August 15 peace.[7]

STILL REELING FROM their September 24 telegram, the Mandebergs called Sonya in New York. Her father answered the telephone, and said little as he listened to the caller's message. Her father's ashen face answered that something terribly wrong had happened to Eugene.

The Mandebergs learned additional details a few days later when they received a letter written on September 9 by Ensign John J. Willis, one of Eugene's best friends. Willis explained that as he knew Mandy "better than anyone else in the squadron," he had the unpleasant task of writing "this very undesirable letter" about Mandy, "as he was affectionately called." Willis provided whatever material he had about Mandeberg's last flight in hopes that the information

> will put your mind more at ease. Ironically enough it was on the very morning the peace was signed. Six of our boys were to go over Tokyo and make an attack on an air field in the vicinity. Just as they got almost to the target a dispatch was sent over the air that the war was over and all flights were to return to the carrier. Our boys were overjoyed I know at the prospects of no more fighting. While on the way home they were jumped by twenty enemy fighters. Of course during a melee such as this must have been, our fellows lost contact with each other. Two only of the six returned. No one seems to know what happened to the other four among whom was Mandy. The two returning had definitely shot down five and they said they saw four or five others. Our gains were noticeable but our losses were overwhelming.

Willis then wrote words that must have been difficult for Nathan and Zelda Mandeberg to read. "We hoped that perhaps a couple of the boys would have gotten to earth safely and been taken prisoner. I don't want to say for you to give up hope but at the same time I don't want you to build your hopes too high." Willis explained that pilots of the fighting squadron had investigated every prison camp in the area and checked camp rosters, but had unearthed no news about their son or the other three fliers. "Perhaps I'm wrong in saying these things," wrote Willis, "but I believe anxiety to be much more difficult to bear than resignation. That's the way I'd like my mom to know." Willis continued that he had inventoried Eugene's belongings, and that the parents would soon receive a box containing their son's personal belongings and a money order for the cash left in Eugene's effects.

Hoping to lend a few comforting words, Willis said that it was easy for him to become friends with Mandy because of the flier's "ever present wit and ability to make you laugh in the direst circumstances." He added, "It wasn't very long before everyone in this squadron learned to love him and cherish his intelligence and witticism. He became quite popular by his various anecdotes on personages in the squadron. The world I know has lost a fine fellow and an intelligent compatriot but myself and the rest of my squadron mates have lost a friend."

Willis admitted that "it's so difficult to express in writing what a man feels in his heart. I'm not capable of the fluency in writing that was one of your son's many accomplishments." He asked Nathan Mandeberg to extend Willis's sympathy to his wife, "for there is no loss as great to a mother as the loss of a son." He ended his letter by expressing "my sincerest regrets to you who have suffered so much," and that "I'll close now with sorrow in my heart."[8]

NEAR THE END of September, the flour families received a letter from Commander H. B. Atkinson, the commanding officer of the Casualty Section at the Navy's Bureau of Personnel in Washington, D.C. Atkinson confirmed that their sons were officially listed as missing in action, and that while he had little information on their final flight, "because of the intensive search which is being carried out in all areas at the present time," he received updates almost every day. "It is hoped that a report will be received concerning your son in the near future," and if so, he promised to relay that news to the families.[9] Atkinson added his sympathies, and enclosed a booklet handed out by the Navy to the families of personnel listed as missing.

Still uncertain about their sons' fates, early the next month Hattie Hobbs sent a letter to Zelda Mandeberg. "I am taking the liberty of writing to you in regards of the status of our missing sons." She explained that she had obtained the Mandebergs' Detroit address from her representative in Washington, D.C., Congressman Forest Harness, and mentioned that "I have repeatedly made requests for information regarding all four of them, and today we received additional assurance that everything possible is being done." She enclosed a copy of Harness's letter, and added in closing, "I hope that you will be able to get a little comfort from this statement, which I feel is reliable. Hoping we get some good news soon."[10]

In the letter she received from Congressman Harness, dated October 2, the politician assured Hattie "that I am continuing [to be] in touch with the Navy Department in the matter, and that I will do everything I can to insure that no effort is spared in the search." He explained that the military was still scouring Japan for traces of her son. "In fact, you may be sure that our forces are going, and will continue to go, over Japan with a fine tooth comb in the work of finding and returning every American who has fallen into Japanese hands. The procedure includes thorough and repeated search of the area in which a man is known to have been lost, exhaustive review of all enemy records, and close interrogation of natives who might be able to offer any specific information."[11]

The next month Ensign Komisarek extended his condolences to the Hobbs family and provided a few details about matters in the Pacific. "I put off writing this letter to you sooner hoping all this time that we would have more definite news for you as to what happened to your son Wright," he wrote on October 16. "Since we know so very little more about it now than we did at the time I'm sure this letter will be disappointing. However I do want to mention the fact that a lot has been done towards finding out what happened to those four boys but all with very poor results." He added his "heartfelt sympathy for the misfortune that befell your son. It was especially hard on us because Wright was so well liked by everyone. His flying ability was never questioned by anyone because he was one of the best pilots in the squadron.

"Ensign [Robert N.] Kelly and myself inventoried Wright's personal effects and sent them on to a Navy center where they will be checked and later forwarded to you folks. I am sending Wright's wallet with this letter and they'll be mailed as soon as our ship reaches San Francisco on or about Oct. 24." He closed with his regrets: "I couldn't get myself to write this letter sooner but I was so sure that we would hear something about it, and I had hoped then that they were alright."[12]

The day after Komisarek's letter to the Hobbs family, Lieutenant Commander Cagle provided further details to the Mandebergs, but as two months had passed without learning anything, he was no longer optimistic about Eugene's fate. "It is indeed difficult for me to write to you that no further news is available concerning your son Eugene; who was lost in action on the 15th of August. We all had great hopes that upon our occupation of Japan your son would be found. All prisoners in the area have been accounted for, and all efforts in searching, both official and unofficial, have been to no avail." He explained that "when the *Yorktown* anchored in Tokyo Bay, I sent out several investigating parties for information; to the hospital clearing ship for prisoners, to the airfield over which the flight occurred, and to Allied Intelligence Headquarters." Because his efforts yielded no results, Cagle became the first to mention what most everyone else had declined to utter. "I am sorry to say, but I am sure you want only the truth, that we can now hold no further hope for the life of your son. We all feel the loss of your son, and we feel also that our country has lost much, for through his gift of humorous writing he could have added much happiness to all in the difficult years following the war."[13] Cagle's referral to death—the Navy would not officially list a man as deceased until he had been missing for one year—devastated the Mandebergs, who like the Hobbs, Harrison, and Sahloff families, held on to the slim hope that their loved one was alive.

So did Page Du Pre. The Hobbs family forwarded frequent updates to Billy's girlfriend, whom they had expected to become a member of the family after Billy returned from the Pacific. She appreciated their efforts, and informed Billy's sister, Joyce, that her brother remained ever in her thoughts. Page's worries extended into the night, when she dreamed of Billy. "Joyce darling, this may sound odd to you, but I also had a dream about Bill. He came riding up on a white horse. I can't remember the details but I saw him so plainly. I dreamed it on a Friday or Saturday nite before I received your letter. I told Barbara about it the next day. She said that white horses meant good news. She is my roommate, and has been so helpful lately. Since then I keep believing that Bill will come back. At first I thought it was even hopeless to even think he could, but now I feel different. Do you understand what I'm trying to say?"

Page said that when she first heard that Billy was missing, she planned to quit work and shut herself inside her home, but "everyone said no [underline hers], that I should keep busy and I wouldn't think about it so much. And they have been right. I honestly think that if I had gone home with nothing to do, I would have been a wreck by now."

Despite her efforts to maintain a normal schedule, the constant strain wore her down. "I too have lost a lot of weight. In fact, I'm down to 92," and she admitted that "it's silly for me to try and write any personal news as my mind is constantly on Bill. Maybe when I see you, we can get our feelings ironed out. Sometimes I just can't keep the tears back. My life has ended too Joyce. I shouldn't write that, but I just can't hold it in any longer."[14]

HOPES FADED AS the months passed. In August 1946, the government informed the four families that as one year had expired without additional information, the aviators' status had been changed from missing to deceased. In a letter to the Mandebergs—with similar letters sent to the other three families—Secretary of the Navy James Forrestal wrote, "In view of the strong possibility that the plane in which your son was flying crashed, and that he lost his life as a result thereof," and because the Navy had received no reports that he survived, from "any lists or reports of personnel liberated from Japanese prisoner of war camps, and in view of the length of time that has elapsed since he was reported to be missing in action, I am reluctantly forced to the conclusion that he is deceased." He added that the law stated for purposes of payment of death gratuities, pay, and allowance, that Eugene's death was presumed to have occurred as of August 16, 1946, "which is the day following the expiration of twelve months in the missing status." Forrestal ended by trying to offer comfort in an impossible situation. "I know what little solace the formal and written word can be to help meet the burden of your loss, but in spite of that knowledge, I cannot refrain from saying very simply, that I am sorry. It is hoped that you may find comfort in the thought that your son gave his life for his country, upholding the highest traditions of the Navy."[15]

Newspapers in the four hometowns, now more concerned with postwar world news, national politics, and sports, included brief articles about the government's notification. "The casualty status of Ensign Esmond Mandeberg, USNR," stated an article in the September 22, 1946, issue of the *Detroit Free Press*, "had been officially changed from 'missing' to 'dead' by the Navy Department. He was the son of Mr. and

Mrs. Nathan Mandeberg, of 18472 Monica." The phrase "he was the son," rather than "he is the son," could not have more bluntly conveyed the grief felt by Zelda in Detroit, Hattie in Kokomo, and the mothers of Howdy Harrison and Joseph Sahloff. They would have agreed with Sonya Levien, who said of their deaths, "They died knowing the war was over."[16]

With the official notification of Billy's death, Hattie Hobbs put into motion the plans she had made for a service to be held in the city's Memorial Hall in his honor. Hundreds of Kokomo residents turned out, and the *Kokomo Tribune* covered the event, calling Hobbs the last "Howard county youth to give his life in combat for his country in World War II."[17] Similar services were held for Eugene Mandeberg, Howard Harrison, and Joseph Sahloff.

The final four servicemen to die in a World War II action were now officially laid to rest.

"WE JUST KEPT LOOKING FOR BILLY TO COME HOME"

Memorial services for their loved ones may have eased the anguish, but because they buried memories and mementos, not remains, an open wound persisted. Without the remains, Hattie Hobbs, Zelda Mandeberg, and the other parents lacked closure. For the rest of her life Hattie sat on the front porch, glancing down the road as if expecting to see her son stroll up. "Mother, until she died," said Nancy Exmeyer, "would sit and look down the lane. She was always looking to see if he might be coming back."[18]

In hopes of keeping Billy's memory alive, Woodson Hobbs, Billy's uncle, nominated the aviator in a contest to rename Bunker Hill Air Base near Kokomo. Woodson wrote to the selection committee that Billy "was one of the last four heroic boys who were lost in World War II. It would be fitting as a timeless reminder of the futility of war, emphasized by the tragic and ironic end of these last four who perished Aug. 15, 1945 in an ill-advised strike against Atsugi Air Base, Tokyo, even as the long prayer for news of the Japanese capitulation was ringing in their headphones above the din of one of the most furious air battles of all time." He added that they "wrote the final glorious, bitter page to the history of World War II."[19]

The Hobbs family kept in touch with Howdy Harrison's widow. They visited each other's homes, and when the Harrison family added a dog, they named it "Hobby" in honor of Howdy's wingman, Billy Hobbs.

Billy's parents had little use for the military after the war. Hattie, in particular, blamed Halsey for her son's death. Each year on the anniversary of his death, which was also Billy's birthday, Hattie submitted to the *Kokomo Tribune* brief poems to print in the newspaper. In the August 1946 poem that she titled "Missing," Hattie introduced Billy and his three squadron mates. "In memory of our loving son, Ens. Wright C. Hobbs, and his three buddies, Lieut. Howdy Harrison, Ens. Eugene Mandeberg and Joe Sahloff, who were lost on V. J. Day over Tokyo." She then added her poem, a single stanza that expressed the love of a mother who missed her son.

His smiling way and pleasant face
Are a pleasure to recall.
He had a kindly word for each,
And was beloved by all.
The years may wipe out many things
But the bond of love won't sever
The memory of those happy days
When we were all together.

Hattie ended with, "Sadly missed by mother and father, Mr. and Mrs. Wright Hobbs and family."[20]

She continued this practice until her passing in 1971, once or twice repeating past favorites, but mostly offering original stanzas that when combined with the others, composed a lengthy ode to Billy. "Dad never said anything about Mom putting in the yearly memorials," said Nancy Exmeyer. "Mom, though, never got over it."[21]

During the fiftieth anniversary memorials honoring Hobbs's death and the end of World War II, a reporter who interviewed family members concluded that August 15 was a date "that still haunts the family's memories." Joyce Hobbs Clelland said, "We just kept looking for Billy to come home."[22]

Ten years later another reporter wrote that the Hobbs family continued to mourn Billy's death. Their sorrow over his loss had deepened because they lacked knowledge of what had happened on that last day of the war, and because they were unable to bring Billy's remains back to Kokomo. Hattie and Wright refused to remove a photograph of Billy in uniform that rested on a living room table, and niece Constance Grove said the parents "talked about him all the time. There was a lot of grief and a lot of bitterness about the Japanese. They talked about him to me all my life, and I spent a lot of time with them. Billy's memory was definitely kept alive all their lives." Constance's mother, Joyce, gave the name Page to one of her daughters, JoEllen Page Clelland, after her brother's girlfriend, Page Du Pre, and Nancy Exmeyer freely admits of the big brother she admired as a youth, "He's still my hero."[23]

His name is etched in a brick at a local chapel, but otherwise the memory of Billy Hobbs has faded in Kokomo. The Hobbs family understands why this is so, as many friends in the city have lost sons, and now daughters, in warfare, but they believe that the mystery surrounding Billy's death, and that he was one of the last four Americans to die in the war, should be remembered.

In November 2017 Natalie Schneider, Billy Hobbs's grandniece, wrote a story for her freshman English Honors Class. Although she could have selected any topic, she chose to depict the moment in 1945 when Hattie Hobbs told Billy's siblings that their brother had died. In the story, Hattie collected her thoughts before talking to her children. "I paused for a moment," Natalie had Hattie reflect, "and then through tears continued, 'On August fifteenth, many soldiers were killed by the Japanese before they all knew Japan had surrendered.' I paused to look at my precious children, and with tears running down my cheeks, thought to myself, 'I cannot believe I got this far through telling the children this. It isn't easy telling your children their role model, the best person in their world, their eldest brother, my firstborn, died after the ceasefire.'" Natalie ended her paper by writing, "World War II was a horrible and tragic event."[24] A death that occurred seventy-two years before Natalie entered high school so affected the Hobbs family that Billy's grandniece chose to write of it and its impact on Hattie.

The Hobbs members take consolation that Billy, the boy who snuck away from home during high school to take flying lessons and soar above verdant Indiana cornfields, perished while doing what he most loved. "He was doing what he wanted to do when he died," said Joyce Clelland. "That's important."[25]

"HE'S REACHING OUT ACROSS THE YEARS TO US"

Zelda Mandeberg's emotions mirrored those of Hattie Hobbs. "Zelda was angry," said Eugene's nephew, Richard Mandeberg. "Zelda hated Admiral Halsey, who made the boys go out on all these missions when he knew the war was winding down." Richard said that because of her anger at Halsey and the Navy, his grandmother refused to attend a 1946 military ceremony to honor all the servicemen who had given their lives during the war, and that whenever they visited their grandparents, "there was no laughter. I think due to Gene's loss. Zelda became a different person."[26] Like Hattie, Zelda would sometimes stand on the front porch as if waiting for news that her son, whose body had not been found, was somehow alive.

THE U.S. MILITARY continued to investigate the disappearance of the four aviators. In 1946 an American Graves Registration Service team from Headquarters, Eighth Army recovered the remains that had been buried near the temple. The next year the team visited the site of the plane that crashed near the Watanabe farm. They recovered additional remains twelve inches below the surface they believed to be Mandeberg, as well as portions of a small porcelain baby bear they concluded was a pilot's good luck charm. Multiple aircraft parts—a tail section, two landing gears, wing sections, two rubber tires, pieces of the fuselage, a smashed radio, propellers, machine guns—confirmed that the plane was an F6F Hellcat, and the presence of an "R" marking on some of the pieces indicated that the aircraft most likely came from the *Yorktown*, whose planes carried the same "R" imprint.

In the days before DNA testing, the American Graves Registration Service had insufficient evidence to provide a positive identification because the remains only consisted of the upper torso. The surgeon general, Rear Admiral C. A. Swanson, contacted the four families and briefed them about the efforts that had been made and of their conclusion that the remains were most likely one of the final four men to die in the war. In a separate communication, he informed the Mandebergs that in examining the evidence, it appeared reasonable to the Army team that the remains were those of their son. The surgeon general asked the family if Eugene carried any good luck charms, in this case the porcelain bear, but no one recalled such an item. Swanson offered the remains to the family, but Zelda and Nathan felt that since the government could not deliver a positive identification, they chose to have the remains interred and marked "Unknown" in a military cemetery overseas. The remains were subsequently buried at the American military cemetery in Yokohama before being later moved to the American cemetery in Manila in the Philippines. Lacking a definitive identification, each of the four families held on to the belief that the individual buried in the Philippines was their loved one.

Decades later, and with DNA testing common, government analysts contacted the four families to obtain DNA samples, and as of this writing are testing those samples against that of the American pilot downed near Yokohama in hopes of informing one of the four that they had located their loved one. Jean Mandeberg, Eugene's niece and namesake, said that the possibility of the remains being identified as her uncle, whom the family would love to bury next to Zelda and Nathan in Detroit, was like a dream come true. "I remember as a kid, that my fantasy in school was being called to the principal's office because my uncle had been found."[27]

The government's action renewed the faint hope for the Hobbs family that Billy's remains would return to Kokomo. Because Billy's sister, Nancy, was alive and well in Kokomo, the analysts are confident that they will be able to, at a minimum, conclusively state whether or not the remains are those of Billy. If they are not, the government hopes to match that DNA with the samples from the Mandebergs, Harrisons, and Sahloffs.

SONYA MOVED ON with her life, eventually marrying and raising a family in New York. Eugene's memory never faded though, and according to daughter Susan Sussman, "My mother's old wound was opened" when she and other family members compiled information for a 2014 documentary about Sonya. "I always knew about Mandy," said Susan, "because Mom talked about him. There was always this other part to our family."[28]

While researching the story Susan, in an effort to learn more about Eugene Mandeberg, sent emails to Jean Mandeberg and her brother, Richard (Eugene's niece and nephew), who knew only that their uncle had been engaged to a woman named Sonya when he died. The families shared memories, and according to daughter Susan her mother "was visibly relieved to hear" that Eugene might not have "died a watery death in Tokyo Bay," but instead had possibly been "treated with respect by a Buddhist monk who later turned them over to American forces." Sonya admitted that while it was at first painful to think of Eugene's loss and share stories of their brief time together, "now there's nothing but pleasure when I think of Eugene."[29]

Almost seventy years after Eugene's death, the two families had reconnected. Each had always sensed a gap in their lives, as if something had been whisked away that by right should have been present, but the reunion served to fill that hole. Jean, a talented artist, grew up believing that Uncle Eugene's death prodded her to pursue her artistic path. Since he never had the opportunity to return from the war and become the writer he always hoped to be, she could in a way fulfill his dreams by fulfilling her own. "Very early in my life it was made very clear to me, that I was named after someone very important to the family," Jean explained. "It was clear to me that I was named after someone who had died, and that I would have a girl's version of his name. It was clear to me that he was a writer, a creative person, and that there was profound grief over the death of this person, and that my birth represented hope."[30]

Susan Sussman said that "we found in each other some missing pieces of our puzzle. We may not be connected by blood but each of us feels like cousins through the shared love of Sonya and Mandy." She added, "It was like twins split apart at birth, and now they were together."[31]

It seemed almost as if Eugene had orchestrated the implausible reunion. "Sonya is the last person alive who knew Eugene," said Richard Mandeberg. "It's like he's reaching out across the years to us. After seventy years, Eugene was reaching out, telling the last remaining individual that he wanted to be put to rest." Jean agreed, and added that while she hoped the government identified the remains as her uncle, she would be pleased with any conclusion. "Our grandparents didn't hear the end of this story," she said, referring to Zelda and Nathan. "Let's at least let Eugene's fiancé hear the end."[32]

"BUT WE REMEMBER WHEN OTHERS FORGET"

Although Air Group 88 remained off the Japanese coast fewer than three months, they participated in some of the most dangerous attacks conducted by carrier aviators. They faced opposition from skilled enemy gunners manning the hundreds of antiaircraft guns surrounding the targets, played a crucial role in sinking the last vestiges of a Japanese fleet that had insulted a nation and embarrassed a military at Pearl Harbor, and brought the war directly from island battlefields to Japan's major cities and industries, all while operating in horrible weather that caused the loss of Lieutenant Commander Crommelin and others.

Since her commissioning in April 1943, the *Yorktown* had taken five air groups into action, and only Air Group 1 had a greater percentage of daily losses than did Air Group 88, which recorded eighteen aviators killed in forty-six days off Japan. By comparison their predecessor, Air Group 9, remained in combat almost twice as long and flew more than double the number of sorties, yet lost one fewer man than did Air Group 88.

"Air Group 88 reported aboard *Yorktown* in June, 1945, just prior to intensive air operations against the Japanese mainland," reported Captain Boone. "The Air Group, with little chance for training, buckled down to the serious task ahead with enthusiasm and a keen interest. During the entire operation they performed their duties in a very satisfactory manner despite poor weather and a relatively high number of combat losses in personnel. The Air Group Commander and the Squadron Commanders are to be commended for their excellent planning and able leadership in the execution of their duties. The accomplishments of Air Group 88 form a record of which they may well be proud."[33]

Lieutenant Commander Cagle added that while the enemy declined to mount an air arm in opposition, Air Group 88 "was a gallant outfit" that "had the satisfaction of being in on the kill, the surrender ceremonies, the liberation of prisoners and the occupation of Japan. It was a job well done."[34]

Merald Woods claims that even today, he still has dreams about his time with the Air Group "because that time means so much to me." John Haag, whose father flew in the fighting squadron with Hobbs and Mandeberg, spends hours researching Air Group 88's time in the war because "I want to honor Dad and his squadron. I feel I have to touch base with him."[35]

John Haag is rightly proud of his father's accomplishments, and Reverend Robert Vrooman, Joseph Sahloff's nephew, was delighted when he unexpectedly came across his uncle's name inscribed in a memorial wall in Hawaii. The USS *Yorktown* Association keeps the story vibrant in Patriots Point, South Carolina, where the aircraft carrier still proudly bobs at anchor and welcomes the visitors who come to walk her decks and scrutinize the ready rooms once used by the World War II aviators and ship's company. But if Lieutenant (jg) Haag or Lieutenant (jg) Sahloff were still alive, they would agree with Lieutenant (jg) Bernard Hamilton of the fighting-bombing squadron. If someone tells Hamilton he is a hero, he politely declines the appellation. "I didn't do anything special," he explains. "It was my job."[36]

The families appreciate the work performed at Patriots Point, whose curator and staff lovingly maintain the *Yorktown* and help guide visitors on their tours, but sometimes they wonder if their World War II relative, whether he was a father, grandfather, son, brother, or uncle, is too speedily and irrevocably vanishing into the past. Outside of family, Billy Hobbs is today an unknown figure in Kokomo, and the Mandebergs, who along with Susan Sussman have helped preserve Eugene's story, have dispersed from the Detroit area. The Harrisons and Sahloffs offer similar stories.

Sonya, as of this writing, remains in New York, where she will freely talk to people about the young man with whom she fell in love seven decades ago. Billy's sister, Nancy, resides in Kokomo with numerous other members of the Hobbs clan, and family members of the other two aviators lost in the war's final action labor to keep memories fresh.

The Hobbs, Mandeberg, Harrison, and Sahloff families have a powerful ally in someone who died almost fifty years ago. Hattie Hobbs, so deeply affected by Billy's death, left words she hoped would ensure that her son would never be forgotten. Writing in behalf of the entire Hobbs family, but using words that convey the grief of every family of the last four men to die in World War II, Hattie wrote in her 1968 memorial poem marking the anniversary of her son's death:

> *Nothing but memories as we journey on,*
> *Longing for a smile from a loved one gone.*
> *None know the depths of our deep regret,*
> *But we remember when others forget.*[37]

NOTES

CHAPTER 1: "And Then Came the War"

1. Lieutenant Paul E. Williams, "Fighting Eighty-Eight," poem printed in the Commissioning Party Program, September 1, 1944, in the "CAG-88" Box, Patriots Point Naval & Maritime Museum Archives, Mount Pleasant, South Carolina (hereafter referred to as Patriots Point Archives).

2. Author's interview with Nancy Exmeyer, October 11, 2017.

3. Exmeyer interview, October 11, 2017.

4. "Sisters Remember Loss of Brother on Last Day of War," *Kokomo Perspective*, August 31, 2005, H-19, in the Cary Hobbs Collection.

5. Exmeyer interview, October 11, 2017.

6. James W. Vernon, *The Hostile Sky: A Hellcat Flier in World War II* (Annapolis, MD: Naval Institute Press, 2003), 15.

7. "There's No Substitute for Marksmanship!" Training Division, Bureau of Aeronautics, United States Navy, November 1942, 1–4, 13, from the "John Ponder Collection, *Yorktown*, WWII," Patriots Point Archives.

8. "Dunking Sense," Training Division, Bureau of Aeronautics, United States Navy, February 1943, 5, 9, 19, 21, from the "John Ponder Collection, *Yorktown*, WWII," Patriots Point Archives.

9. "Prisoner Sense," Training Division, Bureau of Aeronautics, United States Navy, May 1943, 1–2, 15, from the "John Ponder Collection, *Yorktown*, WWII," Patriots Point Archives.

10. Gerald Hennesy email to the author, March 29, 2018.

11. Hennesy email, March 29, 2018.

12. Author's interview with Jean Mandeberg, December 28, 2017.

13. *The Eaglet,* July 9, 1943, 2, in the Jean Mandeberg Collection.

14. Untitled May 1940 article; "Anti-Strike Legislation—Is It Fair to Labor?," December 1940. Both articles in Sonya Levien Kamsky and Susan Kamsky Sussman, "A Loving Engagement: Letters to Sonya Levien from the Mandeberg Family, 1944–1945," June 2015 (hereafter cited as "A Loving Engagement").

15. "The Optimist," July 1940; "Short Order Man," January 1941; "In These Hands," January 1941; all three in "A Loving Engagement."

16. "Private Party," July 1940, in "A Loving Engagement."

17. "First Leave," December 1940, in "A Loving Engagement."

18. Eugene Mandeberg letter to his parents, undated but from "U.S. Naval Air Station, Melbourne, Florida," in the Jean Mandeberg Collection.

19. Vernon, *Hostile Sky,* 48–49.

20. Hennesy email, March 29, 2018.

21. Vernon, *Hostile Sky,* 52.

22. Kay Luna, "WWII Vet Still Has Fighter Pilot's Eye," September 22, 2007, accessed January 17, 2018, http://qctimes.com/news/local/wwii-vet -still-has-fighter-pilot-s-eye/article_3c499349-21e3-55f9-9b08-2c0f c00ea5b1.html.

23. Eugene Mandeberg letter to his parents and Eugene Mandeberg letter to his mother, both undated but from "U.S. Naval Air Station, Melbourne, Florida," both in the Jean Mandeberg Collection.

24. "The Service Parade," *Detroit Free Press,* April 11, 1944, 15.

25. Inscription in Wright Hobbs Diary, in the Denny Clelland Collection (hereafter cited as Hobbs Diary).

26. Hobbs Diary, April 8, April 12, April 14, April 16, and April 17, 1944.

27. Wright Hobbs letter to his mother, undated, but stationery letterhead is "U.S. Naval Air Station, Miami, Florida," in the Denny Clelland Collection.

28. Wright Hobbs letter to Henry Hobbs, May 6, 1944, in the Cary Hobbs Collection.

29. Wright Hobbs letter to his mother, undated, but stationery letterhead is "U.S. Naval Air Station, Miami, Florida," in the Denny Clelland Collection.

30. Hobbs Diary, April 28, April 29, April 30, and May 2, 1944.

31. Dick Halvorsen, *Steeds in the Sky* (New York: Lancer Books, 1971), 116, 118.

32. Hobbs Diary, April 16, April 20, and April 26, 1944.

33. Wright Hobbs letter to Henry Hobbs, May 6, 1944.

34. Hobbs Diary, May 23, 1944.

CHAPTER 2: "Kids Jerked Right Out of High School"

1. Julie McClure, "Day of Victory Also Day of Loss," *Kokomo Tribune*, August 13, 1995, A1.

2. Commanding Officer to the Chief of Naval Operations, "History of Torpedo Squadron Eighty-Eight from 15 August 1944 to 31 December 1944," January 5, 1945, 1.

3. *Martha's Vineyard to Tokyo: A Historical Record of VT-88* (New York: New Era Lithograph Company, undated, but soon after war's end), in USS *Yorktown* Archives, Patriots Point Archives, 14.

4. Author's interview with William Watkinson, November 9, 2017.

5. "History of Torpedo Squadron Eighty-Eight from 15 August 1944 to 31 December 1944," January 5, 1945.

6. Author's interview with Bernard Hamilton Jr., November 19, 2017.

7. "Heroes: The Indestructibles," *Time*, January 24, 1944, 61.

8. "The 'Dixie Demons' of Alabama," accessed August 18, 2017, www.crommelin.org/history/Biographies/Alabama/.

9. "Heroes: The Indestructibles," 61.

10. *Martha's Vineyard to Tokyo*, 15.

11. Author's interview with Arthur Briggs, March 20, 2018.

12. Commander, Bombing Squadron Eighty-Eight to Commander-in-Chief, U.S. Fleet, "War Diary for September 1944," September 30, 1944.

13. Commander, Bombing Squadron Eighty-Eight to Commander-in-Chief, U.S. Fleet, "War Diary for October 1944," October 31, 1944.

14. "History of Torpedo Squadron Eighty-Eight from 15 August 1944 to 31 December 1944," 10; *Martha's Vineyard to Tokyo*, 22.

15. Author's interview with Arthur Briggs, March 16, 2018; Briggs interview, March 20, 2018.

16. Author's interview with Merald Woods, March 15, 2018.

17. *Martha's Vineyard to Tokyo*, 23.

18. Commander S. S. Searcy Jr., *The Story of Air Group 88*, undated, but compiled by the commanding officers of the four air squadrons shortly after the war, 20.

19. Commander, Bombing Squadron Eighty-Eight to Chief of Naval Operations, "Unit History of Bombing Squadron Eighty-Eight from 15 August 1944 to 1 January 1945," January 1, 1945, 4; "History of Torpedo Squadron Eighty-Eight from 15 August 1944 to 31 December 1944," 14.

20. Author's interview with Merald Woods, November 20, 2017.

21. *Martha's Vineyard to Tokyo*, 24.

22. Author's interview with Merald Woods, November 16, 2017.

23. *Martha's Vineyard to Tokyo*, 13.

24. Briggs interview, March 20, 2018.

25. Wright Hobbs letter to Henry Hobbs, January 7, 1945, in the Cary Hobbs Collection.

26. Masatake Okumiya with Jiro Horikoshi and Martin Caidan, *Zero* (New York: Simon & Schuster, Inc., 1956), 221.

27. Commander Gerald C. Hennesy, "My Duty with Air Group 88," personal reminiscence written for the author, December 23, 2017; author's interview with Gerald Hennesy, December 23, 2017.

28. Watkinson interview, November 9, 2017.

29. Woods interview, November 20, 2017.

30. Searcy, *Story of Air Group 88*, 21.

31. Wright Hobbs letter to Henry Hobbs, January 7, 1945.

32. Commander, Bombing Squadron Eighty-Eight to Commander-in-Chief, U.S. Fleet, "War Diary for December 1944," January 6, 1945.

33. Commanding Officer, Fighting Squadron Eighty-Eight to Commander in Chief, U.S. Fleet, "War Diary for December 1944," January 1, 1945.

34. *Martha's Vineyard to Tokyo*, 19.

35. Wright Hobbs letter to Henry Hobbs, January 7, 1945.

36. Author's interview with Sonya Levien, May 30, 2018.

37. Letter from Zelda Mandeberg to Sonya Levien, November 30, 1944, in "A Loving Engagement."

38. Letter from Zelda Mandeberg to Sonya Levien, December 27, 1944, in "A Loving Engagement."

39. Letter from Eugene Mandeberg's aunt, unnamed, to Zelda and Nathan Mandeberg, November 20, 1944, in "A Loving Engagement."

40. Letters from Zelda Mandeberg to Sonya Levien, January 7, January 13, January 20, January 23, and January 27, 1945, in "A Loving Engagement."

CHAPTER 3: "Moved, Always West, Toward the Combat Zone"

1. *Martha's Vineyard to Tokyo*, 16.

2. Woods interview, March 15, 2018.

3. Box given by Wright Hobbs to his brother Henry, in the Cary Hobbs Collection.

4. Exmeyer interview, October 11, 2017.

5. Letter from Zelda Mandeberg to Sonya Levien, February 15, 1945, in "A Loving Engagement."

6. Searcy, *Story of Air Group 88*, 1; "History of Torpedo Squadron Eighty-Eight from 15 August 1944 to 31 December 1944," 14.

7. Letter from Zelda Mandeberg to Sonya Levien, February 21, 1945, in "A Loving Engagement."

8. Woods interview, November 20, 2017.

9. Searcy, *Story of Air Group 88*, 16.

10. Commanding Officer to the Chief of Naval Operations, "History of Torpedo Squadron Eighty-Eight from 1 January 1945 to 31 March 1945," April 1, 1945, 5.

11. Commanding Officer to History Unit, Office of Editorial Research, Office of the Chief of Naval Operations, Navy Department, "Historical Report of Fighting Squadron Eighty-Eight from 1 March to 3 September 1945," October 22, 1945, 1 (hereafter cited as "Historical Report of Fighting Squadron Eighty-Eight").

12. Hobbs Diary, March 9, 1945; Wright Hobbs letter to his sister, Nancy, April 3, 1945, in the Nancy Exmeyer Collection; "Historical Report of Fighting Squadron Eighty-Eight," 2.

13. *Martha's Vineyard to Tokyo*, 38.

14. "Historical Report of Fighting Squadron Eighty-Eight," 1.

15. Wright Hobbs Flight Log, April 26, 1945, in the Cary Hobbs Collection (hereafter cited as Hobbs Flight Log and the date).

16. Commander, Bombing Fighting Squadron Eighty-Eight to Commander-in-Chief, United States Fleet, "War Diary for April 1945," June 6, 1945.

17. Wright Hobbs letter to his sister, Nancy, April 3, 1945; Hobbs Diary, March 16, March 17, March 29, and April 29, 1945.

18. Wright Hobbs letter to his sister, Nancy, April 3, 1945; Hobbs Diary, March 18, 1945.

19. Hattie Hobbs letter to Wright Hobbs, February 27, 1945, in the Denny Clelland Collection.

20. Letters from Zelda Mandeberg to Sonya Levien, February 27, March 18, March 20, April 10, April 18, April 23, April 26, 1945, in "A Loving Engagement."

21. Commander, Bombing Fighting Squadron Eighty-Eight to the Chief of Naval Operations, "History of Bombing Fighting Squadron Eighty-Eight from 1 March 1945 to 31 May 1945," October 17, 1945.

22. "Historical Report of Fighting Squadron Eighty-Eight," 1.

23. Searcy, *Story of Air Group 88*, 6; "Historical Report of Fighting Squadron Eighty-Eight," 2, 4.

24. Hobbs Diary, April 30, 1945.

25. Hobbs Diary, May 1, 1945; "Historical Report of Fighting Squadron Eighty-Eight," 1–5.

26. Letter from Zelda Mandeberg to Sonya Levien, May 16, 1945, in "A Loving Engagement."

27. Hobbs Diary, May 8, 1945; "Historical Report of Fighting Squadron Eighty-Eight," 3, 5.

28. C. P. Trussell, "Blackout Lifted on Capitol Dome," *New York Times*, May 9, 1945, 1; Hanson W. Baldwin, "Blows to Crush Japan Are Now Foreshadowed," *New York Times*, May 20, 1945, 1.

29. Letter from Zelda Mandeberg to Sonya Levien, May 7, 1945, in "A Loving Engagement."

30. Searcy, *Story of Air Group 88*, 28.

31. "Historical Report of Fighting Squadron Eighty-Eight," 6.

32. *Martha's Vineyard to Tokyo*, 40.

33. The Commanding Officer to the Chief of Naval Operations, "History of Bombing Squadron Eighty-Eight from 1 March 1945 to 20 October 1945," October 18, 1945, 2.

34. "Historical Report of Fighting Squadron Eighty-Eight," 7.

35. Author's interview with Bernard Hamilton Jr., March 20, 2018.

36. Searcy, *Story of Air Group 88*, 16.

37. Searcy, *Story of Air Group 88*, 13.

38. Letters from Zelda Mandeberg to Sonya Levien, two undated May 1945 letters, in "A Loving Engagement."

39. "Historical Report of Fighting Squadron Eighty-Eight," 7.

40. Commanding Officer to the Chief of Naval Operations, "History of Torpedo Squadron Eighty-Eight from 1 April 1945 to 20 October 1945," October 20, 1945.

CHAPTER 4: "An Aircraft Carrier Is a Noble Thing"

1. "Historical Report of Fighting Squadron Eighty-Eight," 8.

2. Clark G. Reynolds, *The Fighting Lady* (Missoula, MT: Pictorial Histories Publishing, 1986), 304.

3. Searcy, *Story of Air Group 88*, 6.

4. Searcy, *Story of Air Group 88*, 22.

5. Ernie Pyle, *Last Chapter* (New York: Henry Holt and Company, 1946).

6. George E. Jones, "Lethal Sea Weapon and Powder Keg, Too," *New York Times*, July 29, 1945, 6.

7. Commanding Officer to the Chief of Naval Operations, "Ship's History—U.S.S. *Shangri-La* (CV-38)—Submission of," October 25, 1945, 111–112.

8. Lieutenant Commander J. Bryan III, *Aircraft Carrier* (New York: Ballantine Books, 1954), 109.

9. Morris Markey, *Well Done!* (New York: D. Appleton-Century Company, 1945), 41; Lieutenant Oliver Jensen, USNR, *Carrier War* (New York: Simon & Schuster, 1945), 7.

10. Lieutenant William H. Hessler, "The Carrier Task Force in World War II," *Naval Institute Proceedings*, November 1945, 1276, 1279–1281.

11. Watkinson interview, November 9, 2017.

12. Hennesy interview, December 23, 2017.

13. Pyle, *Last Chapter,* 69.

14. Pyle, *Last Chapter,* 59.

15. Searcy, *Story of Air Group 88,* 28.

16. Letter from Zelda Mandeberg to Sonya Levien, June 28, 1945, in "A Loving Engagement."

17. "Historical Report of Fighting Squadron Eighty-Eight," 8.

18. "Waiting," *Time,* July 9, 1945, http://content.time.com/time/subscriber/article/0,33009,852318,00.html.

19. "The Task Ahead," *New York Times,* June 2, 1945, 14.

20. The Reminiscences of Robert Bostwick Carney, Naval History Project, Oral History research Office, Columbia University, 1964, 442 (hereafter cited as Carney Oral History).

21. Fleet Admiral William F. Halsey and Lieutenant Commander J. Bryan III, *Admiral Halsey's Story* (New York: McGraw-Hill Book Company, 1947), 81.

22. Admiral William F. Halsey, as told to Frank D. Morris, "A Plan for Japan," *Collier's,* April 28, 1945, 18; Transcript of NBC Radio Interview, February 19, 1945, found in "Speeches 1939–45," William F. Halsey Collection, Library of Congress; Carney Oral History, 465.

23. Reynolds, *Fighting Lady,* 299–300.

24. Reynolds, *Fighting Lady,* 305; Hobbs Diary, July 1, 1945.

25. Commander S. S. Searcy Jr., "Combat Summary," found in "CAG-88" Box, Patriots Point Archives.

26. Searcy, *Story of Air Group 88,* 6.

27. "The Surrender of Japan," an undated document found in "Halsey Operational Plans to September 1945," William F. Halsey Papers, Library of Congress, 1.

28. Samuel Eliot Morison, *History of United States Naval Operations in World War II, Volume XIV: Victory in the Pacific, 1945* (Boston: Little, Brown, 1960), 310; Halsey and Bryan, *Admiral Halsey's Story,* 257.

29. "Historical Report of Fighting Squadron Eighty-Eight," 8.

30. Hobbs Diary, July 1–3, 1945.

31. Eugene Mandeberg letter to his parents, July 4, 1945, in the Jean Mandeberg Collection.

32. Hobbs Diary, July 4, 1945.

33. Main Headline, and "Hoosiers to Celebrate Fourth in More Traditional Methods," *Kokomo Tribune*, July 4, 1945, 1.

34. Briggs interview, March 20, 2018.

35. Hobbs Diary, July 6, 1945.

36. Admiral Matome Ugaki, *Fading Victory: The Diary of Admiral Matome Ugaki, 1941–1945* (Pittsburgh: University of Pittsburgh Press, 1991), 642.

37. Hobbs Diary, July 8, 1945; *Martha's Vineyard to Tokyo*, 47.

38. Reynolds, *Fighting Lady*, 305.

39. Hobbs Diary, July 9, 1945.

CHAPTER 5: "Today Our Group 88 Starts Raising Hell with the Japs"

1. Air Intelligence Group Division, Naval Intelligence Office, "Flak Information Bulletin No. 8," April 1945, 20, 21, 23.

2. Reynolds, *The Fighting Lady*, 306.

3. Lieutenant Clarence E. Dickinson, *The Flying Guns* (New York: Charles Scribner's Sons, 1943), 71–72.

4. Hamilton interview, March 20, 2018.

5. Watkinson interview, November 9, 2017.

6. Barbara Stahura, *USS* Yorktown *CV-10: The Fighting Lady, Volume II* (Paducah, KY: Turner Publishing, 1997), 108.

7. Jones, "Lethal Sea Weapon and Powder Keg, Too," 6.

8. Markey, *Well Done!*, 79.

9. "Historical Report of Fighting Squadron Eighty-Eight," 5.

10. Bryan III, *Aircraft Carrier*, 32.

11. Watkinson interview, November 9, 2017.

12. Woods interview, March 15, 2018.

13. Pyle, *Last Chapter*, 83.

14. Morison, *History of United States Naval Operations in World War II, Volume XIV*, 311.

15. "Historical Report of Fighting Squadron Eighty-Eight," 8–9.

16. Hennesy interview, December 23, 2017.

CHAPTER 6: "Carrier Pilots Were the Best in the World"

1. Commanding Officer to Commander, Carrier Air Group Eighty-Five, "ACA-1, Aircraft Action Reports, CVG-85," August 18, 1945, Torpedo Squadron 85 Report No. 27, July 10, 1945, Kasumigaura Airfield.

2. Commander Carrier Group Eighty-Eight to Commander-in-Chief, United States Fleet, "Air Operations against Shikoku, Honshu, and Hokkaido, aboard U.S.S. *Yorktown*—Period 1 July to 15 August," September 12, 1945, Torpedo Squadron 88 Report No. 1, July 10, 1945, Kasumigaura Airfield (hereafter cited as Air Group 88 Action Report, followed by squadron, report number, date, target).

3. Air Group 88 Action Report, Fighter Squadron Report No. 4, July 10, 1945, Kashiwa, Imba, Shiroi Airfields.

4. Air Group 88 Action Report, Bomber Squadron Report No. 2, July 10, 1945, Konoike Airfield.

5. Air Group 88 Action Report, Torpedo Squadron Report No. 2, July 10, 1945, Konoike Airfield.

6. Woods interview, November 20, 2017.

7. Pyle, *Last Chapter*, 62.

8. Pyle, *Last Chapter*, 90.

9. Pyle, *Last Chapter*, 62–63.

10. Lieutenant Max Miller, USNR, *Daybreak for Our Carrier* (New York: McGraw-Hill, 1944), 91.

11. Hobbs Flight Log, July 10, 1945.

12. Air Group 88 Action Report, Fighter Squadron Report No. 4, July 10, 1945, Konoike Airfield.

13. Commanding Officer to Commander-in-Chief, United States Fleet, "War Diary—Month of July 1945," July 31, 1945 (hereafter cited as *Yorktown* War Diary and the date).

14. Searcy Jr., "Combat Summary."

15. Fleet Admiral William F. Halsey, *Life of Admiral W. F. Halsey*, undated typewritten memoirs dictated by Halsey after the war (hereafter cited as Halsey, *Memoirs*).

16. Okumiya, Horikoshi, and Caidan, *Zero*, 397; Ugaki, *Fading Victory*, 644.

17. "Bull's-Eye," *Time*, July 23, 1945, 27–28.

18. "1,500 American Planes Rake Jap Home Islands," *Kokomo Tribune*, July 10, 1945, 1, 7.

19. George E. Jones, "Fighters Sweep in at Dawn in Opening of Halsey's Attack," *New York Times*, July 11, 1945, 1; W. H. Lawrence, "Japan Battered," *New York Times*, July 11, 1945, 1.

20. "Unconditional Surrender," *New York Times*, July 11, 1945.

21. Hobbs Diary, July 10, 1945.

CHAPTER 7: "Somebody Said We Are to Hit Hokkaido"

1. Hobbs Diary, July 11, 1945.

2. Hobbs Diary, July 12, 1945.

3. "Yanks Unopposed During Jap Raids," *Kokomo Tribune*, July 13, 1945, 1; "Hobbs Reports Wheat Yield of 47 Bu. Per Acre," *Kokomo Tribune*, July 13, 1945, 2.

4. Hobbs Diary, July 13, 1945.

5. Woods interview, November 20, 2017.

6. Air Group 88 Action Report, Fighter Squadron Report No. 5, July 14, 1945, Hakodate Area.

7. Air Group 88 Action Report, Bomber Squadron Report No. 3, July 14, 1945, Hakodate Area.

8. Air Group 88 Action Report, Torpedo Squadron Report No. 3, July 14, 1945, Muroran Area.

9. Air Group 88 Action Report, Bomber Squadron Report No. 3, July 14, 1945, Hakodate Area.

10. Commander, Bombing Fighting Squadron Eighty-Eight to the Chief of Naval Operations, "History of Bomber Fighting Squadron Eighty-Eight from 1 June 1945 to 15 September 1945," October 21, 1945.

11. Air Group 88 Action Report, Bomber Squadron Report No. 3, July 14, 1945, Hakodate Area.

12. Air Group 88 Action Report, Torpedo Squadron Report No. 3, July 14, 1945, Muroran Area.

13. Air Group 88 Action Report, Fighter Squadron Report No. 5, July 14, 1945, Hakodate Area.

14. Air Group 88 Action Report, Fighter Squadron Report No. 5, July 14, 1945, Hakodate Area.

15. Wyatt Emmerich, "Malcolm Cagle," *Northside Sun* (Jackson, MS), April 20, 2000, 26.

16. Air Group 88 Action Report, Torpedo Squadron Report No. 3, July 14, 1945, Muroran Area.

17. Air Group 85 Action Report, Bomber Squadron Report No. 35, July 14, 1945, Hakodate Area.

18. Air Group 88 Action Report, Bomber Fighter Squadron Report No. 8, July 14, 1945, Hakodate Area.

19. Gerald Hennesy, "August 15th, 1945—The Japs Surrender," reminiscence given to author, December 23, 2017.

20. Reynolds, *Fighting Lady*, 307.

21. Air Group 88 Action Report, Torpedo Squadron Report No. 5, July 15, 1945, Muroran Area.

22. "Air Operations against Shikoku, Honshu, and Hokkaido, aboard U.S.S. *Yorktown*—Period 1 July to 15 August," September 12, 1945, 4.

23. Reynolds, *Fighting Lady*, 307–308.

24. "History of Bomber Fighting Squadron Eighty-Eight from 1 June 1945 to 15 September 1945."

25. Hennesy, "August 15th, 1945—The Japs Surrender."

26. Halsey and Bryan, *Admiral Halsey's Story*, 260; Halsey, *Memoirs*, 575–576.

27. "Halsey Turns Surface Craft Loose on Japan; Planes Support Strike," *Kokomo Tribune*, July 14, 1945, 1; "Bull's-Eye," *Time*, July 23, 1945, 1–3, www.time.com/time/magazine/article/0,9171,803564,00.html.

28. "Air Operations against Shikoku, Honshu, and Hokkaido, aboard U.S.S. *Yorktown*—Period 1 July to 15 August," September 12, 1945, 18.

29. Air Group 85 Action Report, Bomber Squadron Report No. 34, July 14, 1945, Hokkaido Area.

30. Air Group 85 Action Report, Torpedo Squadron Report No. 33, July 14, 1945, Hokkaido Area.

31. "Historical Report of Fighting Squadron Eighty-Eight," 10.

32. "Air Operations against Shikoku, Honshu, and Hokkaido, aboard U.S.S. *Yorktown*—Period 1 July to 15 August," September 12, 1945, 4; Woods interviews, November 20, 2017, and March 15, 2018.

33. Ugaki, *Fading Victory,* 645.

34. "Halsey Turns Surface Craft Loose on Japan," *Kokomo Tribune.*

35. Hobbs Flight Log, July 14, 1945.

36. Hobbs Diary, July 14, 1945.

37. Letters from Zelda Mandeberg to Sonya Levien, July 12 and July 15, 1945, in "A Loving Engagement."

CHAPTER 8: "Stay Away from Kure"

1. Hennesy email, March 29, 2018.

2. Barrett Tillman, *Whirlwind: The Air War Against Japan, 1942–1945* (New York: Simon & Schuster, 2010), 219; Commander Gerald C. Hennesy personal recollection, "The Shootdown," December 23, 2017.

3. Searcy, *Story of Air Group 88,* 36; "Air Operations against Shikoku, Honshu, and Hokkaido, aboard U.S.S. *Yorktown*—Period 1 July to 15 August," September 12, 1945, 6.

4. Vernon, *Hostile Sky,* 157.

5. "Air Operations against Shikoku, Honshu, and Hokkaido, aboard U.S.S. *Yorktown*—Period 1 July to 15 August," September 12, 1945, 6.

6. Air Group 88 Action Report, Torpedo Squadron Report No. 6, July 18, 1945, *Nagato.*

7. "Ship's History—U.S.S. *Shangri-La,*" 87.

8. Halsey, *Memoirs,* 581.

9. Briggs interview, March 20, 2018; Watkinson interview, November 9, 2017.

10. Watkinson interview, November 9, 2017.

11. Reynolds, *Fighting Lady,* 308.

12. "The Week with Christ Catholic Services," July 22, 1945, Sunday Mass program in "*Yorktown* Chaplains, WWII" Box, Patriots Point Archive.

13. Reynolds, *Fighting Lady,* 308.

14. Air Group 88 Action Report, Bomber Fighter Squadron Report No. 17, July 24, 1945, Kure Harbor.

15. Air Group 88 Action Report, Fighter Squadron Report No. 15, July 24, 1945, Kure Harbor.

16. Air Group 88 Action Report, Bomber Squadron Report No. 7, July 24, 1945, Kure Harbor.

17. Reynolds, *Fighting Lady*, 309.

18. Air Group 88 Action Report, Fighter Squadron Report No. 15, July 24, 1945, Kure Harbor.

19. Air Group 88 Action Report, Fighter Squadron Report No. 16, July 25, 1945, Yonago Airfield.

20. Air Group 88 Action Report, Bomber Fighter Squadron Report No. 20, July 25, 1945, Miho & Yonago Airfield; Searcy, *Story of Air Group 88*, 36.

21. Air Group 88 Action Report, Bomber Fighter Squadron Report No. 22, July 28, 1945, Miho & Yonago Airfield.

22. "Yanks Find Many Dummy Planes on Jap Air Field," *Harlingen (Texas) Valley Morning Star*, August 5, 1945, 8.

23. Air Group 88 Action Report, Torpedo Squadron Report No. 10, July 28, 1945, Kure Harbor.

24. "Air Operations against Shikoku, Honshu, and Hokkaido, aboard U.S.S. *Yorktown*—Period 1 July to 15 August," September 12, 1945, 10.

25. Commanding Officer Fighting Squadron Eighty-Eight to Commanding Officer, U.S.S. *Yorktown*, (CV-10), "Attack Against Reveted and Hidden Japanese Aircraft—Suggested Plan of," July 19, 1945; Air Group 85 Action Report, Torpedo Squadron Report No. 37, July 18, 1945, *Nagato*.

26. "Attack Against Reveted and Hidden Japanese Aircraft—Suggested Plan of."

27. Air Group 88 Action Report, Fighter Squadron Report No. 12, July 18, 1945, *Nagato*.

28. Air Group 88 Action Report, Torpedo Squadron Report No. 7, July 24, 1945, Kure Harbor.

29. Hennesy, "Shootdown."

30. "Halsey Says Blows Open 'Final Plunge,'" *New York Times*, July 25, 1945, 1–2.

31. "U.S. Fleet Within 80 Miles of Tokyo," *Kokomo Tribune*, July 17, 1945, 1.

32. "Greatest Superfort Fleet Fires Japan," *Kokomo Tribune*, July 19, 1945, 1; "With Our Boys in the Service," *Kokomo Tribune*, August 30, 1945, 45; McClure, "Day of Victory Also Day of Loss," A-1.

33. "Jap Battleship Sunk by Airmen," *Kokomo Tribune*, July 28, 1945, 1, 9.

34. Wright Hobbs letter to sister, Joyce Hobbs, July 28, 1945, in the Denny Clelland Collection.

35. Letters from Zelda Mandeberg to Sonya Levien, July 18, July 20, July 28, July 29, and July 31, 1945, in "A Loving Engagement."

36. Searcy Jr., "Combat Summary"; *Yorktown* War Diary, July 28, 1945.

37. Halsey and Bryan, *Admiral Halsey's Story*, 264.

CHAPTER 9: "The Navy Would Be in to Get You"

1. Saburo Sakai, with Martin Caidin and Fred Saito, *Samurai!* (New York: Simon & Schuster, 1957), 323, 361.

2. Henry Sakaida, "Unknown American Pilot Now Identified," posted in WWII History Articles, February 7, 2018, accessed February 20, 2018, http://ww2awartobewon.com/wwii-articles/american-pilot-identified/.

3. Air Group 88 Action Report, Fighter Squadron Report No. 15, July 24, 1945, Kure Harbor; Sakaida, "Unknown American Pilot Now Identified."

4. Air Group 88 Action Report, Fighter Squadron Report No. 15, July 24, 1945, Kure Harbor.

5. "Historical Report of Fighting Squadron Eighty-Eight from 1 March to 3 September 1945."

6. "Dumbo," *Flying*, October 1944, 52.

7. Commander Air Sea Rescue, Ryukyus to Chief of Naval Operations Aviation History Unit, "Air Sea Rescue, Ryukyus—History of," August 26, 1945, 1.

8. "Dumbo," *Flying*, 232.

9. "Life on a Carrier," *Flying*, October 1944, 248.

10. Leo M. Litz, "Navy Pilot Is Rescued as Awed Kobe Stares," *Indianapolis News*, August 8, 1945, 11.

11. Hennesy, "Shootdown."

12. Air Group 88 Action Report, Bomber Fighter Squadron Report No. 19, July 24, 1945, Kure Harbor.

13. Litz, "Navy Pilot Is Rescued," 11.

14. Litz, "Navy Pilot Is Rescued," 11.

15. Hennesy, "Shootdown."

16. Litz, "Navy Pilot Is Rescued," 11.

17. Richard W. Johnston, "Pilot Is Saved by Rescue Plane Under Jap Fire," *Sayre (Pennsylvania) Evening Times,* August 4, 1945, 2.

18. James Lindsley, "Saved Under Nose of Jap Destroyer," *Danville (Virginia) Bee,* August 4, 1945, 7.

19. Lindsley, "Saved Under Nose of Jap Destroyer," 7.

20. Johnston, "Pilot Is Saved by Rescue Plane," 2.

21. "Lt. Sueyres Aids in Rescue Under Jap Fire," *Tampa Bay Times,* August 12, 1945, 21.

22. Father Joseph Moody, "They Brought Him Back Alive," supplement to Commanding Officer to Commander in Chief, U.S. Fleet, "Actions Covering Attacks on Aircraft, Shipping, and Strategic Targets in Northern Kyushu, Shikoku, Tokyo Plain Area, Northern Honshu, and Southern Hokkaido, from 2 July 1945 to 15 August 1945," September 6, 1945.

23. S. P. Walker, "Operation Dumbo," *Our Navy,* March 1, 1946, 4.

24. Walker, "Operation Dumbo," 5.

25. "Dunking Sense," 9, 21.

26. Moody, "They Brought Him Back Alive."

27. Walker, "Operation Dumbo," 4–5.

28. Moody, "They Brought Him Back Alive."

29. Richard W. Johnston, "Dumbo Saves Flyers Under Jap Noses on Failing Engine," *Albany Democrat-Herald,* July 28, 1945, 2.

30. Walker, "Operation Dumbo," 5–6.

31. "Glendale Flyer Saves Two in Jap Sea," *Los Angeles Times,* July 28, 1945, 4.

32. Lyman Hellman, "The Trials and Tribulations of Playmate 9 of VH-4," in *Mariner/Marlin: Anywhere, Anytime* (Paducah, KY: Turner Publishing, 1993), 87.

33. Walker, "Operation Dumbo," 6; Johnston, "Dumbo Saves Flyers," 2.

34. Walker, "Operation Dumbo," 6.

35. Walker, "Operation Dumbo," 60.

36. Moody, "They Brought Him Back Alive."

37. Johnston, "Dumbo Saves Flyers," 2; Moody, "They Brought Him Back Alive."

38. "News of Our Men and Women in Uniform," *Altamont (New York) Enterprise,* April 5, 1946, 1.

39. Walker, "Operation Dumbo," 60.

40. Moody, "They Brought Him Back Alive"; Hellman, "Trials and Tribulations of Playmate 9," 87.

41. Hellman, "Trials and Tribulations of Playmate 9," 88; Walker, "Operation Dumbo," 61.

42. Moody, "They Brought Him Back Alive."

43. Walker, "Operation Dumbo," 61.

44. "Glendale Flyer Saves Two in Jap Sea," 4.

45. "Airmen from 'Fighting Lady' Take 1,000 to 1 Chance, Span Japan in Solid Fog to Save Pal," *Plainfield (New Jersey) Courier News,* September 27, 1945, 13; "Glendale Flyer Saves Two in Jap Sea," 4; Johnston, "Dumbo Saves Flyers," 2.

46. "News of Servicemen," *Ravena (New York) News Herald,* August 10, 1945, 1.

47. Moody, "They Brought Him Back Alive."

48. Hellman, "Trials and Tribulations of Playmate 9," 88.

CHAPTER 10: "Fighting a War That Had Already Been Won"

1. "Ship's History—U.S.S. *Shangri-La*," 96; Admiral Arthur W. Radford, edited by Stephen Jurika Jr., *From Pearl Harbor to Vietnam: The Memoirs of Admiral Arthur W. Radford* (Stanford University: Hoover Institution Press, 1980), 63.

2. "1,546 Small Jap Craft Sunk by U.S. Airmen," *Kokomo Tribune,* August 1, 1945, 1; "Sheets of Fire Blanket Japan," *Kokomo Tribune,* August 2: 1945, 1.

3. John D. Chappell, *Before the Bomb* (Lexington: University Press of Kentucky, 1997), 49, 191n32.

4. Joyce Hobbs Clelland letter to Wright Hobbs, August 1, 1945, in the Denny Clelland Collection.

5. Joyce Hobbs Clelland birthday card to Wright Hobbs, August 2, 1945, in the Denny Clelland Collection.

6. Letter from Zelda Mandeberg to Sonya Levien, August 2, 1945, in "A Loving Engagement."

7. "The Peace Rumors," *New York Times*, July 19, 1945, 22.

8. John Wukovits, "V-J Day," *World War II Presents Victory in the Pacific*, Summer 2005, 78–79.

9. Sakai, Caidin, and Saito, *Samurai!*, 369.

10. "The Ultimatum," *New York Times*, July 28, 1945, 10; "The Japanese Emperor," *New York Times*, July 31, 1945, 18.

11. "Atomic Bomb Loaded with Untold Power Loosed Against Japs," *Kokomo Tribune*, August 6, 1945, 1; John Costello, *The Pacific War 1941–1945* (New York: Quill Books, 1982), 592.

12. "Truman Discloses New Atomic Bomb," *Kokomo Tribune*, August 6, 1945, 9.

13. Herbert P. Bix, *Hirohito and the Making of Modern Japan* (New York: HarperCollins, 2000), 502; Costello, *Pacific War 1941–1945*, 593.

14. Wukovits, "V-J Day," 79.

15. Reynolds, *Fighting Lady*, 313.

16. Searcy Jr., "Combat Summary."

17. McClure, "Day of Victory Also Day of Loss," A-1.

18. "Sober City Awaits Official V-J Word," *New York Times*, August 11, 1945, 9.

19. Letter from Zelda Mandeberg to Sonya Levien, August 8, 1945, in "A Loving Engagement."

20. Letter from Mitchell Mandeberg to Sonya Levien, August 7, 1945, in "A Loving Engagement."

21. "Words Are Weapons," *Time*, August 6, 1945, http://content.time.com/time/subscriber/article/0,33009,803657,00.html.

22. Wukovits, "V-J Day," 81.

23. Reynolds, *Fighting Lady*, 317.

24. Reynolds, *Fighting Lady*, 317; *Martha's Vineyard to Tokyo*, 58.

25. *Martha's Vineyard to Tokyo*, 58; J. Clifford Huddleston letter to Ruben P. Kitchen Jr., December 13, 1978, Patriots Point Archives.

26. Searcy Jr., "Combat Summary."

27. Reynolds, *Fighting Lady*, 318; "Ship's History—U.S.S. *Shangri-La*," 99.

28. Reynolds, *Fighting Lady*, 318.

29. *Martha's Vineyard to Tokyo*, 59.

30. E. B. Potter, *Bull Halsey* (Annapolis, MD: Naval Institute Press, 1985), 346; Commander Third Fleet to Commander in Chief, U.S. Pacific Fleet and Pacific Ocean Areas, "Report on the Operations of the Third Fleet, 16 August 1945 to 19 September 1945," October 6, 1945, 2.

31. "Air Operations against Shikoku, Honshu, and Hokkaido, aboard U.S.S. *Yorktown*—Period 1 July to 15 August," September 12, 1945, 13; Air Group 88 Action Report, Bomber Fighter Squadron Report No. 34, August 10, 1945, Kisarizu [*sic,* Kizarazu] Airfield; Air Group 88 Action Report, Fighter Squadron Report No. 29, August 10, 1945, Niigata Airfield.

32. Peggy Townsend, "The Last Dogfight," *Santa Cruz Sentinel,* July 27, 2003, 22.

33. Hamilton interview, November 19, 2017.

34. Commanding Officer to Chief of Naval Operations, History Unit, "History of Torpedo Squadron Fifty from 10 August 1943 to 29 October 1945," October 29, 1945, 21; Air Group 88 Action Report, Torpedo Squadron Report No. 17, August 13, 1945, Shibaura Electric Company.

35. Commanding Officer to Commander, Carrier Air Group Eighty-Five, "ACA-1, Aircraft Action Reports, CVG-85," August 18, 1945, Torpedo Squadron Report No. 42, August 13, 1945, Shibaura Electric Company.

36. Commanding Officer to Commander, Carrier Air Group Eighty-Five, "ACA-1, Aircraft Action Reports, CVG-85," August 18, 1945, Bomber Squadron Report No. 48, August 13, 1945, Shibaura Electric Company; Reynolds, *Fighting Lady*, 316.

37. "Kokomo Churches Announce Plans for Union 'Thanksgiving' Service," *Kokomo Tribune,* August 11, 1945, 1.

38. "Allies Impatiently Await Reply from Jap Leaders," *Kokomo Tribune,* August 13, 1945, 1.

39. "Halsey's Third Fleet Blasts Jap Homeland," *Kokomo Tribune,* August 13, 1945, 1.

40. "Air Operations against Shikoku, Honshu, and Hokkaido, aboard U.S.S. *Yorktown*—Period 1 July to 15 August," September 12, 1945, 15.

41. U.S.S. *Yorktown*, "Radio Free News," August 14, 1945, in "Radio News Distributed on CV-10, WWII" Box, Patriots Point Archive.

42. Tillman, *Whirlwind*, 242.

43. "Parents Plan Memorial Services for Ensign Hobbs on Next Sunday," *Kokomo Tribune*, October 14, 1946, 24.

44. Vernon, *Hostile Sky*, 177–178.

45. "Parents Plan Memorial Services for Ensign Hobbs," 24.

CHAPTER 11: "Failed to Return with This Flight; Shot Down over Target"

1. McClure, "Day of Victory Also Day of Loss," A-2.

2. Much of this information about preparing for the final strike came from Gerald Hennesy, "August 15th, 1945—The Japs Surrender," reminiscence given to author, December 23, 2017.

3. Radford, *From Pearl Harbor to Vietnam*, 65.

4. Commanding Officer to Chief of Naval Operations, History Unit, "History of Torpedo Squadron Fifty from 10 August 1943 to 29 October 1945," October 29, 1945, 21–22.

5. *Martha's Vineyard to Tokyo*, 59.

6. Hennesy, "August 15th, 1945—The Japs Surrender."

7. Air Group 88 Action Report, Fighter Squadron Report No. 35, August 15, 1945, Chosi Point.

8. Huddleston letter to Kitchen, December 13, 1978.

9. Huddleston letter to Kitchen, December 13, 1978; "History of Torpedo Squadron Fifty from 10 August 1943 to 29 October 1945," 22; Reynolds, *Fighting Lady*, 319–320.

10. Hennesy, "August 15th, 1945—The Japs Surrender."

11. *Yorktown* War Diary, August 15, 1945.

12. Reynolds, *Fighting Lady*, 320.

13. Searcy, *Story of Air Group 88*, 39.

14. Radford, *From Pearl Harbor to Vietnam*, 65.

15. Air Group 88 Action Report, Fighter Squadron Report No. 35, August 15, 1945, Chosi Point.

16. Flight Log of Lieutenant (jg) Joseph G. Sahloff, in the Robert G. Vrooman Collection; Radford, *From Pearl Harbor to Vietnam*, 65.

17. Father Joseph N. Moody, "Recollections of Duty on the *Yorktown*," in *"Yorktown* Chaplains, WWII" Box, Patriots Point Archive, 3.

18. Halsey, *Memoirs*, 592.

19. Hennesy, "August 15th, 1945—The Japs Surrender."

20. Reynolds, *Fighting Lady*, 320.

21. Al Dopking, "Wayne Hansen of Santa Cruz Was in the Middle of Final Battle," *Santa Cruz Sentinel*, August 16, 1945, 1; Leonard Komisarek letter to the Hobbs Family, October 16, 1945, in the Nancy Exmeyer Collection.

22. Dopking, "Wayne Hansen of Santa Cruz Was in the Middle of Final Battle," 1; Watkinson interview, November 9, 2017.

23. Statement by Iwajiro and Teruo Watanabe, "Report of Investigation Division, Legal Section," December 9, 1947.

24. Halsey and Bryan, *Admiral Halsey's Story*, 272.

25. Potter, *Bull Halsey*, 348.

26. Halsey and Bryan, *Admiral Halsey's Story*, 273.

27. Searcy Jr., "Combat Summary."

28. "Historical Report of Fighting Squadron Eighty-Eight," 12–13.

29. "Air Operations against Shikoku, Honshu, and Hokkaido, aboard U.S.S. *Yorktown*—Period 1 July to 15 August," September 12, 1945, 15–16.

30. *Yorktown* War Diary, August 15, 1945.

31. Sakai, Caidin, and Saito, *Samurai!*, 370.

32. Henry Sakaida and Koji Takaki, *Genda's Blade* (Hersham, Surrey: Classic Publications, 2003), 170.

33. "Kokomo Screams Joy at War's End as Autos Flood Downtown Streets," *Kokomo Tribune*, August 14, 1945, 1.

34. Author's interview with Carolyn Hobbs, August 23, 2017.

35. "Kokomo Screams Joy," 1.

36. "Crack Yankee Pilots Shoot Down 26 Japs in Final Air Engagement," *Kokomo Tribune*, August 16, 1945, 1.

37. Author's interview with Susan Sussman, November 17, 2017.

38. Halsey, *Memoirs*, 608–609; Halsey and Bryan, *Admiral Halsey's Story*, 283.

39. "The Week with Christ Catholic Services," September 23, 1945, Sunday Mass program in "*Yorktown* Chaplains, WWII" Box, Patriots Point Archive.

40. Leonard Komisarek letter to the Hobbs Family, October 16, 1945, in the Nancy Exmeyer Collection.

41. Reynolds, *Fighting Lady,* 324.

42. Reynolds, *Fighting Lady,* 334.

CHAPTER 12: "Two Only of the Six Returned"

1. "People Here Prepared for Rest Period," *Kokomo Tribune,* September 1, 1945, 1.

2. Exmeyer interview, October 11, 2017.

3. Joyce Hobbs Clelland letter to Wright Hobbs, August 22, 1945, in the Denny Clelland Collection.

4. Lt. Comdr. Malcolm W. Cagle, Commanding Officer, VF-88, letter to Mr. and Mrs. Mandeberg, August 16, 1945, in the Jean Mandeberg Collection.

5. Letters from Zelda Mandeberg to Sonya Levien, August 19, August 22, August 26, August 29, September 3, September 6, and September 11, 1945, in "A Loving Engagement."

6. Western Union Telegram from Vice Admiral Louis Denfield, Chief of Naval Personnel, to Mr. and Mrs. Nathan Mandeberg, September 24, 1945, in the Jean Mandeberg Collection.

7. "Ensign W. C. Hobbs Reported Missing Since August 15," *Kokomo Tribune,* September 20, 1945, 1.

8. Ensign John J. Willis letter to Mr. Nathan Mandeberg, September 9, 1945, in the Jean Mandeberg Collection.

9. Commander H. B. Atkinson letter to Mr. and Mrs. Nathan Mandeberg, September 29, 1945, in the Jean Mandeberg Collection.

10. Mr. and Mrs. Wright Hobbs letter to Mrs. Zelda Mandeberg, October 4, 1945, in the Jean Mandeberg Collection.

11. Forest A. Harness, Congressman, Fifth District, Indiana, letter to Mr. Wright Hobbs, October 2, 1945, in the Jean Mandeberg Collection.

12. Leonard Komisarek letter to the Hobbs Family, October 16, 1945, in the Nancy Exmeyer Collection.

13. Lt. Comdr. Malcolm W. Cagle, Commanding Officer, VF-88, letter to Mr. and Mrs. Mandeberg, October 17, 1945, in the Jean Mandeberg Collection.

14. Page Du Pre letter to Joyce Hobbs Clelland, November 10, 1945, in the Denny Clelland Collection.

15. James Forrestal, Secretary of the Navy, letter to Mr. and Mrs. Nathan Mandeberg, August 21, 1946, in the Jean Mandeberg Collection.

16. "Detroit Ensign Listed as Dead," *Detroit Free Press,* September 22, 1946, 6; Sonya Levien interview, May 30, 2018.

17. "Parents Plan Memorial Services for Ensign Hobbs," 24.

18. "Sisters Remember Loss of Brother on Last Day of War," H-19, in the Cary Hobbs Collection.

19. "Proposes Name of W. C. Hobbs for Air Field," *Kokomo Tribune,* August 27, 1953, 4.

20. "In Memoriam," *Kokomo Tribune,* August 14, 1946.

21. Exmeyer interview, October 11, 2017.

22. McClure, "Day of Victory Also Day of Loss," A-1.

23. Author's interview with Constance Grove, February 1, 2018; Exmeyer interview, October 11, 2017.

24. Natalie Schneider, "The Last Letter," a story written for her freshman English Honors Class, November 30, 2017.

25. "Sisters Remember Loss of Brother on Last Day of War," H-19, in the Cary Hobbs Collection.

26. Author's interview with Richard Mandeberg, December 28, 2017; Exmeyer interview, October 11, 2017.

27. Author's interview with Jean Mandeberg, December 28, 2017.

28. Sussman interview, November 17, 2017; "A Loving Engagement," 2.

29. "A Loving Engagement," 2; Sussman interview, November 17, 2017.

30. Jean Mandeberg interview, December 28, 2017.

31. "A Loving Engagement," 2; Sussman interview, November 17, 2017.

32. Author's interview with Richard Mandeberg, October 30, 2017; Richard Mandeberg interview, December 28, 2017; Jean Mandeberg interview, December 28, 2017.

33. Commanding Officer U.S.S. *Yorktown* to Commander-in-Chief, U.S. Fleet, "Action Report of Commander, Carrier Air Group Eighty-Eight, Air Operations against Shikoku, Honshu, and Hokkaido, aboard U.S.S. *Yorktown*—Period 1 July to 15 August 1945," October 13, 1945, 2.

34. Searcy, *Story of Air Group 88*, 7.

35. Woods interview, November 16, 2017; author's interview with John Haag, November 17, 2017.

36. Hamilton interview, November 19, 2017.

37. "In Memoriam," *Kokomo Tribune*, August 15, 1968, 37.

BIBLIOGRAPHY

ACTION REPORTS—AIR GROUP 88

Commander Carrier Group Eighty-Eight to Commander-in-Chief, United States Fleet. "Air Operations over Honshu, aboard U.S.S. *Yorktown*, during Armistice Phase. Period 16 August to 2 September 1945," September 12, 1945.

Commander Carrier Group Eighty-Eight to Commander-in-Chief, United States Fleet. "Air Operations against Shikoku, Honshu, and Hokkaido, aboard U.S.S. *Yorktown*—Period 1 July to 15 August," September 12, 1945. They include, organized by date:

VF-88

Report No. 1, July 10, 1945, Katori, Konoike, Hokoda Airfields

Report No. 2, July 10, 1945, Mapping

Report No. 3, July 10, 1945, Mapping

Report No. 4, July 10, 1945, Kashiwa, Imba, Shiroi Airfields

Report No. 5, July 14, 1945, Hakodate Area

Report No. 6, July 14, 1945, Tomakomai Area

Report No. 7, July 15, 1945, Mapping

Report No. 8, July 15, 1945, Photo

Report No. 9, July 15, 1945, Hokkaido

Report No. 10, July 15, 1945, Hokkaido

Report No. 11, July 18, 1945, Kasumigaura & Konoike

Report No. 12, July 18, 1945, *Nagato*

Report No. 13, July 24, 1945, Miho Area

Report No. 14, July 24, 1945, Osaka Area

Report No. 15, July 24, 1945, Kure Harbor

Report No. 16, July 25, 1945, Miho & Yonago Airfields
Report No. 17, July 25, 1945, Miho & Yonago Airfields
Report No. 18, July 25, 1945, Miho & Yonago Airfields
Report No. 19, July 28, 1945, Kure Harbor
Report No. 20, July 28, 1945, Hanshin Airfield
Report No. 21, July 30, 1945, Photography
Report No. 22, July 30, 1945, Miyakawa
Report No. 23, July 30, 1945, Tsuguru
Report No. 24, July 30, 1945, Utsonomiya
Report No. 25, July 30, 1945, Tsugaru Straits
Report No. 26, July 30, 1945, O'Meara Rescue Operation
Report No. 28, August 9, 1945, Iwaki Airfield
Report No. 36, August 9, 1945, Niigata Airfield
Report No. 29, August 10, 1945, Niigata Airfield
Report No. 30, August 10, 1945, Miyakawa Airfield
Report No. 31, August 13, 1945, Tokyo Airfields
Report No. 32, August 13, 1945, Tateyama Airfield
Report No. 33, August 13, 1945, CAP
Report No. 34, August 13, 1945, CAP
Report No. 35, August 15, 1945, Chosi Point

VBF-88

Report No. 1, July 10, 1945, Narimasu & Chofu Airfields
Report No. 2, July 10, 1945, Tokorozawa Airfield
Report No. 3, July 10, 1945, Kasumigaura Airfield
Report No. 4, July 10, 1945, Konoike Airfield
Report No. 5, July 14, 1945, Muroran Harbor
Report No. 6, July 14, 1945, Mapping
Report No. 7, July 14, 1945, Muroran Harbor
Report No. 8, July 14, 1945, Mapping
Report No. 9, July 15, 1945, Chitori and Mizutaiu Airfields
Report No. 10, July 15, 1945, Sapporo and Otaru
Report No. 11, July 15, 1945, Otaru Harbor
Report No. 12, July 15, 1945, Muroran Area Airfields
Report No. 13, July 18, 1945, Photo
Report No. 14, July 18, 1945, Katori Airfield

Report No. 15, July 24, 1945, Miho & Yonago Airfields

Report No. 16, July 24, 1945, Himeji Airfield

Report No. 17, July 24, 1945, Attack on *Settsu*

Report No. 18, July 24, 1945, Ships off Shikoku

Report No. 19, July 24, 1945, Rescue of Ensign Heck

Report No. 20, July 25, 1945, Miho & Yonago Airfields

Report No. 21, July 25, 1945, Targets of Opportunity

Report No. 22, July 28, 1945, Miho & Yonago Airfields

Report No. 23, July 28, 1945, Miho & Yonago Airfields

Report No. 27, July 28, 1945, Kure Harbor

Report No. 24, July 30, 1945, Mapping

Report No. 25, July 30, 1945, Kisarazu Airfield

Report No. 26, July 30, 1945, Maizuru Naval Base

Report No. 28, July 30, 1945, Mapping

Report No. 29, July 30, 1945, Targets of Opportunity

Report No. 30, August 9, 1945, Yabuki & Iwaki Airfields

Report No. 31, August 9, 1945, Koriyama Airfield

Report No. 32, August 9, 1945, Harano Airfield

Report No. 33, August 9, 1945, Koriyama & Iwaki Airfields

Report No. 34, August 10, 1945, Kisarazu Airfield

Report No. 35, August 10, 1945, Iwaki Airfield

Report No. 36, August 10, 1945, Kisarazu Airfield

Report No. 37, August 10, 1945, Koriyama Airfield

Report No. 38, August 13, 1945, Shibaura Electric Company

Report No. 39, August 13, 1945, Kasumigaura Airfield

Report No. 40, August 13, 1945, Tokorozawa Airfield

Report No. 41, August 13, 1945, Tokyo Area Airfields

Report No. 43, August 15, 1945, Kasumigaura Lake

VB-88

Report No. 1, July 10, 1945, Kasumigaura Airfield

Report No. 2, July 10, 1945, Konoike Airfield

Report No. 3, July 14, 1945, Muroran Harbor

Report No. 4, July 14, 1945, Muroran Harbor

Report No. 5, July 15, 1945, Hakodate, Otaru, Muroran Harbors

Report No. 6, July 18, 1945, *Nagato*

Report No. 7, July 24, 1945, Kure Harbor

Report No. 8, July 24, 1945, Kure Harbor

Report No. 9, July 28, 1945, Kure Harbor

Report No. 10, July 28, 1945, Kure Harbor

Report No. 11, July 30, 1945, Kisarazu Airfield

Report No. 12, July 30, 1945, Maizuru Harbor

Report No. 13, August 9, 1945, Yabuki Airfield

Report No. 14, August 9, 1945, Harano Airfield

Report No. 15, August 10, 1945, Iwaki Airfield

Report No. 16, August 10, 1945, Koriyama Airfield

Report No. 17, August 13, 1945, Shibaura Electric Company

VT-88

Report No. 1, July 10, 1945, Kasumigaura Airfield

Report No. 2, July 10, 1945, Konoike Airfield

Report No. 3, July 14, 1945, Muroran Harbor

Report No. 4, July 14, 1945, Muroran Harbor

Report No. 5, July 15, 1945, Otaru Harbor

Report No. 6, July 18, 1945, *Nagato*

Report No. 7, July 24, 1945, Kure Harbor

Report No. 8, July 24, 1945, Kure Harbor

Report No. 9, July 24, 1945, Susake

Report No. 10, July 28, 1945, Kure Harbor

Report No. 11, July 28, 1945, Kure Harbor

Report No. 12, July 30, 1945, Tsuruga Harbor

Report No. 13, August 9, 1945, Koriyama Airfield

Report No. 14, August 9, 1945, Koriyama Airfield

Report No. 15, August 10, 1945, Iwaki Airfield

Report No. 16, August 10, 1945, Koriyama Airfield

Report No. 17, August 13, 1945, Shibaura Electric Company

VF-88 REPORTS

Commanding Officer Fighting Squadron Eighty-Eight to Commanding Officer, U.S.S. *Yorktown*, (CV-10). "Attack Against Reveted and
Hidden Japanese Aircraft—Suggested Plan of," July 19, 1945.

Commanding Officer to History Unit, Office of Editorial Research, Office of the Chief of Naval Operations, Navy Department. "Historical Report of Fighting Squadron Eighty-Eight from 1 March to 3 September 1945," October 22, 1945.

VBF-88 REPORTS

Commander, Bombing Fighting Squadron Eighty-Eight to Commander-in-Chief, United States Fleet, "War Diary for January 1945," February 1, 1945.

Commander, Bombing Fighting Squadron Eighty-Eight to Commander-in-Chief, United States Fleet, "War Diary for February 1945," March 1, 1945.

Commander, Bombing Fighting Squadron Eighty-Eight to Commander-in-Chief, United States Fleet, "War Diary for March 1945," April 6, 1945.

Commander, Bombing Fighting Squadron Eighty-Eight to Commander-in-Chief, United States Fleet, "War Diary for April 1945," June 6, 1945.

Commander, Bombing Fighting Squadron Eighty-Eight to Commander-in-Chief, United States Fleet, "War Diary for May 1945," June 6, 1945.

Commander, Bombing Fighting Squadron Eighty-Eight to the Chief of Naval Operations. "History of Bomber Fighting Squadron Eighty-Eight from 2 January to 1 March 1945," March 23, 1945.

Commander, Bombing Fighting Squadron Eighty-Eight to the Chief of Naval Operations. "History of Bombing Fighting Squadron Eighty-Eight from 1 March 1945 to 31 May 1945," October 17, 1945.

Commander, Bombing Fighting Squadron Eighty-Eight to the Chief of Naval Operations. "History of Bomber Fighting Squadron Eighty-Eight from 1 June 1945 to 15 September 1945," October 21, 1945.

VB-88 REPORTS

Commander, Bombing Squadron Eighty-Eight to Commander-in-Chief, U.S. Fleet. "War Diary for August 1944," August 31, 1944.

Commander, Bombing Squadron Eighty-Eight to Commander-in-Chief, U.S. Fleet. "War Diary for September 1944," September 30, 1944.

Commander, Bombing Squadron Eighty-Eight to Commander-in-Chief, U.S. Fleet. "War Diary for October 1944," October 31, 1944.

Commander, Bombing Squadron Eighty-Eight to Commander-in-Chief, U.S. Fleet. "War Diary for November 1944," December 8, 1944.

Commander, Bombing Squadron Eighty-Eight to Commander-in-Chief, U.S. Fleet. "War Diary for December 1944," January 6, 1945.

Commander, Bombing Squadron Eighty-Eight to Commander-in-Chief, U.S. Fleet. "War Diary for January 1945," March 7, 1945.

Commander, Bombing Squadron Eighty-Eight to Commander-in-Chief, U.S. Fleet. "War Diary for February 1945," March 30, 1945.

Commander, Bombing Squadron Eighty-Eight to Commander-in-Chief, U.S. Fleet. "War Diary for March 1945," April 25, 1945.

Commander, Bombing Squadron Eighty-Eight to Commander-in-Chief, U.S. Fleet. "War Diary for April 1945," May 31, 1945.

Commander, Bombing Squadron Eighty-Eight to Commander-in-Chief, U.S. Fleet. "War Diary for May 1945," July 8, 1945.

The Commanding Officer to the Chief of Naval Operations. "History of Bombing Squadron Eighty-Eight from 2 January 1945 to 1 March 1945," April 7, 1945.

The Commanding Officer to the Chief of Naval Operations. "History of Bombing Squadron Eighty-Eight from 1 March 1945 to 20 October 1945," October 18, 1945.

VT-88 REPORTS

Commanding Officer to the Chief of Naval Operations. "History of Torpedo Squadron Eighty-Eight from 15 August 1944 to 31 December 1944," January 5, 1945.

Commanding Officer to the Chief of Naval Operations. "History of Torpedo Squadron Eighty-Eight from 1 January 1945 to 31 March 1945," April 1, 1945.

Commanding Officer to the Chief of Naval Operations. "History of Torpedo Squadron Eighty-Eight from 1 April 1945 to 20 October 1945," October 20, 1945.

AIR GROUP 88 WAR DIARIES

Commander, Bombing Squadron Eighty-Eight to Chief of Naval Operations. "Unit History of Bombing Squadron Eighty-Eight from 15 August 1944 to 1 January 1945," January 1, 1945.

Commander, Carrier Air Group Eighty-Eight to Commander-in-Chief, U.S. Fleet. "War Diary for October 1944," October 31, 1944.

Commander, Carrier Air Group Eighty-Eight to Commander-in-Chief, U.S. Fleet. "War Diary for February 1945," March 1, 1945.

Commander, Carrier Air Group Eighty-Eight to Commander-in-Chief, U.S. Fleet. "War Diary for March 1945," April 1, 1945.

Commander, Carrier Air Group Eighty-Eight to Commander-in-Chief, U.S. Fleet. "War Diary for April 1945," May 21, 1945.

Commander, Carrier Air Group Eighty-Eight to Commander-in-Chief, U.S. Fleet. "War Diary for May 1945," June 2, 1945.

Commander, Torpedo Squadron Eighty-Eight to Commander-in-Chief, U.S. Fleet. "War Diary for March 1945," April 1, 1945.

Commanding Officer, Fighting Squadron Eighty-Eight to Commander in Chief, U.S. Fleet. "War Diary for August 1944," September 1, 1944.

Commanding Officer, Fighting Squadron Eighty-Eight to Commander in Chief, U.S. Fleet. "War Diary for September 1944," October 2, 1944.

Commanding Officer, Fighting Squadron Eighty-Eight to Commander in Chief, U.S. Fleet. "War Diary for October 1944," November 2, 1944.

Commanding Officer, Fighting Squadron Eighty-Eight to Commander in Chief, U.S. Fleet. "War Diary for November 1944," December 1, 1944.

Commanding Officer, Fighting Squadron Eighty-Eight to Commander in Chief, U.S. Fleet. "War Diary for December 1944," January 1, 1945.

Commanding Officer, Fighting Squadron Eighty-Eight to Commander in Chief, U.S. Fleet. "War Diary for January 1945," February 1, 1945.

Commanding Officer, Fighting Squadron Eighty-Eight to Commander in Chief, U.S. Fleet. "War Diary for February 1945," March 2, 1945.

Commanding Officer, Fighting Squadron Eighty-Eight to Commander in Chief, U.S. Fleet. "War Diary for March 1945," April 5, 1945.

Commanding Officer, Fighting Squadron Eighty-Eight to Commander in Chief, U.S. Fleet. "War Diary for May 1945," June 1, 1945.

HISTORIES

Commander Carrier Group Eighty-Eight to History Unit, Office of Editorial Research, Office of the Chief of Naval Operations, Navy Department. "History of Carrier Air Group Eighty-Eight to 31 December 1944," January 1, 1945.

Commander Carrier Group Eighty-Eight to History Unit, Office of Editorial Research, Office of the Chief of Naval Operations, Navy Department. "History of Carrier Air Group Eighty-Eight from 1 January to 28 February 1945," March 1, 1945.

Commander Carrier Group Eighty-Eight to History Unit, Office of Editorial Research, Office of the Chief of Naval Operations, Navy Department. "History of Carrier Air Group Eighty-Eight from 1 March to 31 May 1945," June 12, 1945.

Commander Carrier Group Eighty-Eight to History Unit, Office of Editorial Research, Office of the Chief of Naval Operations, Navy Department. "History of Carrier Air Group Eighty-Eight from 1 June to 25 October 1945," October 25, 1945.

ACTION REPORTS—USS *YORKTOWN* (CV-10)

Commanding Officer to Commander-in-Chief, United States Fleet. "War Diary—Month of July 1945," July 31, 1945.

Commanding Officer to Commander-in-Chief, United States Fleet. "War Diary—Month of August 1945," August 31, 1945.

Commanding Officer to Commander in Chief, U.S. Fleet. "Actions Covering Attacks on Aircraft, Shipping, and Strategic Targets in Northern Kyushu, Shikoku, Tokyo Plain Area, Northern Honshu, and Southern Hokkaido, from 2 July 1945 to 15 August 1945," September 6, 1945.

Commanding Officer to Commander in Chief, U.S. Fleet. "Operations from 15 August 1945 to 2 September 1945, which Consisted of Airfield Surveillance and Searches for Prisoner of War Camps during Initial Occupation Phases," September 12, 1945.

Commanding Officer to Commander-in-Chief, United States Fleet. "War Diary—Month of September 1945," September 30, 1945.

Commanding Officer U.S.S. *Yorktown* to Commander-in-Chief, U.S. Fleet. "Action Report of Commander, Carrier Air Group Eighty-Eight, Air Operations against Shikoku, Honshu, and Hokkaido, aboard U.S.S. *Yorktown*—Period 1 July to 15 August 1945," October 13, 1945.

Commanding Officer to the Secretary of the Navy. "*Yorktown* Historical Report, from date of commissioning, 15 April 1943, to 2 September 1945," October 19, 1945.

Commanding Officer to Commander-in-Chief, United States Fleet. "War Diary—Month of October 1945," October 31, 1945.

ACTION REPORTS—USS *SHANGRI-LA* (CV-38)

Commanding Officer to the Chief of Naval Operations. "Ship's History—U.S.S. *Shangri-La* (CV-38)—Submission of," October 25, 1945.

Commanding Officer to Commander, Carrier Air Group Eighty-Five. "ACA-1, Aircraft Action Reports, CVG-85," August 18, 1945. They include:

VF-85

Report No. 35, July 10, 1945, Tokyo Area Airfields
Report No. 36, July 10, 1945, Tokyo Area Airfields
Report No. 37, July 14, 1945, Hokkaido
Report No. 38, July 14, 1945, Submarine CAP
Report No. 39, July 14, 1945, RAPCAP
Report No. 40, July 15, 1945, Hokkaido
Report No. 41, July 15, 1945, Hokkaido
Report No. 42, July 18, 1945, Tokyo Area Airfields
Report No. 43, July 24, 1945, Miho & Yonago Airfields
Report No. 44, July 24, 1945, Himeji and Miki Airfields
Report No. 45, July 24, 1945, Rescue Mission
Report No. 46, July 25, 1945, Miho & Yonago Airfields
Report No. 48, July 25, 1945, Miho & Yonago Airfields
Report No. 52, July 28, 1945, Miho & Yonago Airfields

Report No. 53, July 28, 1945, Miho & Yonago Airfields

Report No. 55, July 30, 1945, Tokyo Area

Report No. 57, August 9, 1945, Koriyama Airfield

Report No. 58, August 9, 1945, Iwaki Airfield

Report No. 61, August 10, 1945, Miyakawa Airfield

Report No. 63, August 10, 1945, Niigata Airfield

Report No. 65, August 13, 1945, Shibaura Electric Company

Report No. 68, August 13, 1945, Kasumigaura Airfield

VBF-85

Report No. 32, July 10, 1945, Narimazu Airfield

Report No. 33, July 10, 1945, Kasumigaura Airfield

Report No. 34, July 10, 1945, Tokyo Area Airfields

Report No. 35, July 10, 1945, Konoike Airfield

Report No. 36, July 14, 1945, Hokkaido

Report No. 37, July 14, 1945, Shiroai

Report No. 38, July 14, 1945, Muroran

Report No. 39, July 15, 1945, Hokkaido

Report No. 40, July 15, 1945, Muroran

Report No. 41, July 15, 1945, Hokkaido

Report No. 42, July 15, 1945, Hokkaido

Report No. 43, July 18, 1945, Tokyo Area

Report No. 44, July 18, 1945, *Nagato*

Report No. 45, July 24, 1945, Osaka Area

Report No. 46, July 24, 1945, Kure Harbor

Report No. 47, July 24, 1945, Miho Area

Report No. 48, July 24, 1945, Kure Harbor

Report No. 49, July 25, 1945, Miho & Yonago Airfields

Report No. 50, July 28, 1945, Miho & Yonago Airfields

Report No. 51, July 28, 1945, Kure Harbor

Report No. 52, July 28, 1945, Osaka

Report No. 53, July 28, 1945, Kure Harbor

Report No. 54, July 30, 1945, Tokyo Area

Report No. 55, July 30, 1945, Maizuru Area

Report No. 56, July 30, 1945, Maizuru Area

Report No. 57, July 30, 1945, Utsonomiya Area

Report No. 58, August 9, 1945, Niigata Airfield

Report No. 59, August 9, 1945, Yabuki Airfield

Report No. 60, August 9, 1945, Harano Airfield

Report No. 61, August 9, 1945, Koriyama Airfield

Report No. 62, August 10, 1945, Kisarazu Airfield

Report No. 63, August 10, 1945, Harano Airfield

Report No. 64, August 10, 1945, Kisarazu Airfield

Report No. 65, August 10, 1945, Yabuki Airfield

Report No. 66, August 13, 1945, Kasumigaura Airfield

Report No. 67, August 13, 1945, Kasumigaura Airfield

Report No. 68, August 13, 1945, CAP

Report No. 69, August 13, 1945, Kasumigaura Airfield

Report No. 71, August 13, 1945, Kasumigaura Airfield

Report No. 72, August 15, 1945, Kasumigaura Lake

VB-85

Report No. 32, July 10, 1945, Kasumigaura Airfield

Report No. 33, July 10, 1945, Konoike Airfield

Report No. 34, July 14, 1945, Hokkaido

Report No. 35, July 14, 1945, Hokkaido

Report No. 36, July 15, 1945, Muroran

Report No. 37, July 18, 1945, *Nagato*

Report No. 38, July 24, 1945, Kure Harbor

Report No. 39, July 24, 1945, Kure Harbor

Report No. 40, July 28, 1945, Kure Harbor

Report No. 41, July 28, 1945, Kure Harbor

Report No. 42, July 30, 1945, Tokyo Area

Report No. 43, July 30, 1945, Maizuru Harbor

Report No. 44, August 9, 1945, Yabuki Airfield

Report No. 45, August 9, 1945, Yabuki Airfield

Report No. 46, August 10, 1945, Harano Airfield

Report No. 47, August 10, 1945, Yabuki Airfield

Report No. 48, August 13, 1945, Shibaura Electric Company

VT-85

Report No. 27, July 10, 1945, Kasumigaura Airfield

Report No. 28, July 10, 1945, Konoike Airfield

Report No. 29, July 14, 1945, Hokkaido

Report No. 30, July 14, 1945, Muroran

Report No. 31, July 15, 1945, Muroran

Report No. 32, July 18, 1945, *Nagato*

Report No. 33, July 24, 1945, Kure Harbor

Report No. 34, July 24, 1945, Kure Harbor

Report No. 35, July 28, 1945, Kure Harbor

Report No. 36, July 28, 1945, Kure Harbor

Report No. 37, July 30, 1945, Maizuru Harbor

Report No. 38, August 9, 1945, Koriyama Airfield

Report No. 39, August 9, 1945, Koriyama Airfield

Report No. 40, August 10, 1945, Harano Airfield

Report No. 41, August 10, 1945, Yabuki Airfield

Report No. 42, August 13, 1945, Shibaura Electric Company

Commanding Officer to Commander in Chief, United States Fleet. "Action Report of Operations, U.S.S. *Shangri-La* (CV-38) for the Period 2 July 1945 to 15 August 1945," August 24, 1945.

Commanding Officer to Commander in Chief, United States Fleet. "Action Report of Operations, U.S.S. *Shangri-La* (CV-38) for the Period 16 August 1945 to 2 September 1945," September 3, 1945.

Commanding Officer to the Commander in Chief, U.S. Fleet. "War Diary, U.S.S. *Shangri-La* (CV-38) for Period 1 July, 1945 to 31 July, 1945," August 10, 1945.

Commanding Officer to the Commander in Chief, U.S. Fleet. "War Diary, U.S.S. *Shangri-La* (CV-38) for Period 1 August, 1945 to 31 August, 1945," September 10, 1945.

Commanding Officer to the Commander in Chief, U.S. Fleet. "War Diary, U.S.S. *Shangri-La* (CV-38) for Period 1 September, 1945 to 30 September, 1945," October 6, 1945.

Commanding Officer to the Commander in Chief, U.S. Fleet. "War Diary, U.S.S. *Shangri-La* (CV-38) for Period 1 October, 1945 to 31 October, 1945," November 8, 1945.

Commanding Officer to History Unit, Office of Editorial Research, Navy Department. "History of Fighting Squadron Eighty-Five from 1 April 1945 to 10 September 1945," September 10, 1945.

Commanding Officer to History Unit, Office of Editorial Research, Navy
    Department. "History of Torpedo Squadron Eighty-Five from 1 April
    1945 to Date of Decommissioning," October 10, 1945.

Commander Bombing Fighting Squadron Eighty-Five to Commander
    Carrier Air Group Eighty-Five. "Comments and Recommendations,
    Following Combat Operations for the Period 14 June 1945 to 15 Au-
    gust 1945," August 29, 1945.

Commander Bombing Fighting Squadron Eighty-Five to the Chief of
    Naval Operations, History Unit, Office of Editorial Research, Navy
    Department. "History of Bomber Fighting Squadron Eighty-Five
    from 1 July 1945 to 30 September 1945." No date.

ACTION REPORTS—OTHERS

AIR SEA RESCUE, RYUKYUS

Commander Air Sea Rescue, Ryukyus to Chief of Naval Operations Avi-
    ation History Unit "Air Sea Rescue, Ryukyus—History of," August
    26, 1945.

Commander Task Unit 95.9.2 to CinCPac Advance Headquarters. "Air
    Sea Rescue of Ens. Edwin A. Heck," July 26, 1945.

Commander Task Unit 95.9.2 to CinCPac Advance Headquarters. "Air
    Sea Rescue of Ens. J. H. Moore and Lieut. Howard Harrison," Au-
    gust 7, 1945.

Commanding Officer Rescue Squadron Four to the Commander-in-
    Chief, U.S. Fleet. "War Diary—July, 1945," August 30, 1945.

USS COWPENS (CV-25)

Commanding Officer to Chief of Naval Operations, History Unit. "His-
    tory of Fighting Squadron Fifty from 1 January 1945 to 29 October
    1945," October 29, 1945.

Commanding Officer to Chief of Naval Operations, History Unit. "His-
    tory of Torpedo Squadron Fifty from 10 August 1943 to 29 October
    1945," October 29, 1945.

Commanding Officer to the Commander-in-Chief, United States Fleet. "Report of Actions during the Period 1 July to 15 August," August 28, 1945.

USS INDEPENDENCE (CVL-22)

Commanding Officer to the Chief of Naval Operations, Aviation History Unit. "War History—Submission of," October 8, 1945.
Commanding Officer to Chief of Naval Operations, History Unit. "History of Torpedo Squadron Twenty-Seven," October 26, 1945.
Commanding Officer to Commander in Chief, U.S. Fleet. "Action Report for 1 July 1945 through 15 August 1945," August 30, 1945.
Commanding Officer to Commander in Chief, U.S. Fleet. "Action Report for 15 August 1945 through 2 September 1945," September 6, 1945.

MISCELLANEOUS

Air Intelligence Group Division, Naval Intelligence Office. "Flak Information Bulletin No. 8," April 1945.
Commander Air Group Fifty to Commander-in-Chief, U.S. Pacific Fleet. "Aircraft Action Reports for the Period: 1 July 1945 through 15 August 1945," August 26, 1945. They include:

VF-50

Report No. 9, July 10, 1945, CAP
Report No. 11, July 10, 1945, Kasumigaura Airfield
Report No. 12, July 14, 1945, CAP
Report No. 13, July 14, 1945, Muroran & Hakodate
Report No. 16, July 14, 1945, SubCAP

AG-50

Report No. 8, July 10, 1945, Konoike Airfield

Commander CVLG Twenty-Seven to Commander-in-Chief Pacific Fleet and Pacific Ocean Areas. "Aircraft Action Reports—Submission of—Period from 10 July to 10 August," August 26, 1945. They include:

VT-85

Report No. 1, July 10, 1945, Kasumigaura Airfield
Report No. 2, July 10, 1945, Konoike Airfield

Commander, Second Carrier Task Force, Pacific to Task Force Thirty-Eight. "Selection of Japanese Targets for Carrier Based Attack," June 26, 1945.

Commander Task Group Thirty-Eight Point Four to Commander in Chief, United States Fleet. "Action Report, 2 July to 15 August 1945," September 7, 1945.

Commander Third Fleet to the Commander-in-Chief, United States Fleet. "War Diary," 1 June 1945 to 31 October 1945.

Commander Third Fleet to Commander in Chief, U.S. Pacific Fleet and Pacific Ocean Areas. "Report on the Operations of the Third Fleet, 1 July 1945 to 15 August 1945."

Commander Third Fleet to Commander in Chief, U.S. Pacific Fleet and Pacific Ocean Areas. "Report on the Operations of the Third Fleet, 16 August 1945 to 19 September 1945," October 6, 1945.

"The Surrender of Japan," an undated document found in "Halsey Operational Plans to September 1945," William F. Halsey Papers, Library of Congress.

Statement by Iwajiro and Teruo Watanabe. "Report of Investigation Division, Legal Section," December 9, 1947.

SUBMARINES

Commanding Officer to the Commander-in-Chief, United States Fleet. "U.S.S. *Scabbardfish* (SS-397)—Report of War Patrol Number Five," August 25, 1945.

Commanding Officer to the Commander-in-Chief, U.S. Fleet. "U.S.S. *Perch* (SS-313)—Report of War Patrol Number Seven," August 30, 1945.

USS *WASP* (CV-18)

Commander Carrier Air Group Eighty-Six to Chief of Naval Operations, Historical Division. "History of Carrier Air Group Eighty-Six for Period from 1 March 1945 to 10 September 1945—Submission of," September 9, 1945.

Commander, Fighting Squadron Eighty-Six to the Chief of Naval Operations, History Unit, Office of Editorial Research. "History of Fighting Squadron Eighty-Six from 1 March 1945 to 2 September 1945," October 20, 1945.

Commander Torpedo Squadron Eighty-Six to the Chief of Naval Operations. "Squadron History from 1 March 1945 to 2 September 1945," October 1, 1945.

Commander VB-86 to Chief of Naval Operations, History Unit. "Squadron History, 1 March 1945 to 10 September 1945," September 10, 1945.

Commanding Officer, Bomber Fighting Squadron Eighty-Six to the Chief of Naval Operations. "Squadron History from 2 January through 2 September 1945—Submission of," October 21, 1945.

COLLECTIONS

The Reminiscences of Robert Bostwick Carney, Naval History Project, Oral History research Office, Columbia University, 1964

William F. Halsey Collection, Library of Congress

Kathleen Hansen Collection

Gerald Hennesy Collection:
"My Duty with Air Group 88," personal reminiscence written for the author, December 23, 2017
"August 15th, 1945—The Japs Surrender," reminiscence given to author, December 23, 2017
"The Shootdown," December 23, 2017

Sonya Levien Kamsky and Susan Kamsky Sussman, "A Loving Engagement: Letters to Sonya Levien from the Mandeberg Family, 1944–1945," June 2015

Sonya. Video. Directed by James Spione. Produced by Susan Kamsky Sussman, April 7, 2015

Marvin R. Odom Collection, Veterans History Project, American Folklife Center, Library of Congress, no date given

Patriots Point Archives, including the boxes:
"CAG-88"

"Miscellaneous"

"Plans of the Day"

"Radio News Distributed on CV-10, WWII"

"Rosters and Memorandums, 1943–1945"

"WWII Seav Tens & After Action Reports"

"*Yorktown* Chaplains, WWII"

Robert G. Vrooman Collection

INTERVIEWS

Arthur Briggs, VB-88: Telephone interviews on March 16, March 20, and October 25, 2018.

Denny Clelland, nephew of Wright Hobbs: Personal interview on October 26, 2017.

Nancy Exmeyer, Wright Hobbs's sister: Personal interview on October 11, 2017.

Constance Grove, niece of Wright Hobbs: Telephone interviews on February 1, 2018 and June 25, 2018.

John Haag, son of Lieutenant (jg) John Haag, VF-88: Telephone interview on November 17, 2017.

Bernard Hamilton Jr., VBF-88: Telephone interviews on November 19, 2017 and March 20, 2018.

Gerald Hennesy, VBF-88: Personal interview on December 23, 2017; Gerald Hennesy email to the author, March 29, 2018.

Carolyn Hobbs, sister-in-law of Wright Hobbs: Personal interview on August 23, 2017.

Cary Hobbs, nephew of Wright Hobbs: Personal interview on August 23, 2017; telephone interview on August 14, 2017.

Greg Hobbs, nephew of Wright Hobbs: Personal interview on August 23, 2017.

Sonya Levien, fiancé of Eugene Mandeberg, VF-88: Personal interview on May 30, 2018.

Jean Mandeberg, niece of Eugene Mandeberg: Skype interview on December 28, 2017.

Richard Mandeberg, nephew of Eugene Mandeberg: Personal interview on December 28, 2017; telephone interview on October 30, 2017.

Margie Odom, widow of Lieutenant (jg) Marvin R. Odom, VF-88: Telephone interview on March 5, 2018.

Betty Proctor, widow of Lieutenant (jg) Maurice Proctor, VF-88: Telephone interview on January 16, 2018.

Susan Sussman, daughter of Sonya Levien: Personal interview on May 30, 2018; telephone interview on November 17, 2017.

Robert Vrooman, nephew of Lieutenant (jg) Joseph G. Sahloff, VF-88: Telephone interview on April 3, 2018.

William Watkinson, VF-88: Personal interview on November 9, 2017; telephone interview on July 13, 2017.

Merald Woods, VBF-88: Telephone interviews on November 16 and November 20, 2017; and March 15, 2018.

BOOKS

Allison, Robert. *One Man's War*. Self-published memoir, 2012.

Bix, Herbert P. *Hirohito and the Making of Modern Japan*. New York: HarperCollins, 2000.

Boyington, Colonel Gregory. *Baa Baa Black Sheep*. New York: G. P. Putnam's Sons, 1958.

Bryan, Lieutenant Commander J., III, and Philip Reed. *Mission Beyond Darkness*. New York: Duell, Sloan and Pearce, 1945.

———. *Aircraft Carrier*. New York: Ballantine Books, 1954.

Campbell, David. *Save Our Souls: Rescues Made by U.S. Submarines During World War II*. Lulu.com, 2016.

Chappell, John D. *Before the Bomb*. Lexington: University Press of Kentucky, 1997.

Clark, Admiral J. J., with Clark G. Reynolds. *Carrier Admiral*. New York: David McKay Company, 1967.

Costello, John. *The Pacific War, 1941–1945*. New York: Quill Books, 1982.

Dickinson, Lieutenant Clarence E. *The Flying Guns*. New York: Charles Scribner's Sons, 1943.

Ewing, Steve. *Reaper Leader: The Life of Jimmy Flatley*. Annapolis, MD: Naval Institute Press, 2002.

————. *Thach Weave: The Life of Jimmie Thach.* Annapolis, MD: Naval Institute Press, 2004.

Frank, Richard B. *Downfall: The End of the Imperial Japanese Empire.* New York: Random House, 1999.

Gadbois, Robert. *Hellcat Tales.* Bennington, VT: Merriam Press, 2011.

Galdorisi, George, and Tom Phillips. *Leave No Man Behind.* Minneapolis, MN: Zenith Press, 2008.

Gilbert, Alton Keith. *A Leader Born.* Philadelphia: Casemate, 2006.

Halsey, Fleet Admiral William F., and Lieutenant Commander J. Bryan III. *Admiral Halsey's Story.* New York: McGraw-Hill, 1947.

Halsey, Fleet Admiral William F. *Life of Admiral W. F. Halsey,* undated typewritten memoirs dictated by Halsey after the war.

Halvorsen, Dick. *Steeds in the Sky.* New York: Lancer Books, 1971.

Hanson, Norman. *Carrier Pilot.* Cambridge: Patrick Stephens, 1979.

Hata, Ikuhiko, with Yasuho Izawa and Christopher Shores. *Japanese Army Fighter Aces, 1931–1945.* Mechanicsburg, PA: Stackpole Books, 2002.

Hellman, Lyman. "The Trials and Tribulations of Playmate 9 of VH-4," in *Mariner/Marlin: Anywhere, Anytime.* Paducah, KY: Turner Publishing, 1993.

Hornfischer, James D. *The Fleet at Flood Tide.* New York: Bantam Books, 2016.

Jensen, Lieutenant Oliver, USNR. *Carrier War.* New York: Simon & Schuster, 1945.

Johnston, Stanley. *The Grim Reapers.* New York: E. P. Dutton & Co., 1943.

Kinney, Brig. Gen. John F., with James M. McCaffrey. *Wake Island Pilot.* Washington, DC: Brassey's, 1995.

Kitchen, Ruben P., Jr. *Pacific Carrier: The Saga of the USS* Yorktown *(CV-10) in WWII.* Charleston, SC: Nautical & Aviation Publishing Company of America, 2002.

Lambert, John G. *USS* Independence *CVL-22.* Published and Edited by John G. Lambert, 2015.

Mariner/Marlin: Anywhere, Anytime. Paducah, KY: Turner Publishing, 1993.

Markey, Morris. *Well Done!* New York: D. Appleton-Century, 1945.

Martha's Vineyard to Tokyo: A Historical Record of VT-88. New York: New Era Lithograph, undated, but soon after war's end.

Mason, John T., Jr., ed. *The Pacific War Remembered.* Annapolis, MD: Naval Institute Press, 1986.

Miller, Lt. Max, USNR. *Daybreak for Our Carrier.* New York: McGraw-Hill, 1944.

Miller, Nathan. *The Naval Air War, 1939–1945.* Annapolis, MD: Naval Institute Press, 1991.

Morison, Samuel Eliot. *History of United States Naval Operations in World War II, Volume VII: Aleutians, Gilberts and Marshalls, June 1942–April 1944.* Boston: Little, Brown, 1951.

———. *History of United States Naval Operations in World War II, Volume XIV: Victory in the Pacific, 1945.* Boston: Little, Brown, 1960.

———. *The Two-Ocean War.* Boston: Little, Brown, 1963.

Okumiya, Masatake, with Jiro Horikoshi and Martin Caidan. *Zero.* New York: Simon & Schuster, 1956.

Polmar, Norman. *Aircraft Carriers: A History of Carrier Aviation and Its Influence on World Events, Volume I, 1909–1945.* Washington, DC: Potomac Books, 2006.

Potter, E. B. *Bull Halsey.* Annapolis, MD: Naval Institute Press, 1985.

Pyle, Ernie. *Last Chapter.* New York: Henry Holt, 1946.

Radford, Admiral Arthur W. *From Pearl Harbor to Vietnam: The Memoirs of Admiral Arthur W. Radford.* Edited by Stephen Jurika Jr. Stanford University: Hoover Institution Press, 1980.

Reynolds, Clark G. *The Fast Carriers.* Annapolis, MD: Naval Institute Press, 1968.

———. *The Carrier War.* Alexandria, VA: Time-Life Books, 1982.

———. *The Fighting Lady.* Missoula, MT: Pictorial Histories Publishing, 1986.

———. *On the Warpath in the Pacific.* Annapolis, MD: Naval Institute Press, 2005.

Sakai, Saburo, with Martin Caidin and Fred Saito. *Samurai!* New York: Simon & Schuster, 1957.

Sakaida, Henry, and Koji Takaki. *Genda's Blade.* Hersham, Surrey: Classic Publications, 2003.

Searcy, Commander S. S., Jr. *The Story of Air Group 88*. Undated, but compiled by the commanding officers of the four air squadrons shortly after the war.

Sherman, Frederick C. *Combat Command*. New York: E. P. Dutton, 1950.

Stahura, Barbara. *USS* Yorktown *CV-10: The Fighting Lady, Volume II*. Paducah, KY: Turner Publishing, 1997.

Taylor, Theodore. *The Magnificent Mitscher*. Annapolis, MD: Naval Institute Press, 1954.

Tillman, Barrett. *Whirlwind: The Air War Against Japan, 1942–1945*. New York: Simon & Schuster, 2010.

Ugaki, Admiral Matome. *Fading Victory: The Diary of Admiral Matome Ugaki, 1941–1945*. Pittsburgh: University of Pittsburgh Press, 1991.

Vernon, James W. *The Hostile Sky: A Hellcat Flier in World War II*. Annapolis, MD: Naval Institute Press, 2003.

Wooldridge, E. T., ed. *Carrier Warfare in the Pacific*. Washington, DC: Smithsonian Institution Press, 1993.

ARTICLES

Adams, Frank S. "Wild Crowds Greet News in City While Others Pray." *New York Times*. May 8, 1945, 1, 7.

———. "Millions Rejoice in City Celebration." *New York Times*. May 9, 1945, 1, 18.

"Air and Sea Forces Erase 3 Jap Cities." *Kokomo Tribune*. July 16, 1945, 1.

"Airmen from 'Fighting Lady' Take 1,000 to 1 Chance, Span Japan in Solid Fog to Save Pal." *Plainfield (NJ) Courier News*. September 27, 1945, 13.

"Allies Impatiently Await Reply from Jap Leaders." *Kokomo Tribune*. August 13, 1945, 1, 9.

"Allies Rain Shells on Jap Coast Areas." *Kokomo Tribune*. July 18, 1945, 1.

"Allies Will Land in Japan Sunday." *Kokomo Tribune*. August 21, 1945.

"And Now Japan." *New York Times*. May 8, 1945, 1.

"Another Group of Trainees Is Awaited Here." *Muncie Evening Press*. December 31, 1942, 3.

"Atomic Bomb Loaded with Untold Power Loosed Against Japs." *Kokomo Tribune*. August 6, 1945, 1, 9.

"Attention, Tokyo!" *Time*. August 6, 1945. http://content.time.com/time /subscriber/article/0,33009,803665,00.html.

Axelsson, George. "Stockholm Hears Tokyo Peace Tale." *New York Times*. June 16, 1945, 1.

Baldwin, Hanson W. "Problems of the Pacific." *New York Times*. May 10, 1945, 1.

———. "Blows to Crush Japan Are Now Foreshadowed." *New York Times*. May 20, 1945, 1.

———. "Okinawa in Retrospect." *New York Times*. July 13, 1945, 2.

———. "Ideas Can Fight Japan." *New York Times*. July 18, 1945, 4.

"Bargaining with Japan." *New York Times*. July 25, 1945, 22.

"Battle of Japan: Plans & Planes." *Time*. July 16, 1945. http://content .time.com/time/subscriber/article/0,33009,792170,00.html.

"Battle of the Pacific: To the Last Line." *Time*. June 18, 1945. http:// content.time.com/time/subscriber/article/0,33009,775911,00.html.

"Battleship Park Plaque to Honor Five Crommelins." *Montgomery Advertiser*. May 22, 1970, 3.

Berger, Meyer. "City's Celebration Chilled by Mayor." *New York Times*. May 8, 1945, 1.

"Birth of an Era." *Time*. August 13, 1945. http://content.time.com/time /subscriber/article/0,33009,792239,00.html.

"Blow on Blow." *New York Times*. July 22, 1945, 1.

Bosworth, Brandon. "USS *Crommelin* Decommissions." *Honolulu Star-Advertiser*. November 2, 2012, A1–A2.

Brown, Bill. "Aviation Hall to Honor 7 Alabamians." *Montgomery Advertiser*. May 9, 1999, C3–4C.

"Bull's-Eye." *Time*. July 23, 1945, 23–28.

"Cadet Training Is Intensified." *Muncie Evening Press*. December 16, 1942, 11.

"'Cease Fire' Order Spans Pacific but U.S. Fleet Remains on Alert." *Kokomo Tribune*. August 15, 1945, 1, 15.

"Checks Record." *Kokomo Record*. September 8, 1945, 10.

"Chief Cities Take Victory in Stride." *New York Times*. May 8, 1945, 1.

"Clark Gable Invited to Induction of 'Lombardier' Flying Cadets." *Indianapolis News*. October 12, 1942, 7.

"Controversial Navy Admiral Crommelin Dies." *Anniston Star*. November 12, 1996, 5.

"Crack Yankee Pilots Shoot Down 26 Japs in Final Air Engagement." *Kokomo Tribune*. August 16, 1945, 1.

"Crippled Warships of Japanese Navy Smashed by Fliers." *New York Times*. July 29, 1945, 1, 3.

"Crushing Invasion of Japan Planned." *New York Times*. July 30, 1945, 3.

"Daring Raid." *Kokomo Tribune*. July 27, 1945, 1.

Davis, Spencer. "7 Jap Planes Brought Down in 4 Minutes." *Danville (VA) Bee*. January 21, 1944, 2.

"Declare War Aims, Churchmen Urge." *New York Times*. June 18, 1945, 1.

"Destroyers Batter Jap Aluminum Plant." *Kokomo Tribune*. July 31, 1945, 1.

"Detroit Ensign Listed as Dead." *Detroit Free Press*. September 22, 1946, 6.

"Dick Dozier Dies in Action." *Newport News (VA) Daily Press*. September 9, 1945, 14.

"Die, But Do Not Retreat." *Time*. January 4, 1943, 21–22.

"The 'Dixie Demons' of Alabama." http://www.crommelin.org/history/Biographies/Alabama/. Accessed August 18, 2017.

Dopking, Al. "Wayne Hansen of Santa Cruz Was in the Middle of Final Battle." *Santa Cruz Sentinel*. August 16, 1945, 1.

———. "War Runs into Overtime for Group of U.S. Fliers." *Tampa Bay Times*. August 16, 1945, 1.

"Dumbo." *Flying*. October 1944, 52, 228, 232.

Emmerich, Wyatt. "Malcolm Cagle." *Northside Sun (Jackson, MS)*, April 20, 2000, 26.

"Enemy in Hideout." *New York Times*. July 19, 1945, 1, 4.

"Ensign Robert C. Baker." New England Aviation History. https://www.newenglandaviationhistory.com/tag/ensign-robert-c-baker. Accessed February 23, 2018.

"Ensign T. W. Hansen Escaped in Last Battle with Japs." *Santa Cruz Sentinel*. November 12, 1945, 4.

"Ensign W. C. Hobbs Reported Missing Since August 15." *Kokomo Tribune*. September 20, 1945, 1.

"500 Superfortresses Hammer Jap Plants." *Kokomo Tribune*. July 4, 1945.

"1,500 American Planes Rake Jap Home Islands." *Kokomo Tribune*. July 10, 1945, 1, 7.

"1,546 Small Jap Craft Sunk by U.S. Airmen." *Kokomo Tribune.* August 1, 1945, 1.

"First Conquering Yanks Reach Japan." *Kokomo Tribune.* August 28, 1945.

"Five Naval Officer Brothers Appear to Bear Charmed Lives." *Tampa Tribune.* December 15, 1943, 4.

"Fleet Baits Foe." *New York Times.* July 15, 1945, 1.

"Fleet Envisages Trip in Tokyo Bay." *New York Times.* August 6, 1945, 1.

"Fliers at Atsugi Find Strip Usable." *New York Times.* August 29, 1945, 1, 6.

"Fliers Battle Japs in Dogfight After Surrender." *Minneapolis Morning Tribune.* August 16, 1945, 1.

"Fliers Drop Gifts to Tokyo Captives." *New York Times.* August 26, 1945, 1.

"Ford Starts Assembly Production of New Model of Passenger Autos." *Kokomo Tribune.* July 3, 1945.

"Former Findlay Athlete Killed." *Fremont (OH) News-Messenger.* November 27, 1944, 8.

Gantt, Marlene. "WWII Flying Ace Recalls Dog-fighting Days." June 19, 2005. http://qconline.com/opinion/wwii-flying-ace-recalls -dog-fighting-days/article_9a1b0ac7-ed88-5da3-8e90-f561bb9fadb4 .html.

"Glendale Flyer Saves Two in Jap Sea." *Los Angeles Times.* July 28, 1945, 4.

"Greatest Superfort Fleet Fires Japan." *Kokomo Tribune.* July 19, 1945, 1.

"Grew Puts Stress on Fight in Pacific." *New York Times.* May 9, 1945, 1.

Halsey, Admiral William F., as told to Frank D. Morris. "A Plan for Japan." *Collier's.* April 28, 1945, 18.

"Halsey Fleet Shells Japan Homeland." *New York Times.* July 14, 1945, 1.

"Halsey Minimizes Foe." *New York Times.* January 7, 1943, 4.

"Halsey Moves In." *New York Times.* August 27, 1945, 1 2.

"Halsey Says Blows Open 'Final Plunge.'" *New York Times.* July 25, 1945, 1–2.

"Halsey Turns Surface Craft Loose on Japan; Planes Support Strike." *Kokomo Tribune.* July 14, 1945, 1.

"Halsey's Third Fleet Blasts Jap Homeland." *Kokomo Tribune.* August 13, 1945, 1, 9.

"Halsey Views Situation." *New York Times.* August 13, 1945, 4.

"Hansen." *Santa Cruz Sentinel.* October 13, 1943, 1.

"Hansen Awarded Navy DFC." *Santa Cruz Sentinel.* October 31, 1945, 4.

"Heart of Japan Hit by Airmen." *Kokomo Tribune.* July 30, 1945, 1, 9.

"Herbert Wood." June 13, 2017. http://qconline.com/obituaries/herbert -wood/article_a58f61e2-bd60-5650-9a54-742604127205.html. Accessed January 17, 2018.

"Heroes: The Indestructibles." *Time.* January 24, 1944, 61. Found at http:// content.time.com/time/subscriber/article/0,33009,803089,00.html. Accessed August 18, 2017.

"Hero's Son Given Medals." *Los Angeles Times.* November 29, 1947, 8.

Hessler, Lieutenant William H. "The Carrier Task Force in World War II." *Naval Institute Proceedings.* November 1945, 1271–1281.

"Hobbs Reports Wheat Yield of 47 Bu. Per Acre." *Kokomo Tribune.* July 13, 1945, 2.

"Hoosiers to Celebrate Fourth in More Traditional Methods." *Kokomo Tribune.* July 4, 1945, 1.

"Hoosiers Shriek Delight over End of Hostilities." *Kokomo Tribune.* August 15, 1945, 1, 15.

"Huge Fleet Gets Cease-Fire Order Near Zero Hour for a New Attack." *New York Times.* August 15, 1945, 1.

"Hurly-Burly Thoroughfare." *Time.* August 6, 1945, found at http:// content.time.com/time/subscriber/article/0,33009,803656,00.html. Accessed February 15, 2018.

Hutchinson, David. "WWII Naval Fighter Pilot to Be Honored at Pearl Harbor." NJ.com, updated December 3, 2016. Found at https://www .nj.com/somerset/2016/12/nj_wwii_naval_fighter_pilot_to_be _honored_at_pearl.html. Accessed February 27, 2018.

Ignasher, Jim. "Off Nantucket, MA—December 10, 1944." written July 12, 2017. Found at https://www.newenglandaviationhistory.com/tag /ensign-john-daniel-cassidy/. Accessed January 29, 2018.

"In Memoriam." *Kokomo Tribune.* August 14, 1946.

"In Memoriam." *Kokomo Tribune.* August 14, 1948, 16.

"In Memoriam." *Kokomo Tribune.* August 13, 1949, 6.

"In Memoriam." *Kokomo Tribune.* August 15, 1950, 12.

"In Memoriam." *Kokomo Tribune.* August 15, 1951, 38.

"In Memoriam." *Kokomo Tribune.* August 16, 1952, 8.

"In Memoriam." *Kokomo Tribune.* August 15, 1953, 10.

"In Memoriam." *Kokomo Tribune.* August 17, 1954, 14.

"In Memoriam." *Kokomo Tribune.* August 15, 1955, 30.

"In Memoriam." *Kokomo Tribune.* August 14, 1965, 15.

"In Memoriam." *Kokomo Tribune.* August 15, 1968, 37.

"Insult & Injury." *Time.* July 30, 1945, 1–3. Found at http://www.time .com/time/magazine/article/0,9171,801633,00.html. Accessed February 6, 2018.

"Jap Battleship Sunk by Airmen." *Kokomo Tribune.* July 28, 1945, 1, 9.

"Jap Surrender Envoys to Reach Manila Sunday." *Kokomo Tribune.* August 18, 1945.

"Japan Blasted by Ship and Plane." *New York Times.* July 15, 1945, 1.

"Japan Fears New U.S. Plane Strike." *Kokomo Tribune.* July 11, 1945, 1, 11.

"Japan Rejects." *New York Times.* July 30, 1945, 18.

"Japanese Are Open to Terms Minus Threats, Says Domei." *New York Times.* July 23, 1945, 1, 4.

"Japanese Cabinet Weights Ultimatum." *New York Times.* July 28, 1945, 1–2.

"The Japanese Emperor." *New York Times.* July 31, 1945, 18.

"Japanese Planes Attack." *New York Times.* August 10, 1945, 4.

"Japs Surrender Tonight—Kokomo Time." *Kokomo Tribune.* September 1, 1945, 1, 9.

"Japs Told to Tighten Belt." *Kokomo Tribune.* July 3, 1945.

"Jittery Japs Draw Troops from China." *Kokomo Tribune.* July 20, 1945.

"Job for an Emperor." *Time.* August 27, 1945, found at http://content. time.com/time/subscriber/article/0,33009,792335,00.html. Accessed February 15, 2018.

Johnston, Richard W., "Dumbo Saves Flyers Under Jap Noses on Failing Engine." *Albany Democrat-Herald.* July 28, 1945, 2.

Johnston, Richard W. and Earnest Hoberrecht. "'Supreme Insult' to Enemy." *New York Times.* July 25, 1945, 1.

———. "Pilot Is Saved by Rescue Plane Under Jap Fire." *Sayre (PA) Evening Times.* August 4, 1945, 2.

————. "Savage Aerial Dogfight Flamed Above 3rd Fleet Even After War Had Ended." *Honolulu Star-Advertiser*. August 16, 1945, 1, 3.

Jones, George E. "Fighters Sweep in at Dawn in Opening of Halsey's Attack." *New York Times*. July 11, 1945, 1, 3.

————. "Battleships' Risk Part of Strategy." *New York Times*. July 18, 1945, 1, 5.

————. "Halsey Busy Again." *New York Times*. July 28, 1945, 1, 3.

————. "Lethal Sea Weapon and Powder Keg, Too." *New York Times*. July 29, 1945, 6, 28.

————. "Halsey Keeps It Up." *New York Times*. August 1, 1945, 1–2.

————. "Sea and Air Assaults Pave Way for Invasion." *New York Times*. August 5, 1945, 1.

Kinney, Aaron. "WWII Navy Aviator 'Komo' Dies at 86." *East Bay Times*. January 12, 2007. Found at https://www.eastbaytimes.com/2007/01 /12/wwii-navy-aviator-komo-dies-at-86. Accessed February 27, 2018.

"Kokomo Churches Announce Plans for Union 'Thanksgiving' Service." *Kokomo Tribune*. August 11, 1945, 1.

"Kokomo Makes Plans for V-J Celebration; Business Will Stop." *Kokomo Tribune*. August 10, 1945, 1.

"Kokomo Plants Ready for Peacetime Work." *Kokomo Tribune*. August 11, 1945, 1.

"Kokomo Roars Joy at Jap Surrender." *Kokomo Tribune*. August 15, 1945, 1, 15.

"Kokomo Sailor Reported Dead in Pacific Area." *Kokomo Tribune*. August 21, 1945.

"Kokomo Screams Joy at War's End as Autos Flood Downtown Streets." *Kokomo Tribune*. August 14, 1945, 1.

Lackeos, Nick. "Brothers Nominated for Aviation Honor." *Montgomery Advertiser*. January 23, 1998, 25.

"Lanark Flier Aids in Destruction of Jap Transport in Pacific." *Freeport (IL) Journal-Standard*. January 27, 1944, 1.

"Last Days." *Time*. August 20, 1945, found at http://content.time.com /time/subscriber/article/0,33009,797667,00.html. Accessed February 15, 2018.

"Largest Air Raid of War Hits Japs." *Kokomo Tribune*. July 7, 1945.

Lawrence, W. H. "Japan Battered." *New York Times.* July 11, 1945, 1, 3.

———. "New Big Carrier Attack." *New York Times.* July 14, 1945, 1–2.

———. "Nimitz's Report a Challenge." *New York Times.* July 15, 1945, 1.

———. "Offensive Mounts." *New York Times.* July 17, 1945, 1–2.

———. "Fleet's Challenge off Tokyo Bay Fails to Stir Japanese to Action." *New York Times.* July 22, 1945, 1.

———. "Foe's Fleet Target." *New York Times.* July 24, 1945, 1, 3.

———. "Japanese Ripped." *New York Times.* July 25, 1945, 1–2.

———. "'Superforts' Give 3d Notice." *New York Times.* August 5, 1945, 1, 4.

———. "GI's in Pacific Go Wild with Joy; Let 'Em Keep Emperor,' They Say." *New York Times.* August 11, 1945, 1, 4.

"Lieutenant Joseph G. Sahloff." *Poughkeepsie Journal.* April 10, 1946, 10.

"Life on a Carrier." *Flying.* October 1944, 151–152, 246, 248.

Lindsley, James. "Pilot Saves Navy Fliers from Japan Sea Under Foe Guns." *Oakland Tribune.* July 27, 1945, 2.

———. "Saved Under Nose of Jap Destroyer." *Danville (VA) Bee.* August 4, 1945, 7.

Litz, Leo M. "Navy Pilot Is Rescued as Awed Kobe Stares." *Indianapolis News.* August 8, 1945, 1, 11.

"The Lovely Dumbos." *Time.* August 6, 1945, found at http://content.time.com/time/subscriber/article/0,33009,803659,00.html. Accessed February 15, 2018.

"Lt. Dorney Is Missing over Atlantic." *Portsmouth (NH) Herald.* October 18, 1944, 1.

"Lt. Robert S. Willaman Obituary." *Chicago Tribune.* August 29, 1944, 10.

"Lt. Sahloff Declared Dead." *Poughkeepsie Journal.* September 18, 1946, 2.

"Lt. Sueyres Aids in Rescue Under Jap Fire." *Tampa Bay Times.* August 12, 1945, 21.

"Location of U.S. Fleet Is Secret." *Kokomo Tribune.* July 20, 1945.

Lodge, J. Norman. "Halsey Predicts Victory This Year." *New York Times.* January 3, 1943, 14.

Luna, Kay. "WWII Vet Still Has Fighter Pilot's Eye." September 22, 2007. Found at https://qctimes.com/news/local/wwii-vet-still-has-fighter-pilot-s-eye/article_3c499349-21e3-55f9-9b08-2c0fc00ea5b1.html. Accessed January 17, 2018.

"MacArthur Hopes 'This Is the End,'" *New York Times*. August 11, 1945, 4.

"MacArthur Sets 2-Way Landing of Americans in Japan for Tuesday." *Kokomo Tribune*. August 22, 1945.

"MacArthur 'Soon' to Arrive in Japan." *Kokomo Tribune*. August 20, 1945.

Mahoney, W. J. "Last Crommelin Takes over 'Lex'." *Montgomery Advertiser*. June 14, 1964, 5.

Maki, Kevin. "WWII Fighter Pilot Awarded Medals for Heroism." NBC Montana, May 12, 2016. Found at http://nbcmontana.com /news/local/wwii-fighter-pilot-awarded-medals-for-heroism _20160512135644271. Accessed February 23, 2018.

"Mapleton Aviator Reported Missing." *Council Bluffs (IA) Nonpareil*. October 21, 1944, 8.

Mastin, Frank Jr. "Honor and Courage." *Montgomery Advertiser*. May 27, 1996, 1, 15.

———. "Burial Today for Retired Admiral, WWII Hero." *Montgomery Advertiser*. November 5, 1996, 13, 2B.

———. "WWII Hero Crommelin Dead at 78." *Montgomery Advertiser*. April 30, 1997, 13.

"McCain Sees Foe Saving for 'Sunday Punch' in Air." *New York Times*. July 24, 1945, 1.

McClure, Julie. "Day of Victory Also Day of Loss." *Kokomo Tribune*. August 13, 1995, A1–A2.

"Mighty Allied Pacific Fleet Composed of 133 'Line Ships'." *Kokomo Tribune*. August 16, 1945, 4.

Milliman, Leonard. "Allies Rapidly Crush Jap Air, Sea Defense." *Kokomo Tribune*. July 26, 1945, 1.

"Navy Casualties." *Detroit Free Press*. October 13, 1945, 13.

"Navy Chennault." *Time*. June 14, 1943, 63–68.

"Navy Claims Rule Up to Rim of Japan." *New York Times*. July 11, 1945, 1.

"New Attack at 'Full Power'." *New York Times*. August 13, 1945, 4.

"New Blows Are Planned Against Japan." *Kokomo Tribune*. August 4, 1945, 1.

"News of Our Men and Women in Uniform." *Altamont (NY) Enterprise*. April 5, 1946, 1.

"News of Servicemen." *Ravena (NY) News Herald.* August 10, 1945, 1.

"Nimitz Arrives in Tokyo to Accept Jap Surrender." *Kokomo Tribune.* August 29, 1945.

"Nippon Islands Are Blockaded." *Kokomo Tribune.* August 3, 1945.

"Nomura Attacks Our Peace Terms." *New York Times.* July 9, 1945, 1.

"Noose Tightens On Japs' Home Islands." *Kokomo Tribune.* August 4, 1945, 1.

"Notre Dame Holiday." *Kokomo Tribune.* August 16, 1945, 3.

"133 Warships Hit Foe in Last Blows." *New York Times.* August 17, 1945.

"Pacific Fleet Blasting at Tokyo's Front Gate." *Kokomo Tribune.* July 23, 1945, 1, 9.

"Parents Plan Memorial Services for Ensign Hobbs on Next Sunday." *Kokomo Tribune.* October 14, 1946, 24.

Parrott, Lindesay. "Shortages Blight Japan's Air Power." *New York Times.* July 16, 1945, 5.

"Peace Bid News Hailed on McCain's Flagship" *New York Times.* August 13, 1945, 1.

"The Peace Rumors." *New York Times.* July 19, 1945, 22.

"People Here Prepared for Rest Period." *Kokomo Tribune.* September 1, 1945, 1, 9.

"Pilot Missing." *Marshfield (WI) News-Herald.* December 14, 1944, 7.

"Pilots Describe Havoc." *New York Times.* July 29, 1945, 3.

"Power v. Statesmanship." *Time.* July 16, 1945, found at http://content .time.com/time/subscriber/article/0,33009,792153,00.html. Accessed February 15, 2018.

"President Urges Signing of Charter." *Kokomo Tribune.* July 2, 1945.

"Proposes Name of W. C. Hobbs for Air Field." *Kokomo Tribune.* August 27, 1953, 4.

Rae, Bruce. "Okinawa Is a Lesson for Invasion of Japan." *New York Times.* May 27, 1945, 1.

"Rampaging Airmen Pound Land, Sea." *Kokomo Tribune.* July 21, 1945.

"Reconversion Put into High Gear." *Kokomo Tribune.* July 2, 1945.

"Report Hitler in Antarctic at Nazi Base." *Kokomo Tribune.* July 18, 1945, 1.

"The Road to Tokyo." *New York Times.* May 26, 1945.

Rosenberg, Richard A. "Navy to Honor Montgomery Brothers with Christening of USS *Crommelin.*" *Montgomery Advertiser.* June 26, 1981, 19.

"Russian War Entry Is Radioed Pilots of Carrier Planes." *Morning Herald (Hagerstown, MD).* August 10, 1945, 19.

"Sahloff, Missing in Action, Lauded for His Part in Rescue." *Poughkeepsie Journal.* April 7, 1946, 9A.

Sakaida, Henry. "Unknown American Pilot Now Identified." posted in WWII History Articles, February 7, 2018. Found at http://ww2awar tobewon.com/wwii-articles/american-pilot-identified/. Accessed February 20, 2018.

Schneider, Natalie. "The Last Letter." A story written for her freshman English Honors Class, November 30, 2017.

Sears, David. "Fire in the Skies, Ceasefire on the Ground." *World War II* Magazine, August 14, 2015, found at http://www.historynet.com/the -battle-that-spanned-war-and-peace.htm. Accessed June 22, 2017.

"The Service Parade." *Detroit Free Press.* April 11, 1944, 15.

"Sheets of Fire Blanket Japan." *Kokomo Tribune.* August 2, 1945.

"Shefloe Reported as Missing." *Missoula (MT) Missoulian.* September 21, 1945, 2.

"Shift to the Pacific." *New York Times.* May 12, 1945, 1.

"Short Cut?" *Time.* August 13, 1945, found at http://content.time.com /time/subscriber/article/0,33009,792250,00.html. Accessed February 15, 2018.

"Signers of Terms to Japs Announced." *Kokomo Tribune.* August 23, 1945.

"Sisters Remember Loss of Brother on Last Day of War." *Kokomo Perspective.* August 31, 2005, H-19.

"Sober City Awaits Official V-J Word." *New York Times.* August 11, 1945, 1, 9.

"South Japan Hit by Rocket Planes." *Kokomo Tribune.* July 12, 1945, 1.

"Spaatz Takes Over Japan Bombing Job." *Kokomo Tribune.* July 5, 1945.

"Superforts Continue Hammering Japanese." *Kokomo Tribune.* August 7, 1945.

"Superforts Take Up Task of Jap Raids." *Kokomo Tribune.* August 8, 1945, 1.

"The Surrender." *Time.* August 20, 1945, found at http://content.time .com/time/subscriber/article/0,33009,797640,00.html. Accessed February 15, 2018.

"Surrender Gives Japs to MacArthur." *Kokomo Tribune.* September 3, 1945.

"Surrender Plans Ahead of Program." *Kokomo Tribune.* August 24, 1945.

"250 B29s Pound Jap Home Islands." *Kokomo Tribune.* July 6, 1945.

"2,000 U.S. Airmen Rip Jap Homeland." *Kokomo Tribune.* July 24, 1945, 1.

"3,000 American Fliers Lost in Operation of Superforts." *Kokomo Tribune.* August 17, 1945.

"The Task Ahead." *New York Times.* June 2, 1945, 14.

"Terms for Japan." *New York Times.* July 4, 1945, 12.

"Terms for Japan." *New York Times.* July 23, 1945.

"Terms for Japan Suggested." *New York Times.* July 24, 1945, 22.

"Terrific Pounding of Japs Continues." *Kokomo Tribune.* July 25, 1945, 1.

Thach, Admiral John S. "Butch O'Hare and the Thach Weave." *Naval History.* Spring 1992. Found at https://www.usni.org/magazines/naval history/1992-03/butch-ohare-and-thach-weave. Accessed October 21, 2017.

"Tighten Grip on Japs in All Areas." *Kokomo Tribune.* July 9, 1945.

"To the Bitter End." *Time.* August 20, 1945, found at http://content .time.com/time/subscriber/article/0,33009,797655,00.html. Accessed February 15, 2018.

"Tokyo Calls Japan Fortress of Caves." *New York Times.* June 7, 1945.

Townsend, Peggy. "The Last Dogfight." *Santa Cruz Sentinel.* July 27, 2003, 21–22.

"Truman Discloses New Atomic Bomb." *Kokomo Tribune.* August 6, 1945, 1, 9.

Trumbull, Robert. "Geiger Sees Japan Ripe for Invasion." *New York Times.* July 7, 1945, 1, 3.

———. "Fleet Bombards Kamaishi; Carriers Hit Honshu Again." *New York Times.* August 10, 1945, 1, 4.

———. "Fleet Is Inactive after 2-Day Blows." *New York Times.* August 11, 1945, 1.

———. "Dawn Strike Made." *New York Times.* August 13, 1945, 1, 4.

———. "Fleet Fliers Bag 138 Enemy Planes." *New York Times*. August 13, 1945, 1.

———. "U.S. Units Operate Base at Yokosuka." *New York Times*. August 31, 1945, 1, 3.

Trussell, C. P. "Blackout Lifted on Capitol Dome." *New York Times*. May 9, 1945, 1.

Tully, A. P. "*Nagato*'s Last Year: July 1943–July 1946," 1–18. http://www.combinedfleet.com/picposts/Nagatostory.html. Accessed February 14, 2018.

"Two Brothers Killed." *New York Times*. August 9, 1945, 1.

"Typhoon Forces Surrender Delay." *Kokomo Tribune*. August 25, 1945.

"The Ultimatum." *New York Times*. July 28, 1945, 10.

"Unconditional Surrender." *New York Times*. July 11, 1945.

"Union Service of Thanksgiving to Be at Grace Church Tonight." *Kokomo Tribune*. August 15, 1945, 1.

"U.S. Fleet Clears Path in Tokyo Bay." *Kokomo Tribune*. August 27, 1945.

"U.S. Fleet Within 80 Miles of Tokyo." *Kokomo Tribune*. July 17, 1945, 1.

"U.S. Third Fleet Steams into Action." *Kokomo Tribune*. August 9, 1945, 1, 10.

"Vinson's Report on the Prospects Facing Americans in the Second Phase of the War." *New York Times*. May 10, 1945, 13–17.

Waite, Elmont. "Ensign Marvin R. Odom, 21, Saved after Halting Japs." *Rocky Mount (NC) Telegram*. May 6, 1944, 1.

"Waiting." *Time*. July 9, 1945. http://content.time.com/time/subscriber/article/0,33009,852318,00.html.

Walker, S. P. "Operation Dumbo." *Our Navy*. March 1, 1946, 1–5.

Walz, Jay. "Japan Is Warned to Give Up Soon." *New York Times*. July 22, 1945, 1, 4.

"Wayne Hansen in Last Bomb Run Over Tokyo as War Ends." *Santa Cruz Sentinel*. August 17, 1945, 1.

"We Interrupt This Program." *Time*. August 20, 1945. http://content.time.com/time/subscriber/article/0,33009,797641,00.html.

"What Is Military Necessity?" *Time*. July 2, 1945. http://content.time.com/time/subscriber/article/0,33009,776037,00.html.

"What Will It Take to Beat the Jap?" *Kokomo Tribune*. July 23, 1945, 20.

"With Our Boys in the Service." *Kokomo Tribune.* August 30, 1945, 45.

"Words Are Weapons." *Time.* August 6, 1945. http://content.time.com /time/subscriber/article/0,33009,803657,00.html. Accessed February 15, 2018.

Wukovits, John. "V-J Day." *World War II Presents Victory in the Pacific.* Summer 2005, 73–83.

"Yankees Triumphantly Enter Japan." *Kokomo Tribune.* August 30, 1945.

"Yank Troops Move to Edge of Tokyo." *Kokomo Tribune.* August 31, 1945.

"Yanks Find Many Dummy Planes on Jap Air Field." *Harlingen (TX) Valley Morning Star.* August 5, 1945, 8.

"Yanks Parade City of Tokyo." *Kokomo Tribune.* September 7, 1945.

"Yanks Unopposed During Jap Raids." *Kokomo Tribune.* July 13, 1945, 1, 9.

"Young Hoosier Pilot Was One of World War II's Last Casualties." *Muncie Evening Press.* August 15, 1995, 2.

INDEX